Waterloo, ON
519 888 7748

International Faust Studies

Continuum Reception Studies

International Reception of T. S. Eliot
Edited by Elizabeth Däumer and Shyamal Bagchee

Laurence Sterne in France
by Lana Asfour

Reception of Blake in the Orient
Edited by Steve Clark and Masashi Suzuki

Reception of Jane Austen and Walter Scott
by Annika Bautz

Forthcoming titles from Continuum:

International Reception of Emily Dickinson
Edited by Domnhill Mitchell and Maria Stuart

International Reception of Samuel Beckett
Edited by Mathew Feldman and Mark Nixon

Reception of Wordsworth in Nineteenth-Century Germany
by John Williams

International Faust Studies
Adaptation, Reception, Translation

Edited by Lorna Fitzsimmons

continuum

Continuum International Publishing Group
The Tower Building   80 Maiden Lane
11 York Road   Suite 704
London SE1 7NX   New York, NY 10038

www.continuumbooks.com

© Lorna Fitzsimmons and contributors 2008

All rights reserved. No part of this publication may be reproduced or transmitted in any form or by any means, electronic or mechanical, including photocopying, recording, or any information storage or retrieval system, without prior permission in writing from the publishers.

British Library Cataloguing-in-Publication Data
A catalogue record for this book is available from the British Library.

ISBN: 978-1-8470-6004-4 (Hardback)

Library of Congress Cataloging-in-Publication Data
A catalog record of this book is available from the Library of Congress.

Typeset by Newgen Imaging Systems Pvt Ltd, Chennai, India
Printed and bound in Great Britain by the MPG Books Group

Contents

Notes on Contributors   vii

Introduction   1
Lorna Fitzsimmons

PART I   ANTERIORITIES

1 **Global Dominion: Faust and Alexander the Great**   17
Arnd Bohm

2 **Hanswurst, Kasperle, Pickelhäring and Faust**   36
Jane Curran

PART II   *FAUST*: IN CONTEXT

3 **'Why all this noise?': Reading Sound in Goethe's *Faust I* and *II***   55
Alan Corkhill

4 **Technology as Timelessness: Building and Language in *Faust***   70
Claudia Brodsky

5 **Faust and Satan: Conflicting Concepts of the Devil in *Faust I***   88
Ehrhard Bahr

PART III   *FAUST*: ROMANTIC INTERTEXTS

6 **'Much in the mode of Goethe's Mephistopheles': *Faust* and Byron**   107
Fred Parker

7 **'An orphic tale': Goethe's *Faust* Translated by Coleridge**   124
Frederick Burwick

PART IV   ASIA

8 **On the Reception of *Faust* in Asia**   149
Adrian Hsia

9 Goethe's *Faust* in India: The Kathakali Adaptation 161
David G. John

10 Faust's Spectacular Travels through China: Recent *Faust* Productions and Their History 177
Antje Budde

PART V THE AMERICAS, EUROPE, AFRICA AND BRITAIN

11 Faust and the Magus Tradition in Robertson Davies' *The Rebel Angels* 205
Richard Ilgner

12 They Sold Their Soul for Rock'n'Roll: Faustian Rock Musicals 216
Paul M. Malone

13 The Faustian Disguise of Edoardo Sanguineti and Luca Lombardi 231
Gabriele Becheri

14 Contemporary African and Brazilian Adaptations of Goethe's *Faust* in Postcolonial Context 244
Katharina Keim

15 Reality Just Arrived—Mark Ravenhill's *Faust is Dead* 259
Bree Hadley

Index 277

Notes on Contributors

EHRHARD BAHR is Distinguished Professor Emeritus of German at the University of California, Los Angeles, United States. His publications include *Weimar on the Pacific: German Exile Culture in Los Angeles and the Crisis of Modernism*, *The Novel as Archive: The Genesis, Reception, and Criticism of Goethe's Wilhelm Meisters Wanderjahre* and *Die Ironie im Spätwerk Goethes: '... diese sehr ernsten Scherze ...' Studien zum West-östlichen Divan, zu den Wanderjahren und zu Faust II*. He was President of the Goethe Society of North America 1995–7.

GABRIELE BECHERI teaches piano and music theory at Il Trillo, Florence, Italy. He has written books and essays on the music of the second half of the twentieth century and the relationship between music and poetry. He has given both solo and ensemble performances internationally.

ARND BOHM is Associate Professor of English at Carleton University, Canada. His research interests include German literary history and Anglo-German literary relations. He is the author of *Goethe's 'Faust' and European Epic: Forgetting the Future* and many pieces on both German and British literature.

CLAUDIA BRODSKY is Professor of Comparative Literature at Princeton University, United States. She is the author of *The Imposition of Form: Studies in Narrative Representation and Knowledge*, *Lines of Thought: Discourse, Architectonics, and the Origin of Modern Philosophy* and *In the Place of Language: Goethe and the Architecture of the Referent*.

ANTJE BUDDE is Assistant Professor in the University College Drama Program and the Centre for Comparative Literature at the University of Toronto, Canada. Her research interests include experimental theatre in China, intercultural theatre, independent theatre in Germany and East German television. Her publications include a book on the history of Chinese experimental theatre. She is also active as a theatre director and performer and has staged productions in Germany and China.

FREDERICK BURWICK is Professor Emeritus of English at the University of California, Los Angeles, United States. His publications include twenty books and over ninety articles. He has been named Distinguished Scholar by both the British Academy (1992) and the Keats–Shelley Association (1998). He is co-editor of *Faustus, from the German of Goethe. Translated by Samuel Taylor Coleridge* (2007) and editor of the *Coleridge Handbook*.

JANE CURRAN is Professor and Chair of the German Department at Dalhousie University, Canada. Her field of concentration is the eighteenth century and most of her publications have been in this area (Wieland, Goethe, Schiller). Her current research topic focuses on reading aloud in Goethe's world.

ALAN CORKHILL is Reader/Associate Professor in German in the School of Languages and Comparative Cultural Studies at the University of Queensland, Australia. He has published extensively on aspects of German letters since the

Age of Goethe and on German–Australian literary and cultural cross-currents. He is the author of four books, the latest entitled *Glückskonzeptionen im deutschen Roman von Wielands 'Agathon' bis Goethes 'Wahlverwandtschaften'*. He is the Australasian co-editor of *Seminar: A Journal of Germanic Studies*.

LORNA FITZSIMMONS is Associate Professor and Coordinator of the Humanities Program at California State University, Dominguez Hills, in Los Angeles, United States. She has taught an interdisciplinary comparatist Faust course for ten years. Her publications include *The Lives of Faust: The Faust Theme in Literature and Music. A Reader* and Faust studies in *The Germanic Review*, *Studies in French Cinema* and elsewhere. She is currently working on several interdisciplinary books on Faust discourse.

BREE HADLEY is Lecturer in Performance Studies in the Creative Industries Faculty at Queensland University of Technology, Australia. She has research interests in contemporary, multimedia and physical performance and has worked as a writer, dramaturge, director and arts administrator.

ADRIAN HSIA is Professor of German Studies at McGill University, Canada (retired 2007) and Honorary Professor of Chinese at the University of Hong Kong. He has published twenty-one books and eighty articles, including *Zur Rezeption von Goethes 'Faust' in Ostasien, Goethe und China—China und Goethe* and 'Goethe's "Faust" in Four Chinese Translations'.

RICHARD ILGNER taught German and Comparative Studies at Dalhousie University until 1980, and since then German and Interdisciplinary Graduate Studies in the Humanities at Memorial University, Canada. His publications include *Die Ketzermythologie in Goethes Faust* and *Das Geschäft der Lemuren: Der Tod des Schöpferischen*, as well as over a hundred presentations and articles on topics in German and Interdisciplinary Studies.

DAVID G. JOHN is Professor of German, Department of Germanic and Slavic Studies, at the University of Waterloo, Canada. His publications include *Images of Goethe through Schiller's 'Egmont'*, *The German Nachspiel in the Eighteenth Century* and *Johann Christian Krüger. Werke. Kritische Gesamtausgabe*. Recent articles address Goethe and Schiller, as well as intercultural performances of Goethe's *Faust* in the United States, the Philippines and India. He is currently writing a book on the East German director Fritz Bennewitz.

KATHARINA KEIM is Assistant Professor of Theatre Studies at Ludwig-Maximilians-University, Germany. Her research and teaching areas include classical and contemporary German and French theatre and postcolonial theatre. She has published the study *Theatralität in den späten Dramen Heiner Müllers* and co-edited the collection *Theater ohne Grenzen*. She also contributed to H.-P. Bayerdörfer's collection, *Im Auftrieb: Grenzüberschreitungen mit Goethes 'Faust' in Inszenierungen der neunziger Jahre*.

PAUL M. MALONE is Associate Professor of Germanic and Slavic Studies at the University of Waterloo, Canada. His research interests include adaptation, performance theory, Faust music, Kafka and Ödön von Horváth. He has published in *Faust: Icon of Modern Culture*, *Processes of Transposition: German Literature and Film*, *Mediated Drama/Dramatized Media* and *Film/Fiction: Classics*.

FRED PARKER is Fellow and Director of Studies, Clare College and University Senior Lecturer in English, University of Cambridge, United Kingdom. He specializes in eighteenth-century and Romantic English literature and also teaches *Faust* for a foreign literature module. His publications include *Scepticism and Literature: An Essay on Pope, Hume, Sterne, and Johnson* and *Johnson's Shakespeare*. He is currently working on a study of the devil as muse in literature from Milton to Thomas Mann.

Introduction

Lorna Fitzsimmons

> *For he accompanied himself with divers that were seen in those Devilish Arts and that had the Chaldean, Persian, Hebrew, Arabian, and Greek tongues . . .*
> The Historie of the damnable life, and deserued death of Doctor Iohn Faustus

This book is an international interdisciplinary collection of chapters on Faust discourse from the early modern period to the present. Written with the bicentenary of Goethe's *Faust* (1808) in mind, these studies extend much beyond Goethe's text in their engagement with the heterogeneous matrix of discourses marked by the sign of 'Faust' over the centuries. The scope of the book is broadly, multiply internationalist. It draws together scholars from around the world whose work on the Faust thematic and its reception falls within comparative frameworks. Our concern in this book is not only Goethe's *Faust*, but also Faustian discourse that precedes it and, even more so, the myriad, increasingly global variants of the Faust theme in its wake. While the proliferation of Faustian discourse in diverse tongues, increasingly evident from the nineteenth century to the present, is a phenomenon that clearly testifies to the widespread appeal of the fantasy of defying death—'That time may cease and midnight never come!' (Marlowe 1993: V.ii.69)—or no doubt, for many, the stirring munificence of the imperative to strive, it nevertheless also articulates the sociopolitical agendas to which ends Faustian ambitions have not infrequently been deployed, and which still, in some contexts, mark the meaning(s) of the Faustian today. If the Faustian project is internationalist from its (asymptotic) beginnings, this collection scrutinizes its internationalism reflexively, re-engaging the traditional themes through critical prisms acutely attentive to questions of power raised, or obscured, by Faustian discourse in its multiple configurations from the early modern to the postmodern, up to the early twenty-first century.

The focus of the book is on questions of adaptation, reception and translation pertaining to Faustian discourse in a diversity of cultural traditions, including the Chinese, African, Indian, Japanese, Brazilian and Canadian, as well as the European. The Faust figure is engaged in multiple contexts, from the European and African puppet theatre to opera, Indian Kathakali dance and in-yer-face performance. The fifteen studies gathered here engage previously neglected Faustian materials or bring to bear alternative perspectives on the better-known texts.

2 International Faust Studies

The collection is arranged in five sections: Parts I, II and III engage European and British Faust discourse from the sixteenth to the nineteenth centuries (with some extension to post-1945 examples), while Parts IV and V focus on the Faustian of the twentieth and early twenty-first centuries, in global contexts. Part I examines two significant yet neglected axes in the history of Faust reception: 'Alexander' material and the Faust puppet plays. Part II comprises three readings of Goethe's *Faust* in context. Part III considers the import of the Faustian for two British Romantics, Byron and Coleridge. Part IV consists of three studies of Faust reception in the Middle East, India, Japan and China. The five studies in Part V engage the Faust theme in theatre, literature, music and film from Canada, the United States, Brazil, Africa, Europe and the United Kingdom.

As a comparatist undertaking, the objectives of this collection are marked by Goethe's 'Weltliteratur' ('world literature') concern with the processes and potentialities of transnational cultural exchange. In the current era of globalization, critical engagement with the implications of the concept of 'Weltliteratur', in all its ambiguities, is increasingly called for (Prendergast 2004; Damrosch 2006, 2003; Koch 2002; Pizer 2006, 2005, 2000; Julien 2006; Birus 2003; Grabovszki 2003; Agathocleous and Gosselink 2006; Atkinson 2006). Within the contemporary critical debate, the familiar trope of the 'Faustian pact' circulates with politicized apotropaic purpose. David Barry's 'Faustian pursuits: The political-cultural dimension of Goethe's *Weltliteratur* and the tragedy of translation' is a case in point. Recalling Goethe's concern with the potential of 'Weltliteratur' to counter nationalism, Barry (2001: 165) considers the goals of 'Weltliteratur' vitally relevant as a 'humanizing counter to the greed and political economical expediency driving the processes of contemporary globalization'. It is a Faustian irony, however, that the cosmopolitanism envisaged as 'Weltliteratur' has been 'misappropriated' in the service of Western economic and political interests (Barry 2001: 173). Of the alliance between 'Weltliteratur' and translation there is also reason to be wary, Barry warns, due to the latter's 'dangerous, dubious, mephisthophelean associations', Goethe's support of translation, despite its vulnerabilities, notwithstanding (2001: 182). More recently, South Korean critic Yoo Hui-Sok (2006) deploys the Faustian pact trope to critique Franco Moretti's theory of world literature, within which Goethe's *Faust* is reframed as a '*world*' rather than a 'German' text, in the sense that its 'geographical frame of reference is no longer the nation-state, but a broader entity—a continent, or the world-system as a whole' (Moretti 1996: 50; 2006; 2004). Contending that 'world literature in no way has an integral meaning but in its particular topography, that is, as a part of national literature', Yoo finds Moretti's aims 'too globally vain to confront locally unequal reality', and hence 'rather dangerously close to the impertinently ambitious Faustian pact' (2006: 136).

The internationalist thrust of this collection is one that seeks to expand knowledge of both the 'peripheral' and the 'canonical' while interrogating such conceptualizations and the contingencies thereof. Its aim is to broaden the scope of Faust studies and the range of perspectives by which the sign 'Faust' can be understood and, in so doing, to advance recognition of its multiplicity. Deeper knowledge of the hybridity of Faustian discourse and its multiple reception histories, in local, regional and international contexts—whether pertaining to the Faustus *Historia* of the European Reformation or the parodic *Daoban fushide* (盗版浮士德)(*Bootleg Faust*) of the Chinese fin-de-siècle—can eventuate in the generation of alternative decodings and constructions, or the complication of existing practices, and facilitate greater cross-cultural understanding.

The field of transcultural reception studies takes on increasing relevance and urgency within the context of contemporary globalization (Bharucha 2000, 1990; Damrosch 2006, 2003; Cronin 2003; Schmitz-Emans 2004). Adaptation and translation are two key nexuses of transcultural reception of central concern to this book. The cultural, or 'power', turn in adaptation and translation studies has sharpened awareness of the political nature of both practices, rendering the performative qualities of adaptation and translation processes more visible (Tymoczko and Gentzler 2002; Venuti 1995, 1992; Ungar 2006; Loffredo and Perteghella 2006; Apter 2004; Cronin 2003; Pavis 1989). By interrogating the political implications of such practices—the choices and interests they entail—work in the field is enriched and can be productive of a 'better understanding of the foreign and . . . [deeper] confrontation with the common, i.e., the self' (Schmitz-Emans 2004: 19).

Although the chapters in this collection raise questions of translation pertaining to Faust material in a variety of contexts, scholarly focus often converges on the translation of the metaphysical. Chantal Wright has argued that 'Goethe's *Faust* requires perpetual retranslation to reflect the constant change in society's thinking on metaphysical concepts such as the nature and provenance of good and evil . . .' (2006: 153). As a number of contributors demonstrate, the metaphysical is a particularly problematic and generative nexus in the translation and adaptation of Faustian material. Ehrhard Bahr's analysis of conflicting concepts of the devil in *Faust*, in Chapter 5, provides an apparatus for engaging this crucial theme, which remains a fertile matrix of hybridity in Faust adaptation histories. In Chapter 7, Frederick Burwick contends that the metaphysics of *Faust* posed a serious moral dilemma for the anonymous translator of *Faustus, from the German of Goethe* (1821), whom Burwick traces to the outstanding British 'poet of the supernatural and demonic', Samuel Taylor Coleridge. In Part IV, questions of translation within the reception of Faust discourse in Asia, including the problems of translating and adapting the metaphysical, are addressed in Adrian Hsia's study of *Faust* reception in the Middle East, India, Japan and China in Chapter 8, David G. John's case study of a Kathakali *Faust* adaptation in Chapter 9 and Antje Budde's work on Faust productions in China in Chapter 10. Other, suggestive conceptualizations of 'translation' are raised in Claudia Brodsky's Heideggerian reading of *Faust* in Chapter 4 and Gabriele Becheri's analysis of Lombardi's operatic version of Sanguineti's *Faust. Un Travestimento* (*Faust. A Disguise*) in Chapter 13.

The resourcefulness often stimulated by the challenge of adapting Faustian discourse is amply evidenced in this collection. The 'adaptive faculty is the ability to repeat without copying', as Hutcheon observes, 'to embed difference in similarity, to be at once both self and Other' (2006: 174). In Chapter 1, Arnd Bohm delineates the variegations of a 'reciprocal mimesis' between the figures of Faustus and Alexander, tracking its traces in Marlowe's and Goethe's adaptations. In Chapter 2, Jane Curran explores the nuances of embeddedness within the mutually fertile, yet often marginalized, relation between the early Faust puppet theatre and Goethe's *Faust*. In Chapter 3, Alan Corkhill contextualizes figurations of sound in *Faust* and distinctive sound effects in recent theatrical productions, including Peter Stein's monumental *Faust* of 2000. In Chapter 6, Fred Parker examines mutations of the Mephistophelean in major works of Byron.

The post-1945 period witnessed a striking proliferation of Faustian adaptation in theatre, music, literature, film and other media, not only in the West but around the world. In music, cross-fertilization between traditions of Faust opera (Kreutzer 2003; Grim 1988–92; Cerf 1987; Kelly 1976) and rock was productive, as Paul M. Malone and Gabriele Becheri show in Chapters 12 and 13. In Chapter 11, Richard Ilgner examines Robertson Davies' novel *The Rebel Angels* as a major example of the Faustian discourse that rose to international prominence in the Canadian novel and cinema of the 1980s. The 1990s produced several provocative Faust adaptations, such as Mark Ravenhill's *Faust is Dead* (1997), as Bree Hadley discusses in Chapter 15. In the self-consciously 'hybrid cultural space' (Bhabha 1994) of postcolonial Faust adaptation, a number of notably creative reinterpretations were produced, as Antje Budde and Katharina Keim show in Chapters 10 and 14. These studies suggest that the significance of such postcolonial productions is multifold and lies, not the least, in social critique and transcultural generative potential: 'When fragment A and fragment B belonging to different localities come into contact, deeper and wider strata of sense are revealed, strata no longer confined to narrow spaces and moments, to a time *a* and a place *b*' (Guillén 1993: 44; Bharucha 2000, 1990).

Jane K. Brown has concluded that the challenge in reading Goethe's *Faust* is 'not in the play's resistance to interpretation, but rather its incorrigible responsiveness to any question posed to it' (1994: xiv). In the twentieth and early twenty-first centuries, the questions posed to the canonic Faust texts have come from increasingly diverse contexts around the world, with many noteworthy results. Only in recent years have scholars in the field made a start at engaging such 'other' works, however. The traditional, European focus of Faust studies has been prevalent in much of the scholarly reception, with a gradual broadening of the field since the 1980s (Bianquis 1935; Dédéyan 1954–67; Dabezies 1967; Henning 1966–76; Kimura 1988, 1989, 1993; Balmas 1989; Thinès 1989; Hsia 1993; Csobádi 1993; Möbus et al. 1995; Mahl 1999; Rhie 2000; Seifert 2000; Doering 2001; Bayerdörfer 2002; Ost and van Eynde 2002; Masson 2003; Kreutzer 2003; Jakuseva 2005; Orvieto 2006). English-language Faust studies are comparable in this regard (Meek 1930; Butler 1952; Smeed 1975; Grimm and Hermand 1987; Ugrinsky 1987), although somewhat slower to expand into non-European reception than Faust studies in German, as exemplified by Kimura Naoji's studies of Japanese *Faust* reception in the 1980s and 1990s and Adrian Hsia's milestone collection *Zur Rezeption von Goethes 'Faust' in Ostasien* (*The Reception of Goethe's 'Faust' in Asia*) in 1993. Boerner and Johnson included Kimura's work and also Erwin Theodor Rosenthal's study of Brazilian Faust material in the dual-language *Faust through Four Centuries: Retrospect and Analysis. Vierhundert Jahre Faust: Rückblink und Analyse* in 1989. In 1994, Brown, Lee and Saine included Stuart Atkins' (1994b: 237–8) list of Chinese, Japanese, Korean, Portuguese (Brazil) and Turkish *Faust* translators in *Interpreting Goethe's 'Faust'*

Today, but the focus of the collection remains European, as does that of Singer and Schlunk's *Doctor Faustus: Archetypal Subtext at the Millennium* (1999), and it was not until Osman Durrani's landmark study *Faust: Icon of Modern Culture* (2004) that 'Faust Globalized' was engaged at length in English-language criticism. Significant advances were achieved at the 'Faust in the 21st Century: Modernity, Myth, Theatre' symposium held at the University of Toronto in 2004 and 'The Reception of *Faust* in non-Christian Cultures/Zur Faustrezeption in nicht-christlichen Kulturen/Réception de Faust dans les cultures non-chrétiennes' conference that Adrian Hsia and Jochen Golz organized at McGill University in Canada in 2006. Two recent critical studies, *Hidden Mutualities: Faustian Themes from Gnostic Origins to the Postcolonial* (Mitchell 2006) and *The Faust Myth: Religion and the Rise of Representation* (Hawkes 2007), include sections addressing postcolonial contexts.

At the present time, there is considerable scholarly investment in the area of Faust studies conceived both traditionally, in Eurocentric terms, and, increasingly, as reconceived in postmodern terms that interrogate the traditional hierarchies and open alternative critical spaces. We are beginning to forge significant international exchanges of knowledge about Faust materials previously neglected in scholarly circles. The field of Faust studies today encompasses a domain of far-reaching scope, unprecedented in its international, interdisciplinary dimensions and implications. We have in the twentieth and early twenty-first centuries witnessed the vast diversification of Faust discourse in theatre, literature, music, film, television and new media. The Faust figures have undergone myriad permutations in the service of many, often divergent, interests. In acknowledging the multiplicity of this domain, our undertaking in this book is reflexively bounded, compacted, in a way, by the necessity to contradict the pretensions to mastery for which the 'Faustian' is notorious. We begin by tracing some anteriorities of the 'Faustian' and pursue a series of alterities, interrogating the mutations, the 'disguises' and the 'divers' agendas with which they are associated.

Part I of this book presents two chapters that advance scholarship in the area of early Faust discourse and also help us put contemporary Faust discourse in broader perspective. Reflexive upon the trope of 'Faust Globalized', Arnd Bohm, in Chapter 1, marshals evidence of a neglected prototype for the global ambitions the figure of Faust embodies—Alexander the Great. Author of *Goethe's 'Faust' and European Epic* (2007), Bohm deepens the internationalism of early modern Faust studies by demonstrating the importance of classical and medieval sources on Alexander in the construction of the Faustus persona. Reception of the sign of 'Alexander' laid the groundwork for that of Faustus. Bohm demonstrates that there are significant parallels between the legends of both. The flight fantasy, descent to hell, desire for power, intellectual curiosity and early death of Faustus bear comparison to those associated with Alexander in the histories and romances. The Alexander themes in Marlowe's *Doctor Faustus* foreground the 'politics of ambition'. Goethe's adaptation of Alexander material subtends the tyrannical aspirations of Faust in Part II. The violence of the crucial Philemon and Baucis incident, a nodal point in several chapters in this collection, Bohm asserts has a classical precedent in accounts of the conqueror Alexander's pursuit of dominion.

In Chapter 2, Jane Curran's work on the reception history of the Faust puppet theatre raises important contexts for understanding not only Goethe's

Faust but also contemporary postcolonial puppet performance such as *Faustus in Africa!*, which Katharina Keim discusses in Chapter 14. Although Goethe's enthusiasm for the puppet theatre is well-known, the imprint of the 'humble' puppet conventions in *Faust* tends to be marginalized in scholarship. Curran reverses this by bringing into relief an array of thematic, idiomatic and structural parallels, including instances of cross-fertilization. Johann Christoph Gottsched's controversial 'crusade' against the 'vulgarities' of Faust puppet theatre remains a significant moment in the history of Faust reception and the disciplining of 'taste'. Gottsched's reaction to the hybridity of the Faust puppet theatre denigrated the signs of the Italian commedia dell'arte and sought to banish the clown Hanswurst. Considering the impact of this 'banishment' on Goethe's work, Curran delineates signs of the puppet theatre 'dispersed and distributed throughout' the fabric of *Faust*.

Part II consists of three studies of Goethe's *Faust* in context. Alan Corkhill's discussion of sound images in *Faust* and recent theatrical adaptations, in Chapter 3, engages the topic with a broad, interdisciplinary apparatus gracefully attuned to ancient myth and linguistic theory no less than modern physics. The author suggests the (meta)physics of sound in *Faust* evokes the Pythagorean while anticipating Big Bang theory. Corkhill calls attention to the intriguing question of the human threshold for (meta)physical sounds raised in *Faust II*. Goethe's own theory of acoustics, in his *Zur Farbenlehre* (*Theory of Colors*), gives a 'progressive' approach to the issues of the day. *Faust* is shown to be deeply marked by contemporary debate over the origins of the earth and human speech. Corkhill suggests that the 'aesthetics of words' becomes a particular 'preoccupation' of Part II, related to Goethe's theory of acoustics. In the Philemon and Baucis episode Faust's 'aesthetic conditioning' is most acutely called into question. Corkhill concludes with a survey of innovative sound effects in post-1945 *Faust* theatre productions by Fritz Kortner, Christoph Schroth, Peter Stein and others.

Claudia Brodsky, in Chapter 4, deploys Heidegger's work on technology to critique the 'land-reclamation' project of *Faust II*. In Faust's will to construct a *'place which is an origin, an origin which is a place'* Brodsky detects Socratic traces distinctively non-Socratic in the demand for the 'immediate identity of thought and action, theory and practice'. For Brodsky, the instrumentalist practice Faust enacts exploits the 'enslaved'. The will to 'aesthetic absolutism', evident in the Philemon and Baucis episode, annihilates the 'temporal'. Brodsky contends that the system of 'translation' constitutive of Faust's architectonic project parallels Heidegger's conceptualization of technology as caesural recontextualization, redistributing power in the way that language entails the 'deracination' of those who use it.

The problem of 'misreading' is pivotal to the conflicting configurations of the devil Ehrhard Bahr discusses in Chapter 5. Bahr tracks the cultural phases of the 'biography' of Satan and finds them to be at odds throughout *Faust*. In his view, 'Goethe never solved the problem because he avoided the problem of evil'. Mephistopheles, in part, evokes Satan of the Book of Job. Yet his 'self-characterization' is contradictory, bearing marks of the Christian re-interpretation of Satan as Lucifer as well as Goethe's own mythology of Lucifer. As a 'personification of irony' Mephistopheles plays many roles, which Bahr illustrates in his scene-by-scene analysis of *Faust I* and the end of Part II. The author concludes by relating the redemption of Faust to Goethe's mythology.

Part III consists of two studies of Faust discourse from the Romantic period. For Mephistophelean multiplicity, Fred Parker demonstrates in Chapter 6, Byron had an especial affinity. Parker argues that the attraction was profound, amounting to an 'influence that changed him as a writer'. Parker's analysis fine-tunes critical understanding of the extraordinary significance of Goethe's *Faust* within the Romantic movement. Beginning with *Manfred*, Parker delineates the Faustian strains and counter-strains in Byron's work. In *Cain*'s devil, the author detects the negativity and modern idiom of Goethe's. *The Vision of Judgment*, like Goethe's 'Prologue in Heaven' ('Prolog im Himmel'), projects a devil of the Job tradition. In *Don Juan*, the shift from the Miltonic to the Mephistophelean, while unappreciated by contemporaneous readers such as Southey, is multiply evinced, and suggestively creative.

In Chapter 7, Frederick Burwick, co-editor of *Faustus, from the German of Goethe. Translated by Samuel Taylor Coleridge* (2007), presents further discussion and documentation in support of the claim he and James C. McKusick have recently put forth that Coleridge was the translator of the anonymous English translation of *Faust* published in 1821. Burwick discusses the reception of the translation by contemporaneous critics, including Thomas Carlyle, and demonstrates parallels between phrases used in the translation and Coleridge's poetry. Addressing the question of Goethe's knowledge of Coleridge's involvement, Burwick details unpublished correspondence to Goethe from London, and, charting Goethe's interest in Coleridge's work, demonstrates Goethe's own translation and appropriation of lines by Coleridge.

Part IV of the collection consists of three chapters on Faustian discourse from Asia. In Chapter 8, Adrian Hsia discusses the reception history of *Faust* in the Middle East, India, Japan and China. Hsia reviews key translations and adaptations from each region and identifies factors that eased or hindered reception. He concludes that 'cultural affinity plays an important role in the process of transcultural reception'. Whereas Islamic culture was 'well-equipped' to receive *Faust*, Hindi reception was 'more ambivalent', although both areas have a history of Faustian adaptation. In the case of East Asia, Japan has been highly instrumental in the dissemination of Faust discourse in the region. It produced a large number of translations and stage adaptations, and academic reception is also highly developed. Although Chinese translation and adaptation of *Faust* have developed at a slower pace, the Chinese have valued the 'Faustian element of striving'.

David G. John, in Chapter 9, provides an in-depth study of a Kathakali adaptation of *Faust* in India. John has documented five *Faust* adaptations in India since the 1970s. This chapter focuses on the *Faust I and II* Aymanam Krishna Kaimal directed in Kerala and elsewhere in 1976. Kathakali is a classical dance-drama with characters typically drawn from the Indian epics or Puranas. In this case, Faust was assimilated to the Hindu legend of King Rugmamgatha. John discusses in detail the adaptation of Faust sources to the traditional dance-drama form, referencing the playbills and a videotaped performance. The Indian reception context is represented by K. M. George's Malayalam text on the 'Hinduizing' of the theme, illustrating the biographical interpretation often followed in Indian scholarly reception. John concludes that Kaimal's *Faust* remains an 'outstanding' example of 'transcultural enrichment'.

In Chapter 10, Antje Budde discusses two recent *Faust* productions in China, *Faust I and II* (1994) and *Bootleg Faust* (1999), in the context of Chinese Goethe reception, Western colonialism and twentieth-century Chinese history. Her survey of Goethe and *Faust* reception in China sets the stage for an extended contextualization of the plays in relation to trends in modern Chinese theatre and culture. Lin Zhaohua's big-budget production *Faust I and II* is indicative of the recent 'explosion' in the performing arts of China. Budde analyzes the production in detail and identifies the play's hybrid qualities, relating it to the concept of 'Weltliteratur'. She concludes with a discussion of Meng Jinghui's *Bootleg Faust*, a smaller scale, avant-garde parody using innovative collage techniques.

The chapters in Part IV discuss Faustian discourse produced since the 1970s in Canada, the United States, Europe, Africa, Brazil and the United Kingdom. In Chapter 11, Richard Ilgner discusses some major Canadian Faust works of the 1980s, focusing on Robertson Davies' widely acclaimed novel *The Rebel Angels* (1981). Ilgner brings his expertise in shamanism to bear on Davies' narrative, delineating its significant parallels with Goethe's *Faust*. Of particular interest are the underground smith and goddess figures in the shaman paradigm. Through analysis of their traces in the novel and Goethe's *Faust*, Ilgner suggests how both texts subvert patriarchal traditions, effecting the 'restoration of the feminine'.

In Chapter 12, Paul M. Malone analyzes the adaptation of Faustian material in rock musicals. His focus is on four musicals that emplot the Goethean triad (Faust, Mephistopheles and Gretchen) in a rock music setting: Brian De Palma's film *The Phantom of the Paradise* (1974), with songs by Paul Williams; the Canadian stage musical *Starboy* (1983), composed by Randall Paris Dark, with music by Ian Crowley; *Randy Newman's Faust* (1995); and the two versions of Rudolf Volz's *Faust: Die Rockoper (Faust: The Rock Opera)* (1999, 2004). Malone delineates the Faustian plot twists while contextualizing each work with respect to its musical ancestry. He concludes with an assessment of Volz's updated rock opera, a 'work in progress' which claims 'fidelity' to Goethe's *Faust*.

Gabriele Becheri analyzes Luca Lombardi's operatic rendering of Edoardo Sanguineti's *Faust. Un Travestimento (Faust. A Disguise)* in Chapter 13. Sanguineti's treatment of Goethe's *Faust* imbricates translation, modernization and parody. His poetic category of 'disguise' is self-consciously reflexive, setting the 'simulation and dissimulation' of translation into infinite regress. Becheri's elegant analysis of Lombardi's highly syncretic text-libretto, which was first performed in 1990, is rich in detail enhanced by his examination of the composer's preparatory materials. Delineating the chords, and their symbolism, associated with each main character in the opera, Becheri also explains its 'inexhaustible stylistic multiplicity', which ranges from parody of the Rolling Stones' 'Sympathy for the Devil' to allusions to German anthems. Exemplary of the 'disguise' technique, the *Canzone di Greta (Greta's Song)* episode, the multiple intertexts of which include Schubert's 'Gretchen am Spinnrade' ('Gretchen at the Spinning Wheel'), is examined in depth.

Katharina Keim's discussion of South African and Bahian adaptations of *Faust* from the 1990s, in Chapter 14, sets the productions in postcolonial context. Combining aspects of European and local or African performance, both are key examples of 'theatrical syncretism'. Keim contextualizes the productions with respect to 'colonial discourse' in *Faust*, hinging on the Philemon and Baucis episode, and the reception history of the Faustian 'colonization project', including Herman Sörgel's 'Atlantropa' project, which sought to drain land in the Mediterranean. Keim contends that the relation between text and theatrical production in these postcolonial cases is one of 'cultural interaction', rendering 'new semantic potentials of the dramatic text productive'. Márcio Meirelles' production of *Urfaust* (*Fausto Zero*) in Salvador in 1999 draws on Afro-Brazilian Candomblé ritual in its revaluation of the characters and dichotomies of the source. The South African production *Faustus in Africa!*, first staged by William Kentridge and the Handspring Puppet Company in 1995, is comparably syncretic. Drawing on material by South African poet Lesego Rampolokeng, it adapts Faust discourse to enact the empowerment of non-white South Africans.

Bree Hadley's analysis of British playwright Mark Ravenhill's 'radical reinterpretation' of *Faust*—*Faust is Dead* (1997)—concludes the collection, in Chapter 15. Hadley sets the play's disruptive devices and social critique in the context of the confrontational in-yer-face theatre of the 1990s. Caricaturing the 'icons of postmodernity' and social irresponsibility, *Faust is Dead* reinterprets the Faustian conventions to levy a broad critique of 'self-indulgent' practices in contemporary consumer society. Hadley claims, '*Faust is Dead* in fact depicts a whole society that has sold its soul to consumer capitalism, all the characters bearing the cost of the death of God, progress, man, humanity and reality'. Hadley concludes her study with a comparative look at other late-twentieth-century recontextualizations, including Ariane Mnouchkine's *Mephisto* (1979), Elizabeth LeCompte's *House/Lights* (1998), Gustav Ernst's *Faust* (1995) and Pablo Ley's *F@usto: Version 3.0* (1998).

The chapters in this collection thus address configurations of the Faustian in a range of local, regional and international contexts, broadening the field of Faust studies in significant directions. As the sign of 'Faust' continues to diversify in the global economy, the interrelated questions of adaptation, reception and translation raised in this book expand our knowledge of its remarkable appeal and permutability, and the purposes to which the latter has been put.

Bibliography

Agathocleous, T. and Gosselink, K. (2006), 'Debt in the teaching of world literature: Collaboration in the context of uneven development', *Pedagogy: Critical Approaches to Teaching Literature, Language, Composition, and Culture*, 6, (3), 453–73.

Allen, M. De Huszar (1985), *The Faust Legend: Popular Formula and Modern Novel*. New York: Peter Lang.

Anglet, A. (1997), 'Faust-Rezeption', in T. Buck (ed.), *Goethe Handbuch*, v. 2. Stuttgart: Metzler, pp. 478–513.

Anon. (1994), *The Historie of the damnable life, and deserued death of Doctor Iohn Faustus*, P. F. Gent (trans.), in J. H. Jones (ed.), *The English Faust Book: A Critical Edition Based on the Text of 1592*. Cambridge: Cambridge University Press, pp. 90–184.

Apter, E. (2004), 'Global *translatio*: The 'invention' of comparative literature, Istanbul, 1933', in C. Prendergast (ed.), *Debating World Literature*. London and New York: Verso, pp. 76–100.

Atkins, S. (1994a), 'Evaluating a *Faust* translation. On the occasion of Martin Greenberg's version of *Part One*', *Goethe Yearbook*, 7, 210–21.

— (1994b), 'Goethe's *Faust* at the hands of its translators: Some recent developments', in J. K. Brown, M. Lee and T. P. Saine (eds), *Interpreting Goethe's 'Faust' Today*. Columbia: Camden House, pp. 231–8.

Atkinson, W. (2006), 'The perils of world literature', *World Literature Today*, 80, (5), 43–7.
Balmas, E. (1989), *Immagini di Faust nel romanticismo francese*. Fasano: Schena.
Baron, F. (1978), *Doctor Faustus from History to Legend*. Munich: Fink.
— (1992), *Faustus on Trial: The Origins of Johann Spies's 'Historia' in an Age of Witch Hunting*. Tübingen: Niemeyer.
Barricelli, J.-P. (1983), 'Faust and the music of evil', *Journal of European Studies*, 13, 1–26.
Barry, D. (2001), 'Faustian pursuits: The political-cultural dimension of Goethe's *Weltliteratur* and the tragedy of translation', *German Quarterly*, 74, (2), 164–85.
Bates, P. A. (ed.) (1969), *Faust: Sources, Works, Criticism*. New York: Harcourt, Brace and World.
Bayerdörfer, H.-P. (ed.) (2002), *Im Auftrieb: Grenzüberschreitungen mit Goethes 'Faust' in Inszenierungen der neunziger Jahre*. Tübingen: Niemeyer.
Bhabha, H. K. (1994), *The Location of Culture*. London and New York: Routledge.
Bharucha, R. (1990), *Theatre and the World: Essays on Performance and Politics of Culture*. New Delhi: Manohar Publications.
— (2000), *The Politics of Cultural Practice: Thinking through Theatre in an Age of Globalization*. Hanover: Wesleyan University Press.
Bianquis, G. (1935), *Faust à travers quatre siècles*. Paris: Librairie E. Droz.
Birus, H. (2003), 'The Goethean concept of world literature and comparative literature', in S. Tötösy de Zepetnek (ed.), *Comparative Literature and Comparative Cultural Studies*. West Lafayette: Purdue University Press, pp. 11–22.
Bishop, P. and Stephenson, R. H. (eds) (2000), *Goethe 2000: Intercultural Readings of His Work*. Leeds: Northern Universities Press.
Boerner, P. and Johnson, S. (eds) (1989), *Faust through Four Centuries: Retrospect and Analysis. Vierhundert Jahre Faust: Rückblink und Analyse*. Tübingen: Niemeyer.
Bohm, A. (2007), *Goethe's 'Faust' and European Epic: Forgetting the Future*. Rochester: Camden House.
Boyle, N. and Guthrie, J. (eds) (2002), *Goethe and the English-Speaking World*. Rochester: Camden House.
Brown, J. K. (1994), 'Introduction', in J. K Brown, M. Lee and T. P. Saine (eds), *Interpreting Goethe's 'Faust' Today*. Columbia: Camden House, pp. xi–xiv.
Burwick, F. and McKusick, J. (eds) (2007), *Faustus, from the German of Goethe. Translated by Samuel Taylor Coleridge*. Oxford: Oxford University Press.
Butler, E. M. (1952), *The Fortunes of Faust*. Cambridge: Cambridge University Press.
Cerf, S. R. (1987), 'The Faust theme in twentieth-century opera: Lyric modernism', *Zeitschrift für Literaturwissenschaft und Linguistik*, 66, 29–41.
Cronin, M. (2003), *Translation and Globalization*. London and New York: Routledge.
Csobádi, P. (ed.) (1993), *Europäische Mythen der Neuzeit: Faust und Don Juan. Gesammelte Vorträge des Salzburger Symposions, 1992*, 2 v. Anif / Salzburg: Müller-Speiser.
Dabezies, A. (1967), *Visages de Faust au XXe siècle. Littérature, idéologie et mythe*. Paris: Presses Universitaires de France.
Damrosch, D. (2003), *What is World Literature?* Princeton: Princeton University Press.
— (2006), 'World literature in a postcanonical hypercanonical age', in H. Saussy (ed.), *Comparative Literature in an Age of Globalization*. Baltimore: Johns Hopkins University, pp. 43–53.
Dédéyan, C. (1954–67), *Le Thème de Faust dans la littérature européenne*, 4 v. Paris: Lettres modernes.
Doering, S. (2001), *Die Schwestern des Doktor Faust: Eine Geschichte der weiblichen Faustgestalten*. Göttingen: Wallstein Verlag.
Dumiche, B. and Blondeau, D. (eds) (2001), *Faust, modernisation d'un modèle*. Paris, Budapest, Kinshasa, Torino and Ouagadougou: L'Harmattan.
Durrani, O. (2004), *Faust: Icon of Modern Culture*. Mountfield, East Sussex: Helm Information.
Glass, D. (2005), *Goethe in English: A Bibliography of the Translations in the Twentieth Century*. Leeds: Maney Publishing.

Grabovszki, E. (2003), 'The impact of globalization and the new media on the notion of world literature', in S. Tötösy de Zepetnek (ed.), *Comparative Literature and Comparative Cultural Studies*. West Lafayette: Purdue University Press, pp. 45–57.
Grim, W. E. (1988–92), *The Faust Legend in Music and Literature*, 2 v. Lewiston, NY: Edwin Mellen Press.
Grimm, R. and Hermand, J. (eds) (1987), *Our 'Faust'? Roots and Ramifications of a Modern German Myth*. Madison: University of Wisconsin Press.
Grovier, K. (2008), 'Coleridge and Goethe, together at last', *The Times Literary Supplement*, 13 February, http://entertainment.timesonline.co.uk/tol/arts_and_entertainment/the_tls/article3363528.ece (retrieved 5 March 2008).
Guillén, C. (1993), *The Challenge of Comparative Literature*, C. Franzen (trans.). Cambridge: Harvard University Press.
Hamlin, C. (2002), 'Faust in performance: Peter Stein's production of Goethe's *Faust*, Parts 1 and 2', *Theater* 32, (1), 116–36.
Hart, G. K. (2005), 'Errant strivings: Goethe, *Faust* and the feminist reader', in M. Orr and L. Sharpe (eds), *From Goethe to Gide: Feminism, Aesthetics and the French and German Literary Canon 1770–1936*. Exeter: University of Exeter Press, pp. 7–21.
Hartmann, P. (1998), *Faust und Don Juan: ein Verschmelzungsprozess, dargestellt anhand der Autoren: Wolfgang Amadeus Mozart, Johann Wolfgang von Goethe, Nikolaus Lenau, Christian Dietrich Grabbe, Gustav Kühne und Theodor Mundt*. Stuttgart: Ibidem Verlag.
Hawkes, D. (2007), *The Faust Myth: Religion and the Rise of Representation*. New York and Basingstoke: Palgrave Macmillan.
Haynes, R. D. (1994), *From Faust to Strangelove. Representations of the Scientist in Western Literature*. Baltimore: Johns Hopkins University Press.
Hedges, I. (2005), *Framing Faust: Twentieth-Century Cultural Struggles*. Carbondale: Southern Illinois University Press.
Hendrix, H., Kloek, J. J., Levie, S. and van Peer, W. (eds) (1996), *The Search for a New Alphabet: Literary Studies in a Changing World*. Amsterdam: John Benjamins Publishing.
Henning, H. (1966–76), *Faust-Bibliographie*, 3 v. Berlin and Weimar: Aufbau-Verlag.
— (1993), *Faust-Variationen: Beiträge zur Editionsgeschichte vom 16. bis: Jahrhundert*. Munich, London and New York: Saur.
Hilmi, A. (1986), *Die Rezeption Goethes in Ägypten*. Stuttgart: Heinz.
Hsia, A. (ed.) (1993), *Zur Rezeption von Goethes 'Faust' in Ostasien*. Bern: Peter Lang.
Hutcheon, L. (2006), *A Theory of Adaptation*. New York and Abington: Routledge.
Jaeger, M. (2004), *Fausts Kolonie. Goethes kritische Phänomenologie der Moderne*. Würzburg: Königshausen and Neumann Verlag.
Jakuseva, G. V. (2005), *Faust v iskusenijach XX veka: Gëtevskij obraz v russkoj i zarubeznoj literature*. Moscow: Nauka.
Jasper, W. (1998), *Faust und die Deutschen*. Berlin: Rowohlt.
Julien, E. (2006), 'Arguments and further conjectures on world literature', in G. Lindberg-Wada (ed.), *Studying Transcultural Literary History*. Berlin and New York: Walter de Gruyter, pp. 122–31.
Kelly, J. W. (1976), *The Faust Legend in Music*. Detroit: Information Coordinators.
Kimura, N. (1988), 'Eine japanische Ausgabe von Taylors Faust-Übersetzung', *Japanisches Goethe-Jahrbuch*, 30, 159–76.
— (1989), 'Probleme der *Faust*-Rezeption in Japan', in P. Boerner and S. Johnson (eds), *Faust through Four Centuries: Retrospect and Analysis. Vierhundert Jahre Faust: Rückblink und Analyse*. Tübingen: Niemeyer, pp. 143–55; A. Hsia (ed.), *Zur Rezeption von Goethes 'Faust' in Ostasien*. Bern: Peter Lang, pp. 65–80.
— (1993), 'Probleme der japanischen *Faust*-Übersetzung', *Goethe Jahrbuch*, 105, 333–43; A. Hsia (ed.), *Zur Rezeption von Goethes 'Faust' in Ostasien*. Bern: Peter Lang, pp. 23–43.
Koch, M. (2002), *Weimaraner Weltbewohner: zur Genese von Goethes Begriff 'Weltliteratur'*. Tübingen: Niemeyer.
Kreutzer, H. J. (2003), *Faust. Mythos und Musik*. Munich: Beck.

Lindberg-Wada, G. (ed.) (2006), *Studying Transcultural Literary History*. Berlin and New York: Walter de Gruyter.
Loffredo, E. and Perteghella, M. (eds) (2006), *Translation and Creativity: Perspectives on Creative Writing and Translation Studies*. London and New York: Continuum.
Mahal, G. (1997), *Faust. Und Faust. Der Teufelsbündler in Knittlingen und Maulbronn*. Tübingen: Attempto.
Mahl, B. (1999), *Goethes Faust auf der Bühne (1806–1998): Fragment, Ideologiestück, Spieltext*. Stuttgart: Metzler.
Marlowe, C. (1993), *Doctor Faustus: A- and B-texts (1604, 1616)*, D. Bevington and E. Rasmussen (eds). Manchester and New York: Manchester University Press.
Masson, J.Y. (ed.) (2003), *Faust ou la mélancolie du savoir*. Paris: Desjonquères.
Meek, H. (1930), *Johann Faust. The Man and the Myth*. London: Oxford University Press.
Mitchell, M. (2006), *Hidden Mutualities: Faustian Themes from Gnostic Origins to the Postcolonial*. Amsterdam and New York: Rodopi.
Möbus, F., Schmidt-Möbus, F. and Unverfehrt, G. (eds) (1995), *Faust: Annäherung an einen Mythos*. Göttingen: Wallstein Verlag.
Moretti, F. (1996), *Modern Epic: The World-System from Goethe to García Márquez*, Q. Hoare (trans.). London and New York: Verso.
— (2004), 'Conjectures on world literature', in C. Prendergast (ed.), *Debating World Literature*. London and New York: Verso, pp. 148–62.
— (2006), 'Evolution, world-systems, *Weltliteratur*', in G. Lindberg-Wada (ed.), *Studying Transcultural Literary History*. Berlin and New York: Walter de Gruyter, pp. 113–21.
Orvieto, P. (2006), *Il mito de Faust. L'uomo, Dio, il diavolo*. Rome: Salerno.
Ost, F. and van Eynde, L. (eds) (2002), *Faust ou les frontières du savoir*. Brussels: Publications des Facultés universitaires Saint-Louis.
Paulin, R., St Clair, W. and Shaffer, E. (2008), 'A Gentleman of Literary Eminence', Institute of English Studies, University of London, http://ies.sas.ac.uk/Publications/stc-faustus-review.pdf (retrieved 24 March 2008).
Pavis, P. (1989), 'Problems of translation for the stage', in H. Scolnicov and P. Holland (eds), *The Play Out of Context: Transferring Plays from Culture to Culture*. Cambridge: Cambridge University Press, pp. 25–44.
Pizer, J. (2000), 'Goethe's "world literature" paradigm and contemporary cultural globalization', *Comparative Literature*, 52, (3), 213–27.
— (2005), 'Cosmopolitanism and *Weltliteratur*', *Goethe Yearbook*, 13, 165–79.
— (2006), *The Idea of World Literature: History and Pedagogical Practice*. Baton Rouge: Louisiana State University Press.
Prendergast, C. (ed.) (2004), *Debating World Literature*. London and New York: Verso.
Prodolliet, E. (1978), *Faust im Kino: die Geschichte des Faustfilms von den Anfängen bis in die Gegenwart*. Freiburg: Universitätsverlag.
Rhie, W.-Y. (2000), 'Goethes *Faust* auf der koreanischen Bühne: Überlegungen zur Rezeption in Korea'. Goethe-Symposium der Sophia-Universität, Tokyo 1999. *Studien des Instituts für die Kultur der deutschsprachigen Länder*, 18, www.info.sophia.ac.jp/g-areas/DE-Publikation.htm#PublikationenStudien (retrieved 15 August 2007).
Saussy, H. (ed.) (2006), *Comparative Literature in an Age of Globalization*. Baltimore: Johns Hopkins University.
Schanze, H. (1999), *Faust-Konstellationen: Mythos und Medien*. Munich: Fink.
Scherer, L. (2001), *'Faust' in der Tradition der Moderne: Studien zur Variation eines Themas bei Paul Valéry, Michel de Ghelderode, Michel Butor und Edoardo Sanguineti: mit einem Prolog zur Thematologie*. Frankfurt/Main: Peter Lang.
Schmitz-Emans, M. (2004), 'Preface on the project', in M. Schmitz-Emans (ed.), *Transkulturelle Rezeption und Konstruktion; Transcultural reception and/et Constructions transculturelles*. Heidelberg: Synchron Publishers, pp. 17–23.
Schöne, A. (1999), *Johann Wolfgang Goethe, Faust: Kommentare*. Frankfurt/Main: Deutscher Klassiker Verlag.

Segre, G. (2007), *Faust in Copenhagen: A Struggle for the Soul of Physics*. New York: Viking.
Seifert, S. (ed.) (2000), *Goethe-Bibliographie 1950–1990*, 3 v. Munich: Saur.
Simm, H. J. and Lux, C. (eds) (2007), *Zweihundert Jahre Goethes 'Faust'*. Frankfurt/Main: Insel Verlag.
Singer, A. E. and Schlunk, J. (eds) (1999), *Doctor Faustus: Archetypal Subtext at the Millennium*. Morgantown: West Virginia University Press.
Smeed, J. W. (1975), *Faust in Literature*. London and New York: Oxford University Press.
Šormová, E. (ed.) (1993), *Don Juan and Faust in the XXth Century*. Prague: Czechoslovak Academy of Sciences.
Sponsler, C. and Chen, X. (eds) (2000), *East of West: Crosscultural Performance and the Staging of Difference*. New York and Basingstoke: Palgrave.
Thinès, G. (1989), *Le Mythe de Faust et la dialectique du temps*. Paris: L'Age d'homme.
Tötösy de Zepetnek, S. (ed.) (2003), *Comparative Literature and Comparative Cultural Studies*. West Lafayette: Purdue University Press.
Trumpener, K. (2006), 'World music, world literature: A geopolitical view', in H. Saussy (ed.), *Comparative Literature in an Age of Globalization*. Baltimore: Johns Hopkins University, pp. 185–202.
Tymoczko, M. and Gentzler, E. (eds) (2002), *Translation and Power*. Amherst and Boston: University of Massachusetts Press.
Ugrinsky, A. (ed.) (1987), *Goethe in the Twentieth Century*. New York: Greenwood Press.
Ungar, A. (ed.) (2006), 'Writing in tongues: Thoughts on the work of translation', in H. Saussy (ed.), *Comparative Literature in an Age of Globalization*. Baltimore: Johns Hopkins University, pp. 127–38.
Van der Laan, J. M. (2007), *Seeking Meaning for Goethe's Faust*. London and New York: Continuum.
Venuti, L. (ed.) (1992), *Rethinking Translation: Discourse, Subjectivity, Ideology*. London and New York: Routledge.
— (1995), *The Translator's Invisibility: A History of Translation*. New York: Routledge.
Vietor-Engländer, D. (1987), *Faust in der DDR*. Frankfurt/Main and New York: Peter Lang.
Watt, I. (1996), *Myths of Modern Individualism: Faust, Don Quixote, Don Juan, Robinson Crusoe*. Cambridge and New York: Cambridge University Press.
Wende-Hohenberger, W. and Riha, K. (eds) (1989), *Faust Parodien: eine Auswahl satirischer Kontrafakturen, Fort und Weiterdichtungen*. Frankfurt/Main: Insel Verlag.
Williams, J. R. (2002), 'What gets lost? A look at some recent English translations of Goethe', in N. Boyle and J. Guthrie (eds), *Goethe and the English-Speaking World: Essays for the Cambridge Symposium for His 250th Anniversary*. Rochester: Camden House, pp. 213–26.
Wright, C. (2006), '*Faust* goes pop: A translator's rereading(s)', in E. Loffredo and M. Perteghella (eds), *Translation and Creativity: Perspectives on Creative Writing and Translation Studies*. London and New York: Continuum, pp. 145–57.
Yoo, H.-S. (2006), 'A little pact with the devil? On Franco Moretti's conjectures on world literature', in G. Lindberg-Wada (ed.), *Studying Transcultural Literary History*. Berlin and New York: Walter de Gruyter, pp. 133–43.

Part I

Anteriorities

1 Global Dominion: Faust and Alexander the Great

Arnd Bohm

The search for the historical Faust has yielded remarkably little solid evidence, beyond scattered references of dubious reliability (Kreutzer 1988: 62–3; Schöne 1999: 182). What has come together as the 'matter of Faust' was assembled from a wide range of materials (Baron 1992: 95–109; Füssel 1991; Kühne 1868: 149–253). The sources for the Faust Books are one problem, but another central question has been where the contours of Faust's life came from. Various figures have been suggested as possible prototypes (Bevington and Rasmussen 1993: 7–8).[1] All of these are plausible candidates to some extent as men of learning on some sort of quest for illegitimate knowledge through satanic pacts, black magic and the occult. There has also been some suggestion that Faust's career follows that of a negative saint's biography (Baron 1992: 124–5). Looking to men of the world as models, Harold Jantz (1978: 141–3) argued for Timoleon and Caesar, whose biographies Goethe would have known from Plutarch.[2] He might well have suggested someone else prominent in Plutarch, namely Alexander the Great.[3] The concentration upon the epistemological dimensions of the Faust material within the context of the rise of science has tended to occlude another of his defining qualities: his conquering ambition. This is brought into sharp focus by Marlowe when Faustus sketches for himself a future of unlimited imperial power:

> Shall I make spirits fetch me what I please?
> Resolve me of all ambiguities?
> Perform what desperate enterprise I will?
> I'll have them fly to India for gold,
> Ransack the ocean for orient pearl,
> And search all corners of the new-found world
> For pleasant fruits and princely delicates.
> I'll have them read me strange philosophy
> And tell the secrets of all foreign kings.
> ...
>
> I'll levy soldiers with the coin they bring
> And chase the Prince of Parma from our land,
> And reign sole king of all the provinces.
>   (Marlowe 1993: I.i.78–86, 91–3)[4]

He wishes nothing less than power over the entire world and would even wrest 'the secrets' from 'all foreign kings', reducing them to little more than booty. Significantly, an exercise of might will garner the secrets, rather than the study of hermetic texts. The plan may be correct for the man of arms, but for the man of letters knowledge should lead to power, and ultimately knowledge should expose the emptiness of political triumphs. The use of Alexander as the template for Faustus' biography has inverted the relationship. The figure haunting Faust is that of the famous conqueror, the first and enduring example of overweening worldly ambition.

The conjunction of Faustus and Alexander may seem an unlikely one today, but medieval and early modern readers were familiar with a different Alexander than the one we know. The 'historical Alexander' has been stripped of everything except those deeds which can be documented.[5] The main classical sources considered to be reliable remain Arrian's *Anabasis of Alexander* and his *Indica* (1967), Curtius Rufus' *History of Alexander* (1984) and Plutarch's life of 'Alexander' and his orations 'On the fortune or the virtue of Alexander' (1957; 1958). The history books have fallen silent about Alexander's adventures in the realms of the wonderful and the fantastic that captivated audiences for 1500 years. The archive in which his legendary exploits were preserved, varied and amplified included a wide range of texts, including Alexander's 'Epistola Alexandri ad Aristotelem' ('Letter to Aristotle') (Gunderson 1980: 140–56), the Archpriest Leo's *Historia de Preliis* (Bergmeister 1975), the medieval French *Roman d'Alexandre* (La Du 1937; Hilka 1920), Walter of Châtillon's *Alexandreis* (Pritchard 1986), the pseudo-Aristotelian *Secretum Secretorum* (*Secret of Secrets*) (Steele 1898; Manzalaoui 1977), the Middle Dutch *Seelentrost* (*Soul's Consolation*) (Barnouw 1929), the Middle High German *Alexanderlied* by the cleric Lamprecht (Ruttmann 1974) and the Spanish *Libro de Alexandre* (Willis 1934).[6] In the sixteenth century Johann Hartlieb's *Alexander* (Pawis 1991) bridged the transition from manuscript to printed versions of the Alexander legends and overlapped chronologically with the rise of the Faust story, which quickly absorbed and displaced the Alexander tales.

Readers were most interested in the lessons that could be drawn from Alexander's actions, his qualities and the meanings of his life and death. Those who admired him praised his virtues, down to Montaigne, who cited personal ones ('justice, temperance, liberality, fidelity to his word, love for his people, humanity toward the vanquished') as well as his military ones ('diligence, foresight, patience, discipline, subtlety, magnanimity, resolution, good fortune') (1965: 571–2). Because of his generosity and magnanimity, he was presented as a model for kings, knights and courtiers[7] and was canonized as one of the Nine Worthies (Schroeder 1971). In addition to sharing the achievements ascribed to the historical Alexander, the legendary Alexander was also credited with fantastic exploits: going to paradise and to hell, encountering fairy-maidens who turn out to be flowers, exchanging letters with the Amazons, seeking advice from the talking trees and, not least, ascending into the air by the aid of griffins and going underwater by means of a diving bell. Of these episodes none caught the medieval imagination more than the heavier-than-air flight.[8]

Most detractors stressed the negative implications of Alexander's exploits without disputing that they might have happened. Accomplishments such as winning battles and undertaking explorations were no more admirable than fabulous gests. Harshest among the critics was Lucan:

> There lies the mad son of Macedonian Philip, that fortunate freebooter, cut off by a death that avenged the world. The limbs that should have been scattered over the whole earth they laid in a hallowed shrine; Fortune spared his dead body, and the destiny of his reign endured to the last. (1997: 591–3; 10.20–8)[9]

Christian commentators were less interested in Alexander's political legacy than in the problem of where to insert him in history framed eschatologically (Pfister 1976: 333–42; Cary 1956: 118–42; Bunt 1982; Cölln 2000: 171–4). Some aspects of the legends were taboo, especially where they touched on Alexander's divinity, whether as the putative son of Jove or in his elevation to godhead under the influence of oriental rites (Badian 1976). Other incidents could be glossed to reveal how Christians should understand Alexander's behavior. The key criterion, the mean, was taken from Aristotelian philosophy: whatever smacked of excess was condemned, whatever worked toward maintaining or re-establishing the mean was praiseworthy. Hence Alexander's largesse was good when it redressed imbalances in the social order, but was bad when it was too magnificent (as when the Macedonians began to imitate the luxuriant gift economy of the Persians). Alexander's violations of the mean were evident in two essential aspects of his undertakings, his curiosity and his political ambitions. Both came together in the episode of his flight. On the one hand, his curiosity was relatively harmless, indeed amusing, and consistent with the inquiring mind represented by his 'Letter to Aristotle'. On the other, it was perilously close to forbidden prying into secret realms, perilously close to the sin of 'curiositas'.[10] Consequently the German accounts Christianize the text by having God imposing a limit to the ascent (Cary 1956: 258; Kugler 1987: 9–10; Franke 2000: 135–7; Pawis 1991: 312).

The same conjunction between curiosity and conquest is revealed when Walter of Châtillon has Nature descend into the underworld to demand that limits be set on Alexander's plans:

> For you must be aware of the great upheaval and annoyance that warlike Alexander is causing the elements. After subduing the Pamphylian Sea with his fleet, he has thrice conquered Darius, and, crushing all Asia, he has compelled Porus, hitherto invincible in wars, to be his vassal.
>
> Nor is he content with this. He now searches the hiding-places of the East, and like a lunatic thunders against the Ocean itself. Should the fates guide his sails with favorable winds, he proposes to track down the source of the Nile, hitherto hidden from the world, and then surround and besiege Paradise. (Pritchard 1986: 220)

The denizens of hell are outraged and resolve to have him poisoned. Alexander meanwhile 'had crushed the Ocean with his menacing fleet' and planned 'to take the Macedonian lances over into the land of the Carthaginians, once he had settled the affairs of Asia, and then, crossing the Numidian border, to proceed beyond the limits of Spain, where Rumour reported the pillars [sic] of Hercules to be, and to force the western sun to submit to him in war' (Pritchard 1986: 222). Walter's narrator can no longer restrain himself from anxious apostrophe, echoing Lucan's invective:

> To what lengths does your hunger go, Alexander? What end will there be to your possessions, what limit to your requirements, what goal for your labours? Madman, you are accomplishing nothing! You have confined all kingdoms under one rule and subdued the entire world, yet you will always be in need. (Pritchard 1986: 223)[11]

To what extent the rumors of future plans corresponded to reality may never be fully known, but a recent sober assessment of the evidence concludes: 'in his last years his concept of his own greatness had become obsessive. His intention was not merely to surpass what had gone before but to leave posterity no hope of equalling him' (Bosworth 1988: 211).

After having been so dominant in the medieval imagination, the figure of Alexander receded in the fifteenth century. 'Alexander' largely ceased to be a productive signifier around which stories could be collected and organized as coherent historical narratives. The rise of a new critical philology meant that readers were increasingly skeptical about the authority for wonderful tales (Cary 1956: 235–41; Pfizer 1975: 77–8). To replace Alexander other figures emerged, such as Fortunatus and Faustus, and the all-encompassing genre of the travelogue provided scope for reports of marvelous lands and creatures. Curiosity itself was no longer to be condemned as a sin, but with the significant stipulation that it be directed at the real, observable world (Peters 2001; Eamon 1994: 269–300).

The Prose History of Faustus

Beside the empirical scientist there were people who used the opportunity afforded by the legitimation of curiosity to dabble in magic, witchcraft and the occult. The representative for this type was the notorious 'Faustus' and to him were transferred key features of the Alexander in romance. The ground had been prepared by the image of Alexander as too curious, too greedy and too proud. Seeing Alexander as an embodiment of 'superbia' opened the way for an allegorical identification of him 'as a type of Lucifer's supreme attempt against the throne of God' (Loomis 1918: 184; Cary 1956: 258–9). Hence the Alexander legends could be coupled with the stories of Satan/Lucifer/the devil. The contours of the life of Faustus look as though they had been scripted with close reference to those of Alexander's career. Faustus too is bound by the conqueror's desires for power and control and must share his early death.[12] The chapbook history acknowledges the reciprocal mimesis of the two figures when Faustus learns about 'his Lord Lucifer' and recognizes himself in the other (Anon. 1969: 14).

Although his double Lucifer remains occluded, Alexander does appear virtually in the theatre staged at the imperial court. The Emperor Charles V wants to see his splendid predecessor:

> the great and mighty monarch of the world Alexander magnus, was such a lanterne & spectacle to all his successors, as the Cronicles makes mention of so great riches, conquering, and subduing so many kingdomes, the which I and those that follow me (I feare) shall never bee able to attaine unto: wherefore, Faustus, my hearty desire is that thou wouldst vouchsafe to let me see that Alexander, and his Paramour, the which was praysed to be so fayre, and I pray thee shew me them in such form that I may see their personages, shape, gesture & apparel, as they used in their lifetime, and that here before my face; to the ende

> that I may say I have my long desire fulfilled & to prayse thee to be a famous man in thine arte and experience. (Anon. 1969: 50)

One of the real Charles V's ambitions was to outdo Alexander by expanding the Holy Roman Empire past the Pillars of Hercules to include the 'new' world (Walter 1997; Tanner 1993: 109–15).[13] Having no less a figure than Alexander appear at his court would confirm that Charles has overgone, not just succeeded, his ancestor. Within the context of the Faustus and Alexander complex, the episode has contradictory functions. First it indicates the difference between the two and stresses Faustus' modernity and his superiority, since he has power over the great dead man. Faustus' control undermines Alexander's efforts to retain sole authority over the construction of his fame (Braudy 1986: 32–51). Second, the delivery of Alexander confirms Faustus' reputation as a necromancer, indeed as a great one, thus placing him beside Alexander at the apex of achievements.

Another allusion is Faustus' ascent into the sky, immediately recognizable as Alexander's flight:

> beholde, there stoode a Waggon, with two Dragons before it to drawe the same, and all the Waggon was of a light burning fire, and for that the Moone shone, I was the willinger at that time to depart: but the voyce spake againe, sit up and let us away: I will, said I, goe with thee, but uppon this condition, that I may aske after all things that I see, heare, or thinke on: the voyce answered, I am content for this time. Hereupon I get me into the Waggon, so that the Dragons carried me upright into the ayre. (Anon. 1969: 30)

The connection to Alexander's ascent is underscored when Faustus makes explicit that there should be no limitations on what he sees, hears or thinks about: his curiosity is to be absolute. From the air, Faustus sees the tiny earth and the countries spread out below. The extended description of what he observes has always seemed oddly disproportionate and superfluous to the story of Faustus. What is it supposed to show or accomplish? However, the purpose of such a survey is quite logical in the Alexander story, as Michelle Warren explains with reference to the *Roman d'Alexandre*:

> In flight, Alexander rules the world in the imaginative mode . . . Describing this landscape, the narrator adopts Alexander's imperial eyes . . . As of this moment, Alexander has constituted his full imperial power—but only as a memory, preserved in narrative and recoverable through the reading of history. (2002: 147)

Faustus' virtual dominion becomes even more tangible in the following chapter where he criss-crosses the topography of the Holy Roman Empire, literally incorporating all the lands of Europe into his experience and mirroring the endless campaigns with which Alexander made the known world his.[14]

After completing the textual assimilation of the Christian Empire, Faustus goes to the Orient, again imitating Alexander's trajectory. The history blends 'Turkey' with Alexander's 'Persia' and Faustus' sojourn in the Turkish harem revises Alexander's sybaritic activities at the Persian court after the defeat of Darius. The narrator amplifies the topic of Alexander's sexual excesses, transposing them on to Faustus and adding some anti-Islamic propaganda:

> he himselfe appeared amongst the Ladies in all things as they use to paint their Mahumet, at which sight, the Ladies fell on their knees, and worshipped him, then Faustus tooke the fairest by the hand, and led her into a chamber, where

after his maner hee fell to dalliance, and thus he continued a whole day and night: and when hee had delighted himself sufficiently with her, hee put her away, and made his spirite bring him another, so likewise hee kept with her 24 houres play ... (Anon. 1969: 43–4)

The treatment of Faustus by the Turkish women resembles that shown by the conquered family of Darius to Alexander; the comparison to 'Mahumet' is a reminder of the theme of Alexander's divinity.[15] Despite Plutarch's reassurances that Alexander had been self-restrained to the point of asceticism when it came to the Persian women, Arrian's account conveyed a different impression (Arrian 1967: 2215 [VII.4.4–5]). The latter view certainly would appeal more to a popular audience.[16] From Turkey Faustus goes to Egypt, again following Alexander's trajectory. After a digression back to Europe, the narrative takes Faustus to Paradise, where Alexander had also gone (Pfister 1976: 151–9; Cary 1956: 176–7).

Less explicit is the influence upon the construction of Faustus' death from the traditions surrounding Alexander's last days. Both figures die an untimely, early death. In each case the time and cause of their death are known beforehand. Alexander is surrounded by loyal soldiers and Faust by a group of students. Both carefully prepare a will and designate who should inherit. As the end draws near, Alexander's mind filled with anxiety quite out of keeping with the confidence that he had always felt:

Alexander, then, since he had now become sensitive to indications of the divine will and perturbed and apprehensive in his mind, converted every unusual and strange occurrence, were it never so insignificant, into a prodigy and portent; and sacrificers, purifiers, and diviners filled his palace. So, you see, while it is a dire thing to be incredulous towards indications of the divine will and to have contempt for them, superstition is likewise a dire thing, which, after the manner of water ever seeking the lower levels, filled with folly the Alexander who was now become a prey to his fears. (Plutarch 1958: 431–3 [lxxv.2])

Similarly Faustus breaks out in anguished remorse:

Here was the first token, for he was like a taken murtherer or a theefe, the which findeth himselfe guiltie in conscience before the Judge have given sentence, fearing every houre to die: for hee was grieved, and wayling spent the time, went talking to himselfe, wringing of his hands, sobbing and sighing, hee fell away from flesh, and was very leane, and kept himself close: neither could he abide to see or heare of his Mephostophiles anymore. (Anon. 1969: 75)

The end when it comes for Faustus is horrible and violent. The students find his limbs scattered around and his body on the dungheap. The histories and romances spare Alexander such an ignoble end, but the punishment does remind one of Lucan's regret that Alexander had been buried in a grave rather than having his limbs strewn 'over the whole earth'.

Doctor Faustus

Deflected from searching for other sources by Marlowe's evident and extensive borrowing from the prose history of Faustus, critics have shown little interest in the play's allusions to Alexander, despite Marlowe's classical education, which yielded, not least, a partial translation of Lucan. Marlowe mentions Alexander in

The Jew of Malta (Marlowe 1969: III.iv.97–100), *Tamburlaine* (Marlowe 1969: V.i.69) and *Edward II* (Marlowe 1969: I.iv.394), indicating familiarity with the whole of his history. *Tamburlaine* and *Edward II* touch on themes central to Alexander (conquest and the love for Hephaestion, respectively). Nor was Marlowe's concern with Alexander unique, as Lyly's *Campaspe* (1991), Shakespeare's *Henry V* (1973: 736–69) and Daniel's *The Tragedy of Philotas* (1963) indicate.[17] Like his contemporaries Marlowe would have encountered the Alexander tradition directly from Plutarch and Lucan, as well as from professors like William Perkins.[18] The Alexander themes suggest that Marlowe was as much concerned with the politics of ambition as with the theology of damnation.[19] A crucial question is how men of learning should accommodate themselves to their sovereigns. One controversial touchstone for the debate was Plutarch's assertion in his 'On the fortune of Alexander' that through his actions Alexander had been an authentic philosopher, perhaps even greater than Plato:

> Although few of us read Plato's *Laws*, yet hundreds of thousands have made use of Alexander's laws, and continue to use them. Those who were vanquished by Alexander are happier than those who escaped his hand; for these had no one to put an end to the wretchedness of their existence, while the victor compelled those others to lead a happy life. (1957: 395 [328 E])

The claim that actions are more valuable than theories was and remains controversial. Why mourn the death of Socrates as long as there are Alexanders?[20]

Marlowe's antipathy to tyrants might suggest that *Doctor Faustus* should be read in terms of a conflict between power and knowledge, as an allegory on the condition of Elizabethan scholars and courtiers. But Marlowe complicates things since Faustus is neither a philosopher nor a man of action. His flaw is that he desires first to emulate and then to outdo Alexander through illusions and magic. The preposterousness of such ambitions was castigated by Francis Bacon in the *Novum Organum*:

> For there has been no lack of empty talkers and dreamers who, partly from credulity, partly by imposture, have loaded the human race with promises . . . But of these lavish promisers it would be fair to say that there is as great a difference in philosophical doctrine between their baseless utterances and true arts as there is in historical narrative between the exploits of Julius Caesar or Alexander the Great and the deeds of Amadis of Gaul or Arthur of Britain. For those illustrious commanders are found in fact to have done greater things than these shadowy heroes are even feigned to have done, and indeed by ways and means that were neither fabulous nor miraculous. (1994: 97)

In other words, what modern scientists can learn from an Alexander is how to operate in the real world, how to get things done, how to make Nature actually reveal her secrets. Faustus and his ilk declined to do so, preferring to imitate the empty accomplishments of fictional heroes. Faustus explicitly fancies himself the successor to Alexander:

> I'll be great emperor of the world
> And make a bridge through the moving air
> To pass the ocean; with a band of men
> I'll join the hills that bind the Afric shore
> And make that country continent to Spain,
> And both contributory to my crown.

> The Emperor shall not live but by my leave,
> Nor any potentate of Germany.
> (Marlowe 1993: I.iii.103–10)

The plans for expedition to the Straits of Gibraltar and Spain are exactly those attributed to Alexander by Plutarch, Arrian and other historians (Bosworth 1988: 190–7; Pearson 1960: 261). Faustus imagines that he will succeed where Alexander fell short. How high he hopes to vault is measured by his response to the Bad Angel's temptation: 'Be thou on earth as Jove is in the sky,/Lord and commander of these elements' (Marlowe 1993: I.i.75–6). Whereas Alexander was reputed to have been a son of Jove, Faustus grasps at the possibility of being the supreme god. An even more audacious presumption is Faustus' resurrection after his dismemberment by Martino, Benvolio and Frederic:

> And had you cut my body with your swords,
> Or hewed this flesh and bones as small as sand,
> Yet in a minute had my spirit returned,
> And I had breathed a man made free from harm.
> (Marlowe 1993: IV.ii.73–6)

The parody of Christ's resurrection is blasphemous, but also an ironical anticipation of Faustus' end. Moreover the lines evoke the fate Lucan had wished upon Alexander, that his body should have been widely scattered.

The precision with which Marlowe indicts Faustus' imitation of Alexander is highlighted when he grandiloquently refers to 'all corners of the new-found world'. Of course, Alexander had not been able to conquer the undiscovered Americas, so Faustus is easily able to make himself appear greater than his precursor, taking advantage of an accident of history. Also in the same speech Faustus alludes to Alexander's encounter with the Gymnosophists (Brahmans): 'I'll have them read me strange philosophy/And tell the secrets of all foreign kings'.[21] As Plutarch tells the story (1958: 405–9 [XIV]), Alexander had captured ten foreign philosophers and 'put difficult questions to them, declaring that he would put to death him who first made an incorrect answer'. The allusion is significant because it suggests that Marlowe had grasped that the episode of Faustus' encounter with the Old Man in Act V ultimately derived from the Alexander legends. The connection is not immediately apparent, for the authors of the chapbooks had replaced the original pagan philosophy with a Christian sermon while retaining the situation of the original episode (Anon. 1969: 67–9). The Gymnosophists, who go naked and possess no worldly goods, dare to resist their omnipotent adversary. The otherwise unidentified humble Old Man, who resembles a 'traditional Morality figure' (Spinrad 1982: 250), makes a final effort to rescue Faustus by reminding him of God's love and the dangers of sorcery, holding out the possibility that it is not too late for Faustus to change his ways. Although the specifics have been adapted to the Christian context, the thrust of the Old Man's counsel is close to the message delivered by the Gymnosophists. They had challenged Alexander to abandon his course of conquest and to pursue a life of renunciation instead. Both Alexander and Faustus lend a respectful ear but ultimately reject the alternative path. Their reasons for doing so follow similar logic. Alexander does not deny the Gymnosophists' teaching but avers that he no longer has a choice, since he must fulfill his destiny (Stackmann 1983: 334). Similarly, Faustus is moved by the Old Man's words to reflect and to repent, yet he fatalistically accepts his doom. Their respective encounters bring both men face to face with the reality of their mortality. When asked by the Gymnosophists to grant them immortality, Alexander admits that he cannot do so since he himself must die. The Old Man's warnings make Faustus all too aware of impending death. The irony is that neither Alexander nor Faustus can benefit from wisdom when they do encounter it.

The circumstances of conjuring up Alexander on the stage reveal key differences between Marlowe's version and the episode in the chapbook. Word of his skill has reached the Emperor, who flatters him most courteously, yet Faustus is pressed to provide visible evidence of his skill; reputations seem unreliable. The confrontation of the two emperors moves Faustus to the margins, since he has never reigned or earned any glory through historical deeds. The best that Faustus can do is to assert control by instructing the Emperor about the rules regarding illusions:

> My lord, I must forewarn your Majesty
> That when my spirits present the royal shapes
> Of Alexander and his paramour,
> Your Grace demand no questions of the king,
> But in dumb silence let them come and go.
> (Marlowe 1993: IV.i. 92–5)

The courteous Emperor submits, unlike rude Benvolio who remains skeptical and taunts Faustus. His skepticism is punished cruelly when Faustus makes horns grow from Benvolio's head. After removing them at the Emperor's behest, Faustus warns Benvolio to respect men of learning: 'And hereafter, sir, look you speak well of scholars'. The warning is ineffectual; Benvolio blithely denounces such forceful attempts to shore up unearned fame: 'Speak well of ye? 'Sblood, an scholars be such cuckold-makers to clap horns of honest men's heads o' this order, I'll ne'er trust smooth faces and small ruffs more' (Marlowe 1993: IV. i.164–7). Faustus cannot manipulate popular opinion so as to guarantee that his fame will be secure. His lapse from decorum is hardly worthy of a courtier and may be an overt allusion to Alexander's outrage when Cleitus dared to question his reputation. Faustus' demand for respect also brings to mind Alexander's requirement that the Macedonians show him reverence by prostrating themselves as the Persians did for their kings (Arrian 1967: 2361–9 [IV.7.4–IV.9.10]; Bosworth 1988: 63–4).

The appearance on stage of Alexander and his Paramour intensifies the audience's sense of the profound difference between Faustus and Alexander. Marlowe provides a wordless pantomime that mirrors the climax of Alexander's victory over the Persians, something missing from the chapbook:

> *Enter at one [door] the Emperor* ALEXANDER, *at the other* DARIUS. *They meet; Darius is thrown down. Alexander kills him, takes off his crown, and, offering to go out, his* PARAMOUR *meets him. He embraceth her and sets Darius's crown upon her head; and, coming back, both salute the [German] Emperor, who, leaving his state, offers to embrace them, which Faustus seeing suddenly stays him.* (Marlowe 1993: IV.ii before 103)

It is the most fitting moment to show the Emperor, not just because it represents the zenith of Alexander's might but, more importantly, because it reveals Alexander's noblest virtue, his magnanimity. Unlike the Greeks who enslaved the Trojan women after Troy fell, Alexander spared the lives of the Persian royal women and even married one.²² Such ideal behavior contrasts with Faustus, who never conquered anyone and therefore could not demonstrate largesse, and who is basically incapable of generosity. The mere virtual presence of Alexander makes Faustus' life pale by comparison.

Faustus consoles himself with the thought that he too could be an ancient hero. Again he is following the example of Alexander, whose admiration for Homer, the Homeric world and above all Achilles was well-known (Pearson 1960: 10, 40–1; Mossman 1988: 84). Faustus likewise claims his right to live in the age of heroes: 'Have not I made blind Homer sing to me/Of Alexander's love and Oenone's death?' (Marlowe 1993: II.iii. 24–5). However, whereas Alexander was spurred to greater deeds, Faustus withdraws into fantasy:

> Here will I dwell, for heaven is in these lips,
> And all is dross that is not Helena.
> I will be Paris, and for love of thee
> Instead of Troy shall Wittenberg be sacked,
> And I will combat with weak Menelaus,
> And wear thy colours on my plumèd crest.
> Yea, I will wound Achilles in the heel
> And then return to Helen for a kiss.
> (Marlowe 1993: V.i.99–106)

Alas, Faustus' will cannot be done. Or perhaps fortunately, since his unlimited ambition seems ready to sacrifice an entire modern city in order to satisfy his vanity. That innocent Wittenberg should be sacked for the sake of his delusions is a thought that discloses in a sudden flash why Faustus must never be allowed access to real power. Alexander had sacked Thebes and burned Persepolis in the course of building an empire, not to satisfy personal whims, and he knew first-hand what war was. The friction of reality limited his achievements but also his ambitions, whereas the inventions of Faustus lack all prudent restraint.

Faust

The apparent absence of Alexander from Goethe's *Faust* is unexpected, particularly because his Faust has the same hubristic goals as Faustus. There are only slight traces of the Alexander legends in Part I.²³ However, Part II steadily reveals Alexander's presence as a model as Faust evolves into an absolute tyrant.²⁴ The revelations begin almost immediately:

> The Emperor wants to see, and will brook no delay,
> Helen of Troy and Paris here before him,
> and gaze upon clear counterfeits
> of those two paragons of male and female beauty.
>
> (Der Kaiser will, es muß sogleich geschehn,
> Will Helena und Paris vor sich sehn;
> Das Musterbild der Männer, so der Frauen,
> In deutlichen Gestalten will er schauen.)
> (F, 6183–6)

The difference between this Emperor's desires and those of the Emperors in the chapbook and in *Doctor Faustus* is consistent with the Emperor's ineffectual performance as a ruler. Caring little about properly managing the affairs of state, he does not admire Alexander. Instead he and the court take voyeuristic pleasure from gazing upon ancient lovers. The gossip of the courtiers marks the limited degree to which they can identify with classical heroism. Overwhelmed by his own fantasy, Faust forgets that the spectacle is an illusion and attempts to prevent the abduction of Helena, with catastrophic consequences. Faust cannot control his own feelings or master an illusion, never mind conquering the world.

Goethe has systematically retained traces of the Alexander stories and incorporated them into the play. What matters is the pervading legacy of the tradition that continues to influence, inspire and shape human affairs. But the past has been reduced to a pathetic remnant in a world where wars are entertainment, as the Second Burgher proclaims:

> Sundays and holidays there's nothing I like more
> than to discuss a war and military matters
> when armies far away—off there in Turkey—
> engage in battle with each other.
>
> (Nichts bessers weiß ich mir an Sonn- und Feiertagen,
> Als ein Gespräch von Krieg und Kriegsgeschrei,
> Wenn hinten, weit, in der Türkei,
> Die Völker auf einander schlagen.)
>
> (F, 860–3)

In such a world Faust's aspirations for fame and glory might even be valued as a positive alternative, a striving worthy of an Alexander. Through Mephistopheles' mockery Faust's parallels to Alexander become evident:

> Perhaps I'll guess what's fired your ambition—
> something sublime and daring, I am sure!
> Did you, while floating near the moon, not have
> the lunatic desire for a lunar voyage?
>
> (Errät man wohl wornach du strebtest?
> Es war gewiß erhaben kühn.
> Der du dem Mond um so viel näher schwebtest,
> Dich zog wohl deine Sucht dahin?)
>
> (F, 10177–80)

The legendary ascent has been recast: Faust was borne aloft on Helen's garments that dissolved as he rose. One implication is that griffins will no longer convince a modern audience, which prefers outright fantasies. At the same time, the use of fabric and vapor brings the mechanics of ascent up to date, since flight in balloons was possible in Goethe's time.[25] Faust's monologue from the heights echoes the surveys from the chapbook and *Doctor Faustus*. Mephistopheles alludes to Alexander:

> You've now surveyed, in measureless expanses,
> the kingdoms of the world and all their glory.
>
> (Matt. 4)
>
> Yet I suppose, since nothing ever suits you,
> that you saw nothing you desired.
>
> (Du übersahst, in ungemeßnen Weiten,
> Die Reiche der Welt und ihre Herrlichkeiten;
>
> (MATTH. 4)

Doch, ungenügsam wie du bist,
Empfandest du wohl kein Gelüst?)
(F, 10130–3)[26]

But Mephistopheles does not hide his ultimate contempt for Faust's ambitions, putting them in the category of 'lunatic'. Among other things, Mephistopheles tempts Faust with the possibility that he might build himself a Versailles in the manner of Louis XIV, who was blatantly compared to Alexander by the French (Ranum 1980; Grell and Michel 1988). The set of allusions to Louis XIV had begun in Act I, where the spectacular entrance was based by Goethe on Charles Le Brun's depiction of *The Triumphal Entry of Alexander the Great in Babylon*, of which he owned a copy (Gaier 1999: 608–10). The original painting was part of Le Brun's project of allegorizing Louis XIV as a second Alexander (Grell and Michel 1988: 110–20).

Faust recognizes the topic and cites 'Sardanapalus', a byword for the excesses of tyrants. Nevertheless, he remains intent on a project that will rival Alexander. He will establish dominion over the ocean waves:

> Imbued with strength, wave after wave holds power
> but then withdraws, and nothing's been accomplished—
> a sight to drive me to despair,
> this aimless strength of elemental forces!
> This has inspired me to venture to new heights,
> to wage war here against these forces and subdue them.
>
> (Da herrschet Well auf Welle kraftbegeistet,
> Zieht sich zurück und es ist nichts geleistet.
> Was zur Verzweiflung mich beängstigen könnte,
> Zwecklose Kraft, unbändiger Elemente!
> Da wagt mein Geist sich selbst zu überfliegen,
> Hier möcht' ich kämpfen, dies möcht ich besiegen.)
> (F, 10216–21)

This ambition had a counterpart in the legend, according to which Alexander's army was miraculously spared from drowning in Pamphylia (Pearson 1960: 36–7; Cary 1956: 126–7). Walter of Châtillon had Nature refer explicitly to the incident of the Pamphylian Sea when condemning Alexander's limitless plans for conquest (1986: 220). The hubris of Faust's and Alexander's goals is highlighted when they die without having defeated Poseidon.

The central event of Act IV is the battle between the Emperor and his anonymous opponent. There has been some speculation about which battle Goethe had in mind or where he had learned the relevant tactical theory (Steinmetz 1994). Goethe, like generals down to the present, studied the accounts of Alexander's most famous victory, the decisive defeat of the Persians at Gaugamela (Arbela).[27] The battle became a case study on how an outnumbered army could win through innovative military thinking. Goethe's narrative follows the standard account fairly closely, but he introduces an incongruous twist when Mephistopheles resorts to magic in order to save the day. Alexander did not have such means at his disposal, yet Mephistopheles touches on a key point in tactical thinking when he observes that feints can be crucial in deciding the outcome of a battle and that not all the factors involved are under a commander's control. At stake is the problem posed by Plutarch: were Alexander's successes due to his personal virtue or to good fortune? Plutarch attributed them to virtue but, as Goethe has constructed the history, virtue is in this instance precluded since the Emperor lacks any positive qualities. Even though the battle has been won by cheating, the Emperor is satisfied: 'It does not matter how! What counts is that we've won/and that the scattered foe is fled across the plain' (*F*, 10849–50). The Emperor echoes Plutarch's argument that fortune favors the brave: 'Although our battle did involve some use of tricks,/the fact remains that we were those who did the fighting' (*F*, 10857–8). However, this Emperor can hardly be compared to Plutarch's Alexander, who struggled for his triumphs: 'But what greatness did Alexander acquire beyond his just merits, what without sweat, what without blood, what without a price, what without labour?' (Plutarch 1957: 463 [340]). This Emperor has done nothing except watch.

As he grows into the role of tyrant, Faust's conquests spare no one. The idyll of Philemon and Baucis is a last bit of free terrain. The connection of Faust's rash seizure of their property may be explicated by Goethe's observations in his 'Noten und Abhandlungen zu besserem Verständnis des West-östlichen Divans' ('Notes to the West-Easterly Divan') on Alexander's killing of Cleitus. Goethe links the incident to the Macedonians' burning of Persepolis (Goethe 1982, 2: 176–7). The city and the idyll, both repositories of civility and culture in a conquered world, are burned to the ground by willful excesses of power. Just as Alexander wept bitterly and rued the murder, so Faust sincerely regrets what has happened to Philemon and Baucis, but remorse comes too late. It does not matter whether Alexander or Faust ever intended to harm anyone. The eruptions of violence are contrasted with the possibility for doing good, represented in Alexander by his mercy to the family of Darius after the Persian's defeat. The incident was known to Goethe since he had made a special effort while in Italy to see Paolo Veronese's *The Family of Darius*, which showed the emotional moment (Goethe 1982, 11: 86). He knew how to estimate the gesture and its distance from the conqueror who had had the citizens of Thebes slaughtered.[28] At the same time, he grasped that a life spent pursuing dominion, whether over people or Nature, was not a good one. At the end the Lemures gather around Faust's grave and gravely mock his mortality with fake riddles: 'Who built me such a wretched house/ with shovel and with spade?' (*F*, 11604–5). The episode reminds us of a passage in the *Secretum Secretorum* where wise men gather around Alexander's tomb and contrast the conqueror's ambitions with the corpse's reality, uttering with pithy sayings, such as 'yesterday hym suffisid not all the world full of Precious stonys, ne no Palis of golde; to day hym Suffice a lytill bounde of two ellis othyr thre' (Steele 1898: 151).[29] Dominion over the world, it would seem, has prepared neither Faust nor Alexander for the grave; the dead have no dominion.

Notes

1   Kästner (1993: 109–11) suggests Agrippa von Nettesheim, Johannes Wierus, Paracelsus, Kaspar Peucer, Leonhard Thurneysser, Adam von Bodenstein, Nostradamus, Jehan Thibault, Michael Servet, Nikolaus Kopernikus, Georg Rheticus and Georg Iserin as some figures who audiences might have associated with the figure of Faust.

2   But see the cautions expressed by Boyle (1982–3: 131–2).
3   Two slight hints at the similarity between Alexander and Faust are made by Dronke (1997: 138) and Vercesi (2005: 19).
4   *Doctor Faustus* here and below is quoted from the B-text (1616).
5   Overviews of the historians' approaches and of the difficulties presented by the documents include Bosworth (2000), Demetriou (2001), Pearson (1960), Thomas (2007) and Wirth (1993).
6   Indispensable as a guide through the labyrinth of texts, versions and editions is Cary (1956). The Medieval Alexander Project at the University of Rochester maintains a very useful online bibliography for the British and French traditions. For the German Alexander reception, see Buntz (1973). Ross (1971; 1988) surveys in detail the illustrated manuscripts.
7   The whole of the extremely popular *Secretum Secretorum* was couched as advice from Aristotle to Alexander on how to be a good ruler (Steele 1898; Manzalaoui 1977). By imputation, it was easy to conclude that Alexander had indeed fulfilled the ideal. For the *Roman d'Alexander* see Kibler (2002) and Gosman (2002) and for the *Alexandreis* see Perez (1989). On Alexander and chivalry, see Bologna (1989). His importance for actual rulers is masterfully examined in a case study by Franke (2000).
8   On Alexander and the marvellous, see the thorough exposition by Friede (2003). On his flight see also Schmidt (1995), Kugler (1987) and Merkelbach (1977: 84–8).
9   On Lucan's treatment of Alexander, see Croisille (1990) and Quint (1993: 152–5).
10 Benedict (2001) provides an accessible overview, which can be supplemented, especially on the medieval theories, with Harrison (2001), Zacher (1976) and Peters (1996; 2001). Hadot (2006) is a profound contribution to these topics.
11 On the philosophical background to Walter's critical stance, see Kratz (1980: 61–168).
12 On Faustus and curiosity, see Forster (1981), Kästner (1993: 106–9), Müller (1984) and Benedict (2001: 34–6).
13 There were many attempts by European rulers to claim Alexander as an ancestor; see Borchardt (1971: passim).
14 Cunningham (1559: 'Preface') links mapmaking with Alexander's military successes.
15 In Hartlieb's version, the Persians wanted to worship Alexander but he demurred, saying he was only mortal (Pawis 1991: 187).
16 Compare also Pearson (1960: 50–61).
17 On *Campaspe*, see Scragg (1999); on Alexander in *Henry V*, see Mossman (1994) and Spencer (1996).
18 The Calvinist attack on Alexander as an attack on the Catholic French monarchs warrants closer study. See the complex use of Alexander's construction of fame by Perkins (1604: 509).
19 Suggestive in this regard are the observations by Tate (1997: 270–1) on the 'imperial iconography' of the conjuring for Charles V.
20 See Adler's (2003: 199–206) incisive discussion.
21 For a summary and analysis of the sources, see Hansen (1965), Stackmann (1983), Göller (1989), Bejczy (1990) and Stoneman (1995). The theological implications are outlined by Wallach (1941).
22 See the thorough and balanced reassessment by Carney (1996).
23 I hope to address this issue in a separate study. Some of the necessary background is provided by Fenzi (2003) and the sources cited there. Citations of *F* refer to Goethe (1994a) and the Atkins translation (1994b).
24 My interpretation of the political implications of Act IV is indebted to Schuchard (1935).
25 On Goethe's fascination with balloon flight, see Wenzel (1988).
26 See the commentary by Gaier (1999: 980–1). Without an awareness of Alexander's precedent, the thrust of Goethe's ironic citation of Scripture is blunted: Mephistopheles insinuates that the scene of Christ's temptation copied Alexander's flight.

27 On the sequence of the battle, see Devine (1975). On its significance for the history of war, see Creasy (1900: 57–83). Fuller (1961: 27–248) claims an analysis of Alexander's tactics shaped military thinking in the twentieth century.
28 Cf. the profound essay by Gutwirth (1983).
29 In the *Secretum Secretorum*, which is not organized as a chronicle of Alexander's life, the passage comes in the middle of the text. Already in the thirteenth century Jacob van Maerlant's Dutch *Alexanders Geesten* had made the material part of the closing (De Graaf 1978: 247). Cf. the Middle Dutch and Middle Low German versions edited by Barnouw (1929: 395–6). Barnouw also reprints a version published from a manuscript in 1798 by Bruns (337–66). Goethe thought well of Bruns (1982, 10: 476) and might well have seen the text.

Bibliography

Adler, E. (2003), *Vergil's Empire: Political Thought in the* Aeneid. Lanham and Boulder: Rowman and Littlefield.
Anon. (1969), *The Historie of the Damnable Life, and Deserved Death of Doctor John Faustus (London 1592)*, P. F. Gent (trans.). Amsterdam: Theatrum Orbis Terrarum and New York: Plenum Publishing.
Arrian (1967), *Anabasis Alexandri and Indica*, E. Iliff Robson (trans.). Cambridge: Harvard University Press and London: William Heinemann.
Bacon, F. (1994), *Novum Organum, With Other Parts of The Great Instauration*, P. Urbach and J. Gibson (eds and trans.). Chicago and La Salle: Open Court.
Badian, E. (1976), *The Deification of Alexander the Great*. Berkeley: The Center for Hermeneutical Studies in Hellenistic and Modern Culture, University of California, Berkeley.
Barnouw, A. J. (ed.) (1929), 'A Middle Low German Alexander legend', *The Germanic Review*, 4, 50–77, 284–304, 373–401.
Baron, F. (1992), *Faustus on Trial: The Origins of Johann Spies's 'Historia' in an Age of Witch Hunting*. Tübingen: Max Niemeyer.
Bejczy, I. (1990), 'De "bon sauvage" in de middeleeuwen: Alexander en de Brahmanen: het voorbeeld van Maerlant', *De Nieuwe Taalgids*, 83, 434–45.
Benedict, B. M. (2001), *Curiosity: A Cultural History of Early Modern Inquiry*. Chicago and London: University of Chicago Press.
Bergmeister, H.-J. (ed.) (1975), *Die Historia de Preliis Alexandri Magni (der lateinische Alexanderroman des Mittelalters)*. Meisenheim: Hain.
Bevington, D. and Rasmussen, E. (1993), 'Introduction', in D. Bevington and E. Rasmussen (eds), *Doctor Faustus: A- and B-texts (1604–1616)*. Manchester and New York: Manchester University Press, pp. 1–102.
Bologna, C. (1989), 'La generosità cavalleresca di Alesssandro Magno', *L'Immagine riflessa*, 12, 367–404.
Borchardt, F. L. (1971), *German Antiquity in Renaissance Myth*. Baltimore and London: The Johns Hopkins University Press.
Bosworth, A. B. (1988), *From Arrian to Alexander: Studies in Historical Interpretation*. Oxford: Clarendon.
—(2000), 'Introduction', in A. B. Bosworth and E. J. Baynham (eds), *Alexander the Great in Fact and Fiction*. Oxford: Oxford University Press, pp. 1–22.
Boyle, N. (1982–3), '"Du ahnungsloser Engel, Du!": Some current views of Goethe's *Faust*', *German Life and Letters*, 36, 116–47.
Braudy, L. (1986), *The Frenzy of Renown: Fame and Its History*. New York and Oxford: Oxford University Press.
Bruns, P. J. (1798), *Romantische und andere Gedichte in altplattdeutscher Sprache*. Berlin: F. Nicolai.

Bunt, G. H. V. (1982), 'Alexander and the universal chronicle: Scholars and translators', in P. Noble, L. Polak and C. Isoz (eds), *The Medieval Alexander Legend and Romance Epic: Essays in Honour of David J. A. Ross*. Millwood, NY and London: Kraus International, pp. 1–10.

Buntz, H. (1973), *Die deutsche Alexanderdichtung des Mittelalters*. Stuttgart: Metzler.

Carney, E. D. (1996), 'Alexander and the Persian women', *American Journal of Philology*, 117, 563–83.

Cary, G. (1956), *The Medieval Alexander*, D. J. A. Ross (ed.). Cambridge: Cambridge University Press.

Cölln, J. (2000), 'Arbeit an Alexander: Lambrecht, seine Fortsetzungen und die handschriftliche Überlieferung', in J. Cölln, S. Friede and H. Wulfram, with R. Finckh (eds), *Alexanderdichtungen im Mittelalter*. Göttingen: Wallstein, pp. 162–207.

Creasy, E. S. (1900), *Decisive Battles of the World*. New York: Colonial Press.

Croisille, J. M. (1990), 'Alexandre chez Lucain: l'image du tyran: notes sur. *Ph* X, 1–52', in J. M. Croisille (ed.), *Neronia IV: Alejandro Magno, modelo de los emperadores romanos*. Brussels: Latomus, pp. 266–76.

Cunningham, W. (1559), *The Cosmographical Glasse Conteinying the Pleasant Principles of Cosmographie, Geographie, Hydrographie, or Navigation*. Early English Books Online. Ann Arbor, MI: Proquest.

Curtius Rufus (Quintus Curtius Rufus) (1984), *The History of Alexander*, J. Yardley (trans.). Harmondsworth: Penguin.

Daniel, S. (1963), 'The tragedy of Philotas', in A. B. Grosart (ed.), *The Complete Works in Verse and Prose of Samuel Daniel*, v. 1. New York: Russell and Russell, pp. 95–181.

De Graaf, K. R. (1978), 'The last days of Alexander in Maerlant's *Alexander's Geesten*', in W. J. Aerts, J. M. M. Hermans and E. Visser (eds), *Alexander the Great in the Middle Ages*. Nijmegen: Alfa, pp. 230–66.

Demetriou, K. N. (2001), 'Historians on Macedonian imperialism and Alexander the Great', *Journal of Modern Greek Studies*, 19, 23–60.

Devine, A. M. (1975), 'Grand tactics at Gaugamela', *Phoenix*, 29, 374–85.

Dronke, P. (1997), 'Poetic originality in *The Wars of Alexander*', in H. Cooper and S. Mapstone (eds), *The Long Fifteenth Century: Essays for Douglas Gray*. Oxford: Clarendon, pp. 123–39.

Eamon, W. (1994), *Science and the Secrets of Nature*. Princeton: Princeton University Press.

Fenzi, E. (2003), 'Seneca e Dante: da Alessandro Magno a Ulisse', in J. Bartuschat and L. Rossi (eds), *Studi sul Canone Letterario del Trecento: Per Michelangelo Picone*. Ravenna: Longo Editore, pp. 67–78.

Forster, L. (1981), *The Man Who Wanted to Know Everything*. London: Institute of Germanic Studies, University of London.

Franke, B. (2000), 'Herrscher über Himmel und Erde: Alexander der Große und die Herzöge von Burgund', *Marburger Jahrbuch für Kunstwissenschaft*, 27, 121–69.

Fuller, J. F. C. (1961), *The Conduct of War 1789–1961*. New Brunswick: Rutgers University Press.

Füssel, S. (1991), 'Die literarischen Quellen der *Historia von D. Johann Fausten*', in R. Auernheimer and F. Baron (eds), *Das Faustbuch von 1587: Provokation und Wirkung*. Munich and Vienna: Profil, pp. 15–39.

Gaier, U. (1999), *Johann Wolfgang Goethe, Faust-Dichtungen. Band 2: Kommentar I*. Stuttgart: Reclam.

Goethe, J. W. (1982), *Werke. Hamburger Ausgabe in 14 Bänden*, E. Trunz (ed.). Munich: Deutscher Taschenbuch Verlag.

—(1994a), *Faust: Texte*, A. Schöne (ed.). Frankfurt/Main: Deutscher Klassiker Verlag.

—(1994b), *Faust I and II*, S. Atkins (ed. and trans.). Princeton: Princeton University Press.

Göller, K. H. (1989), *Kontinuität und Transformation der Antike im Mittelalter*, W. Erzgräber (ed.). Sigmaringen: Jan Thorbecke, 1989, pp. 105–19.

Gosman, M. (2002), 'Alexander the Great as the icon of perfection in the epigones of the *Roman d'Alexandre* (1250–1450): The *utilitas* of the ideal prince', in D. Maddox and

S. Sturm-Maddox (eds), *The Medieval French Alexander*. Albany: State University of New York Press, pp. 175–91.

Grell, C. and Michel, C. (1988), *L'École des princes ou Alexandre disgracié: essai sur la mythologie monarchique de la France absolutiste*. Paris: Belles Lettres.

Gunderson, L. L. (1980), *Alexander's Letter to Aristotle about India*. Meisenheim am Glan:Verlag Anton Hain.

Gutwirth, M. (1983), '"By diverse means . . ." (I:1)', *Yale French Studies*, 64, 180–7.

Hadot, P. (2006), *The Veil of Isis: An Essay on the History of the Idea of Nature*, M. Chase (trans.). Cambridge, MA and London: The Belknap Press of Harvard University Press.

Hansen, G. C. (1965), 'Alexander und die Brahmanen', *Klio: Beiträge zur alten Geschichte*, 43–5, 351–80.

Harrison, P. (2001), 'Curiosity, forbidden knowledge, and the reformation of natural philosophy in Early Modern England', *Isis*, 92, 265–90.

Hilka, A. (ed.) (1920), *Der altfranzösische Prosa-Alexanderroman*. Halle: Niemeyer.

Jantz, H. (1978), *The Form of Faust*. Baltimore and London: The Johns Hopkins University Press.

Kästner, H. (1993), '*Fortunatus* und *Faustus*: Glücksstreben und Erkenntnisdrang in der Erzählprosa vor und nach der Reformation', *Zeitschrift für Literaturwissenschaft und Linguistik*, 89, 87–120.

Kibler, W. W. (2002), '"A paine a on bon arbre de malvaise raïs": Counsel for kings in the *Roman d'Alexandre*', in D. Maddox and S. Sturm-Maddox (eds), *The Medieval French Alexander*. Albany: State University of New York Press, pp. 111–25.

Kratz, D. M. (1980), *Mocking Epic: Waltharius, Alexandreis and the Problem of Christian Heroism*. Madrid: José Porrú Turanzas.

Kreutzer, H. J. (1988), '"Der edelste der Triebe": Über die Wißbegierde in der Literatur am Beginn der Neuzeit', in U. Fülleborn and M. Engel (eds), *Das neuzeitliche Ich in der Literatur des 18. und 20. Jahrhunderts*. Munich: Wilhelm Fink, pp. 59–70.

Kugler, H. (1987), 'Alexanders Greifenflug: Eine Episode des Alexanderromans im deutschen Mittelalter', *Internationales Archiv für Sozialgeschichte der deutschen Literatur*, 12, 1–25.

Kühne, A. (ed.) (1868), *Das älteste Faustbuch*. Zerbst: E. Luppe's Buchhandlung.

La Du, M. S. (ed.) (1937), *The Medieval French Roman d'Alexandre*, v. 1: *Text of the Arsenal and Venice Versions*. Princeton: Princeton University Press.

Loomis, R. S. (1918), 'Alexander the Great's celestial journey (conclusion): Western examples', *The Burlington Magazine for Connoisseurs*, 32, 177–8, 180-1, 182–5.

Lucan (M. A. Lucanus) (1997), *The Civil War*, J. D. Duff (trans.). Cambridge, MA and London: Harvard University Press.

Lyly, J. (1991), *Campaspe. Sappho and Phao*, G. K. Hunter and D. Bevington (eds). Manchester and New York: Manchester University Press.

Maddox, D. and Sturm-Maddox, S. (eds) (2002), *The Medieval French Alexander*. Albany: State University of New York Press.

Manzalaoui, M. A. (ed.) (1977), *Secretum Secretorum: Nine English Versions*, v. 1: *Text*. Oxford: Oxford University Press for The Early English Text Society.

Marlowe, C. (1969), *The Complete Plays*, J. B. Steane (ed.). Harmondsworth: Penguin.

—(1993), *Doctor Faustus: A- and B-texts (1604–1616)*, D. Bevington and E. Rasmussen (eds). Manchester and New York: Manchester University Press.

Merkelbach, R. (1977), *Die Quellen des griechischen Alexanderromans*. Munich: C. H. Beck.

Montaigne, M. E. (1965), *The Complete Essays of Montaigne*, D. M. Frame (trans.). Stanford: Stanford University Press.

Mossman, J. (1988), 'Tragedy and epic in Plutarch's *Alexander*', *The Journal of Hellenic Studies*, 108, 83–93.

—(1994), '*Henry V* and Plutarch's *Alexander*', *Shakespeare Quarterly*, 45, 47–73.

Müller, J.-D. (1984), '*Curiositas* und *erfarung* der Welt im frühen deutschen Prosaroman', in L. Grenzmann and K. Stackmann (eds), *Literatur und Laienbildung im Spätmittelalter und in der Reformationszeit*. Stuttgart: Metzler, pp. 252–71.

Pawis, R. (ed.) (1991), *Johann Hartliebs 'Alexander'*. Munich and Zurich: Artemis.
Pearson, L. (1960), *The Lost Histories of Alexander the Great*. London: William Clowes and Sons, for The American Philological Association.
Perez, M. (1989), 'Le Personnage d'Alexandre le Grand dans l'*Alexandréide*', *Bien Dire et Bien Aprandre*, 7, 19–34.
Perkins, W. (1604), *A Commentarie or Exposition, upon the Five First Chapters to the Epistle to the Galatians*. Early English Books Online. Ann Arbor, MI: ProQuest.
Peters, E. (1996), '*Rex curiosus*: A preface to Prospero', *Majestas*, 4, 61–80.
—(2001), 'The desire to know the secrets of the world', *Journal of the History of Ideas*, 62, 593–610.
Plutarch (1957), 'On the fortune or the virtue of Alexander', in F. C. Babbitt (trans.), *Plutarch's Moralia*, v. 4. Cambridge: Harvard University Press and London: William Heinemann, pp. 319–45.
—(1958), 'Alexander', in B. Perrin (trans.), *Plutarch's Lives*, v. 7. Cambridge: Harvard University Press and London: William Heinemann, pp. 223–439.
Pritchard, R. T. (ed.) (1986), Walter of Châtillon, *The Alexandreis*. Toronto: Pontifical Institute of Medieval Studies.
Quint, D. (1993), *Epic and Empire: Politics and Generic Form from Virgil to Milton*. Princeton: Princeton University Press.
Ranum, O. (1980), *Artisans of Glory: Writers and Historical Thought in Seventeenth-Century France*. Chapel Hill: The University of North Carolina Press.
Ross, D. J. A. (1971), *Illustrated Medieval Alexander-Books in Germany and the Netherlands: A Study in Comparative Iconography*. Cambridge: Modern Humanities Research Association.
—(1988), *Alexander Historiatus* (revised edn). Frankfurt: Athenäum.
Ruttmann, I. (ed.) (1974), *Das Alexanderlied des Pfaffen Lamprecht (Strassburger Alexander)*. Darmstadt: Wissenschaftliche Buchgesellschaft.
Schmidt, V. M. (1995), *A Legend and Its Image: The Aerial Flight of Alexander the Great in Medieval Art*. Groningen: Egbert Forsten.
Schöne, A. (1999), *Johann Wolfgang Goethe, Faust: Kommentare*. Darmstadt: Wissenschaftliche Buchgesellschaft.
Schroeder, H. (1971), *Der Topos der Nine Worthies in Literatur und bildender Kunst*. Göttingen: Vandenhoeck and Ruprecht.
Schuchard, G. C. L. (1935), 'Julirevolution, St. Simonismus und die Faustpartien von 1831', *Zeitschrift für deutsch Philologie*, 60, 140–274, 362–84.
Scragg, L. (1999), '*Campaspe* and the construction of monarchical power', *Medieval and Renaissance Drama in England*, 12, 59–83.
Shakespeare, W. (1973), *The Complete Works of Shakespeare*, H. Craig and D. Bevington (eds). Glenview, IL and London: Scott, Foresman and Company.
Spencer, J. M. (1996), 'Princes, pirates, and pigs: Criminalizing wars of conquest in *Henry V*', *Shakespeare Quarterly*, 47, 160–77.
Spinrad, P. S. (1982), 'The dilettante's lie in *Doctor Faustus*', *Texas Studies in Literature and Language*, 24, (3), 243–54.
Stackmann, K. (1983), 'Die Gymnosophisten-Episode in deutschen Alexander-Erzählungen des Mittelalters', *Beiträge zur Geschichte der deutschen Sprache und Literatur* (Tübingen), 105, 331–54.
Steele, R. (ed.) (1898), *Three Prose Versions of the Secreta Secretorum*, v. 1: *Text and Glossary*. London: Kegan Paul, Trench, Trübner, for The Early English Text Society.
Steinmetz, R.-H. (1994), 'Goethe, Guibert und Carl von Österreich: Krieg und Kriegswissenschaft im vierten Akt von *Faust II*', *Goethe-Jahrbuch*, 111, 151–70.
Stoneman, R. (1995), 'Naked philosophers: The Brahmans in the Alexander historians and the Alexander romance', *The Journal of Hellenic Studies*, 115, 99–114.
Tanner, M. (1993), *The Last Descendants of Aeneas*. New Haven and London: Yale University Press.

Tate, W. (1997), 'Solomon, gender, and empire in Marlowe's *Doctor Faustus*', *Studies in English Literature, 1500–1900*, 37, 257–76.
Thomas, C. G. (2007), '"What you seek is here": Alexander the Great', *The Journal of The Historical Society*, 7, 61–83.
Vercesi, M. (2005), 'Alessandro Magno nella letteratura medievale: tracce per un mitologema', *Testo: Studi di Teoria e Storia della Letteratura e della Critica*, 26, 7–19.
Wallach, L. (1941), 'Alexander the Great and the Indian Gymnosophists in Hebrew tradition', *Proceedings of the American Academy for Jewish Research*, 11, 47–83.
Walter, H. (1997), 'Die Säulen des Herkules–Biographie eines Symbols', in H.-J. Horn and H. Walter (eds), *Die Allegorese des antiken Mythos in der Literatur, Wissenschaft und Kunst Europas*. Wiesbaden: Harrassowitz, pp. 170–213.
Warren, M. R. (2002), 'Take the world by prose: Modes of possession in the *Roman d'Alexandre*', in D. Maddox and S. Sturm-Maddox (eds), *The Medieval French Alexander*. Albany: State University of New York Press, pp. 143–60.
Wenzel, M. (1988), '"Buchholz peinigt vergebens die Lüffte . . .": Das Luftfahrt- und Ballonmotiv in Goethes naturwissenschaftlichem und dichterischem Werk', *Jahrbuch des Freien Deutschen Hochstifts*, 1988, 79–111.
Willis, R. (ed.) (1934), *Libro de Alexandre: Texts of the Paris and Madrid Manuscripts*. Princeton and Paris: Princeton University Press.
Wirth, G. (1993), *Der Weg in die Vergessenheit: Zum Schicksal des antiken Alexanderbildes*. Vienna: Verlag der Österreichischen Akademie der Wissenschaften.
Zacher, C. K. (1976), *Curiosity and Pilgrimage: The Literature of Discovery in Fourteenth-Century England*. Baltimore and London: The Johns Hopkins University Press.

2 Hanswurst, Kasperle, Pickelhäring and Faust

Jane Curran

The [comic] actor could teach the preacher the way.[1]
(Ein Komödiant könnt' einen Pfarrer lehren.)

Goethe, Faust *(527)*

The stock comic figure whose presence regularly clashes with more sober and particularly self-righteous roles provides a large proportion of the amusement in the traditional puppet play.[2] In the puppet shows of *Faust* that evolved in Germany in the wake of the visiting English traveling players who brought their version of Christopher Marlowe's play to the continent, the situation is no different. Yet although several of the puppet theatre features do remain, slapstick scenes, dialogues based on coarse humor and habitual punning together with the other antics that typify the German Kasperle, Hanswurst or Pickelhäring are not immediately obvious ingredients of Goethe's *Faust*. While it is true that the somewhat puzzling designation Goethe gave his work, 'a tragedy' ('eine Tragödie'), does not entail a strictly enforced absence of comic elements, nevertheless the traditional clownish figure has not survived in the play as an identifiable and integrated persona. The efforts of the conservative drama theorist Johann Christoph Gottsched (1700–66) to turn the German theatre repertoire into something sophisticated enough to stand up against the French classical stage and even approach the Greek tragedians included strong opposition to the continued provision of roles for the vulgar figure of Hanswurst. The influence of Gottsched's reforms, though no longer as strongly felt as it initially had been, may well have left its mark and contributed to Goethe's disguising of the comic element by distributing features of Hanswurst among a number of characters and scenes.

Any commentary on Goethe's *Faust* would be remiss if it did not begin by mentioning Goethe's earliest brush with the story of Dr. Faust through the medium of a puppet theatre showing, the sediments of which remain throughout Goethe's repeated process of revision.[3] Indeed Goethe is likely to have seen puppet shows of *Faust* both in Frankfurt and in Strasbourg, presumably different versions. In *Dichtung und Wahrheit* (*Poetry and Truth*) he attests to the lasting effect of his visual encounter with the Faust story: 'The remarkable puppet show story . . . sounded and hummed polyphonically inside me' ('Die bedeutende Puppenspielfabel . . . klang und summte gar vieltönig in mir') (Goethe 1986: 451).

However, the other traditions and influences that Goethe worked into his masterpiece, ranging from ancient Greek drama via Calderón, Dante and Shakespeare to contemporary German literary vogues, are so plentiful and varied that the humble puppet theatre is sometimes overlooked.

The puppet version of the saga, which would undergo such a thoroughgoing transformation in Goethe's hands, was itself a radical retelling of the story hitherto known in the rather different chapbook version of 1587. Put succinctly, whereas the chapbook set out to provide moral instruction through negative example and admonition, the puppet show aimed principally at entertainment. Goethe's play, with its distinct stages of development extending over the greater part of the poet's life, emerges ultimately in such a complex form of presentation that one might well wonder at the number of elements it contains whose origins still identifiably belong in that earlier dramatic version of the Faust story, the puppet show. The gift of a puppet theatre is one of Goethe's happy childhood memories and one that he transposed into the reminiscences related by the autobiographically based protagonist in Book One of *Wilhelm Meisters Lehrjahre* (*Wilhelm Meister's Apprenticeship*). Having overcome the unpleasant surprise that puppets are dependent on human handlers for their life, young Wilhelm finds intense pleasure in manipulating the puppets himself. There is an obvious analogy between the puppeteer's control of this small realm and the Creator's control over the theatre of the world, such as we glimpse it in *Faust*, especially in the 'Prologue in Heaven' ('Prolog im Himmel') (Curran 2002: 22). The surprising number of instances in which he preserves traceable puppet show traditions in the telling of Faust's story distinguishes Goethe's play from other versions undertaken by his contemporaries, such as Lessing or Maler Müller (Boyle 1992: 220). Nikolaus Lenau mentions having watched Faust's story performed by marionettes, but the extent to which this contributed to the choice of theme for his *Faust. Ein Gedicht* (*Faust. A Poem*) (1836) is open to debate.

The mechanism of puppetry (and here the discussion is exclusively about marionettes) depends on balance and counterweight; the skill of the puppeteer includes temporary suspension of the law of gravity and precision of timing. On the level of dramatic action and dialogue, the story performed by the puppets needs built-in tension and spectacular contrasts to ensure a lively response from the audience. And here too, gravity, now in its other sense as the antonym of light-heartedness, is altogether out of place. Fast-paced, witty dialogue, generously spiced with pun and innuendo, is an essential tool, supplementing the visual and engaging action and retaining the audience's interest. Because of the flexible and transitory nature of such performances, it is difficult to state with confidence anything concrete about the kind of puppet show Goethe would have seen. As was also the practice among traveling players, the puppet handlers deviated from the basic story line at will, integrating local references to comic effect, and relying on the inspiration of the moment for their unrehearsed, spontaneous repartee. Actual scripts were few and far between. Karl Simrock (1802–76), the German scholar and poet who did so much to preserve literary classics such as *Das Nibelungenlied* (*Song of the Nibelungs*) and *Parzival* (*Parsifal*) from oblivion through his skilful translations into a more modern idiom, performed another great service by gathering together and publishing such remnants of the puppet shows as he could find. Simrock confirms that the sources garnered for his collection, reconstructed and published in 1846, were full of gaps. He had no choice but to fill them in order to preserve the essence of this ephemeral phenomenon in a useful volume: 'I have not added anything of substance. I do not even need to mention that the dialogue and general construction is mostly my own, and that all the verse is attributable to me' ('Wesentliches habe ich nicht hinzugetan. Daß der Dialog, die Ausführung überhaupt, größtenteils mir gehört, und alle Verse auf meine Rechnung kommen, brauche ich nicht erst zu sagen') (1991: 6).

As Simrock openly admits, then, the literal wording of the dialogues cannot be counted as authentic in the usual sense of the word. But the stock components that make up the conflicts and tensions, and the character types who provide the comedy in puppet shows, are much less subject to variation. Observed in a certain light, and by stretching the point a little, Goethe's play could appear to be composed in the same spirit of more or less spontaneously inspired elaboration upon a theme from folklore, reworked over time. After all, Goethe preserves the basic elements of Faust's character and his Mephistopheles, already familiar from the Faust chapbook and the puppet shows, has not strayed too far from his origins as swift and beguiling tempter.[4] An increased emphasis on biblical origins enters through the frame which Goethe creates out of Christian mythology, and a strong analogy between the folk Mephistopheles and the figure of Satan in Job emerges. After this exchange with the Lord, however, Mephistopheles is free to act as he chooses. The angelic voices Faust hears in the opening scene of the puppet show (except in the Ulmer version, which begins in the underworld), embodiments of a struggle of conscience within Faust, also play a prominent role in Christopher Marlowe's play *Doctor Faustus* (1604). These voices can also be said to have survived in Goethe's work, albeit in new forms. Angelic voices are present at various points in *Faust I*, most notably at the opening of the 'Prologue in Heaven', where they sing the praises of the Lord and the heavens. From the point of view of content, however, the debate between Mephistopheles and the Lord that takes place in the Prologue, albeit in the absence of Faust, incorporates some of the same tension between the temptation to do evil and the will to do good as these voices speak of in the puppet version of *Faust*.

Faust's soliloquy, though somewhat expanded in Goethe's version, still deals with substantially similar subject matter to that familiar from its puppet show origins. The puppet Faust also suffers from despair, and is easily as dissatisfied with the limits of earthly existence and the scholarly life as Goethe's protagonist:

> I have reached a stage in my studies
> At which people laugh at me wherever I go.
> I have searched through books from beginning to end
> And still cannot find the philosopher's stone.
>
> (Soweit hab' ichs nun mit Gelehrsamkeit gebracht,
> Daß ich allerorten werd' ausgelacht.
> Alle Bücher durchstöbert von vorne bis hinten
> Und kann doch den Stein der Weisen nicht finden.)
> (Simrock 1991: 9)

The puppet Faust believes that his lengthy scholarly training has not helped him achieve his goal of understanding. He needs money and desires true knowledge as well as recognition, and is even willing to try his hand at the darker arts in the pursuit of these ends.

> Who will pay me for the nights I sat up?
> I haven't a decent coat on my back
> And I've so many debts I don't know which way to turn.
> I'll have to ally myself with Hell
> To find out the hidden secrets of Nature.
>
> (Meine durchwachten Nächte, wer bezahlt mir die?
> Keinen heilen Rock hab' ich mehr am Leibe
> Und weiß vor Schulden nicht wo ich bleibe.
> Ich muß mich mit der Hölle verbünden
> Die verborgenen Tiefen der Natur zu ergründen.)
> (Simrock 1991: 9)

The actual content of Faust's lament is more developed in Goethe's version: his character has moved beyond acute financial distress to a nagging spiritual hunger. Goethe's Faust yearns for true knowledge, while the puppet Faust is preoccupied with material benefits. Yet when one compares these lines with Faust's famous monologue, both the general despairing mood and the prosodical qualities stand out in their similarity.

> Alas, I've studied Philosophy,
> The Law and Physic and also,
> More's the pity, Divinity
> With ardent effort, through and through
> And here I am, about as wise
> Today, poor fool, as I ever was.
>
> (Habe nun, ach! Philosophie,
> Juristerei und Medizin,
> Und leider auch Theologie!
> Durchaus studiert, mit heißem Bemühn.
> Da steh' ich nun, ich armer Tor!
> Und bin so klug als wie zuvor . . .)
> (F, 354–9)

Goethe's Faust sounds like an echo of the puppet Faust here, because Goethe has preserved the four-beat rhymed lines familiar from the puppet theatre with their amusing, entertaining rhythm. Wolfgang Kayser describes the suitability of this choice of verse form in the following terms: 'the Knittel verse comes across as simple, folksy, German' ('der Knittel gilt uns als bieder, vollkstümlich, deutsch') (1982: 22). As Schöne points out, it was from Gottsched's *Versuch einer critischen Dichtkunst vor die Deutschen* (*Essay on a German Critical Poetic Theory*) that Goethe learned all there was to know about meter (Goethe 1994b: 208). Gottsched explicitly associates the 'Knittelvers' with humorous compositions:

> One usually writes jokes in doggerel, that is, in those old Franconian octosyllables with weak rhymes that one used to make before Opitz's day. The beauty of these verses is that they can easily be imitated.
>
> (Man pflegt zum Scherze auch Knittelverse zu machen, das ist, solche altfränkische, achtsylbige, gestümpelte Reime, als man vor Opitzens Zeiten gemacht hat. Die Schönheit dieser Verse besteht darinn, daß sie wohl nachgeahmet sind.)
> (1972: 226)

In his *Reisebilder* (*Travel Pictures*), Heine (who was pleased to call Simrock his friend) also identified the kinship with puppet idiom in Faust's speech. His reference to this monologue is in the context of a plaidoyer or plea on behalf of humor's ability to put a serious point across more effectively:

> Aristophanes shows us the most horrifying images of human insanity but only as laughingly reflected, as a joke; Goethe only dares to express the great sufferings of the thinker who grasps his worthlessness in the doggerel of the puppet show, and Shakespeare places the most fatal complaint about the despair of the world into the mouth of a Fool, and anxiously shakes his cap of bells.
>
> (Die grauenhaftesten Bilder des menschlichen Wahnsinns zeigt uns Aristophanes nur im lachenden Spiegel des Witzes, den großen Denkerschmerz, der seine eigne Nichtigkeit begreift, wagt Goethe nur in den Knittelversen eines Puppenspiels auszusprechen, und die tödlichste Klage über den Jammer der Welt legt Shakespeare in den Mund eines Narren, während er dessen Schellenkappe ängstlich schüttelt.) (1973: 200)

After this speech the rhythm of Goethe's *Faust* settles into the loose iambic pentameter with which the more solemn hexameter will then contrast so strikingly in the exchange between Faust and Helena in *Faust II*.

Wagner, Faust's admiring servant, by times humble, by times self-important, also belongs first in the puppet show before finding his way into Goethe's play. In both settings, he takes himself rather too seriously and his character traits remain substantially unaltered. Simrock's modus operandi is such that his text occasionally uses material anachronistically adopted from Goethe and transposed into his reconstructed earlier source. In editing the text, Günther Mahal notes that the Latin phrase from the Book of Genesis 'Eritis sicut Deus, scientes bonum et malum' is spoken by Faust addressing Mephistopheles in the puppet text and is inscribed by Mephistopheles in the student's notebook in Goethe's *Faust*: it is therefore a possible instance of such transposition (Simrock 1991: 127). His source for the character known as Wagner seems likely to have been Goethe's play, rather than any earlier text, such as the chapbook. As Unseld assumes, 'Goethe had seen the Faust drawing in Auerbach's tavern and probably also met some students and a self-satisfied academic, Wagner' ('in Auerbachs Keller hatte Goethe die Faust-Zeichnung gesehen und wohl auch manchen Studenten und einen selbstgenügsamen Akademiker Wagner erlebt') (1991: 622).

Susceptibility to contemporary influences is not restricted to Simrock, however, as Sahlin's study (1937) shows. In the puppet Faust manuscript from the pen of Jocham August Bille, transcribed by Sahlin, which also adopts the name Wagner, Sahlin detects additional similarities with Schiller's *Räuber* as well.

A love story, a grand scene at court and a carnival, each component familiar from Goethe's play, were also all standard fare on the puppet stage, but there is one crucial component that distinguishes the puppet play from *Faust. Eine Tragödie*: the comic figure. Hanswurst or Kasperle seems to have taken over as the main character in most puppet shows. Much of the tension and drive in puppet shows of *Faust* springs from the need for Kasperle to share the stage with Faust, and confrontation ensues between the actual central figure, Faust, and his comic counterpart, the equally prominent Hanswurst, Kasperle or Pickelhäring character.

The third scene of the first puppet play in Simrock's collection is a soliloquy delivered by Kasperle. This character, with his penchant for puns and complete lack of respect for his superiors, bears a striking resemblance to other members of the court jester and Fool traditions, and yet Goethe has chosen not to include any really close parallel to this figure in his own *Faust*. Kasperle's speech commands attention by being a sort of negative response to Faust's opening soliloquy. Faust laments the emptiness of bookish learning and his inability to gain true knowledge by conventional scholarly methods. Kasperle, in his own way, demonstrates the limits of words by waving a knapsack around to enact a literal interpretation of the saying 'get into the swing of things' ('in Schwung kriegen') and then jokes about owning a new coat and pair of shoes, even though the component parts are still with the tailor and shoemaker respectively and have not yet been paid for. Barely literate, a fact that emerges when he tries to read the spells in Faust's book, he plays with words by separating them from their agreed sense and easily guarantees the audience's laughter. Kasperle's speech actually corresponds very closely to Faust's complaints about his lot in life, only Faust expresses himself in tragic rather than comic idiom. Whereas Faust complains about what he lacks, Kasperle talks about what he does possess, that is, nothing: his knapsack is empty (Sahlin 1937: 167). Faust identifies the lack of connection between the words to which he has devoted so much time as a scholar and any real knowledge or wisdom. This is the cause of his suffering. Faust and Kasperle are concerned with two sides of the same coin: the divorce between words and meaning, one using this disjuncture for comic ends, the other viewing the same phenomenon with deep regret.

Kasperle is also suffering from a financial shortfall, just like Faust. He too has no money to pay for a coat and shoes and the next scene consists of his attempts to gain a meal using only pretence, teasing and riddles. Again, this comic figure shows up the amusing side of Faust's pursuits. The riddles Kasperle trots out are effective, in the end, and gain him access to the desired source of money and nourishment.

> WAGNER. The inn is next door.
> KASPERLE. You don't say! This isn't an inn? I can't get anything to eat and drink for my money here?
> WAGNER. No, I tell you, no!
> KASPERLE. Oh well, I'm not like that. If there's no option, I'll co-operate and accept a meal without paying.
>
> (WAGNER. Das Wirtshaus ist hier nebenan.
> KASPERLE. Was Ihr sagt! Hier ist kein Wirtshaus? Hier kann man nichts haben für sein Geld zu essen und zu trinken?
> WAGNER. Nein, sag' ich, nein!
> KASPERLE. Na, ich bin auch nit so. Wenn's nit anders sein kann, will ich Euch mein gutes Gemüt zeigen und eine Mahlzeit umsonst annehmen.) (Simrock 1991: 13)

Whereas meaningless riddles help Kasperle in the direction of his earthly needs, the fulfillment of Faust's spiritual goal will require other resources. In a continuation of the parallel, these riddles correspond to the sober magical incantations that Faust hopes will help him advance toward his own more spiritual goal. The stage directions merely mention that he mumbles 'incomprehensible words'; when Kasperle gets hold of Faust's magic book he succeeds in making the spirits come and go with the words 'Perlippe' and 'Perlappe'. Both the teasing riddles and the magical incantations are effective in producing dramatic and satisfactory results, satisfyingly material in one case and intriguingly intangible in the other.

Kasperle's aims are all too earthly, mostly having to do with overindulgence in food and drink. One aspect of the humor he generates arises from his ability to dabble in magic—the very exercise Faust has set his heart on—without any previous thought of doing so and without any real expenditure of effort either. Kasperle's poor education is no impediment and, discovering the simple procedure by chance, he calls up spirits with absurd ease and with no purpose in mind other than a moment's entertainment. He regards the ethereal experiences that follow with complete equanimity. This Hanswurst figure easily takes center stage in the puppet version of Faust, by undermining the scholar's earnest pursuits. With his verbal tricks and down-to-earth humor he typically wins the audience's sympathy, unlike the more grave and self-absorbed protagonist.

More pointedly satirical still is the rewarding exchange between Kasperle and Wagner. The latter's pedantry is repeatedly lampooned, even while he himself makes condescending remarks about Kasperle's lack of education. Pretending to be naïve and confused about the relative values of 'Goldgülden' and 'Groschen' ('gold guilder', 'ten-pence piece'), Kasperle easily wins Wagner's sympathy: wit and linguistic ingenuity gain the upper hand over the scholar's superior learning.

Kasperle evades the conditions that restrain Faust and achieves his own goals with greater ease. He has nothing to fear from the devils conjured up or from the threat of his soul's descent into hell, since, as he quips, he has no soul anyway: 'And as regards the soul, Kasperle hasn't got one. You stupid devils, not noticing that! When I came into the world there just weren't any souls available at the moment' ('Und was die Seel' betrifft, eine Seel' hat Kasperle nit. Ihr dumme Teufel, daß ihr das nit gemerkt habt. Als ich zur Welt gekommen bin, waren just keine Seelen vorrätig') (Simrock 1991: 26). Despite this and other significant privations, Kasperle succeeds in remaining carefree; in that ability, he possesses something that Faust lacks (Sahlin 1937: 178).

For puppeteers and traveling players as well, conditions dictated the sort of play that could reasonably be expected to meet with an enthusiastic reception. They were, after all, totally dependent on the income contributed by the audience. Moral and aesthetic scruples had no place in their choice of repertoire; coarse humor was guaranteed to sell tickets whereas theatrical experiments were unlikely to meet with the same degree of enthusiasm.

The next stage in the evolution of the Faust myth is tellingly described by Heinrich Heine in the introductory remarks to his *Der Doktor Faust. Ein Tanzpoem nebst kuriosen Berichten über Teufel, Hexen und Dichtkunst* (*Dr Faust, a Dance Poem, with Interesting Reports on Devils, Witches and the Art of Poetry*) (1851). Heine endorses the view that the puppet performance Goethe witnessed was crucial for his own masterpiece and that his liberal borrowings of both matter and form from it are very evident. On the topic of the puppet-*Faust*, Heine mentions its entertainment value for the lower classes, but he also touches on the controversial presence of Hanswurst.

> It was that puppet show Faust, which came over from England to the continent, traveling through the Netherlands and visiting the market stalls of our country as well and, translated into coarse German dialect and corrupted with German tomfoolery, delighted the lower classes.
>
> (Es ist nun jener Puppenspiel-Faust, der von England herüber nach dem Festland kam, durch die Niederlande reisend auch die Marktbuden unserer Heimat

besuchte, und in derb deutscher Maulart übersetzt und mit deutschen Hanswurstiaden verballhörnt, die unteren Schichten des deutschen Volkes ergötzte.) (Heine 1991: 8)

Heine's own reworking of Faust's story has its entertaining twists as well, including the female character Mephistophela, but nothing more than a cameo appearance is reserved for the stock comic figure. This comes in the fifth act, in a fairground atmosphere. Among various diversions on offer, the puppet show ('Puppenspiel') is mentioned and 'Pickleherrings jumping around' (Heine 1991: 30).

The bowdlerization of plays featuring Hanswurst that Heine refers to proceeds from principles expounded by Johann Christoph Gottsched. In his concern to elevate the level of entertainment offered on the German stage, Gottsched was determined to look back to the French classical stage and the Greek dramatists. In his *Essay on a German Critical Poetic Theory* Gottsched argues against the spontaneous farce characteristic of German traveling players, recommending instead adherence to the classical unities of time, place and action. His campaign to educate the taste of the theatre-going public included the controversial and only briefly successful crusade against the character Hanswurst. Whatever name he may go by, writes Gottsched in the section entitled 'Von Komödien oder Lustspielen' ('On Comedies or Farces'), this figure is devoid of taste and has no equivalent in nature.[5] People who know better may from time to time find themselves laughing at his antics despite their better judgment, but they are nevertheless ashamed of themselves afterward for having succumbed to his base tricks:

> From this it is easy to conclude what kind of work can be made from the Italian theatre and the marketplace theatre, where the fare is totally lacking in taste. A wise man would either not laugh at it at all, or feel ashamed at having laughed. It is the same with all German Fools, whether they have traditional origins, like Hans Wurst or Pickelhering, who were still being used by Weiße, or a new type, like the so-called Peter, or Crispin, or whatever they may be called. The reasons that militate against them are also opposed to all creations of a disordered imagination that have no model in nature.
>
> (Hieraus ist nun leicht zu schließen, was von dem THEATRE ITALIEN und THEATRE DE LA FOIRE, wo lauter abgeschmacktes Zeug vorkömmt, für ein Werks zu machen sey: darüber ein Kluger entweder gar nicht lacht; oder sich doch schämt, gelachet zu haben; imgleichen was von allen deutschen Narren zu halten sey, sie mögen nun von alter Erfindung seyn, wie Hans Wurst oder Pickelhering, dessen sich Weise noch immer bedienet hat; oder auch von neuer Art, wie der sogenannte Peter, oder Crispin, oder wie sie sonst heißen mögen. Eben die Gründe, die wider jene streiten, sind auch allen diesen Geschöpfen einer unordentlichen Einbildungskraft zuwider, die kein Muster in der Natur haben.) (Gottsched 1972: 358)

Gottsched repeatedly attributes the character of Hanswurst and all the buffoonery that goes into his performance to the undesirable influence of Italian theatre. Tricks, deception and farce make up the mainstay of the commedia dell'arte, according to him. 'Harlekin' ranks as principal protagonist there and nothing in these plays resembles normal life, in Gottsched's view: 'Harlequin and Scaramouche are the inevitable principal roles on their stages, and they do not imitate the actions of normal life' ('Harlekin und Scaramutz sind die ewigen Hauptpersonen ihrer Schaubühne: und diese ahmen nicht die Handlungen des gemeinen Lebens nach') (1972: 342–3). Moderation is more effective; the comic element should not be overdone and the imitation of nature is crucial, otherwise the audience will not be able to relate to the characters and no lesson will be learned from their example: 'one should not overdo the amusing characters. As soon as the audience feels that no one in the world would be so foolish, the character has lost its value' ('Man muß aber die lächerlichen Charactere nicht zu hoch treiben. So bald der Zuschauer glauben kann, so gar thöricht würde wohl kein Mensch in der Welt seyn: so bald verliert der Character seinen Werth') (1972: 354). Even more specifically, Gottsched warns poets to avoid using tales like Faust's as the basis for their drama:

> The legend of Dr Faust has amused the masses for long enough, and we have more or less ceased to enjoy watching such foolishness. For this reason a poet must take great care not to present incredible things on the stage and certainly not to make them visible.
>
> (Das Mährchen von Dr Fausten hat lange genug den Pöbel belustiget: Und man hat ziemlicher maßen aufgehört, solche Alfanzereyen gerne anzusehen. Daher muß denn ein Poet große Behutsamkeit gebrauchen, daß er nicht unglaubliche Dinge auf die Schaubühne bringe, vielweniger sichtbar vorstelle.) (1972: 175)

The true root of the comic art, for Gottsched, lies not in ludicrous costumes or silly word games and gestures—techniques of which he claims the ancients knew nothing—but in action. Comedy should make fun of absurd behavior, with a view to leading the onlooker to adopt more reasonable conduct:

> This, then, is the truly comic element in comedy. But inferior intellects, who have no inkling of morality and are unable either to notice the irregularities in human actions or present them satirically, are at a loss for another method. They think the amusing element can be found not in things, but in foolish clothing, words and gestures.
>
> (Dieses ist nun das wahre Belustigende in der Komödie. Allein kleine Geister, die keine Einsicht in die Moral besitzen, und das ungereimte Wesen in den menschlichen Handlungen weder wahrnehmen noch satirisch vorstellen können, haben sich auf eine andre Art zu helfen gesucht. Sie haben das Lächerliche nicht in den Sachen, sondern in närrischen Kleidungen, Worten und Gebärden zu finden gemeynet.) (1972: 357)

Beginning in 1727, Gottsched formed an alliance with the enterprising theatre director and actress Friederike Caroline Neuber (1697–1760) to establish the ideal national German theatre, one that would produce only the types of plays Gottsched approved of and recommended. Most memorably, Hanswurst would never darken its doors. To this end, in 1737 Caroline Neuber performed the part of Hanswurst before a Leipzig audience in an allegorical prologue with the title 'Der alte und neue Geschmack' ('The Old Taste and the New') in which Hanswurst was formally banned from the stage.

Hanswurst was not absent from the German stage for long; indeed his return to Leipzig is recorded as occurring in 1740 (Martini 1984: 179). And while it does seem that Gottsched, with his well-intentioned proposals for the reform of the German theatre, failed to recognize the direction that the theatre would inevitably take, his banishment of Hanswurst did achieve public attention. In the '17th letter on literature' (*Literaturbrief*) Lessing defended Hanswurst against

Gottsched's persecution of him. He writes of Gottsched: 'He had Harlequin ceremoniously driven from the theatre, which was in itself the greatest tomfoolery ever performed; in short, he did not so much want to improve our old theatre as be the creator of a completely new one' ('er ließ den Harlekin feierlich vom Theater vertreiben, welches selbst die größte Harlekinade war, die jemals gespielt worden; kurz, er wollte nicht sowohl unser altes Theater verbessern, als der Schöpfer eines ganz neuen sein') (1973: 71).

In Act V, scene two of J. M. R. Lenz's *Der neue Menoza oder Geschichte des cumbanischen Prinzen Tandi* (*The New Menzoa or The Story of the Cumbanian Prince Tandi*), an exchange between the mayor ('Bürgermeister') and Zierau re-creates the controversy surrounding Gottsched's ban. The mayor gives voice to his enjoyment of puppet shows, and especially of the comic figure 'Hannswurst'. Zierau soberly replies in Gottsched's idiom: 'Pleasure without taste is not pleasure' ('Vergnügen ohne Geschmack ist kein Vergnügen') (Lenz 1967: 177).

Without mentioning Gottsched by name, Goethe mentions the controversial ban with a certain amount of regret in his sketched history of the German stage in *Poetry and Truth*.

> In order to be useful, it had to be ethical, and it trained itself to achieve this even more in north Germany when the clown figure was banished on the grounds of taste, and although intelligent people spoke in its favor, it still had to retreat because it had already contrasted the coarseness of the German Hanswurst with the sweetness and delicacy of the Italian and French Harlequins.
>
> (Um nützlich zu sein, mußte es sittlich sein, und dazu bildete es sich im nördlichen Deutschland um so mehr aus, als durch einen gewissen Halbgeschmack die lustige Person vertrieben ward, und, obgleich geistreiche Köpfe für sie einsprachen, dennoch weichen mußte, da sie sich bereits von der Derbheit des deutschen Hanswursts gegen die Niedlichkeit und Zierlichkeit der italienischen und französischen Harlekine gewendet hatte.) (1986, 14: 617)

Goethe himself makes use of a Hanswurst in the satirical *Jahrmarktsfest zu Plundersweilen* (*Market Festival at Plundersweilen*) (1773) in the fragment *Hanswursts Hochzeit oder der Lauf der Welt* (*Hanswurst's Wedding, or the Way of the World*) (1775), as well as in the allegorical *Epimenides Erwachen* (*Epimenides' Awakening*) (1814), where he appears as Clown ('Lustige Person').

Goethe does not adopt the figure variously known as Kasperle, Hanswurst or Pickelhäring into the list of dramatis personae for his *Faust*, but neither does he suppress all aspects of his role. Glimpses of Hanswurst's presence come to the surface first in the 'Prelude on the Stage' ('Vorspiel auf dem Theater') where he goes by the generic name of Clown ('Lustige Person') that Goethe would use again in *Epimenides Erwachen*. Since this section of the play is really a framing technique, the Clown is not speaking in true character but more or less as a theorist, recommending less emphasis on lofty or fashionable ideas and suggesting that coarser entertainment will do wonders at the box office.

> Come now, show the world the way, be sure that when
> Imagination and all her choruses,
> Reason, Good Sense and Sentiment and Passion,
> Say their lines, the Fool also says his.
>
> (Drum seid nur brav und zeigt euch musterhaft,
> Laßt Phantasie, mit allen ihren Chören,

Vernunft,Verstand, Empfindung Leidenschaft,
Doch, merkt euch wohl! Nicht ohne Narrheit hören.)
(F, 85–8)

The voice of the Clown is heard throughout: in the 'Prologue in Heaven' and then via the witty tongue of Mephistopheles in various other scenes, the spirit of Kasperle lives on. Most obviously, Mephistopheles repeatedly challenges Faust to embrace a lighter mode of pastime. Using a series of minor characters as foils (the drinkers in 'Auerbach's Tavern' ['Auerbachs Keller in Leipzig'], Martha, Wagner and the student, to name but a few) Mephistopheles continues his entertaining provocations right through both Part I and Part II. Obviously Kasperle would feel at home in the atmosphere in 'Auerbach's Tavern', and would easily be included in the revelry and delight at getting something to drink without paying, although the origins of the scene are more firmly rooted in the chapbook *Faust* (Goethe 1994b, 2: 280). In that setting, Faust is able to provide free drinks for all his companions when he wins a wager by miraculously transporting a heavy keg up from the cellar by riding on it as though on horseback, a scene often reproduced in illustrations (Benz 1964: 95–6). The supernatural aspect Mephistopheles introduces into 'Auerbach's Tavern', using magic for frivolous and mischievous ends, is reminiscent of the puppet Kasperle's childish repetition of the conjuring and banishing formulae to make the spirits come and go. In the final exchange between Kasperle and Faust, however, there is a suggestion of an episode similar both to the original chapbook version and to the one that takes place in 'Auerbach's Tavern'. Kasperle is trying, even now, to trick Faust into giving him some money, and he claims that it would be easy to get some since Wagner conjures up money with the magic word 'Papperlapapp' and buys champagne for the students with it (Simrock 1991: 49).

Kasperle's conversations with the puppet Wagner are effective in poking fun at the scholar and bringing him down a peg or two. Wagner puffs himself up with pride as he relates that he has a good position in the service of 'His Magnificence, Doctor Faust' (Simrock 1991: 14). For good measure, he throws in a Latin tag: 'I am his right hand, his alter ego, so to speak'. As might be expected, the rhyming pun which allows Kasperle to call Wagner an ass does not emerge through a literal translation into English:

WAGNER. I am his right hand, his alter ego, so to speak.
KASPERLE. His old ass?

(WAGNER. Ich bin seine rechte Hand, sozusagen sein alter ego.
KASPERLE. Sein alter Esel?) (Simrock 1991: 14)

The translator would need to substitute another expression, which, when slightly altered, has the same sort of deflating effect on Wagner. The phrase 'his alter ego' might perhaps be rendered as 'his older echo' which, while less insulting than the comparison with an ass, does still expose Wagner's pretentious use of Latin, while emphasizing his inferiority. In Goethe's *Faust* it is of course Mephistopheles on whom this function has devolved, principally in his encounter with the student in 'Study' ('Studierzimmer II'). Mephistopheles undermines the student's zeal for study with his confusing speech, so that the student ends up feeling that a millwheel is spinning in his head.

In seemingly banishing Hanswurst as a separate character, Goethe nevertheless preserves much of his contribution to the action. There are also instances in which actual lines in the final edition ('Ausgabe letzter Hand') are very close to the 'Puppenspiel'. One example of this occurs during the scene 'At the Neighbour's House' ('Der Nachbarin Haus'), when Mephistopheles is beginning his campaign to manipulate Marthe: 'Your husband's dead and says hello' ('Ihr Mann ist tot und läßt sie grüßen') (F, 2916). The same logical and linguistic conundrum is familiar from the puppet version Simrock presents as 'Die Geißelbrechtsche Fassung' ('The Geisselbrecht Version') in which the name of the comic figure is Kaspar, rather than the diminutive Kasperle:

> WAGNER. In a word, are your parents still alive?
> KASPAR. Yes they are still alive, but they have died.
>
> (WAGNER. Mit einem Wort, leben deine Eltern noch?
> KASPAR. Ja die leben noch, sie sind aber gestorben.) (Simrock 1991: 54)

An exchange that takes place in the third act of the puppet show involves an explanation, provided by Mephistopheles, as to why Faust should no longer keep company with the aristocratic group at the court but should escape from possible danger. The explanation is that because Kasperle, his servant, has upset hell with his irresponsible invocation of magic spells, the people now superstitiously consider Faust to be a dangerous influence. Mephistopheles and Faust agree to depart for Constantinople. Faust argues against bringing Kasperle along: 'Leave Kasperle behind, so he won't get up to mischief again' ('Den Kasperle laß hier, damit er mir nicht wieder solche Possen spielt') (Simrock 1991: 37). In Goethe's *Faust II* an echo of this situation can be identified in Act II, 'A Laboratory' ('Laboratorium'). Wagner has succeeded in creating the incorporeal Homunculus who now plans to go exploring with Mephistopheles and Faust. Like the puppet Kasperle, who also created spirits, or at least conjured them up, Wagner is to be left behind.

> WAGNER. [*anxiously*] And I?
> HOMUNCULUS.   Why you
> Must stay at home: you have great things to do.
>
> (WAGNER. *ängstlich*
>   Und ich?
> HOMUNKULUS. Eh nun
> Du bleibst zu Hause Wichtigstes zu tun.) (F, 6987–8)

Wagner in Goethe's play and Kasperle in the puppet show are both to be left behind because, despite being able to conjure up or even create a spirit, they do not have any proper understanding of the significance of their accomplishment.

A comparison between the 'Frühere Fassung', or *Urfaust*, and the 'Ausgabe letzter Hand' reveals some more tangible traces of the 'Puppenspiel'. The first conversation between Wagner and Faust in 'Night' ('Nacht') shows a discrepancy at line 194 of *Urfaust* which corresponds to 548 of *Faust I* ('Ausgabe letzter Hand'). The joke is on Wagner, of course, who, on overhearing Faust interrogating his miraculously conjured spirit visitor, imagines that the scholar has been rehearsing lines from a Greek tragedy. He launches into a speech in praise of rhetoric. In the final version, Faust interrupts him with these words:

> Look for your profit in an honest part.
> Don't be the fool who comes on loudly sounding.
>
> (Such' Er den redlichen Gewinn!
> Sei Er kein schellenlauter Tor!)
>
> (F, 548–9)

The *Urfaust* contains an explicit reference to puppet shows in a line that does not survive into Goethe's revised text:

> What delivery! That is fine for a puppet show.
> My dear Master, take control!
> Do not be a loudly sounding fool!
>
> (Was Vortrag! Der ist gut im Puppenspiel
> Mein Herr Magister hab er Krafft!
> Sey er kein Schellenlauter Thor!)
>
> (1994b: 194–6)

Goethe places disparaging remarks about the art of the puppet show into the mouth of Faust, thereby temporarily turning him into a mouthpiece for Gottsched's reforms. These particular remarks are jettisoned in the later text, but the expression 'loudly sounding fool' ('schellenlauter Tor') is used dismissively in both contexts. It may well be a lingering reference to the Kasperle of the puppet show, whose words are indeed often uttered more for show than for their content and for whom the name 'Tor' is not at all out of place.

A very few lines further on, both the early and late versions (with only one minor difference in punctuation) include a sarcastic remark by Faust which again seems to have been derived from a familiarity with Gottsched's writings:

> A rubbish bin
> Of melodramas of affairs of state
> And fine maxims for living fit,
> At best, to be mouthed by a marionette.
>
> (Und höchstens eine Haupt- und Staatsaktion
> Mit trefflichen pragmatischen Maximen,
> Wie sie den Puppen wohl im Munde ziemen!)
>
> (231–2; F, 583–5)

The phrase 'melodramas of affairs of state' relates to the type of repertoire, both bombastic and moralizing, that was performed by German traveling players in the late Baroque period. This type of theatre belonged together with the coarseness associated with the puppet theatre in Gottsched's view: both needed to be eradicated in the general overhaul he envisaged. Here the suggestion is that what binds together these two undesirable dramatic forms is the lack of verisimilitude, not a consideration that weighed heavily on Goethe's mind in relation to *Faust*, it seems.

A major and well-known deviation from the Faust folk tradition resides in Goethe's omission of the time reference from the pact signed between Faust and Mephistopheles. Here the puppet Kasperle has something to contribute.

In the third act he takes on the position of night watchman and calls out the hours as the pact runs out and Faust's end draws nearer. Along with this position, Kasperle has acquired a wife and family, and here the potential for entertaining repartee presents itself. Violent disagreements between husband and wife in the style of Punch and Judy shows can be thoroughly enjoyed by onlookers. Beyond the entertainment, however, is the observable parallel with Faust, who, in the speech immediately prior to Kasperle's first domestic dispute, declares that the image of the Virgin Mary, to whom he is trying to pray, is taking on the features of Helena. So Kasperle's mundane domestic concerns entertain the audience and represent the comic side of Faust's celestial ones, his somewhat supernatural vision and his ideal view of woman.

Although identifiable remains of the puppet Faust are principally to be found in *Faust I*, the phenomenon is not restricted to that part of the play. While the Helena reference brings the image of the woman in 'Witch's Kitchen' ('Hexenküche') to mind, as well as Gretchen's distraught address to the Virgin, it obviously also looks forward to Helena in *Faust II*. In the first scene of Act III of the puppet show the audience is entertained by an exchange between Kasperle and Don Carlos that is reminiscent of the 'Throne Room' ('Kaiserliche Pfalz—Saal des Thrones') scene in Act I of *Faust II*. Whereas in the puppet show Kasperle bargains with Don Carlos and offers to perform magic tricks in exchange for money, in Goethe's play it is Mephistopheles who plays the court jester. By adroit use of wording he convinces the Emperor and his courtiers that he holds the solution to their economic shortfall. And just as Helena and Paris are conjured up there as visible but insubstantial phantoms, so, too, in the puppet show, Faust is able to present the Count ('Herzog'), Countess ('Herzogin') and Don Carlos with figures conjured up from the Bible. The Countess asks, 'Are these images we see more than vain mist,/Can we touch them, too, without fear? ('Sind mehr als eitler Dunst die Bilder, die wir schauen,/So darf man sie wohl auch betasten ohne Grauen?') (Simrock 1991: 36). When Helena actually appears to the puppet Faust in Act IV scene two, she bears little resemblance to the Helena who will ultimately take on such significance in *Faust II*. A domestic arrangement with her seems to be in Faust's plan, but Helena unfortunately takes on the characteristics of an apparition from 'Walpurgis Night' ('Walpurgisnacht'): 'I was clasping a hellish serpent to my chest' ('Eine höllische Schlange drückt' ich an meinen Busen') (Simrock 1991: 44). It is high time at this point for Kasperle to return to the stage, and he soon does, to bring the action down to the level of a common or garden matrimonial clash.

The 'Ulmer Puppentheater' offers Pickelhäring, as he is called there, a much more modest role (Simrock 1991: 63–84). He relates in a monologue how he came upon hell quite by chance and describes its sights and smells. After a brief conversation with Wagner, in which he is hired on as a second servant for his master, he meets Faust in person. His impertinent rather than humorous replies to his new master's questions leave the audience in no doubt of his unsuitability for the position. His reduced role in this play demonstrates how one might come to the conclusion that the comic figure is dispensable. This is not for the reasons Gottsched outlined, but because Pickelhäring contributes no essential element to the dramatic action and the play would not suffer without him. If Pickelhäring's speeches are reduced to an interlude, entertaining or otherwise, if he can no longer be regarded as a worthy challenger to Faust, he is no longer important to the establishment of dramatic tension.

In order for it to be effective, then, Kasperle's role must be substantial enough to issue a challenge to Faust's dominance of the stage and his claim to the audience's attention. But his relation to Faust also needs to incorporate the flexible dialectic of master and servant. Faust is his superior, but like the proverbial court jester, Kasperle is indulged with certain liberties. The jester alone can utter unflattering truths without fear of any reprisal. Stubborn insubordination is not the key, but rather clever and witty parody, which brings about subversion of the power dynamic. The 'Ulmer Puppentheater' contains a poorly constructed Pickelhäring who, instead of trying to manipulate his master with witty words, behaves in an insolent and rigid manner.

Gottsched's view of German folklore's harlequin applies to his appearances among traveling players as well as in the puppet theatre. He argues for subtlety and moderation in the use of humor, and his opposition to Hanswurst is based on the figure's customary exaggerated crassness in both dialogue and actions. Goethe, as we have seen from the passage in *Poetry and Truth*, seems to have considered the act of banishing him altogether somewhat harsh. Nevertheless, Goethe gives up the extreme and provocative language he had placed in the mouth of the main character in his *Hanswurst's Wedding* (composed contemporaneously with *Urfaust*) and allows Hanswurst's influence into his *Faust* only in diluted or refracted forms. As the Clown, he offers measured and objective recommendations for a successful play. Disguised in the words of Mephistopheles debating with the Lord in the later composed 'Prologue in Heaven' he adopts a teasing and irreverent tone, expresses scorn for mankind in amusing images and assumes a status for himself on a level with God. The Lord, however, reasserts the master and servant relationship that properly belongs to Hanswurst and provides the framework for his impertinence. Mephistopheles even addresses the issue of humor, identifying himself as its source: 'Pathos from me would surely make you laugh/ Were laughter not a thing you've learned to do without' ('Mein Pathos brächte dich gewiß zum Lachen/Hätt'st du dir nicht das Lachen abgewöhnt') (*F*, 277–8). These lines appear to contain an oblique comment about the Gottsched phase in the history of German theatre.

Hanswurst's presence is heard in the verse form of Faust's monologue as it suggests the light-hearted rhythms of the puppet stage which is his home. Scenes that include songs about drinking and merrymaking, such as 'Outside the Town' ('Vor dem Tor') and 'Auerbach's Tavern', aim at the same audience that enjoys puppet shows. Mephistopheles' wit defeats his interlocutor in ways that are reminiscent of the resourceful Hanswurst. In *Faust II* he even outwits the Fool ('Narr') in 'A Pleasure Garden' ('Kaiserliche Pfalz—Lustgarten') and is soon involved in beckoning spirits for purely entertainment value. Hanswurst is well and truly embedded in the fabric of Goethe's *Faust*, dispersed and distributed throughout.

Notes

1 *Faust* is hereafter cited as *F*. Translations from *Faust I* are taken from the Constantine (2005a) translation. Those from *Faust II* are from the translation by Luke (1994a).
2 Eversberg (1985: 46): 'This figure . . . becomes the main character on the puppet stage' ('Diese Gestalt . . . wird zur Hauptfigur auf den Marionettenbühnen').

3 Scheithauer (1959: 5); Goethe (1994b: 18); Boyle (1992: 220); Brown (1992: 23); Eversberg (1985: 45); Goethe (2005b: 408).
4 Heine disagrees with this view, as he explains in the context of expressing doubts about whether Goethe was acquainted with the folklore sources while he was working on *Faust I*: 'Here too my view that Goethe was not acquainted with them while writing the first part of Faust gains support. He would not have had Mephistopheles appear in such a filthy and funny, such a cynical and ludicrous mask' ('Auch hier bestärkt sich meine Vermutung, daß Goethe letztere nicht kannte, als er den ersten Teil des "Faustes" schrieb. Er hätte sonst in keiner so säuisch spaßhaften, so zynisch skurrilen Maske den Mephistopheles erscheinen lassen') (1991: 57).
5 Sahlin associates the renaming of Hanswurst as Kasper(le) with his reentry onto the stage after Gottsched's ban lost its effect (1937: 120).

Bibliography

Benz, R. (ed.) (1964), *Historia von D. Johann Fausten*. Stuttgart: Reclam.
Boyle, N. (1992), *Goethe: The Poet and the Age*. Oxford and New York: Oxford University Press.
Brown, J. K. (1992), *Faust: Theater of the World*. New York: Twayne.
Curran, J. V. (2002), *Goethe's Wilhelm Meister's Apprenticeship: A Reader's Commentary*. Rochester: Camden House.
Eversberg, G. (1985), *Johann Wolfgang v. Goethe: Faust Teil I*. Hollfeld: Bange.
Goethe, J. W. (1986), *Sämtliche Werke*, K.-D. Müller (ed.). Frankfurt/Main: Deutscher Klassiker.
—(1994a), *Faust, Part Two*, D. Luke (trans.). Oxford: Oxford University Press.
—(1994b), *Sämtliche Werke*, A. Schöne (ed.). Frankfurt/Main: Deutscher Klassiker.
—(2005a), *Faust, Part I*, D. Constantine (trans.). London: Penguin.
—(2005b), *Faust. Erster Teil. 'Urfaust', Fragment, Ausgabe letzter Hand*, U. Gaier (ed.). Stuttgart: Reclam.
Gottsched, J. C. (1972), *Ausgewählte Werke*, J. Birke (ed.). Stuttgart: Metzler.
Heine, H. (1973), *Historisch-Kritische Gesamtausgabe der Werke*, v. 6, M. Windfuhr (ed.). Hamburg: Hoffmann und Campe.
—(1991), *Der Doktor Faust. Ein Tanzpoem nebst kuriosen Berichten über Teufel, Hexen und Dichtkunst*. Stuttgart: Reclam.
Kayser, W. (1982), *Kleine deutsche Versschule*. Bern and Munich: Franke.
Lenau, N. (1971), *Faust*. Stuttgart: Reclam.
Lenz, J. M. R. (1967), *Werke und Schriften*, v. 2., B. Titel and H. Haug (eds). Stuttgart: Goverts.
Lessing, G. E. (1973), *Werke*, v. 5. Darmstadt: Wissenschaftliche Buchgesellschaft.
Marlowe, C. (2001), *Doctor Faustus*, S. Barnet (ed.). New York: Signet.
Martini, F. (1984), *Deutsche Literaturgeschichte*. Stuttgart: Kröner.
Sahlin, N. G. (1937), The Faust Puppet Play Manuscripts in the William A. Speck Collection of Goetheana, Yale University. Diss. Yale University.
Scheithauer, T. F. L. J. (1959), *Kommentar zu Goethes Faust*. Stuttgart: Reclam.
Simrock, K. (1991), *Doktor Johannes Faust. Puppenspiel in vier Aufzügen*, G. Mahal (ed.). Stuttgart: Reclam.
Unseld, S. (1991), *Goethe und seine Verleger*. Frankfurt/Main: Insel.

Part II

Faust: In Context

3 'Why all this noise?': Reading Sound in Goethe's *Faust I* and *II*

Alan Corkhill

Both parts of Goethe's verse drama contain a multiplicity of sound-related words—most notably 'Hauch', 'Geräusch', 'Klang', 'Laut', 'Ton', 'Schall' and 'Lärm', together with their cognate and associative word fields. This chapter fills a gap in *Faust* scholarship in its linking of these recurring sound images to their broader cosmological, scientific, linguistic and aesthetic contexts. While sound imagery is central to various creation theories that have been strategically woven into the play, Goethe's sketchy, yet sufficiently informative theory of acoustics ('Tonlehre') appended to his *Zur Farbenlehre* (*Theory of Colors*) (1810) provides a point of departure for a consideration of the primacy of sound within eighteenth- and early nineteenth-century scientific discourse. On the linguistic level, sound assumes significance within the contentious philological and anthropological debates of Goethe's day concerning the genesis and acquisition of language. Goethe's own dialectical stance on language origin can be shown to have articulated itself in the *Faust* poem.

This chapter attempts to show how Part II, in particular, is characterized by a sustained preoccupation with the aesthetics of words, especially the effect derived from their acoustic and musical properties ('Lautästhetik'). Arguably, Goethe's oft-quoted supposition, 'one never considers enough that a language is really only symbolic, only pictorial' (GA, 16: 203),[1] falls short of completeness in its failure to take account of the sonority ('Klanglichkeit') of language, that is, words as sound symbols. Inasmuch as sounds—whether they occur in nature or euphonious speech patterns—evoke in the respective listener an intuitive sense of harmony with the totality of existence, this chapter explores the marked hypersensitivity and resistance of several of the dramatis personae to various types of noise. The analysis concludes with an interrogation of the metatextual management of sound, namely, the use of sound effects ('Geräuschkulissen') in some recent theatre productions of *Faust*, such as Peter Stein's marathon staging of the entire unabridged work at the 2000 World Expo in Hanover.

The (Meta)physics of Sound

Sound permeates the creation stories of numerous exoteric and esoteric traditions, both Western and Eastern. In the Book of Genesis we are told that sound preceded the production of light, insofar as the first articulated sound was the voice of the Lord proclaiming, 'Let there be light'. It follows, then, that the Old Testament Yahweh came originally to human kind through the ear, not through the eye. For the Greek Jewish mystic Philo of Alexandria (20 BCE–50 CE) the primordial Word of God referred to in the opening passage of St John's Gospel ('In the beginning was the Word') was synonymous with vibration and movement as the very root of creation. The interchangeability of the Greek 'logos' with 'Thought' (F, 1229),[2] 'Power' (F, 1233) and 'Deed' (F, 1237) becomes apparent in Faust's attempt to translate freely the gospel text into 'the loved accents of [his] native land' (F, 1223). By privileging 'Power' and even 'Deed' over 'the Word' (F, 1224), Faust could be said to have unwittingly described the noisy release of explosive energy associated with the Big Bang ('Urknall')—the micro-second in which the universe is thought to have materialized out of nothingness. But even back in the seventeenth century the mystic theosophist Jakob Böhme, with whose writing Goethe was familiar, underscored the acoustic properties of the 'energia' pulsating through the cosmos and reaching the earth.[3]

The presence of musical sound in the universe was posited by the Pythagoreans some 2,500 years ago, although they could not explain the silence that went before it. In Ptolemaic astronomy the seven known planets were mounted on crystalline spheres that rang out in harmony as they orbited the earth. John Milton gave poetic expression to this phenomenon in his ode 'On the Morning of Christ's Nativity' (1629), where he writes:

> Ring out ye crystal spheres!
> Once bless our human ears
> . . .
> And let your silver chime
> Move in melodious time,
> And let the bass of Heav'n's deep organ blow;
> And with your ninefold harmony
> Make up full consort to the angelic symphony.
> (1957: 46, ll. 125–32)

Even though Pythagoras himself claimed—somewhat fancifully—to have clearly heard the 'musica universalis', it was simply a harmonic and/or mathematical concept within Pythagorean theory.

In terms of the literary appropriation of celestial music, Dante in the *Divine Comedy* identifies the intoning of angels as the echo of the music of the spheres. Similarly, Goethe has his three archangels sing of the majestic sights and sounds of God's wondrous creation in the oratorio-like opening verses of the 'Prologue in Heaven' ('Prolog im Himmel'). The sun, Raphael proclaims, is not only the solar system's provider of heat and light; it resonates, too, in much the same way as the other music-making heavenly bodies ('[w]hile sister-spheres join rival song' [F, 246]).[4] Modern physics has identified such solar emissions as (inaudible) sound waves or vibrations.[5] The reference to 'thunder' (F, 245) rolling about the sun's fixed trajectory is a reminder of the clamorous attributes of Tor in Nordic myth or of Zeus in Greek myth.[6] Turning their gaze to earth, the other two archangels Gabriel and Michael sing of the primal fury of the natural elements as waves swell and dash against the base of cliffs (F, 255–6) or as wild tempests lash the land (F, 259–60).

As to which (meta)physical sounds are humanly discernible, the question is posed in the opening scene of Part II, where Faust awakens from his recuperative sleep to the music of the Elves' chorus accompanied by Aeolian harps. To the extent that 'Pleasing Landscape' ('Anmutige Gegend') is a partial 'Spiegelung' ('mirroring') of the 'Prologue in Heaven', the ethereal strains of the harps approximate the music of the archangels. One wonders whether the 'reborn' Faust can hear the day break, which the stage direction establishes to be an auditory as well as a visual phenomenon: 'A great tumult heralds the approach of the sun' (*F*, before 4666). Ariel, for his part, asserts that the sunrise is inaudible to human ears:

> Hark! The Hours, with furious winging,
> Bear to spirit-ears the ringing
> Rumour of the new day-springing.
> Gates of rock grind back asunder,
> Phoebus comes with wheels of thunder:
> Light spreads tumult through the air.
> Loud are trump and timbrel sounded,
> Eyes are dazed and ears astounded,
> Sounds unheard of none may bear,
> Glide away to petalled bell.
>
> (*F*, 4666–75)

With regard to audibility, today's technology makes use of non-musical 'instruments' to record the sound or pressure waves of interplanetary space that reach the earth after passing through the warm, thin plasma of charged and neutral atoms.

Like Newton (*Opticks*, 1730), Goethe in his *Theory of Colors* was particularly interested in the correspondences, however arbitrary, between light and acoustics—the phenomenon to which the above-quoted line 'Light spreads tumult through the air' pertains. While Goethe's scientific peers failed to take seriously his color theory, premised on the older Aristotelian notion of color arising from the transition between brightness and darkness, rather than on the Newtonian color spectrum, his theory of sound was progressive for the age in which it was formulated.

Goethe's typology encompasses three rubrics of sound: the organic (subjective) category, that is, 'musical sound created by the human voice and perceived by the ear for the pleasure and elevation of the listener'; the mechanical (mixed) category, that is, 'sound generated by certain materials and spatial arrangements'; and the mathematical (objective) sound category, which is 'music defined and determined by physical laws and measurements' (Spaethling 1987: 36). The mechanical designation links Goethe's scientific enquiry to the discoveries of E. F. F. Chladni, the father of vibratory physics, with whom Goethe conferred over aspects of acoustic and color theory during the scholar's frequent visits to Weimar.[7]

The physics of sound in relation to the earth's origins reemerges as a central trope in the scene 'Again on the Upper Peneus' ('Klassische Walpurgisnacht— Am obern Peneios') in Act II of Part II. Here Thales and Anaxagoras debate the viability of the two conflicting doctrines that polarized the scientific community of Goethe's day: Vulcanism, which attributed the geology of the earth to earthquakes and violent volcanic eruptions, and Neptunism, which propagated the derivation of life from the ocean. The Sirens of the deep witness with alarm, and the Sphinxes of the desert with resigned composure, such an upheaval in the making as Seismos sets to work with 'dreadful shaking' and 'thunderous quaking' (*F*, 7523–4): 'I force my passage from the dark abyss,/And summon loudly, as to new-born life,/Another race to sojourn here in bliss' (*F*, 7571–3). The formation of mountain ranges is an act of creation Seismos defends aesthetically as an indispensable contributor to the beauty of the earth (*F*, 7553). For Anaxagoras, the advocate of Vulcanism, the seismic activity is sufficient proof of the contestability of Thales' claim that '[f]rom moisture all organic living came' (*F*, 7856). Perhaps it is just as well that the continuous noise of geological upheavals over millions of years yielded to sporadic outbursts during the ascent of man, given Goethe's speculation in his *Theory of Colors* vis-à-vis thresholds of sound toleration: 'A world that was so continuously filled with sound as it is with light, would be quite unbearable' (*GA*, 16: 589). On a metaphysical level, it would have been arguably far worse had the Roman god Lucifer, the bearer of light, brought to earth the deafening thunderbolts of Zeus. In theosophical thinking the scriptural Fallen Lucifer has a much closer connection with light, given his passage through the sound ether after the sun archangel Michael is reported to have cast him down from the heavens.

Neptunism, to which Goethe subscribed unequivocally, gains ascendancy in *Faust II* by virtue of the corporeal 'becoming' of the allegorical Homunculus (pure spirit) in the waters of the Aegean after its resonant and iridescent glass housing shatters on Galatea's shell-car (*F*, 8472) and the manikin celebrates his paradoxical 'birth-death' (Latimer 1974: 816) through union with the mythical creatures of the sea. Homunculus' beginnings in the retort that has been fired to intense heat in the furnace of Wagner's Gothic laboratory constitute, in a sense, a microcosmic reenactment of the biblical 'fiat lux' process: 'Ay, as a burning jewel, the spark/Flashes a ray to pierce the dark./A light emerges, white and still' (*F*, 6826–8). As a 'source of both sound and light' (Latimer 1974: 815),[8] Homunculus acts as a beacon for the journey back to the southern climes of mythical antiquity. Similarly, a will-o'-the-wisp and a subsequent swarm of glow-worms illuminate the travelers' zigzag path to the summit of the Brocken (*F*, 3903–5).[9]

There is nothing inanimate about the geological strata passed on this steep climb. Instead, the Antiphonal Trio gives weight to the hypothesis of Romantic natural philosophers such as F. W. Schelling, H. Steffens and F. v. Baader that rocks are as much alive with sound ('Snouted rocks in gulches roaring,/Hear their snarling and their snoring') (*F*, 3879–80) as the 'songs' and 'murmurs' of the '[b]rooks and rivers downward streaming' (*F*, 3883–4). Although Goethe was essentially an 'eye'-person, he nevertheless considered it equally important to listen closely to natural objects in order to understand their intrinsic laws ('Gesetzmäßigkeiten'). His highly developed auditory sensitivity enabled him to achieve this.

The Origins of Speech Sound

Paracelsus' alchemical recipe for the creation of an homunculus,[10] a synonym for a human fetus, was to incubate sperm in a hermetically sealed vessel for sixty days at high temperatures.[11] The other ingredients were bones, skin fragments and hair. Goethe details none of the constituent parts of his manikin-to-be. Instead, he is more concerned with the processes of metamorphosis, which include the development of speech. In this respect the 'test-tube' manufacture of Homunculus, is, as I have suggested (Corkhill 1997: 70), a kind of mock creation myth designed to make light of the complex and (self-) contradictory language-genesis and language-acquisition theories advanced by German scholarly circles following the Berlin Academy's release of J. P. Süßmilch's prize-winning tract *Versuch eines Beweises, daß die erste Sprache ihren Ursprung nicht von Menschen, sondern allein vom Schöpfer erhalten habe* (*An Attempt at Proving that the First Language derived its Origin not from Man but from the Creator Alone*) (1766), Hamann's spirited defense of the 'divine' hypothesis and Herder's acclaimed refutation of linguistic innatism in *Abhandlung über den Ursprung der Sprache* (*Treatise on the Origin of Language*) (1772). While Goethe did not contribute publicly to this intellectual debate, four decades later he summarized in *Dichtung und Wahrheit* (*Poetry and Truth*) (1811–14) the basic thrust of the various propositions put forth at the time. Not unlike Fichte in his essay 'Von der Sprachfähigkeit und dem Ursprung der Sprache' ('On the linguistic capacity and the origin of language' (1794), Goethe embraced an even-handed, eclectic approach to the key tenets:

> If God created humans as humans, language was acquired as automatically as erect gait. As quickly as they noticed that they could walk and grasp things, they realised just as quickly that they could sing with their throat and modify these sounds with their tongue, gums and lips in various ways.
>
> . . .
>
> If humans are of divine origin, so is language, and if humans are natural beings in natural surroundings, language is natural as well. I could never keep body and soul apart. (*GA*, 10: 445–6)

If there is any substance to Goethe's observation to Eckermann that Homunculus represents 'pure entelechy . . . spirit as it enters life prior to all experience' and that the manikin is a 'highly gifted' entity,[12] one wonders whether Goethe meant such giftedness to include an innate, 'apriori' predisposition toward language competence. This would contradict Herder's denial of prelinguistic knowledge and Goethe's own 'dialectical' approach. Arguably, by the time Goethe completed *Faust II* in the summer of 1831, more sophisticated anthropological and physiological models, such as those posited by Wilhelm von Humboldt, had defused and marginalized the issue of supernatural/preexperiential versus natural/empirical speech origins. Goethe's own stance had also changed in the intervening years from a self-defeating concern with the genesis of language to a scientifically grounded preoccupation with polylinguistic development.[13]

The intellectual tug-of-war between divine and invention origin-of-language theories actually had little bearing on this 'brave new world' of (al)chemically produced manikins equipped with artificial intelligence. After all, Homunculus is not biologically human. He has no natural parents. There is no womb in which the growing fetus could absorb the aural input of maternal speech patterns and rhythms. There is only a surrogate 'father' (Wagner), as well as a surrogate 'distant relative' (Mephistopheles) who has somehow managed to tamper satanically with the birth process, thus making a mockery of the whole divine creation myth.[14] The manikin is not the incarnation of the Word ('logos'). He is mind without (and in search of) a body, but boasts no genetic lineage, so that even assuming the credibility of the biblical account of the unitary origin of language in the Garden of Eden, he could not have been heir to this God-given Adamic language. Nor do the fundamental suppositions of ontogenetic language-acquisition theory apply when one considers the freakish pace of Homunculus' language development from gesticulation to sporadic sounds and then to mature speech—all in a matter of seconds (F, 6877–88).[15] Interestingly, Goethe fully intended his 'lustrous dwarf' (F, 8245) to sound on stage like a humanoid from the pages of science fiction, having suggested the services of a ventriloquist to make the voice emanate from the vial itself (GA, 24: 378).[16]

Proteus plays a similar trick on Thales ('Rocky Inlets of the Aegean Sea' ['Klassische Walpurgisnacht—Felsbuchten des Ägäischen Meers']) in a kind of hide-and-seek game for which Goethe wrote the stage prompt 'with ventriloquial effect, now at hand, now far off' (F, before 8227). Acoustic tricks also form part of the elaborate hoax of the court pantomime ('Baronial Hall' ['Kaiserliche Pfalz—Rittersaal']) in which the phantoms of Paris and Helen are conjured up after Faust's return from the realm of the Mothers. Thus we are presented here with a (re)creation narrative in the service of art. Mephistopheles' self-assigned role as souffleur enhances the Aristotelian illusion: 'My eloquence should capture every heart,/Since prompting is the devil's special art' (F, 6399–400). Needless to say, the satanic whisper in the ear of the court Astrologer ('You, who of starry courses keep the key,/Will take your cues quite masterly from me' [F, 6401–2]) constitutes the most subversive tool of psychological control Mephistopheles, as a minion of the Great Tempter, wields over Faust during the latter's odyssey ('Irr-fahrt'). The whispering voice of an evil spirit also preys with calculated success on Gretchen's guilty conscience while she attends the funeral mass for her slain brother Valentin ('Cathedral Nave' ['Dom']).[17]

The court pantomime makes use of synesthetic theatrical effects, which Arens (1989: 278) likens to a Wagnerian 'Gesamtkunstwerk'. One such effect is the creation of an artificial mist that envelops the set, a Greek temple, and is 'magically' transformed into sonorous clouds: 'The clouds resolve in music as they go./From airy tones flows strength that none may see,/For, as they move, all, all is melody' (F, 6444–6). Another subtle 'Spiegelung' suggests itself here, for just as the vapors subside in the enclosed space of the 'huge temple singing' (F, 6448) to reveal Paris in all his beauty, so Homunculus comes into view when his clouded resonant retort 'clears' (F, 6872). Analogous to the 'explosion' that abruptly ends the play and returns the legendary pair to the realm of the shades is the shattering of Homunculus' protective flask in a rocky inlet of the Aegean Sea.

The Sonority of Words

Both parts of *Faust* provide fertile ground for interrogating key issues pertaining to the philosophy of language, especially the relationship of thinking to speaking and of concepts to their linguistic representation (Corkhill 1991; 1995). This discourse also encompasses the specific nexus between sound and semantics, albeit a largely problematical one. The (self-evident) Fichtean hypothesis that words remain no more than 'empty noise' (Breazeale 1988: 196) until they are endowed with meaning and are communicated as such is exemplified by Faust's skeptical description ('In Martha's Garden' ['Marthens Garten']) of the names of things and concepts as 'but noise and smoke' (F, 3457). Mephistopheles is no less a language skeptic than his disaffected protégé, as he explains to a fresher with sardonic relish how whole academic disciplines have established their scholarly credibility (or lack thereof) on empty rhetoric, that is, words that sound impressive but are devoid of conceptual meaning. The cognitive inaccessibility of metaphysics ('What things won't fit the human brain' [F, 1951]) is resolved, so Mephistopheles glibly contends, by simply resorting to 'a sounding phrase instead' (F, 1953).[18]

If there was ever a scene in which 'empty noise' remains conspicuously bereft of meaning, it is the intermezzo 'Witch's Kitchen' ('Hexenküche'). The gibberish uttered by the 'crazy crone' (F, 2553) as she intones the magic spell over the rejuvenation draught is even belittled by Mephistopheles: 'And when the people hear a sounding word/They stand convinced that somewhere there's a meaning' (F, 2565–6). Goethe's parody of Catholic liturgy and ritual is evident both here and in the preceding 'mock' Gospel reading at which torch-bearing monkeys substitute for acolytes. Faust, who has freely consented to the hocus pocus, is nonetheless skeptical of such charlatanry:[19] 'How raves this ancient cabalcrier?/Her nonsense makes my head go round!/Stupidity's Gargantuan choir/ Is concentrated in the sound' (F, 2573–6).

Faust II attests to a broadening of the debate on the correspondence between words and their meaning to include the linguistic area of phonosemantics. The earliest critical discussion of the synchronic correlation between phonetics and semantics is traceable to Plato's *Cratylus* dialogue (c. 360 BCE), where Socrates, the principal advocate of this nexus, posited that the spoken word mimicked the 'essence' of the word it denoted.[20] However, since the eighteenth century the phonemic composition of the vast majority of words has been deemed to be quite arbitrary.

Goethe proffers an interesting case study of sound symbolism by probing the etymology of the noun 'Greif' ('griffin'). Indeed, according to one of the 'snarling' griffins, words can sound just like what they mean (onomatopoeia): 'In every word there rings/ An echo of the sense from which it springs:/Grey, grizzled, gruesome, grim, and grave-yard—thus/They tune in etymology' (F, 7094–7). Mephistopheles, who has taunted the griffin in the first place, lays the matter to rest after a further exchange of brilliant punning around the sound-similar infinitive 'greifen' ('to grab').

Such is the disjuncture between a strange-sounding word and its meaning that Faust is confronted by the unfamiliarity of cognitively indefinable Otherness just prior to his descent into the unknown ('A Gloomy Gallery' ['Kaiserliche Pfalz—Finstere Galerie']). Indeed, despite speaking aloud and repeating the word 'Mothers!', a 'sound with wonder haunted' (F, 6219), he still recoils at the strange ring of 'this Word, that I must dread to hear' (F, 6265). A further instance of the attempt to assimilate 'speech', the 'sense' of which was difficult to 'grasp' (F, 11399), occurs when the dying Faust is visited by the four Grey Hags ('Midnight'['Palast—Mitternacht']) and grapples with a phonosemantic quandary: 'A word like *Need* ['Not'] I heard, with bated breath,/And chiming with it came the sound of *Death* ['Tod'],/A hollow, muted note of spectral night' (F, 11400–1).

The *Faust* poem also contains recurring references to the pleasantness or unpleasantness, the mellifluousness or strident quality of the spoken word— what might be termed the aesthetics of sound ('Lautästhetik'). In the 'Prelude in the Theatre' ('Vorspiel auf dem Theater'), the poet who lives for high art but sees his praxis threatened by the dictates of popular taste affirms his vocational mission to morph the 'vexed, uneasy jarring sound' of nature's raw material into the 'rhythmic line euphonious' (*F*, 145–7) and to 'marshal . . . fragments to a ceremonious/. . . music, universal, whole' (*F*, 148–9).

An interconnected trope in the play is the persuasiveness of human speech ('eloquentia'), which in some instances has a significant impact on the course of the dramatic action. While Faust promptly dismisses Wagner's academic penchant for oratory as the trademark of a 'noisy jingling fool' (*F*, 549), ironically, Gretchen's surrender to the seductiveness of Faust's own lofty words ('[t]he sound of his words/Is honey and bliss' [*F*, 3398–9]) proves to be her tragic undoing. The authority of Faust's rhetoric is a double-edged sword, for the same voice speaks kindly to the demented Gretchen as she crouches on the floor of her prison cell amidst 'jangling chains and rustling straw' (*F*, 4422), offering momentary distraction and release from her feelings of abandonment.

Analogous to Gretchen's blind trust in the honorable intentions of her paramour on the strength of his soothing rhetoric is, of course, Helen of Troy's partial reliance on the hypnotically agreeable voice of her liege protector following her 'abduction' to Faust's medieval fortress ('Inner Courtyard of a Castle' ['Innerer Burghof']):

> . . . how comes it that his speech
> Chimed strangely in my ears, so strange, yet kind,
> Each tone in full accord with what came next?
> No sooner has a word well pleased the ear,
> Than comes another, as with a caress.
>
> (*F*, 9367–72)

Faust, himself struck dumb by ineffable emotion, proceeds—in a reversion to Storm-and-Stress thinking—to equate the 'heart' (*F*, 9377) with the wellspring of language itself. What we encounter here is Goethe's organic-subjective acoustical category: the modality of sound playing musically on the senses and impinging on the subconscious. As Schafer (1977: 169) aptly puts it: 'A sound event is symbolic when it stirs in us emotions or thoughts beyond its mechanical sensations or signaling function, when it has numinosity or reverberation that rings through the deeper recess of the psyche'. Not surprisingly, then, the Chorus is moved to tears by the pure melodic strains of Euphorion's string-playing issuing forth from the depths of a cavern. Euphorion, whom Gearey (1992: 129) describes as the 'beautiful expression of self in body and sound', is even capable of charming the cerebral Mephistopheles/Phorkyas with his 'music, sweetly sounding' (*F*, 9679), just as the classical world thrilled to the sounds of Orpheus' music-making. Euphorion's nimbleness is not only the physical embodiment of the flights of fancy he allegorically represents; the youth equally associates movement with the natural sound phenomena of the whistling wind and pounding waves (*F*, 9815–16), to which he is highly receptive. Insofar as his euphonious name intimates the musical quintessence of Romanticism, significantly it is not the visual spectacle of the fallen Icarus with which we are ultimately left, but the echo of his distressed voice rising from the deep.[21]

The fading echo is, in itself, an indicator of what for Goethe was the ephemeral nature of Romantic poesy, as opposed to the enduring plasticity of classical art.

With Helen gone in a puff of smoke, as it were, her retinue Chorus of Trojan women under the leadership of Panthalis finds itself no longer responsive to the narcotically powerful rhythmic flow of Phorkyas' word magic: 'Freed from the strumming, too, of heady wreathing tones/The ear bewildering, and still worse the inward sense./Descend we then to Hades . . .' (F, 9964–6). Panthalis' assertion, 'At last we shake the magic off/With which the old Thessalian hag would bind the soul' (F, 9962–3), foreshadows Faust's all too belated longing ('Midnight') to 'break the spell, all magic spurning,/And clear my path, all sorceries unlearning' (F, 11404–5). Faust has remained forever the language skeptic, lambasting Care for the same 'wretched litany' (F, 11469) of words from which the witch's incantation was once concocted.

Cacophony and Noise

Noise ('Lärm', 'Getöse') manifests itself in a variety of ways in both parts of *Faust*. In autobiographical terms, we know that Goethe was supersensitive to environmental noise. He particularly disliked street din (such as it was in his day), and in this he was not alone. Kant harbored an aesthetic aversion to all sorts of human and animal noises,[22] as did Arthur Schopenhauer (*Parerga und Paralipomena*, 1851). Faust's famulus, Wagner, makes no secret of his distaste for the vulgar and cacophonous 'shouting, fiddle-scraping [and] skittle-banging' (F, 945) of Eastertide merrymakers ('Outside the City Gate' ['Vor dem Tor']), while in 'Auerbach's Cellar' ('Auerbachs Keller in Leipzig') the unworldly Faust stands aloof from the raucous 'bellow[ing]' (F, 2125) of the inebriated drinking party.

On the other hand, Faust reveres a special kind of din: the powerfully deafening sounds of organic and inorganic matter. We witness this in the scene 'Forest and Cavern' ('Wald und Höhle'), where he stands in awe before 'the bounding tempest' that 'tears the forest' (F, 3228), or the 'giant pines' that 'come crashing on the crown/ Of neighbour tree-tops' (F, 3229), or the mountains shaking 'with thud and shock' (F, 3231). The experience of nature's clamorous majesty is replicated in 'Walpurgis Night' ('Walpurgisnacht'), as already exemplified, and again in 'Pleasing Landscape' as the rejuvenated Faust watches the 'cataract pouring, crashing from the boulders' (F, 4716), or the 'thunderous water seeth[ing] in fleecy spume' (F, 4720). In this respect we are reminded of Edmund Burke's celebration of the loud sublimeness of cataracts, raging storms, thunder and other natural phenomena. However, it is an entirely different matter when the distracting intrusiveness of the 'growling' (F, 1202), 'whining' (F, 1238) and 'yelping' (F, 1239) poodle disturbs the scholar's intellectual musing during his attempt to translate from John 1,[23] or when he is confronted on the Blocksberg by a 'cursèd din' (F, 4051), the surreal cacophony of Walpurgis Night reveling. Faust, of course, is not bewitched by the orgiastic shrieks and noisy dance rhythms of the witches' Sabbath—in sharp distinction to Ulysses' mariners who are obliged to plug their eyes with wax to escape the lure of the Sirens.[24]

Further reactions to noise are bound up with folklore, popular superstition and cultural memory. Faust's summoning of the four elementary spirits Salamander,

Sylphide, Undine and Incubus to drive away the devilish apparition from the sacrosanctity of his Gothic study ('Faust's Study (ii)' ['Studierzimmer I']), not to mention his ineffectual use of Judeo-Christian symbols, must have been a noisy affair, given that the first words an emboldened Mephistopheles addresses to the would-be exorcist in the guise of a traveling scholar are: 'Why all this noise?' ('Wozu der Lärm?') (F, 1322). Wagner, for his part, likens the hurdy-gurdy din created by the Easter 'music makers' to the 'roar ... of Satan's hellish clanging' (F, 947).[25] We can equally point to Gretchen's dread of Satan's 'hellish clatter and roar' (F, 4467) as she faces execution and the prospect of eternal damnation,[26] or to Mephistopheles' theologically motivated horror of the peal of church bells.[27]

It is worth dwelling briefly on the associative power of bells which toll, drone and peal at a number of critical junctures in the play. The first and best known example of bell-ringing occurs in 'Night. Faust's Study (i)' ('Nacht'), where the sound of church bells calling the faithful to Easter mass preludes the sung message of hope and salvation through resurrection. It is actually a combination of the fond childhood remembrance of the 'boding fulness' (F, 773) of bells and of the 'heavenly sounds' (F, 763) of devotional music that draws Faust back from the brink of existential despair and contemplated suicide. The full peal of joyous Eastertide bells stands in stark contrast to the association with death and earthly finiteness evoked by the single mournful bell that summons to Valentin's requiem or by Faust's reference to the dire consequences of violating the terms of the pact: 'For I will perish in that day./ 'Tis I for whom the bell shall toll' (F, 1702–3). And for her part the incarcerated Gretchen awaits with trepidation the appointed hour when 'the knell ... is tolled' (F, 4590) that announces her imminent hanging.

Toward the end of Part II the tinkling bell of the chapel on the dunes, where Faust as the mastermind of an ambitious dyke project shows himself to be 'hell-bent' on appropriating Philemon and Baucis' humble abode, reflects the simple piety and hospitality of the cottagers. Yet for Faust the 'silver-sounding' (F, 11072) bell only serves to heighten the affront to his vanity posed by this remaining obstacle: 'Accursèd chime, all solace ending,/It strikes and wounds with treacherous aim' (F, 11151–2). With consummate skill Mephistopheles insidiously fuels Faust's seething indignation: 'This clanging is a grief to hear,/ And this accursed ding-dong bell/Clouds the sweet evening with its knell' (F, 11263–4).[28]

The Philemon and Baucis episode epitomizes more than any other the ethical questionability of Faust's aesthetic conditioning. By blaming a verbal misunderstanding for the fatal consequences of his unambiguous injunction to Mephistopheles' henchmen to dispossess the aged couple—by force if necessary—('[d]eaf to commands you seem to be!' [F, 11370]), Faust has become highly desensitized to distasteful realities. Thus the gruesome details of the torching of the cottage are 'perversely relayed to him over the Watchman's megaphone in a poetically "censored" form ... [T]his is the downside of poetic language: that it is as capable of aestheticizing violence as it is of creating sublimity' (Corkhill, 1997: 66). What is more, the amplified loudness of the megaphone represents a travesty of the pleasant ring of words ('Lautästhetik').

While the battle scenes of Act IV of *Faust II*, in which the aesthetics of myth revert to the 'Machtpolitik' of European history, resonate with the clash of weaponry, the 'non plus ultra' with regard to noise is undoubtedly the invasive and unstoppable din of technical progress as Faust's land reclamation scheme gathers momentum. If Schafer (1977: 75) is right in his contention that the loudest noises in any given soundscape are generated by those who hold the greatest power over it, this is undoubtedly a truism in terms of Faust's grand scheme, and no less applicable to the witches' raucous ascendancy during Walpurgis Night, or even to Mephisto's self-assertive return visit to Faust's professorial study, where, much to the consternation of the aging famulus, the 'penetrating clangour' of the door-bell causes the 'walls to tremble' and the doors to 'fly open' (*F*, before 6620).[29] The 'greybeard' (*F*, 6637) might justifiably ask the same question Mephistopheles first put to Faust: 'Why all this fuss?'

Despite having been blinded by Care ('Midnight'), the dying overseer of public works continues to derive satisfaction from listening to the pick-and-shovel labor of his construction gangs, a noisy activity Baucis had observed with considerable foreboding. Hearing the spades of the Lemures digging his grave ('The Great Outer-Court of the Palace' ['Palast—Großer Vorhof des Palasts']) is, of course, quite a different matter.

Performance Sound

If nineteenth-century artistic directors were faced with technical difficulties over the theatrical performability of certain scenes of the *Faust* poem (Goethe himself was evasive on the subject) (Flax 1979: 154), the new century ushered in the revolving stage, which transformed the logistics of scenography. Max Reinhardt's 1909 *Faust* production was one such milestone. Similarly, major advances have been made in acoustic reproduction. Indeed, over the rich history of *Faust* theatre performances successive dramaturges have incorporated a variety of musical and non-musical diegetic and offstage acoustic events, with or without reference to the original stage instructions. In the thrall of Romanticism, nineteenth-century *Faust* productions embellished the dramatic import of the text through symphonic tone color. This tendency was already evident in the inaugural public performance of *Faust I* in Braunschweig (1829). Here below-stage orchestral accompaniment featured prominently, even if Goethe's instructions did not specify it.[30] Leaving aside the subject of textual musicalization (vocal scoring and instrumentation), which has received a good deal of scholarly attention,[31] this final section will focus on other types of non-musical soundscape innovation in several more recent landmark theatre productions. Until the appearance of disc recordings in the theatre during the 1950s, all such sound effects were produced live offstage. In turn, computer technology has enhanced the experimental richness of the soundscape.

As Mahl (1999) and Schieb (2000) both show, certain scenes have consistently lent themselves more readily than others to the imaginative use of special sound effects, especially 'Prologue in Heaven', 'Witch's Kitchen', 'Walpurgis Night' and 'Laboratory' ('Laboratorium'). The acoustic backdrop to the Walpurgis Night extravaganza in Gustaf Gründgens' avant-garde Hamburg 'Inszenierung' (1957–8) comprised rock music and Brecht-like 'Verfremdungseffekte' such as a wailing siren followed by a filmic back projection of a violent nuclear explosion, both of which were designed to punctuate abruptly the orgiastic tumult

(Mahl 1999: 143). Similarly, Goethe himself 'considered using a volcanic eruption to disperse the crowds after midnight' (Lee 1994: 89). A rock band also played in the 'Witch's Kitchen' scene in Gorgio Strehler's Milan production (1989) and in Michael Thalheimer's version (Berlin, 2004), while in a Dresden staging under the direction of Wolfgang Engel (1990), Euphorion, recast as the lead vocalist in a pop band, deafens his horrified parents with his ear-splitting cacophony (Mahl 1999: 231). What is more, Engel's headstrong youth dies after crashing his motorbike, the noisy roar of which is heard in an interpolated filmic montage.

Another alienation effect widely used in post-1945 productions is the loudspeaker. Fritz Kortner (Residenztheater Munich, 1956) has the entire text of 'Dedication' ('Zueignung') relayed by loudspeaker, as well as Mephistopheles' speaking part in the 'Prologue' (Mahl 1999: 138), while in Christoph Schroth's version (Schwerin 1979) the amplified voice of Homunculus, who is encased not in a vial but in a portable TV, is transmitted into the auditorium (Mahl 1999: 216). The same sound technology is used in the Euphorion sequences (Mahl 1999: 217). Other voice-modification devices feature increasingly in contemporary productions. For instance, a special effect in Peter Stein's 'Walpurgis Night' is Mephistopheles' holding of a microphone up to the speakers of the ancien régime (Schieb 2000: 120).

Stein provided elaborate interpretive notes for the 'Geräuschkulisse' of 'Walpurgis Night' with regard to both musical scoring and general audio effects. For example, acoustic distortion is recommended to convey the incomprehensibly 'exalted nonsense' of the witches' choruses (Schieb 2000: 120). Vocal distortion also underlies the muffled speech of Stein's masked Lemures ('The Great Outer-Court of the Palace').

Stein's sound design throughout the 21-hour long production caters to a range of atmospheric acoustic events, both musical and non-musical. In 'Pleasing Landscape' a high electronic frequency simulates the noise of the approaching sun (Schieb 2000: 125), while a jumble of indistinct musical sounds yields to verbalization as Homunculus acquires the art of 'human' speech (Schieb 2000: 142). Offstage gongs also form part of the sound backdrop, particularly in 'Midnight', where the entrance of the four 'old hags' is eerily heralded by the striking of a gong (Schieb 2000: 173). The sound of ringing or breaking glass is something the Stein production mimics well. Especially subtle in this respect is the explosion marking the end of the court pantomime. The bang is made to sound like splintering glass, as if to suggest that the 'laterna magica' behind the phantasmagorical illusion has itself cracked.

Notes

1. This and all subsequent parenthetical and endnote references to Goethe's writings (except for n. 19) draw on *Gedenkausgabe der Werke, Briefe und Gespräche*, abbreviated in the text and notes to *GA*, followed by the volume number and page number(s). All English translations of citations from *GA* are mine, unless otherwise indicated.
2. This and all subsequent parenthetical and endnote line numbers refer to *Goethe. Faust. Part One* (1949) and *Goethe. Faust. Part Two* (1962) (abbreviated as *F*).
3. Böhme, and Emanuel Swedenborg after him, both taught that knowledge or mystical truth was revealed in resonance. Böhme wrote in his first theosophical work *Aurora, oder*

Morgenröthe im Aufgange (1611–12) that the Word realized itself in sound and that cosmic sound entered all organic and inorganic matter on earth as its shaping force. The 'vox humana' and musical instruments were a faint echo of the 'divine sound that rises up from eternity to eternity' in the Divine Kingdom of Joy (cit. in Haferland 1989: 93).

4 In terms of the nexus between light and sound the ancient Egyptians held the belief that the singing sun created the world through its scream of light. See in this regard Nicklaus (1994: n.p.).
5 The latest helioseismological research suggests that sound waves are trapped inside the sun and make it ring like a bell.
6 According to Arens (1989: 53) Goethe in his 1772 periodical review of Lavater's *Aussichten in die Ewigkeit* spoke of 'the cosmos, the sun's thunder and the rolling of the planets'.
7 Chladni conducted research into vibrating plates using a violin bow and a metal surface sprinkled with sand or sawdust. He was also the inventor of a euphonium consisting of glass rods with different pitches.
8 In Hindu Brahmanic teaching the first humans on earth glowed and resonated.
9 According to popular tradition will-o'-the-wisps are the souls of unbaptized children. Homunculus is also in a sense an unchristened spirit, although the manikin's immersion in the waters of the Aegean is, in terms of the biblical subtext running through so much of *Faust*, a baptismal rite of passage of sorts.
10 See Paracelsus' 'De generationibus rerum naturalium' (1572).
11 The glass flask 'chimes' (6871), we are told. Perhaps it is made of fine crystal which vibrates and emits a clear tone when tapped. In a similar fashion, the stage directions referring to the concoction of the rejuvenation brew in the 'Witch's Kitchen' scene read: 'Meanwhile the glasses begin to ring and the cauldron to hum, making sounds of music' (F, before 2532). As there are physical forces at play here, I cannot agree with the observation by Zimmermann (1997–8: n.p.) that '[the witch] has the power to conjure music and make objects shake and vibrate with her words and gestures'. It only appears magical to the scientifically untrained eye. It is noteworthy that Goethe praised Benjamin Franklin's Glass Armonica, which produced ethereal notes when the player touched a set of rotating glass bowls with his moistened fingers. Perhaps the witch's magic therapy is an allusion to Mesmer's alleged use of glass music to lull his hypnotized patients into a state of mental wellbeing.
12 F. W. Riemer, posthumous note of 30 March 1833, cited in Lohmeyer (1975: 185). My translations.
13 Goethe noted in a conversation with Eckermann (20 June 1831): 'All languages arise from close human needs, human pursuits, as well as from human emotions and observations in general' (*GA*, 24: 758).
14 Homunculus is, in a sense, a bearer of light. In Greek mythology the Roman god Lucifer was called Phosphorus, the shining one.
15 Homunculus' 'revolutionary' capacity to vocalize in the twinkling of an eye runs counter, for example, to E. B. de Condillac's belief in a gradual evolution favoring spoken over gestural language. See his *Essai sur les connaissances humaines* (1746).
16 Gaier (1999: 718–9) mentions the automata invented by the eighteenth-century mechanics Vaucanson and Droz that were able to emit language-like sounds and words. Given the bizarre nature of the manikin's speech production, the resonating property of the glass is unlikely to possess the acoustical significance. Kerényi (1991: 187) fancifully attaches to it: 'Goethe's Homunculus is the pure formula of the . . . music inventing grandchild of cosmogonic mythologems' ('Goethes Homunculus ist die reine Formel . . . des Musik erfindenden Urkindes kosmogonischer Mythologeme').
17 Guardian angels are also known to whisper soothing words in the ears of the distressed, but Gretchen is not vouchsafed this comfort.
18 Goethe noted in a letter to Wilhelm von Humboldt (22 August 1806) that the formulae used to define concepts in mathematics, science, ethics and religion were inadequate and imprecise because they relied on the register of metaphysics. The 'riskiness' of this

metalanguage lay in its frequent substitution of the 'sound' for the 'thing' it was supposed to represent (1990, 4, 51: 197).
19 See Corkhill (2006) for a reading of charlatanic practices in *Faust I* and *II*.
20 It would be hard to imagine how the essence of an object, e.g., a chair, could be imitated by sound, not to mention the complicating factor of cultural and linguistic diversity.
21 In a parallel manner, Gretchen's exiting cry of anguish 'Heinrich, Heinrich' (*F*, 4615) grows ever fainter.
22 Kant articulated his dislike of noise in his little-known treatise *Mussmasslicher Anfang der Menschengeschichte* (*Conjectural Beginning of Human History*) (1785). He railed against the impulse in 'children and thoughtless persons who disturb the thinking members of the commonwealth by rattling, shouting, whistling, singing, and other noisy amusements (the same occurs in religious devotions)' (Kant 1983 [1795]: n. 50). For Kant the ear was less reliable than the eye as a cognitive organ, whereas Herder considered the ear the most important organ for direct access to the soul.
23 Goethe was particularly averse to barking dogs. Cf. Kurt Tucholsky's satirical jibe at Goethe's paranoia in his polemical 'Traktat über den Hund, sowie über Lärm und Geräusch' ('Treatise on Dogs, Noise and Sounds') (1927).
24 Mephistopheles' broadside against popular superstition in 'Imperial Palace' ('Kaiserliche Pfalz—Saal des Thrones'), where the courtiers and officials dismiss as quackery his promise to raise gold, contains an allusion to the aphrodisiacal mandragora ('Of mandrake-roots the one will mumble' [*F*, 4979]). Although the plant was alleged to provide the person who ripped it out of the ground with knowledge of where gold lay hidden, it killed him, so that a black dog, a 'Hound of Hell' (*F*, 4980) was used instead. The link with the Sirens is such that the ears of the digger and/or the bystanders had to be likewise stopped with wax, albeit, in this case, to block out the deadly yells of torment suffered by the deracinated plant.
25 The banging of kettles and other household instruments to ward off evil spirits goes back to heathen practices in most countries of Northern, Central and Eastern Europe.
26 Both Dante, who particularly hated noise, and Milton make much of the infernal hubbub associated with pandemonium (the place of all demons). Indeed, the first thing Dante notices on entering the gates of hell is the noisy sighing and wailing of the condemned (*Inferno*, canto 3, ll. 22–30). Similarly, in Milton's *Paradise Lost* (1667) the angel Raphael, upon approaching the gates of hell, discerns the loud torment and furious rage of lost souls (Book 8, ll. 240–4).
27 In popular superstition devils and demons were thought to be fearful of the metallic tintinnabulation of bells.
28 Arens (1989: 120) mentions another Goethean phobia that finds expression in *Faust*: a dislike of clanging church bells.
29 Gaier (1999: 692) notes that in the chapbook *Historia von D. Johann Fausten* (1587) Mephostophiles always announces his presence to his adept by ringing a bell. According to Schmidt (1999: 225) the loud bell with its earth-shaking reverberations symbolically issues in the new age (of medical science), thereby spelling the demise of the pre-Renaissance worldview. Schmidt, however, fails to explain why he equates Mephisto with the forces of scientific progressivism that have replaced medieval scholasticism.
30 A case in point was the overorchestration of the resonating glasses on the witch's cauldron, which a critic of the time dubbed an 'unnecessary exertion on the ear' (Mahl 1999: 23–4).
31 See 'inter alia' Cotti (1957) and Spaethling (1987).

Bibliography

Arens, H. (1989), *Kommentar zu Goethes Faust II*. Heidelberg: Carl Winter Universitätsverlag (Beiträge zur Neueren Literaturgeschichte 86).

Breazeale, D. (ed.) (1988), *Fichte: Early Philosophical Writings*. Ithaca: Cornell University Press.
Corkhill, A. (1991), 'Goethes Sprachdenken in beziehungsgeschichtlicher Hinsicht', *Neophilologus*, 75, (2), 239–51.
— (1995), 'Sprachphilosophische Fragestellungen in Goethes Faust I', *Neophilologus*, 79, (3), 451–63.
— (1997), 'Language discourses in Goethe's *Faust I*', in K. Dunne and I. R. Campbell (eds), *Unravelling the Labyrinth. Decoding Text and Language*. Bern and Frankfurt: Peter Lang, pp. 57–73.
— (2006), 'Charlatanism in Goethe's *Faust I* and Tieck's *William Lovell*', *Forum for Modern Language Studies*, 2, (1), 80–92.
Cotti, J. (1957), *Die Musik in Goethes 'Faust'*. Winterthur: Keller.
Flax, N. M. (1979), 'Goethe's *Faust II* and the Experimental Theater of his Time', *Comparative Literature*, 31/2, 154-66.
Gaier, U. (1999), *Johann Wolfgang Goethe. Faust Dichtungen*, v. 2. Stuttgart: Reclam.
Gearey, J. (1992), *Goethe's Other Faust. The Drama, Part II*. Toronto, Buffalo and London: University of Toronto Press.
Goethe, J. W. (1948–71), *Gedenkausgabe der Werke, Briefe und Gespräche*, E. Beutler (ed.). Zurich and Stuttgart: Artemis, 24 v. and 3 suppl. v.
— (1949), *Goethe. Faust Part One*, P. Wayne (trans.). Hammondsworth: Penguin.
— (1962), *Goethe. Faust Part Two*, P. Wayne (trans.). Hammondsworth: Penguin.
— (1990), *Werke. Weimarer Ausgabe*, P. Raabe (ed.). Munich: dtv, 3 v. (= suppl. v. 51–3).
Haferland, H. (1989), 'Mystische Theorie der Sprache bei Jacob Böhme', in J. Gessinger and W. v. Rahden (eds), *Theorien vom Ursprung der Sprache*, v. 1. Berlin/New York: Walter de Gruyter, pp. 89–130.
Kant, I. (1795, 1983), *Perpetual Peace, and Other Essays on Politics, History, and Morals*, T. Humphrey (trans.). Indianapolis: Hackett Pub.
Kerényi, K. (1991), 'Das Ägäische Fest. Die Meergötterszene in Goethes "Faust II". Eine mythologische Studie', in W. Keller (ed.), *Aufsätze zu Goethes Faust II*. Darmstadt: Wissenschaftliche Buchgesellschaft (Wege der Forschung 445), pp. 160–89.
Latimer, D. (1974), 'Homunculus as symbol: Semantic and dramatic functions of the figure in Goethe's *Faust*', *MLN*, 89, (5), 812–20.
Lee, M. (1994), 'Faust's Harzreise', in J. K. Brown, M. Lee and T. P. Saine (eds), *Interpreting Goethe's 'Faust' Today*. Columbia: Camden House, pp. 81–93.
Lohmeyer, D. (1975), *Faust und die Welt. Der zweite Teil der Dichtung, eine Anleitung zum Lesen des Textes*. Munich: Beck.
Mahl, B. (1999), *Goethes 'Faust' auf der Bühne (1806–1998)*. Stuttgart: J. B. Metzler.
Milton, J. (1957), *Complete Poems and Major Prose*, M. Y. Hughes (ed.). New York: Odyssey.
Nicklaus, H.-G. (1994), 'Die "Kosmogonie" Marius Schneiders – Wissenschaft, Philosophie, Mythos?', n.p. www.harmonik.de/harmonik/vtr_pdf/Beitraege9407Nicklaus.pdf (retrieved 10 July 2006).
Schafer, R. M. (1977), *The Tuning of the World*. London: Random House.
Schieb, R. (2000), *Peter Stein inszeniert 'Faust' von Johann Wolfgang Goethe. Das Programmbuch 'Faust I und II'*. Cologne: Du Mont.
Schmidt, J. (1999), *Goethes Faust. Erster und Zweiter Teil. Grundlagen – Werk – Wirkung*. Munich: Beck.
Spaethling, R. (1987), *Music and Mozart in the Life of Goethe*. Columbia: Camden House.
Zimmermann, L. D. (1997–8), 'Interiority, power and female subjectivity in Goethe's *Faust I*', *New German Review*, 13, www.germanic.ucla.edu/NGR/ngr13/interiority.htm

4 Technology as Timelessness: Building and Language in *Faust*

Claudia Brodsky

To stand with a free people upon a free foundation.
(Auf freiem Grund mit freiem Volke stehn.)

Goethe, Faust II *(11580)*

Man can, indeed, conceive, form and carry through this or that in one way or another. But over the event of unconcealment, in which at any given time the real shows itself or withdraws, man has no control.
(Der Mensch kann zwar dieses oder jenes so oder so vorstellen, gestalten und betreiben. Allein, über die Unverborgenheit, worin sich jeweils das Wirkliche zeigt oder entzieht, verfügt der Mensch nicht.)

Heidegger, 'Die Frage nach der Technik'
('The question concerning technology')

Faust's Building: Theory as Practice

With the exception of the remarkable discussion of *Faust* by Marshall Berman (1988), whose classic, still searing dialectical analysis of modernity as both constitutive and destructive of history departs from 'the tragedy of development' defined for Berman in Goethe's play, scant if any critical notice has been made of the fact that, of all the acts of transgression Faust commits over the duration of his colorful drama, it is neither seduction, nor desertion, nor even murder that brings about his wager's loss.[1] The erotic 'pull' of 'the eternal feminine' and contrasting pastoral fealty of Philemon and Baucis may have long offered the most fertile ground for commentary on Faust's impassioned trajectory, but it is a decidedly impersonal act that brings the eventful course of his actions to an end. Sitting before the sea toward the close of *Faust II*, a world-weary Mephistopheles at his side, Faust regards natural phenomena—here, the repetitive 'play' of the advancing waves ('With time the game repeats itself' ['Die Stunde kommt, sie wiederholt das Spiel'] [F, 10209])—with the same contemptuous impatience he had reserved for verbal phenomena in *Faust I*. The thrust of Faust's final complaint reflects and reverses his first and, in that inverted symmetry, the arc of development spanning both plays first appears revealed. For, standing with Wagner before the city gate near the beginning of *Faust I*, the disgruntled scholar had described as 'a beautiful dream' the natural scene he now rejects: 'I rush to drink the [goddess'] eternal light,/Before me the day and behind me the night,/The sky above me and under me the waves./A beautiful dream ...' ('Ich eile fort ihr ew'ges Licht zu trinken,/Vor mir den Tag, und hinter mir die Nacht,/Den Himmel über mir und unter mir die Wellen./Ein schöner Traum ...') (*F*, 1086–9). 'Waves' rolling 'below' him, and 'the sky above,' it is no longer the uselessness of human learning and knowledge that inspires Faust's anger ('Precisely what we don't know, is what we could use/And what we do know, is of no use' ['Was man nicht weiss, das eben brauchte man,/Und was man weiss kann man nicht brauchen'] [*F*, 1066]) in *Faust II*, but rather nature's inhuman lack of vision and ambition, the 'purposeless power of unbound elements', 'wave conquering wave ... and nothing accomplished' ('Zwecklose Kraft unbändiger Elemente'; 'Da herrschet Well auf Welle ... und es ist nichts geleistet') (*F*, 10216–19).

Just as Faust's earlier idealization of the pure dynamism of nature has turned in time to disenchantment with its 'purposeless power', so the very mental faculties he had once discounted as impotent now inspire him. Recognizing his separateness from nature as the positive source of an unnatural power—the intertwined abilities to analyze and act upon the 'given' relations of force in nature rather than give oneself to them[2]—Faust 'swiftly forms plans' ('Da fasst'ich schnell im Geiste Plan auf Plan') (*F*, 10227) to do for nature what she cannot do for herself. He will now divert, store and distribute the undirected 'streams' of energy he 'strove' to experience immediately in *Faust I* (*F*, 1078, 1719, 1742) so as to arrive, by means of those natural energies, at an entirely artificial end, a monument not to nature's powers but to man's supernatural ability to turn them about, to yield a certain independent end by intervening in and altering the continuum of cause and effect. Faust's plans would submit 'the unbound elements' of nature to new operations and configurations, funneling the formless dynamism of tidal waters into mechanically sealed containers—canals for shipping—and forming matter by building dams to retrieve ocean breakfront for useable land. Rejecting the instability of the natural power he sees before him, a power always in the course of moving on, negating at every moment its own visible formations, Faust would now coerce substance from force, form from movement, extant ground from what 'is' not.

Always violent in their proposals, husbanders of nature never come bidden. By turns persuasive and despotic, they ply, undermine, compel: their plans, viewed without measure as the material realization of reason itself, mean to subordinate whatever or, by the same token, whomever it is that 'stands' in their way. Having performed the roles of husband and progenitor on the small and large stage with Gretchen and Helen, Faust now turns from all mimetic and allegorical theatre of action to an inimitable scene and its creation, a project, rather than play, of inhuman scope: the reworking of the physical contours and qualities of the given world itself. The dream of experiencing nature as if part of nature's own flowing, motive force ('to flow through nature's veins' ['durch die Adern der Natur zu fliessen'] [*F*, 619]), of being one with the very energy of infinite change ('only restless activity truly occupies man' ['Nur rastlos betätigt sich der Mann'] [*F*, 1759]), is replaced by the opposing dream of imposing permanent change through external means, of transforming nature's fluidity into enclosed liquid masses, and ebbing, visible surfaces into durable solids.

Faust's final act on earth is just that: the founding of a new ground, or ungrounded foundation, upon the earth itself. His 'land-reclamation' project does not truly aim to reclaim, nor even to replace or resituate. It would instead establish, out of natural repetitive movement and displacement, their opposite: *a place which is an origin, an origin which is a place*.³

Thus Faust's original desire, for the immediate, contingent experience of sensuous reality, becomes the will to construct the independent basis for all such experience, an origin anterior to the origin of desire, an absolutely necessary or noncontingent place.⁴ Faust attempts to achieve on and by means of the earth what Plato's interlocutors, unable to define justice in terms of individual experience and perception, are led by his Socrates to view on the nonanalogous model of the state. Socrates' disingenuous comparison of the individual and the organized city as equivalent embodiments of justice distinct merely in scale (or, to recall Socrates' graphic metaphor, as a single text written in 'small' and 'large letters') replaces the irresolvable problem of *knowing* just human practice with an organized *fiction* precluding epistemological quandaries: a purely theoretical 'polis' whose machine-like workings exclude, precisely, the human element, the ability 'to imitate all things' ('mimeisthai panta chremata') personified by but not limited to the poets explicitly banished in *Republic*, Bk. III.⁵ Just as Socrates' new city, according to Socrates' prescriptive theory, will remain free from contingency as long as its constituent elements maintain their prescribed relations, neither transgressing nor exchanging their particular formal functions ('erga'), so Faust's constitution, from newly configured elements, of an original or fully independent, concrete place doubles as the project for a 'polis' ontologically prior to the need for speculative political theory. Faust's 'plans' give rise to a basis for human activity that, from the outset, need never reflect on acting justly, for this is a basis or ground as independent of natural change as it is of human history. It is thus, in the most forceful (and antisocial) sense of those terms, a new or 'free ground' for 'a free people to stand on' ('Auf freiem Grund mit freiem Volke stehn') (*F*,11580), a people literally, empirically set apart from the consequential, if often ontologically ungrounded events historical life entails: a people as free of those chains of historical steps and missteps as it is dependent, in its own existence, on the construction of a previously nonexistent ground.

Like Plato's philosopher-king compelled from a cave of illusory shadow-play to stand in and see the light of the sun, Faust conceives of a place made by force from which the Good may finally be perceived, for, of all the forms of 'the intelligible world'—so Plato's Socrates—'the Good is the last to be seen'.⁶ But whereas Socrates makes clear he considers practice inferior to theory as a means of grasping the true reality of intelligible forms, and that his conception of the well-functioning city may instruct us about justice exactly because it is a theoretical conception, 'formulated in words' rather than 'realize[d] ... in practice', Faust demands the complete and immediate identity of thought and action, theory and practice.⁷ If, for Plato's Socrates, the true measure of 'things ... described in theory' is never and can never be whether they 'exist precisely in practice', for Goethe's Faust *there is and can be no theory*, properly speaking: there is and can only be realization, *and that realization must itself be material*.⁸ That is to say, it must be built: structural rather than individual, hard rather than human, a thing of substance rather than either mimesis or speculation. Faust's 'newest world' ('neusten Erde') (*F*, 11568), like Plato's theoretical state, establishes an origin in architectonic form, the one extracted from physical matter, the other 'formulated in words'. Yet for Faust to see his construction project realized, actually to see the origin of what was not before—a new time embodied in the founding of a new earth—his architectonic design must be put into practice, must be made earthly architecture, *now*: construction must reflect conception as if its own simultaneous mirror image. For in the passage of time between the design and realization, the thinking and building, of a thing, the architectonic moment of its origin is lost, or, rather, loses its identity: once reflected upon that conceptual moment is doubled, reenacted, repeated differently in time. This elision of the new into the old, of an architectonic vision into the painstaking making of architected matter, is precisely what Faust strives to avoid. Speed and immediacy are the inherently violent requirements for the forced subordination of architecture to architectonics:

> What I have thought, I rush to realize;
> Only the word of the master has weight.
> Up from your camps, you slaves! Man for man!
> Let that which I boldly conceived be seen!
> Grab the tools! Stir shovel and spade!
> What has been staked out must immediately come to pass.
> On strict orders, rash industry
> Wins the loveliest prize;
> For the greatest work to be realized
> A thousand hands need but one mind.
>
> (Was ich gedacht ich eil es zu vollbringen;
> Des Herren Wort es gibt allein Gewicht.
> Von Lager auf ihr Knechte! Mann für Mann!
> Lasst glücklich schauen was ich kühn ersann.
> Ergreift das Werkzeug, Schaufel rührt und Spaten,
> Das Abgesteckte muss sogleich geraten.
> Auf strenges Ordnen, raschen Fleiss,
> Erfolgt der allerschönste Preis;
> Dass sich das grösste Werk vollende
> Genügt Ein Geist für tausend Hände.)

(*F*, 11500–10)

Having 'conceived' of a 'work' whose design is itself a conception of matter, a work producing not a particular building but a general ground or foundation for building, Faust's is the ruling 'mind' for which 'a thousand hands' labor in sync, and these synecdochal movers of matter are not only mindless, and faceless, but bodiless. Enslaved to the 'shovel and spade' they animate, the final conduits of an internal physical power they supply, these 'hands' are nothing in themselves but bunches of expendable digits, rudimentary means, akin to their arithmetic namesakes, for performing another's will. Faust's conception of the 'ground' for 'a free people' yields a violently instrumentalist ('Ergreift das Werkzeug'), thoroughly dehumanizing practice because this 'master'-builder acts at once as Socrates and Socrates' hypothesized philosopher-king. His own is the 'mind' which envisions a new earth *and* oversees its realization.[9]

Such an identification of theory with practice, idealized in theory, proves worse than murderous in practice. For, in striving to supplant the temporal difference between the two—'Let that which I boldly *conceived* be *seen*'—Faust's attempt to render theory 'immediately' material must exploit an assembled labor force in a manner unbefitting animals. Extracting energy at all hours and in absolute disregard for the life of its individual repositories, Faust neither intends nor, what is worse, conceives the change that the prosecution of his project imposes upon the corporal economy of the exploitation of labor. For the immediacy of result required by Faust's labor project excludes from its execution even the minimal rational requirement of maintaining the life of the enslaved, favoring in the stead of the rational, a pure consumption of labor, one that effectively supplants labor (the real product alienated from a subject and converted into exchange value by an economy geared instead toward capital accumulation) with the fundamentally antieconomic principle of pure work (lacking a subject of alienation and medium of accumulation whatsoever), which is to say, work which equates to absolute corporal expenditure, work unto death. Individuals die but not so the force of work, which, as the pure, abstract form of labor, provides Faust with an operational concept free from human referents, a self-defining idea as noncontingent as the concrete place Faust would have such force make.[10]

A theory that conceives of itself as a praxis requires pure, universally applicable force, not limited, cognitive particulars, and in order to perform its identity with praxis it proceeds *per force*, with haste. The product it yields must appear unprecedented even by conception if that product, while thoroughly artificial, is nonetheless to be viewed as entirely self-identical: as a replacement of preexisting natural relations that seems instead to predate *rather than* replace these. The ordered removal and consequent, if unplanned, murder of Philemon and Baucis—Faust to Mephistopheles: 'So go and get rid of them [literally: 'put them aside']!' ('So geht und schafft sie mir zur Seite!') (*F*, 11275)—recalls and revises, now as wholly innocent of sensory entrapment and seduction, the deathly consequences of Gretchen's plight in *Faust I*: the condemnation of provincial individuals in the context of a building project is specifically *not* the by-product of corporeal desire satisfied and spent. It is rather violence committed with a view to aesthetic absolutism, Faust's stated desire to 'see' and 'oversee' 'all [he] has done' from a single, dominating perspective, that is, 'in one view'— 'To oversee with one glance/the masterpiece of the human spirit' ('Zu sehn was alles ich getan,/Zu überschauen mit einem Blick/Des Menschengeistes Meisterstück') (*F*, 11246–8), that motivates the destruction of the aged couple.[11] As discussed later in this study, the introduction and 'setting aside' of the importunely located 'Philemon' and 'Baucis' present a perfectly complementary inversion of Goethe's historically precedent use of these conventional pastoral names: 'Philemon, with his Baucis' first appear in *Die Wahlverwandtschaften* (*Elective Affinities*), Chapter One of Part Two, as the narrator describes the pleasant, purely visual effect of Charlotte's removal of all evidence of the location of the dead from the community graveyard.[12]

In direct contrast to their mention in Goethe's novel, in *Faust II* the classically derived Philemon and Baucis represent not complaisant spectators of, but temporal obstacles to, the completion of a fully self-present or exclusively aesthetic 'masterwork'. Like their common history and residence in a 'space' defined only by the presence of 'linden trees' ('Lindenraum'), embodiments of nature that, while, similarly classical in origin, are also equally visually obstructive— 'My high estate, it is not pure/The linden-space with the brown built thing/and decaying little church is not mine' ('Der Lindenraum, die braune Baute,/Das morsche Kirchlein ist nicht mein') (*F*,11157–8)—the shared death of Philemon and Baucis, and grisly report of their incineration alongside linden trees set aflame, confirm the cost exacted upon both historical nature and humanity by the perfection and completion of a predetermined masterplan, the founding of a 'new' context that is also, and *at the same time*, the extracting of a 'free ground' from which that context can be 'viewed' *in its totality*, as if ground and ocular field could ever be rendered entirely coextensive, with or without the removal of any one and any place that interrupted, and so called into question, their visual identity.[13]

Just as it must violently remove the discretely visible from its constructed 'new earth' and visual field, so it is that in Faust's conflation of them, theory-in-practice must in effect replace 're-place-ment', using the mode of substitution to erase its traces by imposing upon preexisting relations a singular place, effacing from the act of replacement all persistent marks of diachrony as if sundering prefix ('re-') and suffix ('-ment') from the word that contains them. Space must be placed where these marks had been before, but in order for such space, and the new 'place' it delimits, to present no grounds for comparisons with places past, this replacement of one locus by another must also effect a necessary temporal contortion.[14] In suppressing the distinction, made only in the mind, between what was before and what came after, the act of replacement must appear to take place even *before* memory can be fully formed, that is, before the mind can recall the difference between 'before' and 'after' to the eye. Forcing disembodied 'hands' to alter the earth over night—'Pick and shovel, blow upon blow . . . There a dam on the next day stood' ('Hack und Schaufel, Schlag um Schlag . . . Stand ein Damm den andern Tag') (*F*, 11124–6); 'The night rang with the cry of pain . . . In the morning it was a canal' ('Nachts erscholl des Jammers Qual . . . Morgens war es ein Kanal') (*F*, 11128–30)—Faust aims to have produced a work which was never a work-in-progress. Completed under cloak of darkness, the rapid work of 'pick and shovel' precludes the work of memory, making the resultant structure appear, like Socrates' Good, a fact as self-evident as the light of day by which it is seen. A noteworthy exception to the common critical idealization of Faust is offered by Kaiser (1994), who, underscoring both the totalizing, antihistorical impulse of Faust's 'idyllic' building project and the profoundly 'unsocial' absolutism required for its realization, calls attention to the dehumanization of labor it requires: 'The newest earth is determined by Faust to be an idyll *in toto* . . . The totalized idyll is everything in everything, and it is a posthistorical state like eschatological fulfillment . . . For the sake of an imaginary free humanity [Faust] reduces human beings here and now into human material' (60–1).

If the contrasting brutality of Faust's building project is the condition of its rapid, non-Socratic realization of theory in practice, the specific form in which that project makes its intellectual origin 'immediately' material is, no less than that of the theoretical Platonic 'polis', architectonic.

Still, Socrates' replacement of the definition of individual human justice by a general fiction of mechanical 'justesse', a theoretical state of individuals reduced to single interlocking, inexchangeable functions, appears a mere verbal sleight-of-hand compared to Faust's violent isolation and impressing of 'hands' into hard labor, for which, appropriately enough, there appears no classical precedent.[15] Indeed, compared to Faust's characteristically modern project of founding 'a free people' on the invisible backs of enslaved laborers, even the imperial design of the ancient gods, forcing a mourning prince to found Latinium, seems mild. The usurpation and pitiless slaying of noble Turnus, with whose bitter, dying glance the *Aeneid* abruptly concludes, can be interpreted as a pure consequence of force or fate depending on one's view of the 'character' of his killer, the political or literary intentions of his decidedly post-Homeric author or the late myth of the divine origin of Roman empire represented—at best ambivalently—in Virgil's poem. By contrast, Faust's ambition to *construct* a new ground is as antimythological as it is impersonal: from the outset it both is and is not his own. The wish to usurp the empire of nature itself has made the question of human *or* divine rule irrelevant for Faust (much as the blood sport of her own usurpation, the war of human empires, did for Helen). Architectural, rather than sexual or imperial, from the ground up—a 'ground' which, in addition, it itself creates—this is an ambition for origin founded in the eradication of all natural and human conditions. Unlike Faust's early erotic drives, or any corporal impulse—actual, remembered or imagined—this desire to build an original place renders the subject or subjects in whom it originates entirely immaterial. The ultimate aim of Faust's ambition is not to be one with the 'body' of nature—indeed not to be, let alone unite with, any sensuous object at all—but *to extract force from that objective body, transfer and store it*.

Already referring to his own 'earthly days' ('Erdetagen') as a 'trace' ('Spur') (*F*, 11583–4), Faust yearns not for more life but to relieve life of its sensory immediacy, to transpose animacy itself into a kind of holding pattern or script. While revealing, through the violence of its installation, a ground previously unexposed, the appearance of a delimited place where fluidity had naturally reigned, such a system of containment and translation destroys life as we know it, disassociating life from the living rather than ensuring the continuity of any being or beings, individual biology, growing empire or group myth. Engendered mechanically, which is to say, concretely *and* abstractly, with force forcefully separated from its particular incorporation in order to be made available for universal application, this is a housing of energy as such in which Faust will not reside; indeed, its very construction anticipates his demise.

Faust's and Heidegger's Technology: Building as 'Poiesis'

The impersonality of Faust's final goal is most adequately described not by Mephistopheles, whose representation of Faust's discontent only extends to the latter's sensuous desires ('No pleasure sates him, no happiness is enough' ['Ihn sättigt keine Lust, ihm gnügt kein Glück'] [*F*, 11587]), but by the later observations of a philosopher who does not appear to have had *Faust*, among Goethe's works, in mind. In his unsurpassed analysis of the 'challenge' to nature and people posed by 'modern technology' ('Technik'), the replacement of natural historical relations with new 'built-in' norms, Heidegger reveals the aim and lure of Faust's building project at its core. Technology, the material interruption and transformation of organic, or self-regulating, physical processes, permits the energy naturally expended by those processes to be extracted, contained, channeled, stored. Heidegger states and responds to the question posed by technology as follows:

> What is modern technology? It too is a revealing ... The revealing that
> rules in modern technology is a challenging, which puts to nature the
> unreasonable demand that it supply energy which can be extracted and
> stored as such. But does this not hold true for the old windmill as well?
> No. Its sails do indeed turn in the wind; they are left entirely to the wind's
> blowing. But the windmill does not unlock energy from the air currents
> in order to store it ...
> The hydroelectric plant is set into the current of the Rhine. It sets the Rhine
> to supplying its hydraulic pressure, which then sets the turbines turning.
> This turning sets those machines in motion whose thrust sets going the electric
> current for which the long-distance power station and its network of cables are
> set up to dispatch electricity. In the context of the interlocking processes
> pertaining to the orderly disposition of electrical energy, even the electric
> plant is not built into the Rhine River as was the old wooden bridge that joined
> bank with bank for hundreds of years. Rather, the river is dammed up into the
> power plant. What the river is now, namely, a water-power supplier, derives
> from the essence of the power station ...
> The revealing that rules throughout modern technology has the character
> of a setting-upon, in the sense of a challenging-forth. Such challenging
> happens in that the energy concealed in nature is unlocked, what is
> unlocked is transformed, what is transformed is stored up, what is
> stored up is, in turn, distributed, and what is distributed is switched about
> ever anew. Unlocking, transforming, storing, distributing, and switching
> about are ways of revealing ...
> Who accomplishes the challenging setting-upon through which what we
> call the real is revealed as standing-reserve? Obviously man. To what
> extent is man capable of such a revealing? Man can, indeed, conceive,
> form, and carry through this or that in one way or another. But over the
> event of unconcealment, in which at any given time the real shows itself
> or withdraws, man has no control.[16]

(Was ist die moderne Technik? Auch sie ist ein Entbergen ...
Das in der modernen Technik waltende Entbergen ist ein Herausfordern,
das an die Natur das Ansinnen stellt, Energie zu liefern, die *als solche*
herausgefördert und gespeichert werden kann. Gilt dies aber nicht auch
von der alten Windmühle? Nein. Ihre Flügel drehen sich zwar im Winde,
seinem Wehen bleiben sie unmittelbar anheimgegeben. Die Windmühle
erschliesst aber nicht Energien der Luftströmung, um sie zu speichern ...
Das Wasserkraftwerk ist in den Rheinstrom gestellt. Es stellt ihn auf
seinen Wasserdruck, der die Turbinen daraufhin stellt, sich zu drehen,
welche Drehung diejenige Maschine umtreibt, deren Getriebe den elektrischen
Strom herstellt, für den die Überlandzentrale und ihr Stromnetz zur
Strombeförderung bestellt sind. Im Bereich dieser ineinandergreifenden Folgen
der Bestellung elektrischer Energie erscheint auch der Rheinstrom als etwas
Betselltes. Das Wasserkraftwerk ist nicht in den Rheinstrom gebaut wie die alte
Holzbrücke, die seit Jahrhunderten Ufer mit Ufer verbindet. Vielmehr ist der
Strom in das Kraftwerk verbaut. Er ist, was er jetzt als Strom ist, nämlich
Wasserdrucklieferant, aus dem Wesen des Kraftwerks ...
Das Entbergen, das die moderne Technik durchherrscht, hat den Charakter
des Stellens im Sinne der Herausforderung. Diese geschieht dadurch, dass

die in der Natur verborgene Energie aufgeschlossen, das Erchlossene umgeformt, das Umgeformte gespeichert, das Gespeicherte wieder verteilt und das Verteilte erneut umgeschaltet wird. Erschliessen, umformen, speichern, verteilen, umschalten sind Weisen des Entbergens . . .
Wer vollzieht das herausfordernde Stellen, wodurch das, was man das Wirkliche nennt, als Bestand entborgen wird? Offenbar der Mensch. Inwiefern vermag er solches Entbergen? Der Mensch kann zwar dieses oder jenes so oder so vorstellen, gestalten und betreiben. Allein, über die Unverborgenheit, worin sich jeweils das Wirkliche zeigt oder entzieht, verfügt der Mensch nicht.)[17]

What does it mean to remove energy from its material source, transform it into a new medium that can be channeled at will, hold it 'ab situ' and implement it in the execution of action with which it would otherwise have nothing to do? Technology, the artificial decontextualization and transfer of power, effects a break with biological time and place: housed in a form not its own, power can remain, for any period of time, impotent or ineffectual, inactive, or practically 'dead'. At the moments it is purposefully 'unlocked' or 'tapped' ('erschliessen'), released from containment in a delimited, directed fashion, its effectiveness can be redoubled, having been shaped by and brought to bear upon alien or extrinsic contexts. Thus our relationship to technology is obviously not that of individual subject to object, or even grammatical subject to predicate, discrete identities brought into temporary relationship by an action or verbal complement. Heidegger names that which is not a subject or something in itself, or is no longer, the 'standing-reserve' ('Bestand'), an assembled stock of means or elements kept accessible for eventual implementation. Like those 'challenged' to bring it forth, and whom it challenges in turn, the standing-reserve neither lives nor perishes on its own. It is the holding pattern whose concrete abstraction from the immediacy of living reveals 'the real' of Being even as it destroys beings, the being of the Rhine as we know it or that of human beings subjected to the power their built technologies release and store.

'*What the river is now, namely, a water-power supplier*': the renaming and redefining of something as a not-thing, a mechanism that stands in waiting, its interlocking, interactive parts available for implementation, is no mere polemical metaphor on Heidegger's part. In substituting an emphatically artificial compound word ('Wasserdrucklieferant') for the natural fluidity of the being of the river, Heidegger brings to mind the larger mechanism this built network of operations, in effect, mimics, the mechanism that supplies the power to connect all objects and actions, with or without propinquity, to distinguish and distribute all attributes as well as command our attention to them. Lacking all natural foundation, *that mechanism is language*, the not-thing that 'is' nothing other than the exercise of its forms and functions. Heidegger's concrete description of power artificially abstracted from given relations and conditions, transformed, housed and directed not only with measurable efficacy but to inestimable, supplemental effect, is as illustrative a parable of the development of language as any characterizing those intellectual acts of modernization which, before the isolation and distribution of electrical power, were collectively named the 'Enlightenment'.[18] Recalling such materialist theorists of language and the machine as Condillac, Diderot and La Mettrie, Heidegger's analysis of technology startles in its own enactment of 'interlocking' concreteness and abstraction: the physical being of the river Rhein, given as such, is also given over to the 'essence' of the water power plant into which it is 'built' ('verbaut'), and of which it thus appears not the occasion but the effect. Indeed, the essence of that 'essence' seems to be metalepsis, the poetic reversal of cause and effect, by which what the Rhein 'is'—a natural source and place of power—'now' 'derives' instead from its functional translation, just as the power of technology owes less to the river than to its own irreversible poetic process, that of exchanging organic nature for its organization and, in so doing, changing self-governing matter into material text and context.

The notion of essential translation pertains as much to the mechanization of 'physis', the natural repositories of energy in the world, as to the conduits and collecting stations, or grammar and words, which compose the mechanics of discourse and whose essence translates 'psyche', that uniquely human energy, into the world, forming and so transforming it, encoding and storing it, for present and future appropriation. It is not difficult, but rather difficult *not* to read in Heidegger's 'standing-reserve' the status and structure of language itself, of language that 'is' what language does, the modality that not only changes the force of meaning it transfers, giving it shape, value, sense and name, but also alters both ends of its own trajectory, the given context it leaves as well as that it makes. This is language not as 'river', a unidirectional flow, spontaneous expression or act, but language as 'water-power-supplier', as articulation and 'metapherein': the activity of identifying, containing and relocating the power of meaning in a script, by means of which that power reemerges at once decontextualized and recontextualized, with or without either a proximate or referential basis. Unforeseeable in its destination and effects, such a distribution of power, while independent of nature, may carry with it at any time some or all of an acquired semantic sediment. Thus it is that the ungrounded technology of language, of storing and releasing energy by way of mechanisms that are always standing by, 'on hand', defines, as it defies, the ratiocination of its 'users' rather than the reverse.

While Heidegger is no more apologetic than Philemon and Baucis for his own enduring attachment to the earth, his questioning of technology removes the latter irrevocably from the realm of practiced, physical interaction with nature eulogized in this essay and others, that which, adhering to the ritual use of 'handtools' ('Werkzeuge'), links the body of nature and the human body across and through their difference, mutual resistance and submission.[19] Yet, it is in technology that Heidegger also recognizes the 'physis' of that formative power that is and has always been at work in the world, the power to transform and reveal 'also' named, he states, 'poiesis', indicating, thereby, not only the congruence of technology and language, but the incongruous or exceptional identity of 'poetry-making' torn between 'techne' and 'physis', 'water-power supplier' ('Wasserdrucklieferant') and 'handtool' ('Werkzeug').[20]

It is in this context that the essay most closely related to, and sharply differing from 'The question concerning technology', Heidegger's 'Der Ursprung des Kunstwerkes' ('The origin of the work of art') (written 1935–6), must be read. Evoked in a series of descriptions of precisely such practiced handwork as technology is here said to replace, works of art constitute 'poiesis' in that earlier essay not as original, dislocating 'techne' but rather as the lived-in, historical locus of Being, 'wohnen' ('residing'). Between them the two essays effectively split Heidegger's conception of 'poiesis' into a poetry of earth and a poetry of language, an architecture for dwelling and the uninhabitable architectonics of the moving and storing machine. This is not to say that Heidegger's conception of 'poiesis' is either too capacious or self-negating, but rather that the work of art resembles 'poiesis' as residing while technology resembles 'poiesis' as power plant, as radically *non*residential building.[21] Thus part of what Heidegger's unearthing of 'poiesis' as mode of revealing or bringing-forth reveals is that 'poiesis' itself is not itself but rather Janus-like in its manifestations, place of Being or no-place, lined handtool bearing traces of the work of historical bodies on earth or temporary storage facility for a power extracted from the earth and necessarily isolated from bodies it can kill, a power put on indefinite hold rather than ever held and implemented by hand.

It is exactly these two faces of Heidegger's 'poiesis'—being of, and not of, the earth and laboring hand—that are conjoined to awful effect in the carrying out of Faust's materialist architectonic plan. For the 'hands' Faust commands work not like hands but like power-suppliers, mechanisms for a transfer of energy occurring at the cost of the bodies from which it derives. Here the 'hands' working to remove and replace the earth to which they are enslaved are themselves 'Werkzeuge', but these are 'handtools' implemented in the mode of nonmanual technology, with all the violence—to body and to earth—that conflating these two mutually unidentifiable ways of 'poiesis' entails.

Extraction, transformation, storage, distribution, exchange or switching—modes of managing the energy concealed in and composing the relations of nature—belong, for Heidegger, to the realm of 'bringing-forth' that may indeed be named for the essence or metalepsis of language, 'metapherein' (generally, 'to move, to transfer'); for language, not as nominal substitution for a nonlinguistic realm, but rather, as mode of appropriating, articulating and revealing that realm by directing, as it defines, the power of understanding. Unruly at first, imposing and winning by design, metaphor is language, the 'natural' flow of grammar and syntax, as technology is 'bios', the naturally flowing Rhein, under new management.

Just as Faust's rejection of the 'old' forms of language for the immediacy of sensuous life turns inevitably into a rejection of the 'old' earth upon which sensuous experience transpires, so Faust's architectonic reconstitution of the earth, *not with but as technology*[22]—as power-supplier that, like language, breaks 'new' ground by breaking the natural chain of cause and effect—must destroy the life that constitutes the earth in order to channel it. Replacing the earth with a 'new earth', the old encumbered ground with a 'free ground', Faust builds not earth but the freedom from earth that is technology. Technology, a nonbeing, 'is' the new basis for freedom, and sole basis for defining the 'new', because its functioning constitutes its own ground precisely by freeing itself from earthly constraints. Rather than a body or an idea, technology dazzlingly embodies the break with bodies and ideas, the caesura that allows these to be stored and transferred at will. Indifferent to any difference between discursivity and sensuousness—and, within these, to historicity and individuality, their strangeness *and* familiarity—technology is defined by a rapidity outstripping the labor of both hand and eye, of tactile contact and cognitive communication alike. In this it will indeed always be 'new', and in this, too, it proves ultimately unmanageable for Faust. For, rather than as earth definitively refashioned into technology, the basis for freedom from all sensuous temporality, Faust views his 'new earth' as the grounds upon which he would have a future 'moment' ('Augenblicke') (*F*, 11581) remain. Already envisioning the prospect of the incomparably 'beautiful' life it will enable—that which, precisely as technology, it holds in store—Faust reiterates in the present the phrase that spells loss of his wager: 'Linger yet a while, you are so beautiful' ('Verweile doch, Du bist so schön!') (*F*, 11582). In seeing the future and addressing it—in speaking not only of, but to his vision—Faust gives shape to the earthly difference between past and future, becomes himself the body of historical being he has sworn to eradicate, and that language, alone among technologies, maintains.

Notes

1   See Berman (1988: 60–86). Citations from *Faust I* and *Faust II* throughout this chapter are from Goethe (1982). Unless otherwise indicated, all translations from the German throughout this study are my own.

   In an essay devoted to the final scene of *Faust II*, and which itself opens, as if by way of analogy, with a discussion of textual study after Auschwitz, Adorno argues that the piecemeal quality of composition in *Faust II* derives from its necessary 'forgetting' of Part I. While Adorno ultimately refers to Faust's intended founding of a 'new ground' for mankind and destruction of Philemon and Baucis, he does not note the contradiction between Faust's exhaustive desire to redesign in its totality the world he sees and the purported saving grace of the pointedly underschematized dramatic structure of Part II. Identifying Faust with Goethe on his deathbed and, perhaps, with Europe on its own, Adorno instead argues that Faust is saved because, by mere 'force of living on', and 'forgetting', he has changed: 'Is not Faust saved because he is no longer at all he who signed the pact; does not the wisdom of the play in pieces lie in how little man is identical with himself . . .? The force of life, as a living on, is equated with forgetting' ('Wird nicht Faust darum gerettet, weil er überhaupt nicht mehr der ist, der den Pakt unterschrieb; hat nicht das Stück in Stücken seine Weisheit daran, wie wenig mit sich selbst identisch der Mensch ist . . .? Die Kraft des Lebens, als eine zum Weiterleben, wird dem Vergessen gleichgesetzt') (Adorno 1967: 366).

   In *Goethe's Faust* (2003), Brandes endorses what he characterizes as Adorno's view of forgetting as 'power of transformation', and traces such a concept of forgetting taking place 'beyond the economy of guilt' from Nietzsche through Kommerell, Adorno and Derrida: 'Faust has become another not through his becoming as striving but through his forgetting, whereby his forgetting is hardly to be designated his own, but is rather the gift, the gift of forgetting' (200–4). Although Brandes recognizes that Derrida's conception of 'radical forgetting' includes its own contradiction of oblivion in the trace, and uses Derrida's notion of trace to discuss the anticipatory articulation of the 'Augenblicke' that precipitates Faust's death, he maintains an uneasy identity of forgetting with 'future-oriented' remembering: 'The forgetting of forgetting is itself a remembering of the possibility of this form of forgetting' (203–4).

2   'Let us crash into the rush of time,/Into the rolling round of givenness' ('Stürzen wir uns in das Rauschen der Zeit,/In's Rollen der Begebenheit!') (*F*, 1754–5). As discussed below, the consciousness of time underpinning Faust's desire in *Faust I*—his view that, by hurling himself into the natural course of things, he will in effect embrace time per se, thus eluding all experience of specific temporal change—is no less determinative of the architectonic project, proceeding from a directly opposite approach to 'givenness', that he oversees in *Faust II*.

   One of the best studies of *Faust* to date, Brown (1986), provides a welcome, in-depth analysis of its 'nonmimetic' structure and content (21, 35, 149, 208ff, passim). Considering 'the fundamental concerns of the play to be epistemological and aesthetic' (26), rather than the illustration of one man's (failed) moral education, Brown indirectly suggests an inherent conflict between artificial forms of knowledge and Goethe's recognition of the unartful movement of time: 'While it may seem obvious that to live in the world and to live in time are identical, it was not obvious to Faust in "Night," when as a human subject to time he sought to transcend the world' (81). Such 'transcend[ence]' can only be effected instead in a complete identification with 'temporal flux' that, as Brown rightly points out, must lead *in literary terms* to naturally ungrounded artificiality. This study argues that it is the architectural project of constructing a ground independent of nature and history that in fact ends Faust's immersion in the temporal. On the allegorical mode of *Faust II*, cf. Schlaffer (1981).

Lange (1980) interprets the openly 'symbolic' and 'citational character' of *Faust II* as 'exceeding all figural and scenic representation'; more than a drama, he states, *Faust II* is 'a poem precisely about language, about the possibilities of communicative speech within an encompassing, realized system of rhetorical and poetological means of representation and expression' (281–312 [287, 293–4]). See also the fine essay by Muenzer (1994: 187–206), in which the 'abruptly changing stage' of the play, like the figure of Helena herself, 'dragged across time and space as *Übertragung* into Faust's palace', is shown to enact Goethe's 'essentially *historical aesthetic*' in Part II (188, 200). Although Muenzer does not discuss the building project of Act V, his observation that 'Goethe has layered the *Faust*-stage temporally' provides an especially fitting description of the layers of temporal nonidentity—of theory and practice, conception and vision—that Faust would violently collapse in the construction of a 'newest earth' 'free' from all previous stagings of time.

3   Benjamin (1972–89, 2: 739) describes Faust's 'reclaiming of land from the sea' as 'an activity which nature prescribes to history and in which nature is itself inscribed—that was Goethe's conception of historical action'. While it is certainly true that Goethe identified history and natural history as a single active and cognitive domain, it is not at all true that we may identify Goethe with Faust, or that nature 'prescribes to history' its own undoing in Faust's land-reclamation project. On the contrary, it is precisely its equal opposition to nature and history that defines Faust's project and, with it, both the peripeteia and dénouement of his drama. For his building of an origin without precedent, a place free from both natural and historical 'prescription', results ultimately in the expressed wish that this origin linger and so constitute its own natural history, a joining of beauty to duration defining not Faust's design but, quite the contrary, his bet.

4   By contrast, Blackhall (1984: 5), even while emphasizing that Faust's final 'concern is . . . with the earth and man's place upon it', describes 'the project of reclaiming land from the sea' as psychologically motivated, 'satisf[ying] [Faust's] desire for power, control and dominion'. Similarly, while noting the explicitly external, 'topographical' language of Faust's final speech, Blackhall interprets that language as 'symbolic' of an 'internal', all too human struggle: 'Faust's vision is topographical, but it can also be interpreted symbolically, with the phrase "im Innern hier" referring not just to the polderlands but to the mind of man' (7). Blackhall had already characterized the external aspect of Faust's project positively even with regard to the people and earth it supplants; Faust's 'vision', he writes, 'involves not just personal dominion but heritage to others, and not just colonization but preservation against the eroding forces—of nature!' (6).

5   Plato (1930, 1982), *Republic*, II 368d–369b3; III 398a. The famous critique of the mimetic arts and resultant argument for censoring or banishing poets from a hypothetical, purely functionalist state, occupies the first half of Bk. III (386–398c), and informs, often in pointedly nonhypothetical terms, the ongoing tradition of 'platonic' literary and art criticism in the West, a tradition itself tending to bifurcate along often incompatible 'aesthetic' and 'moral' lines. I have previously discussed (1999: 19–34) Socrates' originary detour from defining 'the justice of one man' ('dikaiosyne . . . esti men andros enos') to that of 'an entire city' ('esti de pou kai oles poleos') as coordinated state.

6   Plato, *Republic*, VII 517b8–c1 ('en to gnosto teleutaia e tou agathou idea kai mogis orasthai').

7   Plato, *Republic*, V 473a1–b3 ('e physin egei praxin legeos etton aletheias ephaptesthai').
8   Plato, *Republic*, V 473a5–6 ('to logo dielthomen, toiauta pantapasi kai to ergo dien gignomena apophainein').
9   Comparing the ending of *Faust II* with Balzac's contemporaneous *Peau de chagrin*, Lukács (1967: 128) employs metaphors of flooded land to contrast Balzac's 'modern' creation of 'a new epic form' out of the 'ripping apart of the dams of the old forms by the storm flood' of capitalism, with Goethe's 'regulation of the water current through old, newly imaged forms'. Without noting that Faust's enforced labor project aims exactly at the actual, physical creation of 'new ground' from floodland, Lukács gives voice to the modernity of Faust's, if not his author's, project: 'Balzac seeks to ground the inner powerlines of this spilling over [of the old forms], in order to allow a new epic form to arise out of their recognition; Goethe undertakes a regulation of the current through old, newly imaged forms'.
10 Neither epistemological nor aesthetic in function, Faust's final act of building 'new earth' is, I think, mischaracterized by Brown as a coequal part of the tradition of artificial creativity she so ably discusses throughout her study: 'In Act III, Faust created Arcadia "in play"; we recognized this as an artistic act. Now [Faust] creates his Arcadia in the world. To the extent that both temporarily impose a vision on the raw stuff of nature, they are the same' (1986: 239–40). Similar to Brown, Flax concludes that '[t]he culmination of Faust's long education in Mephistopheles's school of art is that he finally transforms himself into an artist, a creator, a conjurer' (1987: 46), and van der Laan views 'the act of technically taming nature' as the culmination of Faust's 'quest for meaning' (2007: 105, 98). Mieth, by contrast, commends Goethe's refusal 'to sublate historical development and dialectic in a utopia', whether of 'creative' or theoretical origin (1980: 90–102 [102]).
11 Hamm (1982: 70–91) observes that no practical 'necessity' but rather aesthetic demands determine Faust's elimination of Philemon and Baucis, adding: 'In that he offers no compelling economic reason for the extermination of this world, Goethe did not intend us to see it as unpreventable' (90–1). Hamm here takes aim at Metscher's thesis (1976: 28–155) that the play heralds the historical and social development of the worker class, an argument strangely identifying a society free of class struggle with Goethe's representation of slave labor. Vaget (1994: 43–55 [53–4]) presents a definitive critique of the use of Saint-Simonian notions of human 'perfectibility' and the 'social and political engineering' which they sanction to justify Faust's actions:

> To an unbiased mind, there is no way to morally justify the expropriation of their property and the death of Philemon and Baucis … Faust's inspired vision [of a free people]—the C-Major fanfare trumpeted by all Marxist readings of *Faust*—is about as trustworthy as the vow of sobriety of a derelict alcoholic … Faust's last speech … marks no conversion in a moral or political sense; it still bears the imprint of an authoritarian, power-hungry mind.

12 See Goethe (1982, 6: 361). For Goethe's explanation to Eckermann of his use of these 'ancient' names, borrowed from Ovid, in *Faust II*—his serene disavowal that their appearance in the play was related in any way to their opposing fate in *Metamorphoses* Bk. 8, in which the gods instead reward Philemon and Baucis for their hospitality with a magnificent palace raised safely on an island above floodwaters—and for an analysis of the relation between their removal in the play and the earlier 'setting aside' of gravestones in the *Wahlverwandtschaften*, see my *In the Place of Language: Goethe and the Architecture of the Referent* (forthcoming from Fordham University Press).
13 It may well be the recognizable, historical humanity of 'that old pair' ('Die jenes alte Paar') (*F*, 11347), 'these good old folk' ('die guten alten Leute') (*F*, 11316), evoked even by the eventual agent of their destruction, that has made Philemon, Baucis and their demise a preferred critical measure of the inevitability of Faust's own rise and fall, just as the radical depersonalization effected by Faust's enslavement of a 'thousand hands'

similarly extends to the many critics who, neglecting to reflect upon this faceless crew, lament the death of Philemon and Baucis with remarkable consistency. Among the most prominent of these are Lukács (1967: 178), Trunz (in Goethe 1982, 3: 479) and Adorno (1967: 336–7); preceding them, Stöcklein (1949: 88); and, more recently, Berman (1988: see below). Böhme oddly interprets the report of Faust's 'slaves' called up from their 'camp' ('Vom Lager auf ihr Knechte!') (*F*, 11503) as 'a magical technological process' and 'allegorical representation' (2005: 159–60).

Perhaps the clearest statement of Faust's rationale for the removal of the couple is offered by Gearey (1992: 168): 'The removal of the old couple does not mean for Faust an extension of the land for the inhabitancy of a greater number for the greater good; it means the opportunity and pleasure of contemplating his achievement . . . This is the Faust who has sought absolute beauty and now seeks absolute completion, which are perhaps the same thing'. When, however, Gearey completes his own lucid analysis by concluding of Faust, '*He remains the idealist*' (168, my emphasis), the brutality as well as the materiality of Faust's aestheticist building project vanish from view, much in the manner of those who instead praise Faust for his 'communal' striving. Along with Lukács and Berman, cited below, these include Blackhall, who omits to mention Philemon and Baucis altogether: 'The ground is free, the people are free—or rather: the ground is to be free . . . full of potentialities for development, uncluttered because new and therefore free for men to develop' (1984: 6–7). Jaeger instead takes the conventional view of Faust as insatiable, which he allies—at great length—with 'modernity' and briefly opposes to Philemen and Baucis' 'resigned life of having enough' (2004: 414).

An excellent account of Lukács' 'dogmatic interpretation of *Faust*'—in which 'the Philemon/Baucis episode', viewed as a necessary representation of 'the brutal attack of capitalism on the pre-capitalist idyll', is itself viewed as necessary to the 'Marxist-Stalinist vista of human development'—is offered by Vazsonyi (1999: 119–26).

14 Derrida offers a closely related perception of the singularly nonreferential status of the name 'U.S.S.R.': 'U.S.S.R. itself is the only name of a state in the world that carries with it no reference to a locality or a nationality. The only proper name of a state which finally carries with it no given proper noun, in the current meaning of the term: the U.S.S.R. is the only name of . . . an individual and singular State which gave to itself or intended to give to itself its own proper name ('son propre nom propre') without reference to any singular place or any national past' (Derrida 2005: 17). The temporal complications inherent in such a 'purely artificial' (18) self-naming are not considered explicitly at this moment by Derrida, nor, retrospectively, need they have been, since the 'U.S.S.R.' to which Derrida traveled, as he states, 'at the moment when certain Republics of the U.S.S.R. have begun to claim their independence', has since become an *historical designation*, the 'technical' name of an idea itself naming a thing of the past.

15 Nor, with the exception of Kaiser (1994), is there preceding critical reflection on Faust's use of enslaved laborers as disposable 'Werkzeuge'. Neither Lukács, nor more recent Marxist criticism by Zabka (1993), presents Faust's absolute expenditure of bodies as anything but consistent with the bourgeois tenet of 'free' markets, even if Zabka recognizes, without noting the contradiction of market principles his observation implies, that in Faust, 'the idea of the free exchange becomes the reality of naked violence' (252). Lukács interprets Faust's violent establishment of 'new ground' as an expression of communal struggle, the 'highest aim of humankind . . . to fight together with his fellow men' (177), while attributing 'the gruesome rhythm of extermination that accompanies and comments on Faust's dream of the future' to Goethe's 'adequate expression' of the 'insolubility of the dissonance' of 'capitalist development' (178). Berman takes an even more romantic view, concluding that, for the witness to the blood shed by Faust's '"[h]uman sacrifices"' and the nightly '"[t]ortured screams"' succeeded by the appearance of dams and canals by day, 'there is something miraculous and magical about all this', while, as the overseer of slave laborers, Faust (much like any 'vision'-driven CEO) is just as tough—although Berman does not say how—on number one: 'if he drives his workers hard, so he drives himself' (64–5).

16 'The question . . .', in *Heidegger* (1977: 283–318 [296–99]), with modifications.
17 Heidegger (1967: 5–36 [18–21]). Although he does not refer to *Faust* in this watershed essay, Heidegger does explicitly cite and incorporate in 'Die Frage . . .' a neologism from the *Wahlverwandtschaften*. Treating Goethe's language much as he would Parmenides', Heidegger notes the introduction, in the 'Novelle' within the novel, of the 'mysterious word' '"fortgewähren"' (roughly, 'to grant permanently'), used instead of the customary '"fortwähren"' ('to endure permanently'), proceeding to include the inserted particle of Goethe's new term in his own novel designation of the enduring essence of technology, 'Ge-stell' (roughly, 'framing') (35).
18 Interestingly, Kant's famous 1784 essay on enlightenment, which expanded the practical definition of the term to encompass the defining human 'inclination and vocation to *think freely*' ('nämlich den Hang und Beruf zum *freien Denken*'), is entitled, like Heidegger's essay on technology, for a question, 'Beantwortung der Frage: Was ist Aufklärung?' ('Answer to the question: What is enlightenment?') (1968, 11: 53–61, A 481–94 [61, A 494] [emphasis in text]). Although the question of enlightenment's definition was a topical one that had already been posed publicly—Moses Mendelssohn's response to it appearing in the *Berlinische Monatsschrift* in the same month Kant wrote his own (September 1784) (see Kant [1968, 11: 61★, A 494★])—Kant's continued use of the term as an object of interrogation implies, as does Heidegger's 'question of technology', that the very operation of the subject posed by the question is and will remain implicated in its answer: that understanding enlightenment requires what it itself entails, namely, a free, or nonfinite, process of thought. Kant's essay also ends by introducing the same distinction that Heidegger makes in 'The question . . .' between human being and machine. While Heidegger emphasizes the nonautonomous status of the machine *viewed as technology*, that is, as a challenge to man, and Kant stresses the permanent challenge to human beings to 'think freely' and to governments to 'treat' people according to their 'worth' as thinking beings, rather than as mere 'machines' ('*den Menschen, der nun mehr als* Maschine *ist, seiner Würde gemäss zu behandeln*') (Kant 1968, 11: 61 A 494 [emphasis in text]), both Kant and Heidegger view the inherently active subjects of their analyses—the thinking involved in becoming enlightened and responding to technology, respectively—in opposition to any version of their mechanistic limitation. (On enlightenment as ongoing action, see Kant [1968, 11: 59, A 491]: 'Do we now live in an *enlightened* age? . . . No, but we do live in an age of *enlightenment*' ['Leben wir jetzt in einem *aufgeklärten* Zeitalter? . . . Nein, aber wohl in einem Zeitalter der *Aufklärung*'] [emphasis in text].)
19 Similar to Benjamin's differentiation between 'practiced', haptic or 'tactile' experience and the temporal and spatial dislocation of experience produced with optical technologies (see Benjamin, 'Das Kunstwerk . . .' and 'Über einige Motive . . .' [1977: 136–69, 185–229; 1976: 155–200, 217–51]), Heidegger's long unraveling of the categories related in Hegelian dialectic as of the mode of dialectical opposition itself can be seen in small in his passing, parenthetical differentiation between the manual 'Werkzeug' and technology in this essay: '(Here would be the place to discuss Hegel's definition of the machine as an autonomous tool. With regard to the tool of manual work his characterization is right. By such a characterization, however, the machine is not thought at all out of the essence of technology to which it belongs. Seen in terms of the standing-reserve, the machine is completely non-autonomous; for it has its standing only from the ordering of the orderable)' (Heidegger 1977: 298–9, with modification) ['(Hier wäre der Ort, Hegels Bestimmung der Maschine al eines selbständigen Werkzeugs zu erörtern. Vom Werkzeug des Handwerks her gesehen, ist seine Kennzeichnung richtig. Allein, so ist die Maschine gerade nicht aus dem Wesen der Technik gedacht, in die sie gehört. Vom Bestand her gesehen, ist die Maschine schlechthin unselbständig; denn sie hat ihren Stand einzig aus dem Bestellen von Bestellbarem)' (1967: 16–17)].
20 '"Physis" also, the arising of something from out of itself, is a bringing-forth, "poiesis"'; 'Once there was a time when the bringing-forth of the true into the beautiful was called "techne". The "poiesis" of the fine arts was also called "techne"' (Heidegger 1977:

293, 315) ('Auch die φύσις, das von-sich-her Aufgehen, ist ein Her-vor-bringen, ist ποίησις'; 'Einstmals hiess τέχνη auch das Hervorbringen des Wahren in das Schöne. Τέχνη hiess auch die ποίησις der schönen Künste' [1967: 15, 38]).

21 The split between 'techne' and 'poiesis' is discussed as historically formative of Heidegger's own course of thought by Riera:

> 'The Origin of the Work of Art' (1935–36) is inextricably implicated in 'The Question Concerning Technology', in the same way that the latter is implicated in 'The Origin of the Work of Art', as the 1956 Addendum bears witness. There are good reasons for this, since there is an *inextricable* relation between *poiesis* and *techne* that took Heidegger several years to explicate . . . The ambiguity of the essence of *techne* points to the secret of unveiling, of truth. *Poiesis* preserves the archi-originary, the *polemos*, the strife that *phusis* is . . . It is more originary than *techne*, since the latter forgets all about it. The essence of technology represses or hides this other mode of unveiling. (2006: 49)

Riera astutely notes that the close proximity of 'techne' and 'poiesis' makes such a staggered delineation of their origination hardly tenable, and that it is 'dwelling' which encompasses both terms under the aegis of 'poiesis', once 'techne', described above as less 'originary' than 'poiesis', is instead understood 'in its origin' as 'poiesis': 'Once again we come across the question of dwelling, since in its origin *techne* meant the unveiling that produces the truth of being . . . that is *poiesis*' (50). The difficulty in understanding 'techne' as both originally 'poiesis' and less originary than 'poiesis' is ultimately described by Riera as constitutive of Heidegger's 'turn toward the work of art and the poem', a turn whose own historical moment seems no less ambiguous, however, than the 'origin' of 'techne', since arising, in Riera's account, 'in this context, punctuated by nihilism and the danger that the essence of technology harbors', which is to say, *after* the turn toward the work of art and the poem in the essay on the origin of art.

22 Cf. Barnouw (1994: 29–42), in which Faust is said to view his building project as 'a technological marvel' and as 'a large-scale housing project' (37). This study argues that Faust's murderous building project aims less at establishing any particular structure than the 'free ground' which, disentangled from the earth, would be that of technology itself.

Bibliography

Adorno, T. W. (1967), 'Zur Schlussszene des Faust', in H. Mayer (ed.), *Goethe im XX. Jahrhundert. Spiegelungen und Deutungen*. Hamburg: C. Wegner, pp. 330–7.
Barnouw, J. (1994), 'Faust and the ethos of technology', in J. K. Brown, M. Lee and T. P. Saine (eds), *Interpreting Goethe's 'Faust' Today*. Columbia: Camden House, pp. 29–42.
Benjamin, W. (1972–91), *Gesammelte Schriften*, 8 v., R. Tiedemann and H. Schweppenhäuser (eds). Frankfurt: Suhrkamp.
— (1976), *Illuminations*, H. Arendt (ed.), H. Zohn (trans.). New York: Schocken Books.
— (1977), *Illuminationen. Ausgewählte Schriften*, S. Unseld (ed.). Frankfurt: Suhrkamp.
Berman, M. (1988), *All That Is Solid Melts Into Air. The Experience of Modernity*. New York: Penguin Books.
Binswanger, H. C. (1985), *Geld und Magie. Deutung und Kritik der modernen Wirtschaft anhand von Goethes Faust*. Stuttgart: Edition Weitbrecht.
Blackhall, E. (1984), *Faust's Last Speech*. London: The University of London Institute of Germanic Studies.
Böhme, G. (2005), *Goethes Faust als philosophischer Text*. Baden-Baden: Die Graue Edition.
Brandes, P. (2003), *Goethes Faust. Poetik der Gabe und Selbstreflexion der Dichtung*. Munich: Wilhelm Fink.

Brodsky Lacour, C. (1999), 'Architecture in the discourse of modern philosophy: Descartes to Nietzsche', in I. Wohlfarth and A. Kostka (eds), *Nietzsche and an 'Architecture of Our Minds'*. Los Angeles: Getty Center, pp. 19–34.
Brown, J. K. (1986), *Goethe's Faust. A German Tragedy*. Ithaca: Cornell University Press.
— (2007), *The Persistance of Allegory*. Philadelphia: University of Pennsylvania Press.
Brown, J. K., Lee, M. and Saine, T. P. (eds) (1994), *Interpreting Goethe's 'Faust' Today*. Columbia: Camden House.
Derrida, J. (1995, 2005), *Moscou Aller-Retour*. Paris: Editions de l'Aube.
Flax, N. M (1987), 'Goethe and romanticism', in D. McMillan (ed.), *Approaches to Teaching Goethe's Faust*. New York: The Modern Language Association, pp. 40–7.
Gearey, J. (1992), *Goethe's Other Faust: The Drama, Part Two*. Toronto: University of Toronto Press.
Goethe, J. W. (1950), *Gedenkausgabe*, 24 v., E. Beutler (ed.). Zurich: Artemis.
— (1982), *Werke*. Hamburger Ausgabe reissued in 14 v. Munich: dtv.
Hamm, H. (1982), 'Julirevolution, Saint-Simonismus und Goethes Abschliessende Arbeit am Faust', *Weimarer Beiträge*, 28, 70–91.
Heidegger, M. (1967), *Vorträge und Aufsätze*, 3 v. Tübingen: Günther Neske Pfullingen.
— (1977), 'The question concerning technology', in D. F. Krell (ed.), W. Lovitt (trans.), *Martin Heidegger: Basic Writings*. New York: Harper and Row, pp. 283–318.
Jaeger, M. (2004), *Fausts Kolonie. Goethes kritische Phänomenologie der Moderne*. Würzburg: Königshausen and Neumann.
Kaiser, G. (1994), *Ist der Mensch zu retten? Vision und Kritik der Moderne in Goethes 'Faust'*. Freiburg: Rombach.
Kant, I. (1968), *Werkausgabe*, 12 v., W. Weischedel (ed.). Frankfurt: Suhrkamp.
Lange, V. (1980), 'Faust. Der Tragödie zweiter Teil', in W. Hinderer (ed.), *Goethes Dramen. Neue Interpretationen*. Stuttgart: Reclam, pp. 281–312.
Lukács, G. (1967), *Faust und Faustus*. Hamburg: Rowohlt.
Metscher, T. (1976), 'Faust und die Ökonomie. Ein literaturhistorischer Essay', *Das Argument*, 3, 28–155.
Mieth, G. (1980), 'Fausts letzter Monolog—poetische Struktur einer geschichtlichen Vision', *Goethe Jahrbuch*, 97, 90–102.
Muenzer, C. (1984), *Figures of Identity. German Novels of the Enigmatic Self*. University Park: Penn State University Press.
— (1994), 'Goethe's gothic classicism: Antecedents to the architecture of history in Faust II, Act III', in J. K. Brown, M. Lee and T. P. Saine (eds), *Interpreting Goethe's 'Faust' Today*. Columbia: Camden House, pp. 187–206.
Plato (1930, 1982), *The Republic*, P. Shorey (trans.). Cambridge: Loeb Classical Library of Harvard University Press.
Riera, G. (2006), *Intrigues: From Being to the Other*. New York: Fordham University Press.
Shell, M. (1980), 'Money and the mind: The economics of translation in Faust', *MLN*, 95, 516–62.
Schlaffer, H. (1981), *Faust Zweiter Teil. Die Allegorie des 19. Jahrhunderts*. Stuttgart: J. B. Metzlersche Verlagsbuchhandlung.
Stöcklein, P. (1949), *Wege zum späten Goethe*. Hamburg: Marion von Schröder.
Vaget, H. R. (1994), 'Act IV revisited: A "post-wall" reading of Goethe's Faust', in J. K. Brown, M. Lee and T. P. Saine (eds), *Interpreting Goethe's 'Faust' Today*. Columbia: Camden House, pp. 43–58.
Van der Laan, J. M. (2007), *Seeking Meaning for Goethe's 'Faust'*. London and New York: Continuum.
Vazsonyi, N. (1999), *Lukács Reads Goethe. From Aestheticism to Stalinism*. Columbia: Camden House.
Zabka, T. (1993), *Faust II—Das Klassische und das Romantische. Goethes Eingriff in die neueste Literatur*. Tübingen: Niemeyer.

5 Faust and Satan: Conflicting Concepts of the Devil in *Faust I*

Ehrhard Bahr

It was an ingenious move by Goethe when he provided his Faust fragment of 1790 with a frame that was based on the book of Job (1.6–12). This frame consisting of the 'Prologue in Heaven' ('Prolog im Himmel'), written in 1800, puts Faust's tragedy on earth into perspective from a higher vantage point. As the three archangels present themselves to the Lord, Mephistopheles is also among them. Both the Lord and the devil decide to monitor and test Faust, whom the Lord calls 'my servant' ('meinen Knecht') (*F*, 299).[1] In the same fashion Satan appears among the sons of God before Yahweh in the book of Job, where Job is identified in the same words by Yahweh as 'my servant' ('mein Knecht') in Luther's translation and given into Satan's hands for the well-known series of his trials and tribulations. Little did Goethe realize that his ingenious move caused him more trouble than he bargained for because Satan is presumably also a son of God in the book of Job, as Henry A. Kelly has argued in his history of the concept of Satan *Satan: A Biography* (2006: 175). In the Old Testament phase of this biography, Satan is in the service of God, not his adversary. This concept is reflected in Goethe's text, when Mephistopheles extends his greetings:

> Since, Lord, You once again are come
> to ask us how we're getting on,
> and before have often welcomed me,
> You see among Your servants me as well.
>
> (Da du, o Herr, dich einmal wieder nahst
> Und fragst wie alles sich bei uns befinde,
> Und du mich sonst gewöhnlich gerne sahst;
> So siehst du mich auch unter dem Gesinde.)[2]
> (*F*, 271–4)

Mephistopheles belongs to the Lord's 'household' ('Gesinde', translated here as 'among Your servants'). In the book of Job, Satan is a celestial functionary who serves as observer, spy and tester, according to Kelly (2006: 21–3). Goethe's Mephistopheles, sent by the Lord with a specific mission statement, fits the job description of such a celestial functionary:

> Human activity slackens all too easily,
> and people soon are prone to rest on any terms;

> that's why I like to give them the companion
> who functions as a prod and does a job as devil.

> (Des Menschen Tätigkeit kann allzuleicht erschlaffen,
> Er liebt sich bald die unbedingte Ruh;
> Drum geb' ich gern ihm den Gesellen zu,
> Der reizt und wirkt, und muß, als Teufel, schaffen.)
> (F, 340–3)

The last line of the above quotation reflects the conceptual dilemma that the intertextual model presented to Goethe. Satan is a member of the Lord's household and he carries out his commands and wishes. Such a position is, however, not compatible with the Christian concept of the devil. Therefore, the line refers to a positive action that Mephistopheles has to perform, although he is a devil. The punctuation marks of the German text support this reading.

The Satan of the book of Job resembles, as Kelly explains, a well-known figure in the 'governments of the time, namely the official inspector and informer employed by the central authorities' (2006: 26). Likewise, Mephistopheles, Goethe's stand-in for Satan, is not God's enemy, but a servant who carries out his Lord's assignments. He is not the rebel out of pride, as was Lucifer who caused Adam and Eve to sin. This character description is part of the 'New Biography of Satan' that was provided by the early Church Fathers. Kelly employs the term 'retro-fitting' for this procedure (2006: 2). This new biography is a reinterpretation of Satan as rebel against God, namely, as the satanic Lucifer. This concept is indirectly referred to by Goethe in the following lines of the 'Prologue in Heaven', when the Lord turns to the archangels for a benediction. Excluding Mephistopheles, he singles them out as 'the true sons of heaven' ('die echten Göttersöhne')[3] and says:

> But may, true sons of heaven, you delight
> in beauty's living richness!
> May the power of growth that works and lives forever
> encompass you in love's propitious bonds.

> (Doch ihr, die echten Göttersöhne,
> Erfreut euch der lebendig reichen Schöne!
> Das Werdende, das ewig wirkt und lebt,
> Umfass' euch mit der Liebe holden Schranken.)
> (F, 344–7)

Yet, Mephistopheles is not Lucifer, but only a minor devil. The Lord calls him a 'rogue' ('Schalk') who bothers him 'the least' of all 'the spirits of negation' (F, 339). The eighteenth-century dictionary definition of German 'Schalk' is not as jocular as the modern meaning of the word. The old definition refers to a person who appears innocent, but is capable of doing harm.[4]

Mephistopheles is aware of Lucifer's fate when he says in the last few lines of the 'Prologue in Heaven' that he takes good care not to offend the Lord (350–3). In the new biography of Satan, Lucifer is based on a misreading of Isaiah 14 by Origen of Alexandria (AD c. 185–c. 250). The original text refers to the King of Babylon who has fallen to earth like the Morning Star, but Origen thought that this statement could not apply to a human being, but only to Satan, or rather Lucifer, the 'Dawn-Bringer' ('Heosphoros'), as he was called in Greek (Kelly 2006: 191–208).[5] Maximilian Rudwin confirmed that due to this misinterpretation, 'the name of Lucifer has been used as a synonym for Satan' (1931: 5). As he further explained, 'the generic term "devil" (*diable* in French and *Teufel* in German) for the evil spirit is a derivation of the Latin *diabolus* (Greek διάβολος) which means an "accuser," an "assailant" and which consequently is the exact Septuagint translation of the Hebrew word *satan*' (1931: 26). The name Mephistopheles (or Mephostophiles) originated from the chapbook, the *Historia von D. Johann Fausten* of 1587. Its etymology is uncertain (Schöne 1999, 2: 167–8).[6]

Goethe developed his own mythology of Lucifer in *Dichtung und Wahrheit* (*Poetry and Truth*, Part II, Bk 8). Although written in 1811, after the completion of *Faust I*, Goethe's autobiography offers an invaluable insight into his belief system. He posited 'a deity that reproduces itself, by itself, from eternity'. Arguing that 'reproduction cannot possibly be imagined without diversity', he envisioned the emergence of a second and third entity. While he acknowledged the second entity under the name of the Son, he did not label the third entity. Goethe's model was obviously the Christian trinity, as he argued for a closed 'circle of divinity'. But then he departed from Christian tradition when he suggested that the three entities created a fourth entity that contained an inner contradiction: 'for while it was absolute, like them, at the same time it was to be kept within them and delimited by them'. Goethe identified this fourth entity as Lucifer. The whole creative power was transferred to Lucifer who gave evidence of his energy by creating the angels. But Lucifer 'forgot that his origin was in a higher source and thought it was to be found in himself . . . And so came to pass what we know as the rebellion of the angels. A group of them formed a concentrate, the rest reverted to their origin'. Goethe concluded that 'from this concentration of the whole universe . . . there arose everything that we perceive in the form of matter' (1987: 261–2). However, this religious mythology had no particular bearing on *Faust I*, except for Mephistopheles' claim that he is 'part of the Darkness that gave birth to Light' (*F*, 1350). Especially all references to Lucifer in Goethe's *Faust* are vague and nonessential.[7]

The reason appears to be that Goethe assiduously avoided establishing a counter-figure of rank, opposite the Lord. As Mephistopheles explains, 'I'm not one of the great myself' ('Ich bin keiner von den Großen') (*F*, 1641). Faust is well aware of Mephistopheles' low rank, when he calls him a 'poor devil' in the second 'Study' scene ('Studierzimmer II'): 'And what have you to give, poor devil' ('Was willst du armer Teufel geben') (*F*, 1675). A clear indication of Mephistopheles' lower rank in Goethe's *Faust* is the fact that he is unable to extract the traditional pact from Faust, but has to be satisfied with a wager. His namesake in the chapbook is also a minor figure, but he has the backing of Lucifer.

For many parts of the drama, Goethe accepted the Christian devil figure that was provided by the Faust tradition, as he first encountered it in the puppet-play and then in some of the later versions of the chapbook: Nikolaus Pfitzer's version of 1674 and an anonymous version of 1725.[8] The Margarete plot is an exception, insofar as there was no chapbook model, but the representation of the devil in the Margarete plot is not conspicuously different. In the chapbook tradition, Mephistopheles is not even similar in rank to Satan, as he is in Goethe's 'Prologue in Heaven' due to the intertextuality with the book of Job, but only a servant spirit sent by Lucifer and under his command. The chapbook of 1587 provides even a detailed topography of hell and an outline of the satanic hierarchy, but rarely mentions Satan by name. Lucifer, who is called 'the Oriental Prince', is the ruler of hell in the chapbook tradition (Haile 1965: 28).[9] The *Historia of D. Johann Fausten* of 1587 devotes a special chapter to Lucifer as a fallen angel and introduces the protagonist to seven different devil figures in hell (Füssel and Kreutzer 1988: 32–3, 49–51).

In Goethe's *Faust*, however, the Satan figure from the book of Job does not disappear completely from the dramatic action, not only due to his commanding role in the 'Prologue in Heaven', but also due to the author's disregard of consistency. The two concepts of the devil from the different stages of Satan's biography are in conflict in Goethe's *Faust*, not only in the 'Prologue in Heaven', but throughout the drama. It is my thesis that Goethe never solved the problem because he avoided the problem of evil. In an early essay of 1771, dedicated to the celebration of Shakespeare, Goethe had declared: 'What we call evil is only the other side of good; evil is necessary for good to exist and is part of the whole, just as the tropics must be torrid and Lapland frigid for there to be a temperate zone' (1986: 165). This statement may well have guided Goethe throughout his life. The concept of Satan in the book of Job corresponded to Goethe's opposition to a strict dualism and favored a solution of his own to the problem of redemption, as he presented it at the end of *Faust II*. Therefore, I will examine the last scenes of the drama that were written between 1825 and 1831, but will otherwise ignore the dramatic action of *Faust II* that has no impact on the final scenes. There is no unequivocal proof that Goethe was aware of the pre-Christian definition of Satan in the book of Job, but the textual evidence points in that direction.

There are a few scenes in *Faust I* that show Mephistopheles involved in his self-definition, but they do not resolve the issue. In the first 'Study' ('Studierzimmer I') scene, he identifies himself as '[a] part of that force/which, always willing evil, always produces good' ('Ein Teil von jener Kraft/Die stets das Böse will und stets das Gute schafft') (*F*, 1335–6). This declaration agrees with the mission statement in the 'Prologue in Heaven' that envisions the devil in the service of the Lord. But when pressed by Faust for a better explanation, Mephistopheles elaborates on the logical consequences of his character that fit the Christian definition of the devil:

> Accordingly, my essence is
> what you call sin, destruction,
> or—to speak plainly—Evil.
>
> (So ist denn alles was ihr Sünde,
> Zerstörung, kurz das Böse nennt,
> Mein eigentliches Element.)
> (*F*, 1342–4)

He does not identify himself as representative of evil, but considers evil a category attributed to him by humans. He presents a different system of values when he introduces himself as 'the Spirit of Eternal Negation' ('der Geist, der stes verneint') (*F*, 1338). He derives his essence not from evil, but from opposition to beneficent creativity:

> ... since all that gains existence
> is only fit to be destroyed; that's why
> it would be best if nothing ever got created.

> (... denn alles was entsteht
> Ist wert daß es zu Grunde geht;
> Drum besser wär's daß nichts entstünde.)
> (F, 1339–41)

But Mephistopheles has to admit that he has not been very successful:

> This awkward world, this Something
> which confronts as foe my Nothing—
> despite all efforts up to now,
> I have failed to get the better of it...
>
> (Was sich dem Nichts entgegenstellt,
> Das Etwas, diese plumpe Welt,
> So viel als ich schon unternommen,
> Ich wußte nicht ihr beizukommen...)
> (F, 1363–6)

P. Michelsen has identified this point of view as the standard explanation of evil in eighteenth-century theodicy (1993: 231). As G.W. Leibniz states in his *Discours de métaphysique*, 'The root of evil exists in nothingness, that is, so to speak, in the deficiencies and limitations of creatures, which God in his mercy remedies through the degree of perfection that he is pleased to dispense' ('La racine du mal est dans le neant, c'est à dire dans la privation ou limitation des creatures, à laquelle Dieu remedie gracieusement par le degre de perfection qu'il luy plaist de donner') (1958: 76).

Later Mephistopheles develops even a new history of his origin that is in contradiction to the Lord's characterization in the 'Prologue in Heaven'. The devil claims to be 'part of the Darkness that gave birth to Light—/proud Light, that now contests the senior rank/of Mother Night, disputes her right to space' ('Ein Teil der Finsternis, die sich das Licht gebar,/Das stolze Licht, das nun der Mutter Nacht/Den alten Rang, den Raum ihr streitig macht') (F, 1350–2). This myth of creation places Mephistopheles into the camp of materialism and Faust is right to call him the 'strange son of Chaos' ('des Chaos wunderlicher Sohn') (F, 1383).

But even more importantly, this self-characterization is one of the few incidents that identifies Mephistopheles as opponent of God, as defined in the Christian stage of Satan's biography. Therefore, Jeffrey Burton Russell discussed Goethe's Mephistopheles as a Christian devil in his four-volume history of the concept of the devil. But he admitted that only one of Mephistopheles' 'components is the Christian devil' (Russell 1986: 157), whereas a German critic called Goethe's Mephistopheles 'the most Christian devil' in the history of representations of the devil in literature (Mahal 1972: 331). Russell characterized him as 'an immensely complex figure' and listed his various impersonations 'as the principle of matter against the principle of spirit, as evil against good, as chaos against order, as a stimulus to creativity', even as 'a nature spirit representing the undifferentiated world' (1986: 157). Rarely does Mephistopheles appear as a representative of evil in Goethe's *Faust*, but rather as a personification of irony. Goethe's legacy, 'the most important literary Devil since Milton's', as Russell concluded (1986: 167), is a devil resurrected in many non-Christian forms, but certainly not totally devoid of his Christian origin. This may be due to Goethe's Enlightenment view of Christianity or his psychological 'avoidance of tragedy',[10] even though his Faust drama was published as a tragedy: *Faust: Eine Tragödie*.

In the scenes following the wager Mephistopheles appears as the devil as prankster in his discussion of university subjects with the student who has come for academic advice to select a major. He steers the young student toward medical school, promising easy access to feminine charms:

> Above all, learn to handle women;
> their myriads of aches and pains,
> that never never cease,
> can all be cured if you know the right spot—
>
> (Besonders lernt die Weiber führen;
> Es ist ihr ewig Weh und Ach
> So tausendfach
> Aus Einem Punkte zu kurieren.)
>
> (F, 2023–6)

When he inscribes the student's album, he quotes scripture: 'Eritis sicut Deus, scientes bonum et malum' (F, 2048).[11] With his sarcastic counsel to follow the advice of his cousin, the serpent, Mephistopheles places himself high in the hierarchy of hell, as Christian tradition identified the serpent in the Garden of Eden with Satan (or Lucifer).[12] Although addressed to a freshman student, the warning is satanic: man's 'likeness to god will some day certainly make him tremble' ('Dir wird gewiß einmal bei deiner Gottähnlichkeit bange!') (F, 2050; my translation).

In 'Auerbach's Wine-Cellar in Leipzig' ('Auerbachs Keller in Leipzig'), Mephistopheles reverts to his prankish behavior, dispensing cheap magic and plying the students with wine that turns into hellish fire when they spill it. When they threaten to attack him and Faust, he hypnotizes them. They are about to cut off each other's noses, when Mephistopheles releases them from the spell, reminding them not to fool with the devil: 'Remove your blindfold from them, Error!/And you! remember well the devil's joke' ('Irrtum, laß los der Augen Band!/Und merkt euch wie der Teufel spaße') (F, 2320–1).

In the 'Witch's Kitchen' ('Hexenküche'), however, Mephistopheles is quoting 'the tradition of devil lore', as W. Koepke called it (1992: 40). He introduces himself as 'lord and master' ('Herrn und Meister') to the Witch, but declines the title of 'Squire Satan' for political reasons. Satan has been relegated to the mythology of the past—there are no 'ravens' ('Raben') (F, 2491), no 'horns or tails or claws' ('Hörner, Schweif und Klauen') (F, 2498) any more. To cover up his 'cloven hoof' ('Pferdefuß') (F, 2490), Mephistopheles has resorted to wearing 'false calves' ('falscher Waden'), as they were the latest fashion in the eighteenth century (F, 2502). Only the red color of his jacket and the cock's feather give him away as devil.[13] Yet despite his conformity to modern fashion, evil still rules the political world after the French Revolution: 'yet mankind is no better off:/the Evil One/they may be rid of, evil ones have still not vanished' ('Allein die Menschen sind nichts besser dran,/Den Bösen sind sie los, die Bösen sind geblieben') (F, 2508–9). In spite of his denial, Mephistopheles exercises his sexual attraction as a satanic figure when he makes '*an indecent gesture*' (before F, 2514) and promises special favors to the Witch at Walpurgis Night: 'And if there's any favor I can do for you,/be sure to tell me on Walpurgis Night' ('Und kann ich dir was zu Gefallen tun:/So darfst du mir's nur auf Walpurgis sagen') (*F*, 2589–90). The Witch, laughing immoderately, is eager to accept the offer: 'I recognize your style!/You always were a rogue, you rascal' ('Das ist in eurer Art!/Ihr seid ein Schelm, wie ihr nur immer war't') (*F*, 2514–15).

The love story between Faust and Margarete that is at the center of *Faust I* shows the different levels at which Mephistopheles operates. To Faust he appears as the procurer, an indispensable, but slightly comic, figure in the seduction of Margarete. He plays the prude in Faust's courtship and rejects the latter's demand to get him the girl within 7 hours:

> You're talking like Jack Reprobate;
> he covets every pretty flower,
> and fancies there's no honest favor
> which can't be plucked if he but tries;
> that isn't always so, however ...
>
> (Du sprichst ja wie Hans Liederlich,
> Der begehrt jede liebe Blum' für sich,
> Und dünkelt ihm es wär' kein Ehr'
> Und Gunst die nicht zu pflücken wär'...)
> (*F*, 2628–32)

After he has provided Faust with necklace and earrings as presents for Margarete, he pretends to be the injured party when the jewelry is lost to the Church, as Margarete's mother suspects its unholy origin and hands it over to a priest: 'I'd have the devil take me here and now/if only I were not myself a devil' ('Ich möcht' mich gleich dem Teufel übergeben/Wenn ich nur selbst kein Teufel wär') (*F*, 2809–10). In his dealings with Martha Schwerdtlein, Margarete's neighbor and confidante, Mephistopheles is the devil as proverbial liar and swindler, pretending to be a messenger from her missing husband: 'your husband's dead and sends regards' ('Ihr Mann ist tot und läßt sie grüßen') (*F*, 2916). He plays upon her credulity and greed to obtain access for Faust to Margarete. Persuading Faust to commit perjury, they both promise to make a deposition to the effect that they were witnesses to Martha's husband's death and funeral in Italy. This false statement enables them to meet both Martha and Margarete in the 'Garden' ('Garten') scene that shows Faust declaring his love for Margarete and Mephistopheles fighting off Martha's amorous advances. In his feigned marriage proposal, he distances himself from his master: 'It's now high time for me to leave—/she'd hold the very devil to his word' ('Nun mach' ich mich bei Zeiten fort!/Die hielte wohl den Teufel selbst bei'm Wort') (*F*, 3004–5). In 'Forest and Cave' ('Wald und Höhle') Mephistopheles is Faust's cynical companion, mocking his self-delusional idealism:

> You're a fine one to cry for shame genteelly.
> Before chaste ears one must not name
> what chase hearts cannot do without.
>
> (Ihr habt das Recht gesittet pfui zu sagen.
> Man darf das nicht vor keuschen Ohren nennen,
> Was keusche Herzen nicht entbehren können.)
> (*F*, 3294–6)

No other scene shows as clearly as 'Forest and Cave' that Mephistopheles is also a manifestation of Faust's alter ego. He says what Faust wants but does not dare to say or do. Not only does he provide self-satisfying reasons for Faust's behavior, but he also offers him the opportunity to blame hell for his transgressions:

> This victim you demanded, Hell!
> Help me, devil, shorten the dread of waiting,
> and let what must be, be quickly done!
>
> (Du, Hölle, mußtest dieses Opfer haben!
> Hilf, Teufel, mir die Zeit der Angst verkürzen!
> Was muß geschehn, mag's gleich geschehn!)
> (F, 3361–3)

Faust must be aware that his argument is as false as it is self-serving, but it provides him with a convenient excuse to blame hell and the devil for his own shortcomings. Although Faust is in control of his actions, he denies his responsibility, calling Mephistopheles 'serpent' ('Schlange') (F, 3324) as well as 'pimp' ('Kuppler') (F, 3338).

Margarete appears to be the only character that is fully aware of the evil represented by Mephistopheles. Although he ensnared her by appealing to her vanity, when he placed the jewelry in her room, she continues to resist him. She minces no words when she tells Faust:

> The person with you all the time
> is someone I detest with all my soul;
> never in my life has anything
> so cut me to the heart
> as has that man's repellent face.
>
> (Der Mensch, den du da bei dir hast,
> Ist mir in tiefer inn'rer Seele verhaßt;
> Es hat mir in meinem Leben
> So nichts einen Stich in's Herz gegeben,
> Als des Menschen widrig Gesicht.)
> (F, 3471–5)

Although Faust knows better, he makes excuses for his companion. Margarete, on the other hand, considers him a villain who is 'incapable of loving anyone' ('Daß er nicht mag eine Seele lieben') (F, 3490). Faust realizes that her intuitions are right, but continues to rely on Mephistopheles' advice and assistance when he hands Margarete the sleeping potion for her mother that will allow him to visit her at night. In the final 'Prison' ('Kerker') scene Margarete will recognize that Mephistopheles is the devil, as she suspected, and will reject the opportunity that he offers her to escape from her death sentence for infanticide.

In the duel with Valentine, Margarete's brother and a professional soldier, Mephistopheles appears as a comrade-in-arms. But instead of helping the inexperienced scholar to ward off the skilled swordsman's attack, he guides Faust's rapier, killing the hapless soldier. Valentine curses his sister as a whore in front of the whole neighborhood that has assembled around the dying soldier. Because of the murder bane that Mephistopheles cannot control, both he and Faust have to leave town.

Mephistopheles' role at the witches' Sabbath on the Brocken mountain in the Harz region casts doubt on his claim to satanic stature, because here he yields this part to the real Satan. Goethe had planned a Black Mass or Satan's Mass for this event, but it was presumably self-censorship that prevented the completion of this scene.[14] Albrecht Schöne reconstructed this scene, but it is not part of the authorized version of *Faust I* of 1808. Even if Goethe had executed this plan, Mephistopheles would not have had a major part in it, except as master of ceremony (Schöne 1999, 2: 737–57). In addition to his concern about obscenity—the witches and warlocks line up to kiss Satan's rump—Goethe must have realized that the Black Mass would have given the Christian Satan a stature of similar rank opposite the Lord of the 'Prologue in Heaven'. It appears that he wanted to avoid such a dualistic confrontation of good and evil.

In the final version neither Mephistopheles nor Faust attends the Black Mass at the mountain summit, but they stop at some campfires, where some questionable characters have assembled for a carnival. Faust dances with a young witch, but leaves the dance when he has a vision of Margarete in chains and with a red line around her neck, predicting her execution for infanticide. Mephistopheles shows his limited power by intimidating a will-o'-the-wisp, who recognizes him as 'lord and master' ('der Herr vom Haus') (*F*, 3866), and by trying to impress witches and warlocks with his title as Squire Nick ('Junker Voland') (*F*, 4023), an archaic name for the devil.[15] His 'cloven hoof is much respected' ('der Pferdefuß [ist] hier ehrenvoll zu Haus') (*F*, 4065), but Mephistopheles is suddenly looking old and tired, declaring that 'this ascent of Witches' Mountain' is his last (*F*, 4093). It is evident from the text that Mephistopheles is holding Faust back from the mountain summit because he does not want him to meet Satan, even in the Christian context of these scenes. Mephistopheles prefers Faust to be entertained by 'petty obscenities', as Jane K. Brown has argued (1992: 58), because that drives Faust to despair and increases his power over him. But it may also have been one of the occasions where Mephistopheles and Satan would meet, and Goethe may have wanted to prevent such a confrontation at all cost because it would have exposed the conflicting concepts of the devil in *Faust*.

In 'An Expanse of Open Country' ('Trüber Tag—Feld'), the only scene from *Urfaust* left in prose, Faust curses Mephistopheles, calling him a '[p]erfidious, contemptible spirit' ('Verräterischer, nichtswürdiger Geist'), 'dog [and] monster!' ('Hund! abscheuliches Untier!'), 'serpent' ('Wurm'), and 'vile companion' ('Schandgesellen'), but never devil or Satan. Nor does Margarete resort to these names in the 'Prison' scene, when Mephistopheles arrives at her cell. But she fully realizes that he ascended from hell when she asks: 'What's that, rising up from below?' ('Was steigt aus dem Boden herauf?') (*F*, 4601). She considers the prison a 'holy place' ('heiligen Ort') (*F*, 4603) because she has placed her trust in '[d]ivine justice' ('Gericht Gottes') (*F*, 4605). Rejecting an escape from prison with Faust and entrusting herself to God, she asks her 'Father' to save her: 'Angels and heavenly hosts/compass me about and keep me safe!' ('Ihr Engel! Ihr heiligen Scharen,/Lagert euch umher, mich zu bewahren!') (*F*, 4608–9). Mephistopheles' sentence that she is condemned is countermanded by a 'VOICE (from above): "She is saved!"' ('STIMME (von oben): "Ist gerettet!"')

(*F*, 4611). This transcendental intervention is a reflection of the 'Prologue in Heaven' and an anticipation of the final judgment of Faust at the end of *Faust II* that Goethe had planned but never wrote (Schöne 1999, 2: 384, 163). There is only a draft of 1830 referring to 'Christ[,] Mother a[nd] Evangelists a[nd] all Saints/Judgment of Faust' ('Christus Mutter u Evangelisten u alle Heiligen/ Gericht über Faust') (Schöne 1999, 1: 731).

This conflict between the biblical Satan and the Christian devil reappears even more pronounced at the end of *Faust II*, where readers expected an 'Epilogue in Heaven' as part of the frame that would settle the dispute between the Lord and Mephistopheles. But there is no such epilogue. Nor does the Lord reappear. In his place the Mater Gloriosa shows up in a scene that is not separated from the rest of the drama as the 'Prologue in Heaven' and concludes the drama as a whole.

Again Goethe avoided the issue of dealing with evil that becomes evident in the murder of the old couple, Philemon and Baucis, and an anonymous traveler in Act V. This scene, reported by Lynceus as watchman and by Mephistopheles (*F*, 11304–77), amounts to the greatest evil committed by the protagonist in *Faust*, but Goethe does not address it. Instead of having a dialogue between the Lord and Mephistopheles or a Judgment Day for Faust, Goethe sends his devil defeated to hell and has Faust rising 'to higher spheres' ('zu höhern Sphären') (*F*, 12094) in the last scene, called 'Mountain Gorges' ('Bergschluchten'). He follows the directions of the Mater Gloriosa and 'a penitent, otherwise named Gretchen', clinging to her (before *F*, 12069; my translation).

After Faust's death, there is a scene in the large outer courtyard of his palace, called 'Interment' ('Palast—Grablegung'), that shows a *'hideous hell-mouth, placed stage-left, [opening] its jaws'* ('*gräuliche[n] Höllenrachen . . . sich links auf [tuend]*') (before *F*, 11644). Here Goethe followed the most traditional conventions of the devil scenes in late medieval drama. As one commentator explained, the devil has never been shown so dumb and cute, as during the Middle Ages (Mahal 1972: 128), and Goethe did not hesitate to employ comedy at this point. His 'Interment' scene is a burlesque farce with *'FAT DEVILS, who have short, straight horns'* ('Dickteufeln vom kurzen, graden Horne') and *'THIN DEVILS, who have long, twisting horns'* ('Dürrteufeln vom langen, krummen Horne') (before *F*, 11656, 11670). Mephistopheles exhorts them to help him catch Faust's soul, to which he is entitled because Faust pronounced the words of the wager: 'Tarry, remain!—you are so fair!' ('Verweile doch! du bist so schön') (*F*, 1700, 11582). But Mephistopheles is cheated out of his duly earned prey. Angels strewing roses defeat the devil and bear away *'the immortal part of FAUST'* ('Faustens Unsterbliches') (before *F*, 11825). Mephistopheles must admit that he has lost the battle against the angels:

> They've robbed me of a great, unequaled treasure;
> the noble soul that pledged itself to me—
> they've tricked me out of it and smuggled it away.
>
> (Mir ist ein großer einziger Schatz entwendet,
> Die hohe Seele die sich mir verpfändet
> Die haben sie mir pfiffig weggepascht.)
>   (*F*, 11829–31)

It is supreme irony that Mephistopheles falls for the same 'love from above' (*F*, 11938–9) that is the decisive factor in the potential salvation of Faust. The devil falls in love with the angels:

> Confounded rascals—though I hate them,
> I find them only too attractive.—
> . . .
>
> You are, I swear, so pretty that I'd like to kiss you;
> I have a feeling you would suit me nicely.
>
> (Die Wetterbuben die ich hasse
> Sie kommen mir doch gar zu lieblich vor.—
> . . .
>
> Ihr seid so hübsch, fürwahr ich möcht euch küssen;
> Mir ists als kommt ihr eben recht.)
> (*F*, 11767–72)

Mephistopheles justifies his homosexual desire for the angels with a reference to their common descent from Lucifer: 'you're descendants too of Lucifer?' ('Seid ihr nicht auch von Luzifers Geschlecht?') (*F*, 11770). But this reference to Lucifer has no theological implication for Mephistopheles' ultimate fate; it serves only to heighten the satiric effect of this scene. He even suffers the trials of Job at the hands of the angels: 'What's happening to me?—Like Job a mass of boils/from head to toe, a horror to myself' ('Wie wird mir!—hiobsartig, Beul an Beule/Der ganze Kerl, dem's vor sich selber graut') (*F*, 11809–10). 'This is Goethe at his most ribald, and Mephisto at his most comical', as J. R. Williams concluded (1987: 207).

Goethe may have contemplated saving Mephistopheles from hell at one time—there are two Goethe conversations documented to that effect (Schöne 1999, 2: 766–7)—but he probably decided against it for pragmatic and aesthetic reasons. He did not have any use for a Christian devil at the end of the drama,[16] but needed an impressive contrast to the following scene. Mephistopheles' return to hell is most effectively set off as tragicomedy against the mystic spectacle of the transfiguration of Faust in the last scene.

This scene is in absolute contrast to the farcical burlesque of the previous scene. But Goethe's Faust is not saved from the sins that he committed. Cosmic love intervenes on Faust's behalf in spite of his sins. The author admitted in a conversation with Johann Peter Eckermann on 6 June 1831 that he chose the Catholic iconography for 'Mountain Gorges' only as mythology, not as an article of faith: 'In dealing with such supersensual, hardly apprehensible things I could easily have lost myself in vagueness, if I had not given my poetic intentions a beneficial confined form and definiteness through the sharply outlined figures and conceptions of the Christian church'.[17] Faust's soul is introduced as a Leibnizian entelechy striving 'to higher spheres above' ('zu höherm Kreise') (*F*, 11918). Goethe used the term 'entelechy' for Faust's soul in an earlier manuscript, but later changed it to 'the immortal part of Faust' in the final version (Schöne 1999, 2: 800). Gottfried Wilhelm Leibniz employed the same terminology—entelechy and striving—in his *Monadologie* (1956: 33–5).[18] The energy displayed by Faust's striving is met by a positive cosmic force that is identified in Goethe's *Faust* as 'love from above' ('die Liebe gar/Von oben'),[19] which is not

Christian love. Neither is 'redemption' ('erlösen') to be understood in Christian terms:

> This worthy member of the spirit world
> is rescued from the devil:
> for him whose striving never ceases
> we can provide redemption;
> and if a higher love as well
> has shown an interest in him,
> the hosts of heaven come
> and greet him with a cordial welcome.
>
> (Gerettet ist das edle Glied
> Der Geisterwelt vom Bösen,
> 'Wer immer strebend sich bemüht
> Den können wir erlösen'.
> Und hat an ihm die Liebe gar
> Von oben Teil genommen,
> Begegnet ihm die selige Schar
> Mit herzlichem Willkommen.)
> (F, 11934–41)

Human beings cannot achieve self-perfection by striving alone; the absolutely necessary ingredient for redemption is cosmic intervention, presented here in the conventions of Christian iconography by the Mater Gloriosa. She stands for a belief departing from church dogma, namely the return of all creatures, including the devil, to God. Some critics have identified this belief as 'apokatastasis panton' ('the return of all'), a heterodox doctrine, proclaimed by Origen of Alexandria.[20] Goethe was familiar with Neo-Platonism and the writings of mystic and Neo-Platonic authors of the sixteenth and seventeenth century who expressed such ideas.[21] While some critics agree that Goethe was influenced by these ideas, when he proposed his interpretation of cosmic love and grace in the conclusion of his Faust drama,[22] others have expressed strong disagreement and suggested other sources, as, for example, Johann Joachim Spalding's *Die Bestimmung des Menschen* (*The Destiny of Man*) of 1748 that went through more than twelve editions until 1794.[23] But it is doubtful that a single book of popular philosophy would have such impact on Goethe. Leibniz' definition of entelechy in his various publications was of greater influence, and, as I suggest, Goethe's own mythology in *Poetry and Truth*. In his autobiography he considered the creation of mankind a duplication of the creation of Lucifer. Man was playing Lucifer's role: 'Ingratitude really implies a separation from one's benefactor, and so rebellion loomed for the second time'. From this analogy Goethe concluded that creation 'was nothing but a rebelling against and returning to the original source'. He introduced the concept of redemption as part of creation and conceived it as 'eternally necessary'. According to Goethe, redemption was an essential part of the process: 'it must always be renewed through the whole period of becoming and being' (1987: 263). Goethe's own mythology appears to me the strongest explanation for the redemption of Faust.

Such a belief in redemption is absent from the representations of the Faust character of the chapbook tradition. The Faust of the chapbook of 1587 was condemned because of his pride. He believed that 'his sins were greater than could be forgiven him' and was convinced that 'in making his written contract with the Devil he had gone too far' (Chapter 68) (Füssel and Kreutzer 1988: 122). Comparing Faust's sins to those of Cain in the Bible, the anonymous author of the chapbook delivered a sophisticated lesson in Luther's theology of grace, explaining that Faust was not lost, if he would 'but turn from [his] evil way' and 'beseech God for Grace' (Chapter 52) (102). The story of the Old Man 'who would have converted Doctor Faustus from his Godless life' (Chapter 52), and the arguments of his students shortly before his death urging him 'to call upon God' and beg 'him for forgiveness' serve this purpose (Chapter 68) (101–3, 122). But Faustus was terrified again and again by the devil and failed this test. Therefore, he met with such a hideous end, as all the other Faust characters in the chapbook tradition: his students find his corpse on a dung heap behind the inn, where they had met the night before to take the evening meal with Faust.

By comparison, the last scene of Goethe's Faust drama is an absolute break with this tradition. Faust is shown moving toward cosmic salvation, for which he does not even have to display any remorse. The scene with the four allegorical Grey Women fails to serve as a demonstration of repentance because they cannot get into Faust's palace, except for the allegorical figure of Care. Faust denies the power of Care. Even though she blinds him, he is even more eager to hasten the fulfillment of his plans of providing land for millions of people: 'Workmen, up from your beds! Up, every man/and make my bold design reality!' ('Vom Lager auf ihr Knechte! Mann für Mann!/Laßt glücklich schauen was ich kühn ersann') (*F*, 11504–5). Koepke is right to argue that Faust 'is saved mostly in spite of himself' (1992: 36). Goethe presents a Faust who appears on his way to redemption by 'love from above' (*F*, 11938–9). This love is not Christian, but part of the eternal process of creation. There is no place for evil in Goethe's universe. The frame installed with the 'Prologue in Heaven' at the beginning of his drama is left open. As in the book of Job, there is no Satan at the end of Goethe's *Faust*.

Notes

1 Goethe (1984) *Faust I and II*, Atkins (ed. and trans.). All quotations from this translation have the same verse numbers as the text of the German edition cited (see n. 2).
2 Goethe (1999) *Faust: Texte*, Schöne (ed.). All German quotations are identical with the verse numbers of the English translation (n. 1).
3 The German word 'Göttersöhne' is a translation of Hebrew 'Bene ha-Elohim' (Sons of God), the term used in the book of Job.
4 J. C. Adelung, *Grammatisch-kritisches Wörterbuch der hochdeutschen Mundart* (Vienna 1811), v. 3: col. 1339, cited in Michelsen (1993: 245).
5 Kelly refers to the misreading of this passage by Origen of Alexandria as 'the hijacking of Isaiah 14' (2006: 191).
6 Etymologies suggested are 'He who does not like light' or 'destroyer of the Good'.
7 For the representation of Lucifer in literature, see Osterkamp (1979). The author deals with Milton, Klopstock and Byron, but not with Goethe. While Goethe became familiar with Klopstock's *Messias* as early as 1762, he read Milton's *Paradise Lost* in 1799 and Byron's *Cain* as late as 1823. For the representation of Lucifer in eighteenth-century art, see Wark (2001: 75–87).

8   See Wilpert (1998: 313–16). Goethe did not read Christopher Marlowe's *Tragicall History of D. Faustus* before 1818.
9   Haile's translation is based on the Faust manuscript in the Duke-August Library in Wolfenbüttel which is similar to, but not identical with, the chapbook printed by Spies in 1587. For a brief analysis of the German chapbook, printed by Spies, and of its seminal importance, see Jones (1994: 3–11).
10 See Heller (1952, 1969: 35–63). See also Anderegg (2004; 2005) and Vaget (2001), who both miss satanic evil in Goethe's representation of the devil. Anderegg (2004; 2005) accepts Brown's definition of Mephistopheles as 'reality principle' (1986: 93) and Vaget quotes Nietzsche, who considered Mephistopheles only 'moderately malicious'. For Vaget (2001: 236), Mephistopheles is an 'homme du monde' representing the French Enlightenment. Michelsen (1993: 251, 247) sees Mephistopheles as an enabler who provides opportunities for human beings to make wrong use of their intelligence.
11 Vulgate text of *Genesis* 3.5: 'Ye shall be as God, knowing good and evil'.
12 Rudwin (1931, 1973: 51–2).
13 For the cock's feather as an iconographic attribute of the devil in German folklore, see Bächtold-Stäubli (1927–42), *Handwörterbuch des deutschen Aberglaubens* (3: 1333). The devil uses the cock's feather also for signing a pact.
14 Schöne (1999), *Faust: Kommentare* (120–9).
15 See MHG. 'vâlant' = 'the frightening one'. This medieval name for the devil is not reproduced in Atkins' translation (see n. 1).
16 For this reason Koepke (1992: 36) considers Mephistopheles 'the real tragic hero of Goethe's great allegory of human destiny'.
17 Eckermann (1984: 435). See Gearey's (1992: 187) comment:

> That the clarification takes the form of a Christian apotheosis results from the fact that it is the only vision of Utopia that has withstood the test of poetic, let alone political, reality. One may not believe in heaven but it is the only image of an afterlife available in Western culture should the thought cross the mind.

See also Schmidt (1990, 1991: 384–417).
18 For 'striving' ('Streben') Leibniz used in his Latin text the term 'appetitus' and in the French text the term 'appetition'.
19 Atkins (n. 1) translates these lines as follows: 'if a higher love as well/has shown an interest in him' (11938–9). I prefer as translation the formulaic 'love from above' with emphasis on its cosmic function.
20 See Henkel (1976, 1991).
21 See Goethe, *Poetry and Truth* (1987: 261).
22 See Henkel (1976, 1991); Breuer (1985: 1–30); Michelsen (1993: 254–5); Schöne, *Kommentare* (1999: 766–7, 788–95).
23 For the disagreement with Henkel and Breuer, see Zimmermann (1994: 171–85) and Bremer (1995: 287–307). For influence by J. J. Spalding, see Eibl (2000: 60–2) and Vaget (2001: 244–5).

Bibliography

Anderegg, J. (2004), 'Wie böse ist der Böse? Zur Gestalt des Mephisto in Goethes *Faust*', *Monatshefte*, 96, 343–59.
— (2005), 'Mephisto und die Bibel', in J. Anderegg and E. A. Kunz (eds), *Goethe und die Bibel*. Stuttgart: Deutsche Bibelgesellschaft, pp. 317–39.
Bächtold-Stäubli, H. (ed.) (1927–42), *Handwörterbuch des deutschen Aberglaubens*, 10 v. Berlin: De Gruyter.

Bremer, D. (1995), '"Wenn starke Geisteskraft...": Traditionsvermittlungen in der Schlußszene von Goethes Faust', *Goethe-Jahrbuch*, 112, 287–307.
Breuer, D. (1985), 'Origines im 18. Jahrhundert', *Seminar*, 21, 1–30.
Brown, J. K. (1986), *Goethe's Faust: The German Tragedy*. Ithaca: Cornell University Press.
— (1992), *Faust: Theater of the World*. New York: Twayne.
Eckermann, J. P. (1984), *Gespräche mit Goethe in den letzten Jahren seines Lebens*, R. Otto (ed.). Munich: Beck.
Eibl, K. (2000), *Das monumentale Ich: Wege zu Goethes Faust*. Frankfurt/Main: Insel.
Füssel, S. and Kreutzer, H. J. (eds) (1988), *Historia von D. Johann Fausten: Text des Druckes von 1587: Kritische Ausgabe*. Stuttgart: Reclam.
Gearey, J. (1981), *Goethe's Faust: The Making of Part I*. New Haven: Yale University Press.
— (1992), *Goethe's Other Faust: The Drama, Part II*. Toronto: University of Toronto Press.
Goethe, J. W. (1984), *Faust I and II*, S. Atkins (ed. and trans.), v. 2, *Goethe's Collected Works*. Cambridge, MA: Suhrkamp/Insel Publishers Boston.
— (1986), *Essays on Art and Literature*, J. Gearey (ed.), E. and E. Nardroff (trans.), v. 3, *Goethe's Collected Works*. New York: Suhrkamp Publishers New York.
— (1987), *Poetry and Truth: Parts One to Three*, T. P. Saine and J. L. Sammons (eds), R. R. Heitner (trans.), v. 4, *Goethe's Collected Works*. New York: Suhrkamp Publishers New York.
— (1999), *Faust: Texte, Kommentare*, A. Schöne (ed.), v. 1: *Texte*; v. 2: *Kommentare*. Darmstadt: Wissenschaftliche Buchgesellschaft. Identical with v. 7.1–2 of the Goethe edition of Deutscher Klassiker-Verlag, 4th rev. ed. Frankfurt/Main 1999.
Haile, H. G. (ed. and trans.) (1965), *The History of Doctor Johann Faustus*. Urbana: University of Illinois Press.
Heller, E. (1952, 1969), 'Goethe and the avoidance of tragedy', *The Disinherited Mind: Essays in Modern German Literature and Thought*. Cleveland: World Publishing Company, pp. 35–63.
Henkel, A. (1976, 1991), 'Das Ärgernis *Faust*', in W. Keller (ed.), *Aufsätze zu Goethes Faust II*. Darmstadt: Wissenschaftliche Buchgesellschaft, pp. 290–315.
— (1993), 'Mephistopheles—oder Der vertane Aufwand', in T. Cramer and W. Dahlheim (eds), *Gegenspieler*. Munich: Hanser, pp. 130–147.
Jones, J. H. (ed.) (1994), *The English Faust Book: A Critical Edition Based on the Text of 1592*. Cambridge: Cambridge University Press.
Kelly, H. A. (2006), *Satan: A Biography*. Cambridge: Cambridge University Press.
Koepke, W. (1992), 'Mephisto and aesthetic nihilism', in E. Timm (ed.), *Subversive Sublimities: Undercurrents of the German Enlightenment*. Columbia: Camden House, pp. 36–44.
Leibniz, G. W. (1956), *Vernunftprinzipien der Natur und Gnade/Monadologie*, H. Hering (ed.). Hamburg: Meiner.
— (1958), *Discours de métaphysique/ Metaphysische Abhandlung*, H. Hering (ed.). Hamburg: Meiner.
Luther, M. (trans.) (1972), *Biblia: Das ist: Die gantze Heilige Schrifft/Deudsch 1545*, 2 v. Munich: Rogner and Bernhard.
Mahal, G. (1972), *Mephistos Metamorphosen; Fausts Partner als Repräsentant literarischer Teufelsgestaltung*. Göppingen: Verlag Alfred Kümmerle.
Michelsen, P. (1993), 'Mephistos "eigentliches Element": Vom Bösen in Goethes *Faust*', in C. Colpe and W. Schmidt-Biggemann (eds), *Das Böse: Eine historische Phänomenologie des Unerklärlichen*. Frankfurt/Main: Suhrkamp, pp. 229–55.
Osterkamp, E. (1979), *Lucifer: Stationen eines Motivs*. Berlin: De Gruyter.
Rudwin, M. (1931, 1973), *The Devil in Legend and Literature*. La Salle, IL: Open Court Publishing Company.
Russell, J. B. (1986), *Mephistopheles: The Devil in the Modern World*. Ithaca: Cornell University Press.

Schmidt, J. (1990, 1991), 'Die "katholische Mythologie" und ihre mystische Entmythologisierung in der Schluss-Szene des *Faust II*', in W. Keller (ed.), *Aufsätze zu Goethes Faust II*. Darmstadt: Wissenschaftliche Buchgesellschaft, pp. 384–417.

Schöne, A. (1999), see Goethe (1999), *Faust: Texte, Kommentare*.

Vaget, H. R. (2001), '"Mäßig boshaft": Fausts Gefährte: Goethes Mephistopheles im Lichte der Aufklärung', *Goethe-Jahrbuch*, 118, 234–46.

Wark, R. R. (2001), 'Blake's Satan, Sin, and Death', in *The Revolution in Eighteenth-Century Art: Ten British Pictures*. San Marino: Huntington Library, pp. 74–87.

Williams, J. R. (1987), *Goethe's Faust*. London: Allen and Unwin.

Wilpert, G. v. (1998), 'Fauststoff', *Goethe-Lexikon*. Stuttgart: Kröner, pp. 313–16.

Zimmermann, R. C. (1994), 'Goethes *Faust* und die "Wiederbringung aller Dinge": Kritische Bemerkungen zu einem unkritisch aufgenommenen Interpretationsversuch', *Goethe-Jahrbuch*, 111, 171–85.

Part III

Faust: Romantic Intertexts

6 'Much in the mode of Goethe's Mephistopheles': *Faust* and Byron

Fred Parker

Visiting Byron in Greece in 1824, the year of his death, George Finlay reported that although Byron had no German to speak of, 'he was perfectly acquainted . . . with Goethe in particular, and with every passage of *Faust*' (Butler 1956: 93). Byron's knowledge of *Faust I* dated from the autumn of 1816, when Matthew Lewis, author of the sensational Gothic novel *The Monk*, was staying with him in the Villa Diodati. Lewis, who had met Goethe in Weimar, spent several days translating *Faust* to him 'viva voce'. Byron recorded that he 'was naturally much struck with it' (Byron 1973–82, 3: 225); when he dedicated *Werner* to Goethe as 'the first of existing masters' (Byron 1980–93,[1] 6: 15) it was *Faust*, we may assume, that he had particularly in mind.

To understand just how Byron was struck by Goethe's great work, we may start with the allusion in the thirteenth canto of *Don Juan*. This comes in one of Byron's recurrent discussions of the process of aging. The narrator writes of how the passions of youth give way, as one passes 'life's equinoctial line' (*P*, 5: 526), to the preoccupations of middle age. In particular, the passion of love gives way to an involvement in politics, and the pleasures of hatred which it brings. This sounds like Byron's 'apologia' for the turn his own work has increasingly taken from the erotic to the social and political. However, the narrator distances himself from *all* such passionate involvement, and he does so in terms which recall the trajectory of Goethe's own poetic career, as Byron would have heard it described by Madame de Staël. In *De l'Allemagne* she wrote that Goethe had no longer that overwhelming ardor that inspired *Werther*, although the warmth of his thoughts was still sufficient to give life to everything. 'It might be said that he is not affected by life and that he describes it only as a painter: he attaches more value now to the pictures which he offers us than to the emotions which he feels. Time has made him a spectator' ('le temps l'a rendu spectateur') (Staël 1968, 1: 190).

> For my part, I am but a mere spectator,
> And gaze where'er the palace or the hovel is,
> Much in the mode of Goethe's Mephistopheles;
>
> But neither love nor hate in much excess;
> Though 'twas not once so. If I sneer sometimes,
> It is because I cannot well do less,

> And now and then it also suits my rhymes.
> I should be very willing to redress
> Men's wrongs, and rather check than punish crimes,
> Had not Cervantes, in that too true tale
> Of Quixote, shown how all such efforts fail.
> (P, 5: 527)

The devil of tradition is full of hate, for God and for mankind. Milton's Satan tells the sun how he hates his beams, and is driven throughout by the passion of envy. He is nothing if not passionate in his anguished revolt. But Goethe's Mephistopheles is diabolical in his seeming indifference, rather than his malice. The characteristic note is struck from the very beginning, in the 'Prologue in Heaven' ('Prolog im Himmel'). (The translator here is Shelley.)

> THE LORD. Have you no more to say? Do you come here
> Always to scold, and cavil, and complain?
> Seems nothing ever right to you on earth?
> MEPHISTOPHELES. No, Lord! I find all there, as ever, bad at best.
> Even I am sorry for man's days of sorrow;
> I could myself almost give up the pleasure
> Of plaguing the poor things. (1824: 396)

Mephistopheles' sympathy with suffering mankind is strictly limited, of course; 'the poor things' is primarily an expression of contempt, as well as a reproach to God for the poor design of his human creation. But still, the clear suggestion is that Mephistopheles has no enthusiasm for his task of tormenting mankind, which he performs as a function of the general badness of things, rather as Byron, as satirist, 'punishes crimes' only because he despairs of any more positive intervention, and sneers only when the rhyme requires it, and because he 'cannot well do less'. Byron's pose of disenchantment and detachment precisely catches the tone of Goethe's devil. The flippancy, the nonchalance, speaks of a deeper negativity; if this is malice, it is a weary malice, 'faute de mieux'.

There is more to be said about Mephistopheles than this, and we shall return to the question of his involvement in a substantial evil. But for the moment, I want to explore the possibility that Byron's reference to Mephistopheles points not only to a coincidence of outlook, but to a moment of encounter and influence that changed him as a writer. Byron has, at all points in his career, many styles: but the difference to which he himself here calls attention, between his signature style and stance (the two are inextricable) in the poetry that made him famous—a mode of passionate declamation—and the dry, ironic, sardonic voice of *Don Juan*, has been much remarked. The change is commonly associated with the effects of exile and of Italy, rather than attributed to any literary influence, although Jerome McGann has sought to link it to Byron's reappraisal of Milton and the figure of Milton's Satan (1976: 23–46). There will, of course, have been many factors in play here, and one might have to assume that Byron felt a deep personal affinity with the devil to explain how Goethe's radically different way of imagining that figure could have opened new possibilities for him. That is not in itself at all implausible. But whatever the biographical truth, it is in any case suggestive that Byron himself, in identifying a turning point in his career, should have associated this with 'the mode of Mephistopheles'.

The work that represents that earlier mode of 'excess', but which was nevertheless written under the sign of *Faust*, is *Manfred*. This was begun in the weeks immediately following Lewis' visit, and shows both how strongly *Faust* had gripped Byron's imagination, and how little he had yet begun to assimilate the part played by Mephistopheles within it. The opening scenes, in particular, closely recall Goethe: Manfred is sitting, like Faust, in a 'Gothic' room at night, passionately unsatisfied by all his knowledge. He rehearses the Faustian starting-point in terms that show how perfectly this had meshed in Byron's mind with his existing fascination with the Fall, and with the consciousness that heroically endures and resents its fallen condition:

> The Tree of Knowledge is not that of Life.
> Philosophy, and science, and the springs
> Of wonder, and the wisdom of the world,
> I have essayed, and in my mind there is
> A power to make these subject to itself—
> But they avail not.
>
> (P, 4: 53)

Manfred, like Faust, invokes the supernatural, calling up spirits that might satisfy his desire. As in *Faust*, they do not give him what he seeks; like Faust, he contemplates suicide, and is barely deflected from taking the fatal step. What torments him is not only the emptiness of 'Knowledge', but also a more specific remorse; Byronic heroes are regularly haunted by some obscure act of crime in their past, but nowhere else is this so clearly identified as the destruction of the beloved. 'I loved her, and destroy'd her!' (*P*, 4: 74), Manfred declares, in a line which—whatever its roots in Byron's own experience—precisely summarizes the Gretchen tragedy. It is striking that Byron so readily follows Goethe in an area which many readers have found difficult, recognizing the connectedness of such a tragedy and the Faustian condition. When Goethe reviewed *Manfred* in *Kunst und Altertum*, he dwelt at length on this act of past crime: 'there are two women whose ghosts haunt [Byron] relentlessly' (Goethe 1994: 176). (Could this be the fragment of an oblique confession, remembering Friederike Brion and Lili Schönemann?) There is a sense in which Manfred can be said to begin the play where Faust ends his: what Manfred seeks from the spirits of earth and air which he calls up is 'oblivion', that forgetting and healing of the trauma of the past which is, in fact, granted to Faust at the start of Part II. Byron could not have known this, and the coincidence of idea attests all the more strongly to the resonance that Goethe's work held for him.

Yet the oblivion that Manfred seeks is denied him, in a way that shows how far Byron was, in his first immediate response to *Faust*, from fully assimilating the mode of Mephistopheles. The passage in which Manfred calls up the spirits closely recalls Faust's conjuration of the 'Erdgeist', the Earth-Spirit; neither protagonist gets what they seek from the encounter, and as Faust 'collapses', so Manfred '*falls senseless*' (Goethe 1972:^{2} 514; *P*, 4: 59). But they do so for opposite reasons. The Earth-Spirit declares itself as the dynamic, ever-changing principle of the totality of life, embracing 'birth and grave—an eternal sea—weaving the living fabric of divinity at the loom of time'. Faust greets its appearance with rapture, and with an impulse of identification: 'Spirit of activity, how near I feel myself to you!', but this presumptuousness meets with an immediate rebuff: 'You resemble the Spirit that you comprehend—not me!' (*F*, 501–13). The spirit disappears; Faust collapses in an agony of chagrin; and the bathos of the actual is consolidated by the arrival of Wagner, who has heard

Faust 'declaiming', as he puts it— 'reading a Greek tragedy, perhaps?' (*F*, 522–3). It is a moment of rejection that burns itself into Faust's consciousness. The spirit that he truly comprehends—and that he therefore resembles—is not the Earth-Spirit, sublime totality of things, but Mephistopheles, the spirit of negation and denial, who is necessarily only ever 'a part', as he himself tells Faust (*F*, 1349), and can never give access to the whole. Indeed, it is the approach to the Earth-Spirit that *generates* Mephistopheles, as aspiration induces bathos, and affirmation induces negation, by a kind of necessary reaction, a rhythm that repeats itself throughout the work. This becomes explicit in Faust's later address to the 'sublime Spirit' (*F*, 3217):

> Oh, but now I feel how nothing comes to perfection for human beings. Along with this joy, which brings me ever closer to the gods, you gave me that companion, whom already I can no longer do without—even though his cold mockery belittles me in my own eyes, and with a word turns all your gifts to nothing. (*F*, 3240–6)

But in *Manfred* there is no such belittling. Faust's mortification was reinforced by the calculated bathos in Goethe's presentation. But Manfred's stature is only enhanced by his encounter with the supernatural; he passes out not because the spirits leave him (they don't) but at the intensity of his own suffering, when he sees in the vision they present to him the woman whom he loved and destroyed. The spirits then discover that there is nothing they could contribute to that suffering, since he is himself his 'proper Hell' (*P*, 4: 61). This concedes the truth of what he had already told them:

> The mind, the spirit, the Promethean spark,
> The lightning of my being, is as bright,
> Pervading, and far-darting as your own,
> And shall not yield to yours, though coop'd in clay!
> (*P*, 4: 58)

This is definitively reasserted at the end of the play. When, as in the Faust legend, the devil arrives to claim his soul, Manfred sends him and his fellow demons most tremendously packing. 'Back to thy hell!'

> What I have done is done; I bear within
> A torture which could nothing gain from thine:
> The mind which is immortal makes itself
> Requital for its good or evil thoughts—
> Is its own origin of ill and end—
> And its own place and time . . .
> I have not been thy dupe, nor am thy prey—
> But was my own destroyer, and will be
> My own hereafter.—Back, ye baffled fiends!
> The hand of death is on me—but not yours!
> (*P*, 4: 102)

Manfred is clearly a Faustian figure, but one whose posture of rebellion and anguished egotism are unequivocally (if melodramatically) heroic. It is a Faust who has never met Mephistopheles. His affiliation is, instead, partly to Prometheus, and partly to Satan of *Paradise Lost*, for whom, also, 'the mind is its own place' (Milton 1998: 76). Satan stands behind many of Byron's brooding protagonists: charismatic yet profoundly isolated figures, exiles or outlaws from conventional society, alienated by the combination of their superior nobility of mind and some obscure act of crime in their past, despising weakness in others as themselves, and disdainful of life itself in its failure to sustain their desires. This Satanic affiliation—the titanic assertion of individual mind, the heroic gesture as compensation for all—was not to be all at once supplanted by Mephistopheles, whose presence can be felt in *Manfred* only in the stridency of the resistance he provokes. In his review, Goethe wrote that Byron 'has used motifs [from *Faust*] which suited his purpose in his own way, with the result that none is the same anymore' (Goethe 1994: 175). That Byron should have reconfigured precisely the Earth-Spirit encounter—the moment when Faust is brought up against his own littleness—as a tribute to Manfred's indomitable mind, can perhaps be understood as an act of resistance to Mephistopheles' deglamorizing, dispassionate gaze.

In his classic essay 'Byron and Goethe', Giuseppe Mazzini argued that Byron's heroes embody the absolutely free, but desperately solitary, individual; each is 'Faust, but without the compact that submits him to the enemy; for the heroes of Byron make no such compact' (Mazzini 1870, 6: 79). In illustration, Mazzini invokes Manfred together with Byron's Cain, since each refuses to kneel to the powers of darkness. That much is true: but *Cain* is a very different work. Written in 1821, when *Don Juan* was well under way, *Cain* is a work which has admitted the influence of Mephistopheles, rather as Cain himself, although he refuses to worship Lucifer, is nevertheless profoundly influenced by his conversation. This is not to say that Byron's Lucifer sounds consistently like Mephistopheles. But they are strikingly comparable in two respects: the negativity which they express, and the ambivalence with which that negativity is represented.

To begin, first, with the negativity. 'I am the Spirit who always denies', Mephistopheles famously introduces himself to Faust,

and rightly so: for everything that comes into being is worthy only of destruction. It would be better, if it never came into being at all! So, what you call sin, destruction, and, in a word, evil, is the element I work in. (*F*, 1338–44)

This spirit of denial is potent in *Faust*. The idea of intellectual vocation, the pleasures of the senses, communion with the natural world, the rapture of passionate love, even the notion of a heroic suicide—all shrink and wither under Mephistopheles' ironic intelligence. This, in Byron's phrase, is what it means to be 'a mere spectator', without the love and hate that come from involvement, seeing things instead with a kind of sublime, corrosive objectivity.

Lucifer, too, offers Cain objective knowledge—knowledge as disenchantment. In the central act of the drama Lucifer takes Cain out into the immensities of the universe, in a great tour through time and space. What he shows him on this tour is the utter insignificance of human life when seen in the long perspectives of astronomy and geological time: he reveals to him the existence of millions of other worlds, the mutations of our own world over eons of distant time, and the shadowy underworld of the dead, which includes the exalted race of pre-Adamite beings, destroyed in geological catastrophe, in line with the recent scientific theories of Cuvier. If the universe looks beautiful, that, Lucifer explains, is merely the effect of distance, promoting delusion—and when Cain opposes to this denial of beauty's substantial reality the loveliness of Adah, his wife and sister, Lucifer replies that her beauty too will pass away, with so much the greater loss for those who cherish it. It is a bleak education, which Cain is inclined to resent:

> CAIN. And to what end have I beheld these things
> Which thou hast shown me?
> LUCIFER. Didst thou not require
> Knowledge? And have I not, in what I show'd,
> Taught thee to know thyself?
> CAIN. Alas! I seem
> Nothing.
> LUCIFER. And this should be the human sum
> Of knowledge, to know mortal nature's nothingness. (*P*, 6: 273)

What connects Byron with Goethe here is the modernity of the idiom in which their devils speak; both command a post-Enlightenment critical consciousness, clearly emancipated from the theological supernaturalism in which the Faust story originates, and standing quite apart from the literary supernaturalism which invoked the devil in contemporary Gothic fiction. Such fiction can be cogently interpreted as the rising up of fears and powers repressed or neglected by Enlightenment rationality. But about Lucifer and Mephistopheles there is nothing of the uncanny or the repressed; they give us, so to speak, the devil seen by daylight. Mephistopheles' ironic consciousness extends to his own role as devil. In the 'Witch's Kitchen' ('Hexenküche') scene he declines the name of Satan, as a figure 'consigned long ago to the book of fables—though humans are no better off: they are rid of the Evil One, but the evil ones remain' (*F*, 2507–9). Mephistopheles knows perfectly well how humans use the devil as scapegoat for their own weaknesses and crimes. When Faust is gripped, belatedly enough, by horror at the consequences for Gretchen of their relationship, he turns on Mephistopheles in passionate reproach, addressing him for the first time as the monstrous figure of evil familiar from tradition and from nightmare ('Roll your devilish eyes furiously in your head'), as if trying to force the register of the play into that of Gothic horror: but he has no reply to Mephistopheles' calmly lethal response: 'Why join with us, if you can't carry it through? ... Who was it, who ruined her? I or you?' (*F*, 'Trüber Tag—Feld' 35–6, 49–50). Byron's Lucifer also knows how to detach himself from his traditional role as tempter to sin. 'I tempt none,/Save with the truth' (*P*, 6: 238), he declares. What he does is little more than offer Cain truths that reinforce and corroborate his initial discontent: the devil's main contribution is to assure Cain that he, the devil, has not contributed to the current painful state of things. When Adam and Eve ate from the tree of the knowledge of good and evil, Lucifer firmly points out, it was God who was really the tempter, 'planting things prohibited within/The reach of beings innocent, and curious/By their own innocence' (*P*, 6: 238).

> CAIN. But didst thou tempt my parents?
> LUCIFER. I?
> Poor clay! what should I tempt them for, or how?
> CAIN. They say the serpent was a spirit.
> LUCIFER. Who
> Saith that? It is not written so on high:
> The proud One will not so far falsify,
> Though man's vast fears and little vanity

> Would make him cast upon the spiritual nature
> His own low failing. The snake was the snake—
> No more. (*P*, 6: 239)

By invoking what is literally written in Genesis, Lucifer accentuates the problem of evil in its sharpest form.

Such passages gave enormous offence. Byron's scandalized readership found it hard to see that he could give such an intelligent voice to the devil without identifying with him altogether.[3] But those who assumed Lucifer to be transparently a spokesman for Byron were missing the finesse of the dramatic situation. The demystifying analysis of the all-too-human motives that construct ideas of the devil as instigator to evil is being offered by the devil himself. In deconstructing the idea of the tempter, is Lucifer acting as tempter indeed? Could the discovery that the traditional narrative of the devil is mere superstition be itself the forbidden knowledge that reinstates the Fall in something like its original form? Crucial here is the way that Byron keeps Lucifer's motives indeterminate, and for this he had the model of *Faust*. In both works the devil speaks with considerable force as a cynic and an ethical nihilist, whose view of life denies it all ultimate value and significance. Yet both works conclude with an act felt to be charged with the greatest significance: the killing of Abel, the fate of Gretchen. How are these two things related? What has the devil's presence to do with the evil done? Mephistopheles rejuvenates Faust in preparation for a life of sexual license, yet it is crucially unclear whether he actively instigates the seduction of Gretchen, whom Faust appears to meet by chance, and we can never be sure how much of what follows is engineered or even foreseen by the devil. His intentions elsewhere are equally hard to ascertain. Although he tells us in a rare soliloquy that he proposes to destroy Faust by leading him into a life of dissipation which will exacerbate his torment of unfulfillment, this plan makes no sense in relation to Faust's wager that he can never be brought to a moment of complete contentment. By Plan A, Mephistopheles should be scheming to frustrate Faust's desires; by Plan B, to fulfill them; and this ambiguity only compounds our doubt as to whether, most of the time, Mephistopheles is scheming against Faust at all, or simply offering his cynical commentaries because that is how—in his view—things truly are, and acting in response to Faust's circumstances and demands with that chilling ultimate indifference which is his trademark. We may wonder: is his detachment in fact the mask for his evil or are those flashes of malice the imperfectly digested remnants of a superseded conception? But this uncertainty is not resolved. The palimpsest or double-exposure effect here may well have originated in the layering processes of composition over thirty years, but it is preserved in the published version as, I think, a stroke of art.

Byron maintains a similar crucial ambiguity in his representation of Lucifer, for we cannot tell whether the devil means well or ill. There are passages where Lucifer seems to speak as the play's 'raisonneur', and acts rather like some rationalist of the eighteenth-century Enlightenment in encouraging his audience—Cain—to emerge from a state of mere superstition. He rebuts the notion that the evils of the human condition are the work of the devil; he reveals the traditional conception of the devil as the projection of our anxieties; and he urges Cain to test the motives to piety against the realities of his own experience. Like a true son of the Enlightenment, Lucifer encourages Cain to open his eyes and think for himself, and speaks of the joy of knowledge and the autonomy of intellect.

> *One good* gift has the fatal apple given—
> Your *reason*:—let it not be over-sway'd
> By tyrannous threats to force you into faith
> 'Gainst all external sense and inward feeling:
> Think and endure,—and form an inner world
> In your own bosom—where the outward fails;
> So shall you nearer be the spiritual
> Nature, and war triumphant with your own.
> (P, 6: 275)

These are Lucifer's last words in the play, his valediction to Cain. They do not sound like an instigation to evil.

Yet what follows on from this enlightenment, and is to some indeterminate degree its consequence, is death and anguish. Was this foreseen and intended by Lucifer? It is impossible to say. He does not suggest the murder, though he does pointedly put Abel's irritatingly acceptable piety into Cain's mind. When he speaks to Cain of 'the joy/ And power of knowledge', it is not only as a child of the Enlightenment, but also with an obliquely sinister exhilaration, a dark investment in that sense of *power*.

> Nothing can
> Quench the mind, if the mind will be itself
> And centre of surrounding things—'tis made
> To sway.
> (P, 6: 239)

This is very different from the calm confidence with which Kant proposes the autonomy of intellect, or the idealism with which Shelley (in some moods) affirms the liberation of the spirit. It identifies enlightenment—or more precisely, the realization of the vigor and freedom of the individual mind—as a Faustian compact, as the devil's bargain. If Lucifer's commentary is, much of the time, convincingly disinterested, there are also passages where he is glad to reinforce Cain's alienation from God, whom he acknowledges as his eternal adversary. He appears sincere in suggesting that a short course in nihilism will have a certain anesthetic value for suffering mankind—understanding the 'nothingness' of human life will spare Cain's children 'many tortures' (P, 6: 273–4)—but if so he misses the way that nihilism itself is painful for human beings, who cannot detach themselves from the conditions of creation with the devil's sublime contempt.

LUCIFER. I pity thee who lovest what must perish.
CAIN. And I thee who lov'st nothing. (P, 6: 270)

Lucifer does not instigate the murder: but the knowledge of 'nothingness' that he gives Cain sharpens his discontent, exacerbating his already dangerous and unreconciled mood.

As a result, in the final act he addresses God in terms full of grudge and virtual accusation; unsurprisingly, his sacrifice is rejected; infuriated, he goes to destroy Abel's altar in repudiation of such a God; and when Abel persists in defending it, strikes him down. The murder is clearly to some degree the consequence of his colloquy with Lucifer—Goethe remarked on the extraordinary beauty of Byron's handling of the motivation (Eckermann 1976: 251)—but we cannot feel sure that it was a necessary or an intended consequence. One effect of this is to give Cain a certain genuinely tragic stature in his remorse and self-horror; there is, truly, no-one else to blame. But more importantly, it also allows us to keep open imaginative relations with the devil, neither demonizing nor yet identifying with the nihilistic intelligence which he offers.

When defending his representation of Lucifer against the storm of protest it aroused, Byron's mind went not simply to *Faust*, but to the 'Prologue in Heaven' in particular.

> What would the Methodists at home say to Goethe's 'Faust'? His devil not only talks very familiarly *of* Heaven, but very familiarly *in* Heaven. What would they think of the colloquies of Mephistopheles and his pupil, or the more daring language of the prologue, which no one will ever venture to translate? (Medwin 1966: 130)

Shelley, in fact, was working on a translation of the Prologue, intended for the first number of *The Liberal*, the radical journal founded by Byron, Shelley and Leigh Hunt. The plan was for Shelley's *Faust* translations—of the Prologue and 'Walpurgis Night' ('Walpurgisnacht')—to accompany a new poem by Byron, *The Vision of Judgment*. *The Vision* is a wonderfully sharp and funny response to, and parody of, Southey's *A Vision of Judgment*, which had solemnly related the poet laureate's vision of the ascension of George III into heaven. Byron's poem is set outside heaven's gate; angels and devils dispute what is to be done with the soul of George, given his abysmal political record, but when Southey himself turns up to testify neither Satan nor the Archangel Michael can endure to listen to his poetry, and in the ensuing chaos King George slips unobserved into heaven.

In the event, the publication of the Prologue was thought too dangerous. What the intended juxtaposition would have made clear to contemporary readers is the close connection between Byron's *Vision* and Goethe's 'Prologue in Heaven'. What both works have in common is not only their setting, but the audacious familiarity with which they address their divine subject-matter. There is one passage in particular, in which the significance of that familiarity is expressed, and Byron shows how intimately he is responding to the spirit of the Prologue. The passage is not part of the topical satire; it describes the encounter of Michael and Satan.

> He and the sombre, silent Spirit met—
> They knew each other both for good and ill;
> Such was their power, that neither could forget
> His former friend and future foe; but still
> There was a high, immortal, proud regret
> In either's eye, as if 'twere less their will
> Than destiny to make the eternal years
> Their date of war, and their 'Champ Clos' the spheres.
>
> But here they were in neutral space: we know
> From Job, that Satan hath the power to pay
> A heavenly visit thrice a year or so;
> And that 'the Sons of God', like those of clay,

> Must keep him company; and we might show,
> From the same book, in how polite a way
> The dialogue is held between the Powers
> Of Good and Evil—but 'twould take up hours ...
>
> The spirits were in neutral space, before
> The gate of heaven; like eastern thresholds is
> The place where Death's grand cause is argued o'er,
> And souls despatched to that world or to this;
> And therefore Michael and the other wore
> A civil aspect: though they did not kiss,
> Yet still between his Darkness and his Brightness
> There passed a mutual glance of great politeness.
>
> (*P*, 6: 322f)

The manner of invoking Job, and the idea of polite relations between the devil and his opposite, are unmistakably after Goethe. The book of Job has, of course, its own Prologue in Heaven. Satan, there, is not yet what he will become in the later tradition: the great enemy of God and man. Instead, he is part of the court of heaven, working in the role of adversary (which is what 'satan' means), a kind of official tester and prosecutor, adversary to Job in questioning the depth of his virtue and in putting him to the test. This will mean the infliction of great and undeserved suffering on earth, of a kind that would seem to demand for its comprehension the hypothesis of some ultimate force of evil. The book of Job as a whole registers this demand with unforgettable power. Yet Satan, although a semi-freelance who roams the earth with disconcerting independence, and despite all the evil connotations which will come to attach themselves to his name and role, is clearly working for God, under license: he suggests the persecution of Job, but it is God who allows him to prosecute it.

Byron's version retains and amplifies this notion of an imaginable liaison between the forces which we would normally think of as eternally opposed. In the special imaginative conditions of 'neutral space', a recognition is possible of the likeness that underlies, or complicates, the great opposites of Good and Evil. At one level, the passage is simply a wicked teasing of the binary orthodoxy of Southey, with his confident allocations of salvation and damnation, and his recent anathematizing of Byron as head of the 'Satanic school' (Rutherford 1970: 181) in poetry. But the unexpected seriousness of the comedy takes it far beyond topical satire. Outside the moment of the poem awaits the idea of an ultimate dichotomy, a final judgment; but meanwhile there can be a civilized meeting between Michael and Satan. It is 'both for good and ill' that they know each other, a knowledge of good and evil as intertwined that weaves that dichotomy into a different pattern. Byron here is drawing intimately on Goethe's Prologue. What I have been describing as the ambiguity that attaches to Mephistopheles concerns not only his intentions, but also what may be called his ultimate ethical orientation. He famously describes himself to Faust as 'a part of that power that always wills evil, and achieves good' (*F*, 1335–6). In Part I, it is for the 'Prologue in Heaven' to suggest what this might mean. There, as in Job, the devil's activity is shown to be licensed by God, who is in no anxiety as to the experiment: error, he declares, is an inevitable part of that striving that marks a good man's dim consciousness of the right path. And although mildly exasperated by Mephistopheles' perpetual fault-finding with the course of life on earth, he can still strike the genial, cordial note. 'I have never hated your kind. Of all the spirits of denial, a rogue like you is the least of a burden to me' (F, 337–9). What is suggested here is a possible reassimilation of the devil into the larger, productive functioning of the whole. In this positive scenario the roguish kind of negativity is ultimately salutary; Mephistopheles, while willing evil, produces good; and Faustian discontent will accordingly escape its traditional end in damnation (as indeed it does at the end of *Faust II*, published twenty-four years after Part I).

This affirmative vision hangs, however, by a thread. Even in the Prologue Mephistopheles is allowed a strongly independent dramatic life. If God regards him with tolerant condescension, at the end of the scene Mephistopheles meets that attitude with a certain irresistible familiarity of his own:

> From time to time I visit the old fellow,
> And I take care to keep on good terms with him.
> Civil enough is this same God Almighty,
> To talk so freely with the Devil himself.
> (Shelley, 1824: 398; F, 350–3)

'Civil enough' is Shelley's equivalent for 'gar hübsch' (F, 352), literally 'pretty', 'really rather sweet'. Shelley's choice of word finely brings out what is clearly implied in the German: the idea of the Lord's *good manners* in receiving and speaking so openly with his social inferior. The liaison between God and the devil is audaciously figured as (merely) a habit of politeness, which keeps on speaking terms two individuals who differ strongly in their attitudes, their interests and their position in the world. It is a fragile bond, and Mephistopheles' feline tribute may well suggest something vulnerable or unwise in God's sublime tolerance of activity which might otherwise be called evil. When Mephistopheles tells us that he takes care to keep on good terms with him, this reminds us that he could, in fact, break with him, and that other stories tell us that he has already done so, and there is in that cool ironic self-possession something still to be fully reckoned with. Nevertheless, the compliment on God, 'civil enough', is itself civil enough; the social decencies are upheld, and grippingly so, because of the degree of potential conflict which they negotiate. Byron has reimagined all this in his own terms, while capturing the spirit of the original with marvelous success. The possibility, indeed the actuality, of real conflict is clear; Satan and Michael have their back-history in *Paradise Lost*. The tension between them is figured, wittily, in terms of social class and hierarchy: Satan nods to his ancient friend with the restrained courtesy, we are told, with which a Castilian nobleman from a great family, but fallen on hard times, might greet a 'nouveau riche', 'a mushroom rich civilian' (P, 6: 323). Their 'great politeness', therefore, is everything; they wear, like Mephistopheles and the Lord, 'a civil aspect'; and an entire poetic could be extrapolated from the 'mutual glance' that temporarily holds in relationship Michael and 'the other'.[4] The other, crucially, remains itself—'they did not kiss'—and there is in this eternal alienation matter for a great regret. Satan will soon return, without enthusiasm, to his role as the enemy and accuser of mankind, just as Byron in a few stanzas will resume his role as polemical satirist, but in the special conditions of 'neutral space' it is possible to feel how one can consort rather intimately with the devil's point of view, without, quite, being taken over by it. This is communicated by the exuberant wickedness, or mock-wickedness, of the writing,

Byron's impudent familiarity with matters of heaven and hell. It is notable that Goethe was a great admirer of the *Vision*; he declared to Crabb Robinson in 1829 that here 'Byron has surpassed himself' (Robinson 1869, 2: 436).

When Byron wrote *The Vision of Judgment*, he had already published the first five cantos of *Don Juan*, the great work which was to occupy him until the end of his life, and in which the narrator looks on and comments, at least some of the time, in the mode of Mephistopheles. It is very possible that the choice of subject—as well as its handling—was more or less directly influenced by *Faust*. The Don Juan story has often been recognized as a kind of comic analogue to that of Faust: each deals with an insatiable protagonist whose desires lead him to transgress the established moral codes in ways which elicit a complex response of admiration and disapproval, and which lead in the end to his death and damnation. (When Goethe asked himself what kind of music could possibly be appropriate for the setting of *Faust*, he thought of *Don Giovanni* [Eckermann 1976: 313].) Like Goethe, moreover, Byron calls the traditional outcome into question: Juan, whom we meet at the very start of his sexual career, is too naïve, too young, and altogether too much seduced rather than seducing, to be a credible candidate for hell. The early cantos in particular refer frequently to damnation, but always with a lesser or greater degree of irony: when Byron promises that in canto twelve he means to show 'the very place where wicked people go', this later turns out, perhaps unsurprisingly, to be London. For Southey, such comic insouciance, flouting the moral decencies, was proof that it was the poet himself who was really damned: *Don Juan* moved him to denounce Byron's 'Satanic spirit of pride and audacious impiety, which still betrays the wretched feeling of hopelessness wherewith it is allied' (Rutherford 1970: 181). But this failed to recognize how Byron's old identification with the Miltonic Satan had been supplanted by his new relationship with Mephistopheles. As a 'mere spectator' who has outgrown the tragedy of passionate excess, the Byronic narrator counterpoints the ardor of his protagonist with the knowing voice of disillusioned, barely amused, formidably worldly wise experience.

The process by which the adolescent Juan falls in love with Julia offers a relatively simple example of a movement that will recur, in increasingly charged and complex forms, throughout the poem. Juan pursues 'his self-communion with his own high soul', lost in his thoughts about the wonders of man, and nature, and the heavens—and also about Donna Julia's eyes:

> In thoughts like these true wisdom may discern
> Longings sublime, and aspirations high,
> Which some are born with, but the most part learn
> To plague themselves withal, they know not why:
> 'Twas strange that one so young should thus concern
> His brain about the action of the sky;
> If *you* think 'twas philosophy that this did,
> I can't help thinking puberty assisted.
>
> (*P*, 5: 38)

This may be compared with Mephistopheles' knowing comment on Faust's longing for the vision of female beauty that he saw in the witch's mirror: 'with that potion in your body, you'll soon be seeing Helen of Troy in every woman' (*F*, 2603–4). Mephistopheles speaks this couplet 'quietly', both to himself, and as a reflection to be shared with us, who become thereby complicit in this devaluation of erotic rapture. Similarly, Byron's mockery is not so much of Juan as of any reader— 'if *you* think . . .'—who might be inclined to take these sublime longings seriously. Mephistopheles' couplet concludes, and so appears to sum up, a sequence of alternating rhymes, as of course does the couplet which concludes Byron's 'ottava rima' stanza; and the heavy, derisive rhyme on 'Leibe'/'Weibe' ('body'/'woman') brings us down, irresistibly, to a terminal bathos—as, in its own way, does the facetiously throwaway four-syllable comic rhyme in Byron's couplet. The voice of denial speaks with compelling force: the sense of privileged insight, as manifested in perfectly controlled comic timing, is irresistible. It comes as no surprise, as we read on, to discover that these 'aspirations high' lead to a scene of marital infidelity realized as bedroom farce.

And yet: Mephistopheles, as he tells Faust at the start, is only and necessarily a part, and can never be the whole (*F*, 1349–78). It is a crucial detail that Faust sees the vision in the mirror *before* he drinks the witch's potion. This is not conclusive as to the value of the vision, for the mirror is itself part of the witch's paraphernalia: but even so, it is enough to introduce an ambiguity, a possibility that Mephistopheles' final lines do not comprehend Faust's rapture as entirely as he may suppose. In the immediately preceding lines he urges Faust to come away from the mirror, to turn to physical realities: the model of all beautiful women will soon be standing before him in the flesh. This seems, at one level, sensible and constructive, part of Mephistopheles' declared strategy of getting Faust out of his miserable study and into the wider world. Yet we also know that Mephistopheles regards this as a strategy for Faust's destruction: so his final couplet may not be so much the exposure of Faust's erotic rapture for what it really is, but a direction of it toward a form of actualization which will diminish it. The devil of nihilist irony may, after all, mask the old devil of malice. And beyond that, to complicate our perception still further, we are aware of the possibility—no more than that—that in willing what is evil, Mephistopheles may bring about what is good, that the actualization of Faust's vision in a real woman may, despite or even because of what seems reductive or diminishing, lead toward good as well as harm.

Does Byron's version of the Mephistophelean voice preserve this ambiguity? Does the spirit of negation keep open, at least, civil relations with his opposite? Francis Jeffrey, the most intelligent of Byron's hostile critics, thought not. The author of *Don Juan*, he wrote, not only laughs at all values as illusions, but does so in a peculiarly pernicious way:

> The moment after he has moved and exalted us to the very height of our conception, resumes his mockery at all things serious or sublime—and lets us down at once on some coarse joke, hard-hearted sarcasm, or fierce and relentless personality—as if . . . to demonstrate practically as it were, and by example, how possible it is to have all fine and noble feelings, or their appearance, for a moment, and yet retain no particle of respect for them—or of belief in their intrinsic worth or permanent reality. (Rutherford 1970: 203)

Among the examples which Jeffrey cites is the wonderfully moving letter which Julia writes to Juan after their parting: this gives us 'the holiest language of the heart' (Rutherford 1970: 203), but is contaminated by the bedroom farce which preceded it, and of course by the fit of seasickness that overcomes Juan while he reads it.

Certainly Byron exposes all things serious or sublime to the commentary of Mephistopheles. But it is not so certain that he rests there. Jeffrey assumes, somewhat against the grain of his perception of the poem's mobility and plurality of voice, that the 'fine feelings' are definitively annulled by the mockery, and that there is an essential Byron in the poem to whose nihilistic vision all roads lead. But this may be disputed. Goethe himself, reviewing the early cantos, described the poem as 'a work of boundless genius, manifesting the bitterest and most savage hatred of humanity, and then again penetrated with the deepest and tenderest love for mankind' (Rutherford 1970: 164), without apparently seeing one of these qualities as subordinated to the other. In the stanza quoted above, Juan's idealistic musings are palpably adolescent, but when in the first two lines the tendency of these is generalized beyond the immediate situation—'In thoughts like these true wisdom may discern/Longings sublime, and aspirations high'—the tone of 'true wisdom' refuses to resolve itself into sarcasm. Like Faust's looking into the mirror, it hints at a limit to the scope, the comprehensiveness, of the Mephistophelean knowingness with which the passage will end. In consequence, when in the rest of the stanza the register is brought down, line by line, until we arrive at open mockery in the final line, this is felt as a deliberate movement by the narrator, akin to Mephistopheles redirecting Faust's attention away from the mirror toward the immediately physical—or akin to the collapse into bathos which marks Faust's inability to comprehend the totality of the Earth-Spirit, in which all opposites coexist. What this means is that we respond to the knowing narrative voice *dramatically*, as a part of the poem, rather than the intelligence from which the poem proceeds. Our uncertainty as to the ultimate tendency of Mephistopheles' interventions is broadly parallel with our uncertainty as to whether this narrator is, at any moment, a comprehensively destructive cynic, or is waging an uninhibited but salutary war on cant. In the terms of the *Vision*, we may say that some flickering connection, some 'mutual glance', is maintained between the darkness and the brightness.

This indeterminacy or dramatic quality makes against closure. 'Nothing so difficult as a beginning/In poesy, unless perhaps the end', writes Byron at the start of canto four,

> For oftentimes when Pegasus seems winning
> The race, he sprains a wing, and down we tend,
> Like Lucifer when hurl'd from heaven for sinning;
> Our sin the same, and hard as his to mend,
> Being pride, which leads the mind to soar too far,
> Till our own weakness shows us what we are.
>
> But Time, which brings all beings to their level,
> And sharp Adversity, will teach at last
> Man,—and, as we would hope,—perhaps the devil,
> That neither of their intellects are vast:
> While youth's hot wishes in our red veins revel,
> We know not this—the blood flows on too fast;
> But as the torrent widens towards the ocean,
> We ponder deeply on each past emotion.
>
> (P, 5: 203)

What makes ending so difficult is the omnipresent possibility of bathos, of falling: a corrective reaction to the pride of Lucifer which may ultimately transform him into a different, more disillusioned form of devil. The bathos with which the Earth-Spirit met Faustian aspiration, which Byron could not in 1817 accept into *Manfred*, has been thoroughly assimilated here. Every idealistic, affirmative or lyrical movement in the poem calls out its negative, ironic countermovement, a voice taught by time and experience. 'As boy, I thought myself a clever fellow', Byron continues, but now 'the sad truth which hovers o'er my desk/ Turns what was once romantic to burlesque' (*P*, 5: 203–4). Such ironic awareness, we may note, is not terminal, or only hypothetically and improbably so; it makes ending difficult, closure almost inconceivable. Byron, like Goethe, takes a story whose protagonist is traditionally bound for hell, and treats it in such a way as to make such definitive ending peculiarly difficult to envisage. Goethe's resistance to concluding *Faust*—epitomized in his publication of the 1790 *Fragment* with the final scenes omitted, and his publication of the completed tragedy in 1808 with the resolute subtitle, *First Part of the Tragedy*—has its analogue in the endlessly digressive, open, non-consequential form of *Don Juan*. (A gesture of imitation may be detected in Byron's publication of *The Deformed Transformed* as a fragment, with a prefatory note announcing that the work is based 'partly on the "Faust" of the great Goethe. The present publication contains the two first Parts only, and the opening chorus of the third. The rest may perhaps appear hereafter' [*P*, 6: 517].)

This antiteleological impulse is central to the precarious hypothesis of Mephistopheles' positive function. In the 'Prologue in Heaven', God suggests that companionship with the devil—that is, with the roguish kind of spirit of negation, which is perhaps as good a short description of the narrator of *Don Juan* as any—is stimulus to activity; striving and negativity exist, it would seem, in a dynamic dialectic:

> The active spirit of man soon sleeps, and soon
> He seeks unbroken quiet; therefore I
> Have given him the Devil for a companion,
> Who may provoke him to some sort of work,
> And must create forever.
> (Shelley 1824: 398; *F*, 340–3)

Is the ultimate effect of Mephistopheles, then, *creative*? 'Must create forever' is Shelley's somewhat elevated rendering of 'muß als Teufel schaffen' (*F*, 343), where Walter Arndt, for example, has merely 'play the deuce' (*F* [2001], 343). In fact, the phrase admits of both emphases, indeed invites us to keep both in play. This idea of the devil as perpetual stimulus, is explored before our eyes in *Don Juan*: the ironic, skeptical, digressive qualities of the detached narrative voice— the mode of Mephistopheles—are felt both as keeping the poem going, and as guaranteeing it against anything that might be felt as a satisfactory conclusion. Bernard Beatty, one of the best modern critics of the poem, has inquired whether, in the later cantos, the poem is beginning to run down, as the narrative voice becomes increasingly predominant, while Juan does less and less; Beatty writes of the allusion to Mephistopheles, 'this sounds plausible enough until we recall that there is no Faust with whom this Mephistopheles can talk' (1985: 46). But to this it can be replied that Byron's extraordinary fluidity of tone itself constitutes a kind of dialogue. The accent, the point of view, are always changing; the effects of bathos and disenchantment are the opposite of teleological, for the nihilistic voice cannot be sustained for more than a line or two without beginning to become its own ironic parody. A narrator who can reflect that he looks on 'much in the mode of Goethe's Mephistopheles', cannot be identical with Mephistopheles; 'mode' carries a certain self-reflexive irony, the extravagance of the sentiment is self-aware, with a degree of comic effect, as the overtly facetious rhyming on 'Mephistopheles' refuses the responsibilities of closure. The narrative voice is a disillusioned voice, yes, but its mobility across a wide spectrum of forms of disillusionment—worldly wisdom, desolation, flippancy, contempt, reader-baiting wickedness, mock-innocence, the elegiac, the relishing of absurdity, moral rage—expresses, through the self-consciousness of its performance, that 'mutual glance' between opposed positions which suspends the absoluteness of their opposition. This mobility is in a real sense Faustian, if one recalls the terms of Faust's wager: Mephistopheles can claim him only if Faust ever feels such fulfillment in a moment of experience that he wishes it to last forever. Until that moment comes, the same incapacity for fulfillment that exposes him to the negativity of Mephistopheles, and that Mephistopheles sustains and symbolizes, also preserves him from Mephistopheles, and from the moment of a final judgment.

Readers have always been divided over whether the mobility of *Don Juan* speaks, finally, more of hollowness or of vitality. In the end, it is perhaps less important to settle that question than to recognize its significance. Can the spirit of negation be assimilated in a way that is ultimately fruitful, or, once admitted as a companion, will it insist on the last word? *Faust* explores that question in one way; Byron's whole poetic career, and the writing of *Don Juan* in particular, explores it in another, which was surely influenced, though to a degree impossible to ascertain with certainty, by his fateful encounter with Mephistopheles.

Notes

1 In subsequent references: *P*.
2 In subsequent references: *F*, followed by line number. Translations are my own, unless otherwise noted.
3 There is a useful anthology of responses in Steffan (1968: 330–426).
4 See McGann (1989: 38–64). McGann sees Byron's way of modulating between oppositions as calling into question Romantic ideals of self-integrity and identity, since these depend, by the Hegelian analysis, on the negation of 'Otherness, that which is not the subject . . . in the process of knowledge we call consciousness' (41).

Bibliography

Beatty, B. (1985), *Byron's Don Juan*. London: Croom Helm.
Butler, E. M. (1956), *Byron and Goethe: Analysis of a Passion*. London: Bowes and Bowes.
Byron (1973–82), *Letters and Journals*, L. A. Marchand (ed.), 12 v. London: John Murray.
— (1980–93), *The Complete Poetical Works*, J. J. McGann (ed.), 7 v. Oxford: Oxford University Press.
Eckermann, J. P. (1976), *Gespräche mit Goethe in den letzten Jahren seines Lebens*, E. Beutler (ed.). Munich: Deutscher Taschenbuch Verlag.
Goethe, J. W. (1972), *Faust*, E. Trunz (ed.). Munich: C. H. Beck.

— (1994), *Essays on Art and Literature*, J. Gearey (ed.). Princeton: Princeton University Press.
— (2001), *Faust. A Tragedy*, C. Hamlin (ed.), W. Arndt (trans.). New York: W. W. Norton.
Mazzini, G. (1870), *Life and Writings of Joseph Mazzini*, 6 v. London: Smith, Elder and Co.
McGann, J. J. (1976), *Don Juan in Context*. London: John Murray.
— (1989), *Towards a Literature of Knowledge*. Oxford: Oxford University Press.
Medwin, T. (1966), *Medwin's Conversations of Lord Byron*, E. J. Lovell (ed.). Princeton: Princeton University Press.
Milton, J. (1998), *Paradise Lost*, A. Fowler (ed.). Harlow: Longman.
Robinson, H. C. (1869), *Diary, Reminiscences, and Correspondence of Henry Crabb Robinson*, T. Sadler (ed.), 3 v. London: Macmillan.
Rutherford, A. (ed.) (1970), *Lord Byron: The Critical Heritage*. London: Routledge.
Shelley, P. B. (1824), *Posthumous Poems*. London: John and Henry Hunt.
Staël, G. de (1968), *De l'Allemagne*, S. Balayé (ed.), 2 v. Paris: Garnier-Flammarion.
Steffan, T. G. (1968), *Byron's Cain*. Austin: University of Texas Press.

7 'An orphic tale': Goethe's *Faust* Translated by Coleridge

Frederick Burwick

On 4 September 1820, Johann Wolfgang von Goethe wrote to his son August that Samuel Taylor Coleridge was translating *Faust*.[1] Because it seemed totally at odds with the available facts, Goethe's confident declaration has long been ignored by critics. No translation of *Faust* by Coleridge was known, and no source for Goethe's assertion has previously been identified. Coleridge, poet of the supernatural and demonic, was recognized as an influential mediator of German thought and was respected as translator of Friedrich Schiller's *Wallenstein*.[2] Many of his contemporaries—among them Henry Crabb Robinson, Sir Walter Scott and Percy Bysshe Shelley—declared that Coleridge was the poet best suited to the task.[3] Twice the attempt had been made by prominent publishers to engage Coleridge as translator of *Faust*: first by John Murray in August 1814, then by Thomas Boosey in May 1820. On both occasions, Coleridge submitted his plan on how the translation might best be conducted, proposing to translate the wide-ranging metrical variations in Goethe's text chiefly into dramatic blank verse, and insisting that his translation be published anonymously.[4] On both occasions there is evidence that Coleridge commenced the task diligently. In 1814, his efforts flagged after less than two months. In 1820, however, he stayed with the project, and his translation was published by Boosey in September, 1821.[5]

Why did Coleridge's accomplishment remain concealed throughout the intervening centuries? The primary factor was the anonymity, compounded by publication in a competitive market as one of six editions of *Faust* to appear between 1820 and 1823: George Soane's translation of some sixty lines as captions to Johann Heinrich Bohte's publication of *Extracts from Göthe's Tragedy of Faustus, explanatory of the plates by Retsch*, January 1820; John Anster's translation of excerpts in *Blackwood's Edinburgh Magazine*, June 1820; Boosey's edition of an anonymous prose translation by Daniel Boileau, illustrated with the Retzsch plates reengraved by Henry Moses, June 1820; Boosey's edition of the anonymous blank-verse translation by Coleridge, also with the reengraved plates, September 1821; Bohte's planned dual-language edition, with a complete translation by George Soane, consisted of only the first 576 lines in English when he sent a set of page proofs for review in the *London Magazine*, November 1821; Bohte sent a second set of the page proofs to Goethe, June 1822;[6] Lord Francis Leveson-Gower's *Faust* published by Murray, 1823; realizing that Soane would not complete the task, Bohte in 1823 published the German text of *Faust* without the parallel English translation.

Among these editions published by Blackwood, Bohte, Boosey and Murray, Coleridge's translation was one of the two anonymous translations published by Boosey. In the course of the nineteenth century Coleridge's translation was falsely attributed to George Soane and subsequently fell into obscurity. His insistence on anonymity was reinforced by his anxiety about its critical reception. Still wincing from William Hazlitt's harsh review of *Christabel*,[7] Coleridge lamented in 1820: 'There is little chance of any work having a fair chance *with my name*'.[8] Friedrich Johann Jacobsen, the commentator on English poets whom Goethe often consulted, also observed in 1820:

> Coleridge had a true paranoia of critics. While Lord Byron and Walter Scott found his Christabel good, he complained that the critics persecuted him so unmercifully that he saw their phantoms wherever he went.
>
> (Coleridge hat eine wahre Wasserscheu vor den Critikern. Er klagt, während Lord Byron und Walter Scott sein Christabel gut gefunden, verfolgte ihn die Critiker so unbarmherzig, daß er ihre Gestalten sehe, wo er gehe und stehe.)
> (1820: 222)

In spite of Coleridge's anxieties, the first published responses to his anonymous translation were relatively benign.

In the *European Magazine* ('R.' 1821: October), the reviewer found the translation, in spite of its 'fidelity', less powerful than it might have been. He complained, with good reason, that Margaret's Song, 'Meine Ruh' ist hin', was awkwardly translated as 'My peace of mind's ruined' (*F*, 3374–413). He granted, however, that the translator 'is evidently a great proficient . . . who seems to feel his subject every where else', and called attention to a passage where the translator 'shews us that it was in his power to do considerably better'. He referred to the passage where Coleridge turned from blank verse and adopted the tetrameter couplets of *Christabel* in describing the ascent of the Brocken (*F*, 3940–55):

> O'er the night a cloud condenses,
> Through the woods a rush commences,
> Up the owls affrighted start;
> Listen! how the pillars part,
> The ever-verdant roofs from under,
> Boughs rustle, snap, and break asunder!
> The trunks incline in fearful forms,
> Roots creak and stretch, as torn by storms
> In startling, and entangled fall,
> Upon each other rush they all,
> And through rent clefts and shattered trees,
> Now sighs and howls the rushing breeze.
> Hear'st thou voices in the air,
> Now far distant, and now near?
> Yes, the mountain's ridge along
> Sweeps a raging, magic song!

The reviewer was ecstatic:

> There is a wild rush in the above lines, which at once make them the very life they describe; they come upon the ear like the night blast over a bleak hill.

> Oh why are not all the other poems so translated, and so versified! Throughout the volume there is not the least hint at the translator, yet it is surely a work of which no man ought to be ashamed. Rumor says the author of Christabelle tried at it and resigned it.

The reviewer then revealed that 'the same worthy authority' also informed him that George Soane was to be Coleridge's 'successor in the undertaking'.⁹ The reviewer's 'worthy' informant had his facts backward: Soane had indeed been commissioned by Bohte to continue with a translation that would present Goethe's dramatic poem in its entirety. But it was Soane who had resigned the task, and, perhaps guessing it, the reviewer had in hand the work as completed by Coleridge.

The set of page proofs with Soane's translation were also sent to the *London Magazine* and were reviewed together with the anonymously published translation by Coleridge. The review was a part of the third installment of 'C.Van Vinkbooms, his dogma for dilettanti', a witty, casual and sometimes scurrilous commentary on importations of European arts and letters. The reviewer began by making the point that Soane was more an adaptor than a translator. Acknowledging the 'many alterations' in his version of Friedrich de la Motte-Fouqué's *Undine, or, The Spirit of the Waters* (staged at Covent Garden 23 April 1821), Soane 'modestly regretted that he had not made many more'. The reviewer then turned to Soane's work on *Faust*:

> Mr. S. is likewise engaged, *or ought to be so*, in the arduous task of pouring the poetry of Goethe from a German into an English vessel— I have 32 pages of it (the Faust) here in print, wherein he appears to have succeeded so far exceedingly well. No doubt the venerable John Wolfgang's inspection of his MS. has been of material utility, and will give his undertaking consequence in the eyes of the public.— 'Allow me to look at those sheets. Ah! this is a very good idea, the inserting of the original on the one side in oblong quarto so as to bind with the original etchings'. So, Soane has turned the sadly pleasing Ottava Rima dedication or address in the Spenserian Stanza. I am afraid he has caught the vulgar notion, that verse in which Tasso sang the woes of Erminia is more adapted to the ludicrous than the pathetic. (Anon. 1821a: 657)

By amending 'engaged' to '*ought to be so*', the reviewer hinted that Soane had in fact already lost enthusiasm for the task. The reviewer was aware, too, that Bohte had been in correspondence with Goethe about the dual-language edition to accompany the plates and intended to present him the same offering of thirty-two quarto pages. As well informed as he was about Bohte's plans for a second edition, he gives no hint that Coleridge was the translator of Boosey's second edition: 'Boosey has published a very pleasing abstract of this Labyrinthine poem, with copious and sufficiently faithful versions of blank verse'. In spite of the explanation in the preface, the reviewer considered the blank verse a misrepresentation of a work, 'written in the most varied metres, principally rhymed, and ... essentially lyrical'. Coleridge had earlier informed Murray of precisely this shortcoming: 'a large proportion of the work cannot be rendered in blank verse, but must be in wild *lyrical* metres'.¹⁰ Having already faulted Soane, as well, for altering Goethe's verse forms, 'Vinkbooms' argued that Soane's endeavor 'will better satisfy the inquisitive and thoughtful student in poetry who may be guiltless of German'. But for fidelity to the language, and to the cadences if not the meter, he granted superiority to Boosey's edition.

The Monthly Magazine featured a review section on the 'New Books' published during the previous month. On 1 June 1821, the reviewer summarized Shelley's *Queen Mab* as 'a continuous declamation, without either "rhyme or reason", and the speaker may pause where he will without injury to the sense or interruption to the monotonous flow of the harangue'. The reviewer went on to dismiss misguided critics who praised Shelley's 'powerful talents' as 'a set of dunces who cannot distinguish between sublimity and bombast,—between poetry and "prose run mad"'(Anon. 1821d: 460–1). The review of *Faustus* in the issue of 1 September 1821, mockingly speculated that the '"prose run mad"' in this translation might have been a hoax of the printer who 'ludicrously arranged' the prose as verse. The reviewer cited the 'Chorus of Invisible Spirits', lines 1607–26, answering the curse of Faustus. Hinting at the identity of the anonymous translator, the reviewer stated:

> We know, perhaps, but one individual in Europe who would be likely to succeed in giving a new dress to the profound thought and daring speculation, the biting sarcasm and deep pathos of this mighty poem. But these qualities, perhaps, the present translator has not perceived, and is content, as his readers must be (with the exception of a scene or two at the opening), to follow a connected tale of the plot, which has in itself nothing very inviting, and is important only as it has been made the vehicle of so much thought and poetry. (Anon. 1821b: 260)

The reviewer concluded with yet another hint at the translator's identity: 'We have said more of this production than it deserves, because we think we trace in it the same hand which has already cruelly disfigured one of the prettiest flowers of modern German literature' (Anon. 1821b: 261). Schiller's *Wallenstein* (1800) would not be referred to as 'one of the prettiest flowers'. The reviewer probably had in mind Coleridge's translation of Tieck's 'Herbstlied', which had appeared as 'Glycine's Song' in *Zapolya* (1815–16) (Coleridge 1912, 1, pt. 2: 922–3).

When Henry Colburn founded *The New Monthly Magazine* in 1821, he wanted a literary journal and therefore enlisted Thomas Campbell as his editor. During his nine years as editor, Campbell published his own poetry and his 'Lectures on Poetry' in its pages, as well as commissioned essays, prose and poetry. The result was a miscellany rather than a critical journal or a review (Elliot 1907–21: 143–6). Campbell travelled in Germany and frequently included articles and reviews on German literature. Not surprisingly, in the December issue appeared a 'Review of *Faustus from the German of Goethe*'.[11] The review was read with delight by Karl Ludwig von Knebel,[12] who prized *The New Monthly Magazine* as one of his 'beloved English journals' ('beliebte englischen Journalen') and had the issues sent to him in Jena.[13] Knebel immediately wrote to his 'Urfreund' Goethe to tell him that the English translation of *Faust* was warmly reviewed. He included this excerpt:

> The subjects represent some of the main passages in the tragedy—a work which very pathetically enforces the dire results of appetite and passion when foresaken by conscience and reason; and the scenes are addressed with a potent effect to the fancy by the visible agency of a demon, witches, etc.—the allegorical personifications of vice and folly. Some of the scenes might be considered, perhaps, too luxuriant, but when attentively reflected upon in connexion with the moral reasonings, illuminations, and miseries entailed in the accompanying analysis of the tragedy, they cannot fail of enforcing the value and beauty of moral rectitude, and the necessity of controlling the senses.[14]

The reviewer for *The New Monthly Magazine*, perhaps Campbell himself, was more concerned with the moral issues than with the poetic qualities of the translation, but his comments were positive.

Coleridge's anticipation of damning criticism was at least partially fulfilled by Thomas Carlyle in *The New Edinburgh Review* (January–April 1822).[15] Carlyle, who set forth his claim as a leading interpreter of German literature with his *Life of Schiller* (1821) and his translation of Goethe's *Wilhelm Meister* (1824) (Ashton 2005: 153–70), had no reservations about clearing the field of any rivals. Carlyle's relationship with Coleridge had been testy. In his *Life of Schiller*, published the year before his review of *Faustus*, Carlyle had declared Coleridge's *Wallenstein* 'the only sufferable translation from the German with which our language has been enriched' (Carlyle 1896–1907, 25: 151n.5). 'Sufferable' is not high praise. In June 1824, Carlyle presented to Coleridge a copy of his translation of *Wilhelm Meister*. Coleridge was already familiar with Goethe's novel, and had translated Mignon's 'Know'st thou the land' ('Kennst du das Land') in 1813 (Robinson 1938: 119–28; Coleridge 1912: 311). In October 1821, the month after his translation of Goethe's *Faust* was published, Coleridge considered following it with a translation of Goethe's *Wilhelm Meister* (Coleridge 1995, 2: 955). Elinor Shaffer argues persuasively that Coleridge's *Confessions of an Inquiring Spirit* (written between 1820 and 1824; published posthumously in 1840) were shaped by his reaction to Goethe's 'Bekenntnisse einer schönen Seele' and to Carlyle's translation, rather clumsily rendered as 'Confessions of a Fair Saint'. Coleridge's *Confessions*, a series of 'Letters to a learned and religious Friend', open with a reference to Carlyle's translation, 'developing it immediately into an account of his own experience, that of one who is "neither fair nor saint"'. Even after Coleridge proposes 'Confessions of a Beautiful Soul' as a preferable translation, he returns to Carlyle's 'fair' and 'saint' as terms that contrast more effectively with his own tormented state. 'Upon the spur of, and under the cover of criticism of, Carlyle's mistranslation', Shaffer declares, Coleridge 'appropriated Goethe's title and set out in a white heat of composition on his own "Confessions"' (Shaffer 2002: 148–52).

Whether or not he was aware that Coleridge was the translator, Carlyle was unable to sustain the harsh indictment with which he began his review of *Faustus*. After the first three paragraphs he turned to a summary of the work as he would like to see it more fully realized (*Abhandlung*, 10–32.). The opening paragraphs attack the translator with persistent undercutting: 'It is no translation of Faust; but merely a pretty full description of its various scenes'. The dialogue is 'rendered into clear and very feeble blank verse'. The translation commits no 'great violence to the meaning of the original', but it makes no 'attempt to imitate the matchless beauties of its diction' (*Abhandlung*, 8). Carlyle then protests that he

> felt mortified at seeing the bright aerial creations of Goethe metamorphosed into such a stagnant, vapid *caput motuum*: and we cannot forbear to caution our readers against forming any judgement of that great foreigner from this representative; or imagining that 'Faustus' affords even the faintest idea of the celebrated drama, the name of which it bears. (*Abhandlung*, 9)

As an example of the translator's distortion, Carlyle cites the translation of 'Bin ich der Flüchtling nicht/ ... / nach dem Abgrund zu' (*F*, 3347–51):

> Oh! am I not
> The fugitive—the houseless wanderer—

> The wild barbarian without an object?
> Or like a cataract that from rock to rock
> With eager fury leaps heralding ruin.

Carlyle objects here to an unwarranted mixing of metaphor: 'Poetic license, and the trammels of verse, are all that can be pleaded in extenuation of this and a thousand unhappy failures' (*Abhandlung*, 9). Unable to compile anything approximating 'a thousand unhappy failures', Carlyle identifies instead three mistranslations: First, 'Hör' auf mit deinem Gram zu spielen' (*F*, 1640) ought to have been translated 'Oh! cease to dally with your misery' and not 'O learn to dally with your misery'. Second, 'alle sechs Tagewerk' (*F*, 3289), as Carlyle points out, 'signifies the universe, not "a whole week's business"'. Third, 'Und dann die hohe Intuition/Ich darf nicht sagen wie—zu schließen' (*F*, 3291–2) are misconceived as 'and then the high, /The wond'rous intuition? (*with a grimace.*) I dare not/Proceed—'(*Abhandlung*,10).

Resting his case on these errors, Carlyle states: 'Perhaps we are too severe on this slender performance: but the sight of it renewed our wish to see Faust in an English dress'(*Abhandlung*, 10). Carlyle then abandons attention to the translation and commences his own commentary on Goethe's work (*Abhandlung*, 10–32), concluding with contrasts to Marlowe's *Faustus* and Byron's *Manfred* (*Abhandlung*, 30–1). Only once again does he excerpt a passage from the translation (*Abhandlung*, 19–20). It is the passage with Faust's curse (*F*, 1583–1606). Significantly, in his own oft-forestalled endeavor to translate *Faust*,[16] Carlyle's rendition of this same passage is the only excerpt he managed to publish (Carlyle 1832: 5). It is the lengthiest passage that he quotes from Coleridge's translation:

> Tho' from my heart's wild tempest
> A sweet remembered tone recovered me,
> And all my youth's remaining hopes responded
> With the soft echo of joys long gone by,
> Yet do I curse them all—all—all that captivates
> The soul with juggling witchery, and with false
> And flattering spells into a den of grief
> Lures it, and binds it there. Accursed be
> All the proud thoughts with which man learns to pamper
> His haughty spirit—cursed be those sweet
> Entrancing phantoms which delude our senses
> Cursed the dreams which lure us to the search
> Of fame and reputation—cursed all
> Of which we glory in the vain possession,
> Children and wife, and slave, and plough—accursed
> Be Mammon, when with rich and glittering heaps
> He tempts us to bold deeds, or when he smoothes
> The pillow of inglorious dalliance—
> Accursed be the grape's enticing juice
> Cursed be love, and hope, and faith—and cursed,
> Above all cursed, be the tame dull spirit
> Which bears life's evils patiently.

Carlyle rightly observed that this translation deviated from Goethe's language. Coleridge was not only translating Goethe's work into another language, but also into another poetic medium. In writing dramatic blank verse Coleridge had learned to martial his imagery in coherent patterns, and he had acquired certain habits of recurrent phrasing. Some recurrences are evident within different parts of the translation. For example, in addressing the Sign of the Macrocosm, Faustus asks: 'Who wrote this sign? it stills my *soul's wild warfare*' (*F*, 435). Later, when Mephistopheles taunts Faust with the fact that he had been ready to drink poison, Faust recalls that the church bells ringing in the Easter services had restored him.

> Wenn aus dem schrecklichen Gewühle
> Ein süß bekannter Ton mich zog,
> Den Rest von kindlichem Gefühle
> Mit Anklang froher Zeit betrog.
> (*F*, 1584–7)

Coleridge uses the same phrasing for taming the 'wild' action:

> Tho' from my heart's wild tempest
> A sweet remembered tone recovered me

In neither case are there words in Goethe's text that would prompt the phrase. But variations recur throughout Coleridge's work:

> *Remorse* (III.ii)
> ...A worse sorrow/Are *fancy's wild hopes* to a heart ...
> *Death of Wallenstein* (II.vi)
> ...incapable of compact,/Thy *heart's wild impulse* only dost thou ...
> *Fall of Robespierre* (Act I)
> ...endearment,/All sacrificed to *liberty's wild riot*.
> 'Ode to the Departing Year' (line 23)
> ...young-eyed Joys! advance! By *Time's wild harp*,
> 'Monody on the Death of Chatterton' (line 73)
> ...of vernal Grace,/And *Joy's wild gleams* that lighten'd o'er ...

In the very speech in which Faust describes how the bells of Easter rescued him from suicidal thoughts, he goes on to pervert the beatitudes of Christ's Sermon on the Mount (Mt. 5.3–11) into a series of curses, beginning with the words:

> So fluch' ich allem, was die Seele
> Mit Lock- und Gaukelwerk umspannt.
> (*F*, 1587–8)

In Coleridge's translation the curse is given a peculiarly Coleridgean turn. Coleridge's vocabulary, like Goethe's, is informed by the lore of curses and spells, as well as by the illusionist arts of swindlers and thieves. Goethe has 'Lock- und Gaukelwerk', 'Blend- und Schmeichelkräften'. Coleridge has 'juggling witchery . . . with false/And flattering spells', 'Entrancing phantoms which delude our senses'. 'Hexerei' is not a word that occurs at all in Goethe's *Faust*. *Witchery*, however, does recur in Coleridge's poetry, and it is used here with almost the same phrasing as in his translation, many years earlier, from Schiller: 'It mocks my soul with *charming witchery*' (*Piccolomini* II.vii.119). Striking in this parallel is not just the 'soul' imperiled by 'witchery', but the animation of that witchery by the active participles, 'juggling' and 'charming'. It is Coleridge's habit to empower witchery with a participle:'... *soothing witcheries*' ('Song of the Pixies', line 45); '... *floating witchery*' ('The Eolian Harp', line 20).

When he came to Faust's doubt, despair and curse, before signing the pact with Mephistopheles, Coleridge recognized the relevance of Job's despair, when his wife tells him to 'curse God and die' (Job 2.9). The litany of the 'cursed', eleven times repeated, darkly parodies the litany of the 'blessed' (the Beatitudes; Mt. 5.1–12). Coleridge had turned often to the literary rhetoric of the curse: the curse from the dead men's eyes in the *Rime of the Ancient Mariner*, Alhedra's curse in *Remorse*, and above all the mother's curse in *The Three Graves*, the 537-line ballad he had begun with Wordsworth in 1797 and completed in 1809.

If Coleridge's role as translator of *Faust* was effectively concealed in London, how could Goethe be fully informed in Weimar? This question could only be answered by searching through the vast collection of correspondence addressed to Goethe, a search made easier by concentrating on unpublished letters from London in 1820.[17] Both Bohte and Boosey were among the correspondents, as well as Johann Christian Hüttner, Goethe's major source of information on the cultural life of London.[18] When Henry Moses completed his reengravings of Retzsch's plates to *Faust*, Boosey had Hüttner forward a set to Goethe with an account of the prose translation. His curiosity aroused, Goethe asked Hüttner to make further inquiries:

> For sending the copper engravings of Faust have the kindness to thank in my name the congenial Mr. Boosey. I desire to see, as well, the sequel, especially the text. If I could learn who the author is, it would be very gratifying to me.
>
> (Für die überschickten Kupfer nach Faust haben Sie die Gefälligkeit in meinen Namen dem freundlichen Herrn Boosey zu danken. Ich bin verlangend auch die Folge zu sehen, besonders des Textes. Könnt ich erfahren, wer der Verfasser ist, so würde es mir sehr angenehm seyn.)[19]

That Daniel Boileau was the anonymous author of the prose translation was a confidence that Boosey did not betray.[20] On 22 August 1820, Hüttner replied to Goethe:

> The bookdealer Boosey & Co. find themselves very flattered, that his Excellency, the Privy Counsellor von Goethe is not unhappy with the copper engravings to Faust and the accompanying descriptions, and they have the honor to forward herewith the conclusion. This [publishing] House has consigned to us the accompanying letter, in which his Excellency will learn something of the anonymous author who translated the descriptions.
>
> (Die Buchhändler Boosey & Comp. finden sich sehr geschmeichelt, daß Sr Excell. Geheimrat Rath von Goethe mit den Kupfern zu Faust und der Beschreibung derselben nicht unzufrieden sind, und haben die Ehre hierbey, den Beschluß davon ergebenst zu übersenden. Dieses Haus hat uns Unterschrieben den hier beygelegten Brief geschickt, woraus Sr. Excellenz etwas über den Anonymnus ersehen werden, welcher die Erklärungen übersetzt hat.)[21]

Hüttner enclosed the letter that Boosey had sent him on 19 August 1820:

> Sir,
> We consider our selves much indebted to you for having transmitted a copy of the outlines to Faust with the Analysis to Mr de Goethe, and feel our selves gratified by the notice he has been pleased to take of them. The author, or rather compiler of the Analysis, is a German in humble circumstances, a man of no little ability, and possessing a very considerable Knowledge of the English Language. The Analysis is merely a literal translation of a portion of the Tragedy to explain the Outlines, and if it have any merit it is its closeness to the original. To have attempted more would have been presumption, and doubtless would not have Succeeded. Mr. Huttner must be well aware of the difficulties of giving a free translation of the whole of the incomparable tragedy, it would require a translator

possessing a thorough knowledge of both languages, a poet, besides other requisites to do it the justice it deserves.

>We remain
>>Sir Your Obliged S^{ts}
>>>Boosey & Sons

PS.

>Perhaps it may be gratifying to Mr. de Goethe to know, that in Consequence of the extensive Sale of the Outlines in this Country, great Curiosity has been excited respecting the tragedy, and of course has had a great Sale lately.[22]

Boosey revealed only that the translator was 'a German in humble circumstances, a man of no little ability, and possessing a very considerable Knowledge of the English Language'. But he also hinted that a new project was underway. In May 1820, a month before his edition with Boileau's prose translation was distributed, Boosey had already commenced negotiations with Coleridge for a blank-verse translation. He does not let Hüttner know that he has already enlisted 'a translator possessing a thorough knowledge of both languages, a poet'. Nevertheless, when Goethe shared Boosey's report with his son August von Goethe (4 September 1820), his letter contained information that Boosey had concealed:

>From England comes the following report, which Mama will surely translate:
>(Aus England meldet man Folgendes, welches die Mama wohl dolmetschen wird:)
>Perhaps it may be gratifying to Mr. de Goethe to know, that in Consequence of the extensive Sale of the Outlines in this Country, great Curiosity has been excited respecting the tragedy, and of course has had a great Sale lately.
>Coleridge translates the piece. They will apparently soon produce it in the theatre, adapted in their manner. The current witch trial can be disposed of only on the witches' mountain.
>
>(Colleridge übersetzt das Stück. Sie werden es nach ihrer Weise wahrscheinlich umgemodelt bald auf's Theater bringen. Der jetzige Hexenprozeß läßt sich wohl auch nur auf dem Blocksberge abthun'.)[23]

In suggesting that 'Mama' may translate the English text, Goethe is referring to his son August's mother-in-law, Henriette von Pogwisch.[24] As Goethe knew, Henriette von Pogwisch was an admirer of Coleridge's poetry. When August von Goethe was married to Ottilie von Pogwisch (17 June 1817), his bride carried with her to Saaletal a copy of *Christabel, Kubla Khan, and The Pains of Sleep* (1816). On 21 June 1817, Ottilie informed August that her mother 'allowed herself to be accompanied home by a lovable Englishman' ('sie sich von einem liebenswürdigen Engeländer nach Hause geleiten läßt'). The 'lovable Englishman' was Coleridge, not in person but as present in Ottilie's copy of his recently published poems. Two days later, 23 June 1817, Henriette von Pogwisch returned *Christabel* to Ottilie, asking her about the projected continuation Coleridge promised in his Introduction, and expressing her concern about the poet's suffering as described in 'Pains of Sleep'.[25]

Neither from Hüttner nor from Boosey had Goethe learned that 'Colleridge übersetzt das Stück'. Reminded, perhaps, that Coleridge was translator of *Wallenstein* and author of *Remorse* and *Zapolya*, Goethe surmised that Coleridge may intend his dramatic blank-verse translation for the stage.[26] To adapt *Faust* for the British stage, and for a British audience, Goethe recognized that changes would be inevitable. 'The present witch trial', he said in a wry reference to the scandalous divorce trial of Queen Caroline, 'can be disposed of only on the Blocksberg'.[27] The news that Coleridge was translating *Faust* was related in Bohte's letter to Goethe (1 August 1820):

> Under the progressive cultivation of German literature in this country one has become especially attentive to your Faust—to which the splendid outline engravings by Retzsch have contributed much. Another commentary with excerpts of remarkable passages appeared in translation in Blackwood's Edinburgh Magazine on the 1st of last month—I hear with pleasure that the poet Coleridge is working on a complete translation of this Dramatic Poem.
>
> (Unter der fortschreitenden Cultivierung der deutschen Literatur in diesem Lande ist man seit einiger Zeit besonders aufmerksam auf Ew: Wohlgeboren Faust geworden—wozu die herlichen Umrisse von Retsch vieles beigetragen.— Eine andre Abhandlung mit Auszügen von merkwürdigen Stellen in Übersetzung erschien in Blackwoods Edinburgh Magazine untern 1ten vorigen Monathes— und vernehme mit Vergnügen, daß der hiesige Dichter Coleridge an einer gänzlichen Übersetzung dieses dramat: Gedichte arbeitet.)[28]

Bohte also sent Goethe a copy of *London Magazine* with George Croly's essay on 'Goethe and Faust'. The 'commentary with excerpts' to which he refers was John Anster's translation from *Faust* in *Blackwood's Edinburgh Magazine* (June 1820). Although he declares that he has learned 'with pleasure' that Coleridge is working on a complete translation, it also meant that there would be significant competition for Bohte's planned edition of a dual-language edition with a translation by Soane.[29]

According to George Bancroft, who visited Goethe one year earlier (12 October 1819), Goethe knew Coleridge's name 'but had forgotten the works'.[30] If so, Goethe had made an effort to review again Coleridge's works upon learning that he was to be his translator. As already mentioned, Goethe could consult the account of Coleridge in Jacobsen's *Briefe ... über die neuesten englischen Dichter* (1820), or he could seek the opinions of Henriette von Pogwisch. Less than two months after receiving Bohte's news that Coleridge was at work on *Faust*, Goethe quoted lines of his poetry approvingly in a conversation with Friedrich Förster (27 September 1820). Förster records:

> He was always of the opinion that the indicated passages had no need of musical support, wherein he completely agreed with the keen-witted Coleridge:
>
> (Er sei immer der Meinung gewesen, daß die bezeichneten Stellen keiner musikalischen Beihilfe bedürften, worin er vollkommen dem geistreichen Coleridge zustimme:)
>
> > An orphic tale indeed,
> > A tale divine of high and passionate thoughts,
> > To their own music chaunted.
> >
> > [(Der Faust) Ein orphisches Gedicht fürwahr,
> > Ein göttliches, voll hoher, leidenschaftlicher Gedanken,
> > Ertönend zu der eigenen Musik.][31]

Goethe not only quoted, he translated and appropriated. The lines in which Coleridge praised the intrinsic musicality of Wordsworth's *The Prelude* are applied by Goethe to his own *Faust*. Goethe cited Coleridge's 'To William Wordsworth. Composed on the Night after his recitation of a Poem on the Growth of an Individual Mind' (lines 45–7). The poem was written in January 1807, but not published until 1817, when it appeared with the same subtitle as 'To a Gentleman' in Coleridge's *Sibylline Leaves*, and later, with a sequence of slight revisions in the first, second and third editions of *Poetical Works* (1828, 1829 and 1834). In the third edition of 1834, Wordsworth's name was first publicly introduced into the title. While it might seem probable that Goethe would be quoting from the version in *Sibylline Leaves*, the variants reveal otherwise. In all these versions the lines in question involve a significant variant: not 'orphic tale' and 'tale divine', but 'orphic song' and 'song divine'.

> An orphic song indeed,
> A song divine of high and passionate thoughts,
> To their own Music chaunted![32]

For Goethe's argument, 'tale' is the more appropriate word, because 'song' would seem to beg the question of the musical nature of poetry itself. The substitution, however, is not Goethe's. The fact that he derived the quotation from yet another source, also renders it impossible that Förster himself interpolated these lines from Coleridge's *Sibylline Leaves* or subsequently from *Poetical Works*. Not the poem as a whole, but lines from the poem had been previously published in the *Biographia Literaria*,[33] among them lines that refer to 'tale' rather than 'song':

> An orphic tale indeed,
> A tale *obscure* of high and passionate thoughts,
> To a *strange* music chaunted!

These lines in *Biographia Literaria* are quoted from *The Friend*, 'though with a few of the words altered'. The purpose for the alteration is clear in context, for the lines appear in the 'letter from a friend', which attempts to persuade Coleridge to omit from the *Biographia* the 'Chapter on the Imagination' as '*strange*' and '*obscure*'. The lines in *The Friend* are exactly as Goethe has quoted them:

> An Orphic Tale indeed,
> A Tale divine of high and passionate thoughts,
> To their own music chaunted![34]

As noted, Bohte had sent news that Coleridge was translating *Faust* at the beginning of August. During the weeks following Goethe apparently attempted to learn more about Coleridge and his works. Also during these weeks, Goethe prepared his 'Urworte, Orphisch', originally written in 1817, for publication in *Über Kunst und Altertum* (1820).[35]

Following Knebel's news of the review, Goethe seems to have given no further attention to Coleridge's translation after it appeared in 1821, nor when a subsequent edition was published in 1824.[36] It was nevertheless in his thoughts, for in his *Tagebuch* (8 May 1826), Goethe referred to the 'Contribution of Coleridge' ('Antheil von Coleridge'), to the 'Various attempts to translate Faust'

('VerschiedeneVersuche Faust zu übersetzen'), as well as to the 'Reengraving of the Copperplates by Retzsch' ('Kupfer von Retsch zu Faust nachgestochen'),[37] which Henry Moses had prepared for the editions published by Boosey. Goethe's interest in Coleridge, never ardent, cooled considerably in the ensuing years. Lord Byron was the British poet whom he most admired, and after him Thomas Moore; about the rest he had little to say, ignoring even Byron's recommendation that he read Wordsworth.[38] Henry Crabb Robinson recorded two evenings he spent with Goethe in August, 1829. On the first evening he read to Goethe from Byron's *Vision of Judgment*; on the second evening he read Coleridge's 'Love' and 'Fire, Famine, and Slaughter'. Predictably, Goethe liked the passages from Byron, but Coleridge's poems he 'damned . . . with faint praise'. Because of Goethe's praise for the speeches of Wilkes and Junius, and his willing endorsement of a few stanzas, Crabb Robinson declared that 'Goethe was in this like Coleridge that he was by no means addicted to contradiction', and possessed a similar readiness to entertain other opinions.[39] Crabb Robinson was being generous in this comparison, for he knew that both could hold to an opinion with stubborn tenacity.

Coleridge varied little in his estimation of Goethe's *Faust*. He had earlier read *Faust, ein Fragment* (1790), but when Henry Crabb Robinson in August 1812 read to him passages from the 'new' *Faust* (1808), he readily 'acknowledged the genius of Goethe'. His objections were primarily against 'the want of religion and enthusiasm'. This deficit was compounded by coarseness of language. Granting that Mephistopheles was well conceived, though not properly 'a character', Coleridge seemed to accept Crabb Robinson's suggestion that as principle of evil 'Mephistopheles ought to be a mere abstraction'.[40] Coleridge also objected to the character of Faust, whose thoughts and actions were 'not *motiviert*'. Coleridge wanted it explained how Faust 'was thrown into a state of mind which led to the catastrophe'. Although Crabb Robinson protested that this does not seem 'a powerful objection', for Coleridge it was precisely the conflict of wisdom and desire that needed to be more adequately revealed. When their conversation was interrupted by the arrival of Captain James Burney, Crabb Robinson noted with admiration Coleridge's ability to give 'a very spirited sketch of Faust'.[41]

Having been 'commissioned by Murray to propose to Coleridge the translation of *Faust*',[42] Crabb Robinson was pleased when Coleridge agreed to the task in August 1814. Accepting Murray's suggestion that he translate in 'a style of versification equal to "Remorse"', Coleridge stressed that the 'blank verse' must be complemented by 'wild *lyrical* metres'.[43] He was especially worried about the public response to the supernatural scenes requiring 'a willing suspension of disbelief':

> The Scenes in the Cathedral and the Prison must delight and affect all Readers not pre-determined to dislike. But the Scenes of Witchery and that astonishing Witch-Gallop up the Brocken will be denounced as *fantastic* and absurd. Fantastic they *are*, and were meant to be; but I need not tell you, how many will detect the supposed fault for one, who can enter into the philosophy of that imaginative Superstition, which justifies it.[44]

When Coleridge later commented on 'The Witch's Kitchen' ('Hexenküche') and 'Walpurgis Night' ('Walpurgisnacht'), he praised Goethe for avoiding the Shakespearean 'Hags'.[45]

Coleridge was still concerned with the work's immorality and the weakness of Faust's character when Boosey persuaded him to return to the task in 1820. In his Introduction, he frankly declares that he must omit those parts that 'would be offensive to English readers, from the free, and occasionally immoral tendency of the allusions which they contain'. Although 'the original is written in a great variety of metres', he has confined himself 'to blank-verse in all parts of the play except those which are strictly lyrical', convinced that this is 'the only measure that would enable him to imitate the tone, without sacrificing the sense of his text'. He praises the conception of Mephistopheles as 'the Principle of Evil':

> He is abject in seducing, diligent in ensnaring, cruel and remorseless in punishing his victim: in human shape he is yet distinguished from his mortal companion by the total want of personal interest which he takes in the scenes through which they pass, and by the bitter, scornful, yet uncomplaining tone of his remarks.

Margaret, in Coleridge's assessment, is the sole character in whom we can invest our sympathy:

> Margaret is the only character for whom we feel undivided interest; she is entangled in the web of temptation, which the fiend has woven to catch the proud soul of his confident disciple; she is betrayed into crime through the kindest of affections: the potion which destroys her mother is unwittingly administered by her hand, and the murder of her child may be supposed to take place in a moment of insanity. Her doom is not, therefore, final. She is punished on earth, but experiences the grace of a repentant sinner.

Coleridge again notes the conflict of reason and passion that splits Faust's character:

> Faustus is a singular compound of strength and weakness. He is daring and timid by turns; ambitious and irresolute; not wholly vicious, yet far from virtuous: he despises the power of the demon to whose arts he yields himself a willing prey, and half detects the snares laid for his destruction.[46]

Perhaps it was because of, rather than in spite of, the weakness and lack of motivation attributed to Goethe's conception of Faust, that Coleridge in his translation wrote himself into the character. He found much with which he could personally identify. One needs only to recall Coleridge's struggle with the meaning of the 'logos' and with the opposition of theism and pantheism to recognize how he might personally engage in Faust's adumbrations, 'In the beginning was the Word'('Im Anfang war das Wort') (*F*, 1224–37), or in Faust's appeal to the Earth-Spirit (*F*, 3217–50). Coleridge, too, experienced the strife of 'two souls'('zwei Seelen') (*F*, 1112–17). Throughout his translation, Coleridge has woven in lines of his own poetry.

An aftermath of disclaimers and denials followed this remarkable achievement. Never has a work been as repeatedly and vociferously disowned by its author. To support his contention that the work was 'stagnant, vapid *caput motuum*', all the evidence that Carlyle could muster were three mistranslated phrases and two passages that depart from Goethe's language but achieve considerable poetic power of their own. As already mentioned, Coleridge was sensitive to harsh criticism, and he was doubtless hurt by Carlyle's hostility. Too, he may have felt that in omitting the 'Prologue in Heaven' ('Prolog im Himmel'), the 'Prelude in the Theatre' ('Vorspiel auf dem Theater'), and much of 'Auerbach's Cellar' ('Auerbachs Keller in Leipzig'),'The Witch's Kitchen' and the 'Walpurgis Night', he had accomplished too little in his translation. With the subsequent editions in 1824 and 1832, and two in 1834, Coleridge's anonymous translation was kept in print throughout the remaining years of his life,[47] but he did not cease to disavow the work.

In a conversation with Dr. Gioacchino de' Prati, Coleridge confessed that in attempting to translate *Faust*, he had to 'give it up in despair':

> I would have attempted to translate your favourite 'Faustus', but I must give it up in despair. To translate it so as to make the English readers acquainted with the plot, is a foolish task. The beauty of this work consists in the colour of the style, and in the tints, which are lost to one who is not thoroughly *au fait* with German life, German philosophy, and the whole literature of that country. The antithesis between the slang of Mephistophiles, the over-refined language of Faustus, and the pastoral simplicity of the child of nature, Margaret, requires a man's whole life to be made self-evident in our language. And therein lies Goethe's peculiarity.[48]

As John Hookham Frere (1874) recalled the conversation of 16 February 1833, he had asked Coleridge whether he had 'ever thought of translating the "Faust"'. 'Yes, Sir, I had', Coleridge replied,'but I was prevented by the consideration that though there are some exquisite passages ... some I reprobate'. As admired passages, Coleridge named 'the opening chorus, the chapel and the prison scenes'. He also admired 'the Brocken scene', praising Goethe for his 'peculiar strength in keeping clear of Shakespear' and restoring 'the real original witch'. He disliked the 'conception of Wagner', and he dismissed as 'dull' the dialogue between Mephistopheles and the Scholar. Mephistopheles 'is well executed, but the conception is not original'. He found that Faust's character is inadequately defined:

> whoever heard of a man who had gained such a wonderful proficiency in learning as to call up spirits &c being discontented. No, it is not having the power of knowledge that would make a man discontented—neither would such a man have suddenly become a sensualist.[49]

The notes for the *Table Talk* add further details to that discussion of *Faust* on 16 February 1833. Coleridge again reaffirmed the complaint, recorded by Crabb Robinson twenty years earlier (20 August 1812), that Faust's motives are inadequately developed:

> In the Faust there is no causation—no progression. The theme intended is, Misology caused by an intense thirst for nature baffled. But a love of knowledge for itself would never produce such a misology—but a love of it for power or base ends. Faust is a ready made sorcerer from the beginning—the *incredulus odi* is felt from the first line. The sorcery and the sensuality are totally unconnected with each other and with the thirst for knowledge. I think Faust himself dull and meaningless.[50]

Coleridge's indictment against Faust is, of course, the self-indictment that Goethe has Faust himself pronounce. His learning has brought him to an impasse: his life, as Coleridge states, has become 'dull and meaningless'. Therefore he lapses into a suicidal despair (*F*, 634–736).[51] His 'sensuality' is in conflict 'with the thirst for knowledge'. Faust is fully aware of the inner conflict: 'Two souls dwell, alas! in my breast' ('Zwei Seelen wohnen, ach! in meiner Brust') (*F*, 1112).[52] Faust's own restless mind and his driving rebellion against 'no causation—no progression' prompt him to make that very stasis the condition of his damnation. If he ever says to a single moment 'Linger, still linger, beautiful illusions'('Verweile doch! du bist so schön!') (*F*, 1700), Mephistopheles can have his soul. Coleridge, who rejected the philosophical materialism of John Locke and Isaac Newton for treating the mind as 'always passive—a lazy *Looker-on*',[53] certainly recognized the ground of Goethe's 'Philosophy of Action' ('Tätigkeitsphilosophie').

It might seem, then, that Coleridge would ultimately reconcile himself to admitting his role as translator. 'Mephistopheles and Margaret', he declared, 'are excellent throughout'. Even scenes from which he had translated only excerpts, 'Auerbach's Cellar' and 'Walpurgis Night', he judged as 'very fine', 'and all the songs are beautiful'. To be sure, he found no coherent whole in *Faust* and considered the scenes to be a mere sequence of 'magic-lantern pictures'. But the real and abiding problem, Coleridge insisted, was that morally he could not 'lend my countenance to language—much of which I thought vulgar, licentious and most blasphemous'. Thus he continued to assert that he 'never put pen to paper as translator of Faust'.[54]

There were, of course, contemporaries who knew better. As rival publishers of *Faust*, Bohte and Boosey knew who was providing their translations. Boosey may have wanted to protect Coleridge's requested anonymity, but Bohte had revealed the fact to Goethe himself. In spite of Coleridge's denials, the fact was still rumored abroad. As late as 1865, William Barnard Clarke, in the Preface to his translation of *Faust*, referred to an earlier translation 'said to be by Coleridge'.[55] With a new critical edition available, it is now possible to appraise Coleridge's remarkable investment in Goethe's major work. No single factor will alter more significantly the understanding of the reception of Goethe's *Faust* in the English-speaking world than the recovery of Coleridge's translation. Long recognized as the most influential mediator of German thought in the first half of the nineteenth century, Coleridge had given to English readers a translation of Schiller's *Wallenstein* of recognized literary merit. His translation of *Faust*, however, has a double significance: it is both a crucial document in the English reception of *Faust* and, at the same time, one of the most personally revelatory texts in Coleridge's entire oeuvre.

Notes

1 Goethe (1887–1919), *Werke,* Weimarer Ausgabe (= *WA*), 4, Bd. 33, S. 199–200; 4, Bd. 42, Zweite Abtheilung, S. 491.
2 Because he worked from a prompter's copy, Coleridge's translation from Schiller's *The Piccolomini* and *The Death of Wallenstein*, 2 v. (1800), appeared prior to their publication in Germany; reprinted in *The Poetical Works*, 3 v. (1828). On Coleridge's translation of *Wallenstein*, the reviewer in *Blackwood's* (Anon. 1823) declared it to be the 'best translation of a foreign tragic drama'.
3 Robinson to Goethe (31 January 1829), recalling his attempt to promote Coleridge's translation for John Murray: 'Coleridge, too, the only living poet of acknowledged genius who is also a good German scholar attempted Faust, but shrunk from it in

despair' (Goethe 1988, 2: 496). Scott: 'Mr Wilson mentioned a report that Coleridge was engaged on a translation of the Faust: "I hope it is so", said Scott. "Coleridge made Schiller's Wallenstein far finer than he found it, and so he will do with this"' (Lockhart 1837–8, 4: 216; cited in Boyd [1932: 216]). Shelley to John Gisborne (January 1822): upon receiving in Italy a copy of *Retsch's Series of Twenty-six Outlines, Illustrative of Goethe's Tragedy of Faust* (1820), Shelley begged Gisborne to 'Ask Coleridge if their stupid misintelligence of the deep wisdom and harmony of the author does not spur him to action'. Shelley referred to Boileau's prose translation (1820b), unaware that Coleridge's blank-verse translation (1821) had been published in September (1964, 2: 376).

4 To Murray, August 1814, (*CL*, 3: 523–5). On 12 May 1820 Coleridge sent Boosey 'My Advice and Scheme', a proposal for translating *Faust*; single sheet dated 12 May 1820 (Huntington Library MS accession number 131334).
5 This text is reprinted with line-by-line annotation in *Faustus From the German of Goethe. Translated by Samuel Taylor Coleridge* (2007).
6 Goethe (*WA*, 4, Bd. 36, S. 61). To Carl Friedrich von Reinhard (10 June 1822): 'In England hat ein Herr Soane meinen Faust bewundernswürdig verstanden und dessen Eigenthümlichkeiten mit den Eigenthümlichkeiten seiner Sprache und den Forderungen seiner Nation in Harmonie zu bringen gewußt; ich besitze die ersten Bogen mit nebengedrucktem Original'.
7 On Hazlitt's negative reviews of Coleridge, especially his *Christabel*, see Wu (2002: 168–94).
8 Coleridge to Robert Southey, 31 May 1820, *Collected Letters of Samuel Taylor Coleridge* (= *CL*, 5: 51). In this letter, Coleridge also speaks of attempting to negotiate a new edition of *Wallenstein* with Thomas Longman, and also regrets the prevailing 'prejudices respecting my supposed German Metaphysics'.
9 'R.' (1821: 362–9). This 'R.' is not the 'R.' identified as the classical scholar Rev. Henry Meen (1744–1817) in Emily Lorraine de Montluzin, Attributions of Authorship in the *European Magazine*, 1782–1826, http://etext.lib.virginia.edu/bsuva/euromag/ (retrieved 1 October 2007).
10 Coleridge to Murray, August 1814, (*CL*, 3: 525).
11 Anon. (1821c: 529–31). The publication had been announced in *The New Monthly Magazine*, September (1821), 468: 'A new Translation of Faustus from the German of GOETHE, will be speedily published in 8vo. with a portrait of the author; and in 4to. with 27 Outlines to illustrate the above-mentioned Tragedy, engraved by Mr. Moses, after Retschs' Designs'. There was also a reference to the Boosey edition of 1820 with Boileau's translation in *The Literary Journal* accompanying *The New Monthly Magazine*, November (1821), 543.
12 Knebel (1744–1834), poet, translator and close friend of Goethe, was best known for his translation of Lucretius, *De rerum natura*, and Alfieri's *Saul*.
13 Knebel to Goethe, 17 November 1821, Letter 578 (Goethe 1851). 'Übrigens suche ich meine Welt so meist wie bisher, in den englischen Journalen, die mir reichlichen Stoff liefern. Zwei interessante Hefte des New Monthly Magazine wird Dir Weller überschickt haben, dafür habe ich die drei neue erhalten'.
14 Knebel to Goethe, 18 December 1821, Letter 580 (Goethe 1851). Introducing his excerpt from *The New Monthly Magazine*, Knebel writes:

> Gestern fand ich in einem von meiner beliebten englischen Journalen, bei Gelegenheit der von H. Moses nachgestochenmen Umrisse des Hern. Retsch nach dem Faust, ein Urteil über das Gedicht selbst, das mich nicht wenig erfreute, zumal da es von einem Engländer kommt. Da ich nicht weiß, ob Du es zu Gesicht bekommen, so will ich es hersetzen.

15 Schröder, *Thomas Carlyles Abhandlung über Goethes Faust aus dem Jahre 1821* (= *Abhandlung*), 8–32; Carlyle (1822: 316–34).

16 Carlyle (Goethe 1887) refers repeatedly to his intended translation of *Faust*: Carlyle to Goethe, 15 November 1830, 240; Eckermann to Carlyle, 7 December 1830, 250; Carlyle to Goethe, 22 January 1831, 254.
17 The pertinent letters were located for me at the Goethe-Schiller Archive by Sabine Schäfer, a coeditor of *Briefe an Goethe: Gesamtausgabe in Regestform*. I thank the administration and staff of the Goethe-Schiller Archive for assistance with the manuscripts and permission to cite those used in this chapter.
18 Recent interest in Hüttner has addressed his role as correspondent for *London und Paris: eine Zeitschrift mit Kupfern* (1798–1810). See especially Proescholdt (2001: 99–110), Guthke (2001: 41–4), Banerji and Donald (1999) and Cilleßen (2006). Still useful are the earlier studies of his career: Hennig (1951: 404–18) and Wadepuhl (1939: 23–7). Hüttner was also known for his *Nachricht von der Britischen Gesandtschaftsreise durch China und einen Teil der Tartarei* (1793, 1996), describing his journey to Peking with the Earl of Macartney in 1793 to meet with the Mandshu Emperor.
19 Goethe to Johann Christian Hüttner, 30 July 1820, (*WA*, 4, Bd. 33, S. 137); Goethe later speculates that a set of Retzsch's prints or the copies by Moses would be an appropriate gift for Miss Dawe, who had presented Goethe with the engravings of his portrait as painted by her brother, George Dawe:

> Wollten Sie nicht die Gefälligkeit haben, mir zu sagen, wie ich Miß Dawe eine Artigkeit erzeigen könnte; vielleicht wären ihr die Original-Radirungen von Retzsch zu meinem Faust angenehm, da doch die Copien jetzt in England so viel Aufsehen machen. Diese Originale werden dadurch merkwürdiger, weil man gewisse Veränderungen bey der Copie beliebte, welche zu denken geben.

Goethe to Johann Christian Hüttner, 22 September 1820, (*WA*, 4, Bd. 33, S. 246).
20 I determined Boileau was the translator only when I found that Boosey was also the publisher of his language text, and that Boileau repeatedly cited his own translation of 1820 in his critique of Abraham Hayward's prose translation of 1833 (Boileau 1820b; 1834).
21 Hüttner to Goethe, 22 August 1820; MS GSA 28/89 Bl. 415.
22 Boosey to Hüttner, 19 August 1820; MS GSA 28/89 Bl. 415.
23 Goethe to Carl August von Goethe, 4 September 1820, (*WA*, 4, Bd. 33, 199–200); Goethe quotes from Boosey's letter, enclosed in Hüttner's letter to Goethe, 22 August 1820.
24 Goethe (*WA*, 4, Bd. 50, S. 181).
25 Letter 1070, from Ottilie von Goethe to August von Goethe, 21 June 1817; Letter 1076, from Henriette von Pogwisch to Ottilie von Goethe, 23 June 1817, (Goethe 2004, 7: 390, 393).
26 Coleridge to Murray, 31 August 1814, (*CL*, 3: 525); when negotiating his translation of *Faust*, Coleridge insisted that he retain the rights to adapt it for the stage.
27 Hüttner to Goethe (4 August 1820) referred to the 'Prozess der Königin der die ganze Aufmerksamkeit des Publikums verschlingt'. See Goethe (*WA*, 4, Bd. 50, S. 181) and Proescholdt (2001: 105–6).
28 Bohte to Goethe, 1 August 1820; MS GSA 28/88 Bl. 362f.; Mappe 8/0068:
    Ew. Wohlgeboren!
    Erlauben mir das Vergnügen beikommend heute erschienenes London Magazine zu überreichen, in der Hoffnung, daß der in diesen Hefte erhaltne erste Abhandlung Ew. Wohlgeboren Intreße und Vergnügen gewähren wird.
    Der Redakteur dieses Journals ist mein Freund John Scott Esq. bekannt wegen Verschiedener achtungswerthen literarischer Produkten—wie z.B. Paris visited etc. etc.
    Soviel mir bekannt ist ihm diesen Aufsatz so wie auch der 4te in diese Magazine, 'Description of certain Frescoes', von meinem Freund eingesandt, der gegenwärtig in

Italien und dessen Bekanntschaft er vor Zwey Jahren auf einer Reise erwähnten Lande gemacht.

Unter der fortschreitenden Cultivierung der deutschen Literatur in diesem Lande ist man seit einiger Zeit besonders aufmerksam auf Ew. Wohlgeboren Faust geworden— wozu die herlichen Umrisse von Retsch vieles beigetragen. Eine andre Abhandlung mit Auszuegen erschien in Blackwoods Edinburgh Magazine untern 1ten vorigen Monathes—und vernahm mit Vergnügen, daß der hiesige Dichter Coleridge an einer gänzlichen Übersetzung dieses Dramat. Gedichte arbeitete.—

In Edinburgh besonders ist man sehr aufmerksam geworden auf die deutsche Literatur. Unter den Titel Florae Germanicae erschienen in vorerwähnten Journale von Zeit zu Zeit Abhandlungen und Übersetzungen der vorzüglichsten Dramatischen

Dichter,—so finde in heute erschienenes Journal eine Abhandlung über Müllners König Yngurd—ohne Zweifel von der Feder meines Edinburgh Freundes Sr. P. Gilles Esq. Dortiger Advocat.—

Auch liefre fortwährend unsern iteressantesten Literärischen Novitäten an Sir Walter Scott in Edinburgh.

Da der kleine Aufsatz in Gegenwärtigen Journale betitelt 'M. Ebert und M. Dibdin' erstern Freunde in Dresden so wie auch H. Buchhändler Brockhaus in Leipzig, sehr interessiere—so wage die Bitte Ew. Wohlgeboren zu bemühen nach Eigner Durchsicht diese ferner eine Durchsicht dieses Journal gütigst zu vergönnen.

Ich habe die Ehre mich zu unterzeichnen mit der größten Hochachtung
 Ew Wohlgeboren
  ganz ergebener
   H. Bohte

29 Because he had already set the German text set for the planned dual-language edition, Bohte decided to bring out a German edition without Soane's parallel English text. For readers of German in England, Bohte published *Faust: eine Tragödie von J. W. von Goethe* (1823).

30 Boyd (1932: 170); also in Goethe [Biedermann (ed.)] (1889–96, 2: 448).

31 Förster (1873: 201–6).

32 'To a Gentleman. Composed on the Night after his recitation of a Poem on the Growth of an Individual Mind' (lines 45–7) (Coleridge 1817: 199).

33 Coleridge (1983), *Biographia Literaria* (= *BL*), 1: 222 (65–75), 225 (lines 92–3), 302 (lines 45–7); 2: 145 (lines 58–60).

34 Coleridge (1969, 2: 258 [28 December 1809]; 1: 368 [1818]).

35 *Über Kunst und Altertum*, Bd. 2, Heft 3, 1820; Goethe [Steiger and Reimann (eds)] (1982–96, 6: 768–9).

36 *Faustus: From the German of Goethe* [trans. by Coleridge] (1821). Counting his edition of Boileau's prose translation as the first edition and Coleridge's blank-verse translation as his second edition, the next printing of Coleridge's translation was Boosey's third edition (1824). Three more anonymous editions of Coleridge's translation followed, one in 1832 and two in 1834.

37 Goethe (*WA*, 1. Bd. 42), Zweite Abtheilung (1907), S. 491.

38 Byron to Goethe, 14 October 1820, (Goethe 1969, 2: 276–9). Byron informed Goethe that 'Peter Bell' was Wordsworth's 'principle publication'. Before his death in Missolonghi, Byron sent a final letter to Goethe (24 July 1823): 'I am returning to Greece to see if I can be of any little use there;—if ever I come back I will pay a visit to Weimar to offer the sincere homage of one of the many Million of your admirers' (Goethe 1969, 2: 353).

39 Robinson (1869), 15 and 16 August 1829; Goethe (1998, 3, pt. 2, 455f; 16 August 1829); also cited in Boyd (1932: 274).

40 Coleridge (1990), *Table Talk* (= *TT*), 13 August 1812, 1: 571; cited from Robinson (1938, 1: 107).

41 Coleridge (*TT*, 20 August 1812, 1: 572); cited from Robinson (1938, 1:108).

42 Robinson (1938, 1: 447–8), 7 October 1834.
43 To John Murray, 23 August 1814, (*CL*, 3: 525); cf n. 12 above.
44 To John Murray, 10 September 1814, (*CL*, 3: 528).
45 Coleridge (*TT*, 1: 381), 15 May 1833: 'Goethe showed good taste in not attempting to imitate Shakespeare's Witches, which are threefold,—Fates, Furies, and earthy Hags o' the cauldron' (*TT*, 1: 573–4). John Hookham Frere remembered the 'threefold' types as 'Witch, Fate and Fairy'. Cf. Schlegel (1846, 2, pt. 2: 153) on Shakespeare's 'Parce, Furien und Zauberinnen'.
46 Introduction, *Faustus* (2007: 6–7).
47 See bibliography and n. 43 above.
48 Coleridge (*TT*, 2: 490–1); Fisch (1943, 4: 111–22).
49 Coleridge (*TT*, 1: 573–4); Frere (16 February 1833).
50 Coleridge (*TT*, 1: 338–9); cf. 2: 197–200 for the text as published in 1836.
51 *Faustus* (1821: 14, 88). Coleridge provides a prose summary for this passage on Faust's attempt at suicide which he did not translate in its entirety.
52 In his comments on *Faust*, Coleridge protested as inappropriate that the 'strong/ But sensual ties' ('Liebeslust' *F*, 1114) should hold such sway over the man of intellectual aspirations. Coleridge nevertheless recognized that the opposition between Faust and Mephistopheles is an externalization of this inner struggle between mental and physical desires. The opposition of Reason and Passion, Hope and Despair, Joy and Sorrow, also informs such poems as 'Two Founts', 'Youth and Age', 'An Old Man's Sigh', and 'Work without Hope'; see Paley (1996: 65–77).
53 Coleridge to Thomas Poole, 23 March 1801 (*CL*, 2: 709).
54 Coleridge (*TT*, 1: 338–9, 343).
55 *Goethe's Faust I. and II Parts*, trans. Clarke (1865: iii).

Bibliography

Anon. (1820), 'Goethe and his Faustus', *London Magazine*, 2, (August), 124–42.
— (1821a), 'C. Van Vinkbooms, his dogma for dilettanti', *London Magazine*, 3, (December), 657.
— (1821b), 'New books published in September', *The Monthly Magazine and British Register*, 52, (1 October), 260.
— (1821c), 'Review of Faustus from the German of Goethe', *The New Monthly Magazine*, (November), in *The New Monthly Magazine*, 1821 to 1830, pp. 529–31. L. Bunnell Jones (ed.), v. 1–14, Feb. 1814–Dec. 1820; [new ser.] v. 1–149, Jan. 1821–Dec. 1871. Ann Arbor: University Microfilms Int., [c. 1971].
— (1821d), 'Shelley's *Queen Mab*', *The Monthly Magazine and British Register*, 51, (1 June), 460–1.
— (1823), 'Schiller's Wallenstein', *Blackwood's Edinburgh Magazine*, (October), 53.
Anster, J. (1820), 'The Faustus of Goethe', *Blackwood's Edinburgh Magazine*, 7, 39, (June), 235–58.
Ashton, R. D. (1977), 'Coleridge and Faust', *Review of English Studies*, n.s. 28, (May), 156–67.
— (2005), 'Carlyle's apprenticeship: His early German criticism and his relationship with Goethe (1822–1832)', *Modern Language Review*, 100, 153–70.
Banerji, C. and Donald, D. (eds) (1999), *Gillray Observed: The Earliest Account of His Caricatures in 'London und Paris'*. Cambridge: Cambridge University Press.
Daumann, L. (1907), *Die englischen Uebersetzungen von Goethes Faust*. Diss Zürich. Halle a. Saale: Erhardt Karras.
Bohte, J. H. (1820), To Goethe, 1 August 1820; MS GSA 28/88 Bl. 362f.; Mappe 8/0068.
Boileau, D. (1820a), *The Nature and Genius of the German Language: Displayed in a More Extended Review of Its Grammatical Forms Than Is To Be Found in Any Grammar Extant, and Elucidated by Quotations from the Best Writers*. London: Printed for T. Boosey and Sons.

— (1820b), *Retsch's Series of Twenty-Six Outlines, Illustrative of Goethe's Tragedy of Faust, Engraved from the Originals by Henry Moses, and an Analysis of the Tragedy*. London: Printed for Boosey and Sons.
— (1834), *A Few Remarks on Mr. Hayward's English Prose Translation of Goethe's Faust: With Additional Observations on the Difficulty of Translating German Works in General*. London: Treuttel, Würtz and Richter; and J. Wacey.
Boosey, T. (1820), To Hüttner, 19 August 1820; MS GSA 28/89 Bl. 415.
Boyd, J. (1932), *Goethe's Knowledge of English Literature*. Oxford: Clarendon Press.
Boyle, N. and Guthrie, J. (eds) (2001), *Goethe and the English-Speaking World*. Rochester: Camden House.
Carlyle, T. (1822), 'Review of Faustus, from the German of Goethe', *New Edinburgh Review*, 2, (January–April), 316–34.
— (1828, 1901), 'Review of *Goethes Sämmtliche Werke*', *Foreign Review*, 2, in *Complete Works of Thomas Carlyle*, v. 13. New York: P. F. Collier & Son, p.148.
— (1832), 'Faust's Curse (translated from Goethe)', *Athenæum*, (7 January), 5.
— (1896–1907), *The Life of Schiller*, in *The Works of Thomas Carlyle*, v. 25, H. D. Trail (ed.). London: Chapman and Hall.
Cilleßen, W. (ed.) (2006), *Napoleons neue Kleider: Pariser und Londoner Karikaturen im klassischen Weimar* [catalogue for the exhibition at the Kunstbibliothek, Staatliche Museen zu Berlin, 20. Oktober 2006 bis 7. Januar 2007]. Berlin: GH-Verlag.
Clarke, W. B. (1865), *Goethe's Faust I. and II. Parts*. Freiburg i. Br.; London: Schmidt.
Coleridge, S. T. (1816), *Christabel, Kubla Khan, and The Pains of Sleep*. London: John Murray.
— (1817), *Sibylline Leaves*. London: Rest Fenner, 23, Paternoster Row.
— (1821), *Faustus: From the German of Goethe*. London: Boosey and Sons, 4 Broad-Street, Exchange, and Rodwell & Martin, New Bond-Street.
— (1824), *Faustus/ From the German of Goethe. Embellished with Retzsch' Series of 27 Outlines, Illustrative of the Tragedy Engraved by Henry Moses. With Portrait of the Author*. 3rd ed. London: Boosey.
— (1832), *Faustus/ From the German of Goethe. Embellished with Retzsch' Series of 27 Outlines, Illustrative of the Tragedy Engraved by Henry Moses*. New ed. with portrait of the author and an appendix containing the May-day night scene translated by Percy Bysshe Shelley. London: E. Lumley.
— (1834a), *Faustus/From the German of Goethe. Embellished with Retzsch' Series of 27 Outlines, Illustrative of the Tragedy Engraved by Henry Moses*. New ed. with portrait of the author and an appendix containing the May-day night scene translated by Percy Bysshe Shelley. London: Hodgson, Boys & Graves.
— (1834b), *Faustus/From the German of Goethe*. London: Simkin and Marshall.
— (1912), *Poetical Works*, E. H. Coleridge (ed.). Oxford: Oxford University Press.
— (1956–1971), *Collected Letters of Samuel Taylor Coleridge* (= *CL*), 6 v., E. L. Griggs (ed.). Oxford: Clarendon.
— (1969), *The Friend*, 2 v., B. Rooke (ed.), *The Collected Works of Samuel Taylor Coleridge*, v. 4. Princeton: Princeton University Press; London: Routledge and Kegan Paul.
— (1983), *Biographia Literaria* (= *BL*), J. Engell and W. Jackson Bate (eds), *The Collected Works of Samuel Taylor Coleridge*, v. 7. Princeton: Princeton University Press; London: Routledge and Kegan Paul.
— (1990), *Table Talk*, 2 v., K. Coburn and B. Winer (eds). *The Collected Works of Samuel Taylor Coleridge*, v.14. Princeton: Bollingen.
— (1995), *Shorter Works and Fragments*, 2 v., H. J. Jackson and J. R. de J. Jackson (eds), *The Collected Works of Samuel Taylor Coleridge*, v. 16. Princeton: Princeton University Press.
— (2007), *Faustus, from the German of Goethe. Translated by Samuel Taylor Coleridge*, F. Burwick and J. McKusick (eds). Oxford: Oxford University Press.
Croly, G. (1820), 'Goethe and his Faustus', *London Magazine*, 2, (August), 125–42.
De Quincey, T. (1824), 'Goethe', *London Magazine*, 10, (August), 189–97; 10, (September), 291–307.

— (2000–3), *The Works of Thomas De Quincey*, 21 v., G. Lindop, E. Baxter, F. Burwick, A. Clej, D. Groves, R. Morrison, J. North, D. Sanjev Roberts, B. Symonds and J. Whale (eds). London: Pickering and Chatto.
Elliot, A. R. D. (1907–21, 2000), 'VI. Reviews and magazines in the early years of the nineteenth century, §10. *The New Monthly Magazine*', in *The Romantic Revival*, v. 12, *The Cambridge History of English and American Literature*, 18 v., A. W. Ward and A. R. Waller (eds). Cambridge: Cambridge University Press; New York: Bartleby.com, pp. 143–6.
Fisch, M. H. (1943), 'The Coleridges, Dr. Prati, and Vico', *Modern Philology*, 41, 111–22.
Förster, F. (1873), *Kunst und Leben. Aus Friedrich Förster's Nachlaß*, H. Kletke (ed.). Berlin: Paetel.
Frere, J. H. (1874), 'Der Nachbarin Haus', *Faust*, lines 2901–31 (December 1835), in *Works*, 3 v., W. E. Frere (ed.). London: Basil Montegu Pickering, rev. 2nd edition, v. 2, pp. 402–3.
Goethe, J. W. (1823), *Faust: eine Tragödie von J. W. von Goethe*. London: J. H. Bohte, Königlich-auswärtiger Hofbuchhändler, York Street, Covent Garden.
— (1851), *Briefwechsel zwischen Goethe und Knebel: 1774–1832*, 2 v. Leipzig: Brockhaus.
— (1887, reprint 1970), *Correspondence between Goethe and Carlyle*, C. E. Norton (ed.). London: Macmillan; New York: Cooper Square Publishers.
— (1887–1919), *Werke*. Weimarer Ausgabe (= *WA*), herausgegeben im Auftrage der Grossherzogin Sophie von Sachsen. 146 v. Weimar: H. Böhlau.
— (1889–96), *Goethes Gespräche*, 10 v., F. W. v. Biedermann (ed.). Leipzig: F. W. v. Biedermann.
— (1969), *Briefe an Goethe*, 2 v., K. R. Mandelkow (ed.). Hamburg: Christian Wegner Verlag.
— (1982–96), *Goethes Leben von Tag zu Tag: eine dokumentarische Chronik*, 8 v., R. Steiger and A. Reimann (eds). Zürich: Artemis Verlag.
— (1988), *Goethes Briefe und Briefe an Goethe*, Hamburger Ausgabe, 6 v., K. R. Mandelkow (ed.). Munich: Beck.
— (1998), *Goethes Gespräche*, 5 v., W. Herwig (ed.). Munich: Dt. Taschenbuch-Verlag.
— (2004), *Briefe an Goethe: Gesamtausgabe in Regestform*, v. 7 (1816–17), Stiftung Weimarer Klassik und Kunstsammlungen, M. Koltes, U. Bischof, S. Schäfer (eds). Weimar: Böhlau.
Guthke, K. S. (2001), 'Hüttners Berichte und Goethe', *Goethes Weimar und 'die große Öffnung in die weite Welt'*. Wolfenbütteler Forschungen Bd. 93. Wiesbaden: Harrassowitz, pp. 41–4.
Hahn, K.-H., Schmid, I. and Schaefer, S. (eds) (1980–), *Briefe an Goethe: Gesamtausgabe in Regestform*, 8 v. Nationale Forschungs- und Gedenkstätten der Klassischen Deutschen Literatur in Weimar, Goethe- und Schiller-Archiv. Weimar: H. Böhlau.
Hamilton, P. (2007), *Coleridge and German Philosophy: The Poet in the Land of Logic*. London: Continuum.
Hauhart, W. F. (1909), *Reception of Goethe's Faust in England during the First Half of the Nineteenth Century*. New York: Columbia University Press.
Hennig, J. (1951), 'Goethe's relations with Hüttner', *Modern Language Review*, 46, (3/4), 404–18.
Hüttner, J. C. (1793, 1996), *Nachricht von der Britischen Gesandtschaftsreise durch China und einen Teil der Tartarei*. Reprint: Ostfildern: Thorbeck Verlag.
— (1820), To Goethe, 22 August 1820; MS GSA 28/89 Bl. 415.
Jacobsen, F. J. (1820), *Briefe an eine deutsche Edelfrau über die neuesten englischen Dichter: herausgegeben mit übersetzten Auszügen vorzüglicher Stellen aus ihren Gedichten und mit den Bildnissen der berühmtesten jetzt lebenden Dichter Englands*. Altona: Hammerich.
Leveson, G. F. (1823), *Faust: A Drama by Goethe; and, Schiller's Song of the Bell*. London: John Murray.
Lockhart, J. G. (1837–8), *Memoirs of the Life of Sir Walter Scott*, 5 v. Edinburgh: Cadell; London: Murray and Whittaker.
— (1834), 'Samuel Taylor Coleridge', *Quarterly Review*, (November), 668–82.
London und Paris: eine Zeitschrift mit Kupfern, (1798–1810), 24 v. Rudolstadt: Verlag der Hof-, Buch-u. Kunsthandlung, 1798–1810; Weimar: Verlag der Industrie-Comptoir, 1798–1803.
McNiece, G. (1991), *The Knowledge That Endures: Coleridge, German Philosophy and the Logic of Romantic Thought*. Basingstoke: Macmillan.

Metzger, L. (1992), 'Modifications of genre: A feminist critique of "Christabel" and "Die Braut von Korinth"', *Studies in Eighteenth-Century Culture*, 22, 3–19.
Nosworthy, J. M. (1957), 'Coleridge on a distant prospect of Faust', *Essays and Studies*, 10, 69–70.
Orsini, G. N. G. (1969), *Coleridge and German Idealism*. Carbondale: University of Southern Illinois Press.
Paley, M. (1996), *Coleridge's Later Poetry*. Oxford: Oxford University Press.
Proescholdt, C. (2001), 'Johann Cristian Hüttner (1766–1847): A link between Weimar and London', in N. Boyle and J. Guthrie (eds), *Goethe and the English-Speaking World*. Rochester: Camden House, pp. 99–110.
'R.' (1821), 'Faustus, from the German of Goethe', *European Magazine*, (October), 80, 362–9.
Robinson, H. C. (1869), *Diary, Reminiscences, and Correspondence*, 3 v., T. Sadler (ed.). London: Macmillan.
— (1938), *On Books and Their Writers*, 3 v., E. J. Morley (ed.). London: J. M. Dent and Sons Ltd.
Schiller, F. (1800), *The Piccolomini and The Death of Wallenstein*, 2 v., S. T. Coleridge (trans.). London: T. N. Longman and O. Rees.
Schlegel, A. W. (1846), *Vorlesungen über dramatische Kunst und Litteratur*, 2 v., in *Sämmtliche Werke*, E. Böcking (ed.). 3rd edition, Leipzig: Weidmann, 2, pts. 1 and 2.
Schreiber, C. F. (1947), 'Coleridge to Boosey—Boosey to Coleridge', *Yale University Library Gazette*, 20, 8–10.
Schröder, R. (1898), *Thomas Carlyles Abhandlung über Goethes Faust aus dem Jahre 1821*. Braunschweig: George Westermann.
Scott. J. [?] (1820), 'The Lion's Head', *London Magazine*, 2, (July), 6–7.
Shaffer, E. S. (2002), 'The "Confessions" of Goethe and Coleridge: Goethe's "Bekenntnisse einer Schönen Seele" and Coleridge's *Confessions of An Inquiring Spirit*', in N. Boyle and J. Guthrie (eds), *Goethe and the English-Speaking World*. Rochester: Camden House, pp. 145–58.
Shelley, P. B. (1964), *Letters of Percy Bysshe Shelley*, 2 v., F. L. Jones (ed.). Oxford: Clarendon.
Soane, G. (trans.) (1820), *Extracts from Göthe's Tragedy of Faustus, Explanatory of the Plates by Retsch, Intended to Illustrate That Work*. London: Printed for J. H. Bohte, 4 York Street, Covent Garden; by G. Schulze, 13 Poland Street, Oxford Street.
Wadepuhl, W. (1939), 'Hüttner, a new source for Anglo-German relations', *The Germanic Review*, 14, (1), 23–7.
Wu, D. (2002), 'Rancour and rabies: Coleridge and Jeffrey in dialogue', *British Romanticism and the Edinburgh Review: Bicentenary Essays*, M. Demata and D. Wu (eds). Houndmills: Palgrave Macmillan, pp. 168–94.

Part IV

Asia

8 On the Reception of *Faust* in Asia

Adrian Hsia

The legend of Faust and the following chapbooks are deeply rooted in Christianity; however, Goethe's drama is a post-Enlightenment product. It is an amalgamation of Christian, classical Greek and modern elements. God and Mephistopheles seem to be on friendly terms, and their bet on Faust is done in apparent friendship. The devil appears to be a necessary component in the plan of creation to benefit, in the final analysis, humankind. Faust's pact with the devil is rather un-satanic and is based on the former's disbelief that his drive for action would ever be satiated. These two elements, the unending striving on Faust's part and the presence of the devil, play the most vital role in the drama's reception in Asia. As a matter of fact, it is, as a rule, Part I of the drama which attracts most attention, while the other components of *Faust*, especially the scenes involving Greek mythology in Part II, catch less attention in Asia.

Asia is probably the most multifaceted continent on Earth, with a multitude of cultures and languages. In this chapter, we have to limit ourselves to examine the reception of *Faust* in three cultural regions. From the Islamic area, we shall focus on the Arabic reaction to Goethe's drama; then we shall study the Hindu reception on the subcontinent India; last, but not least, we shall turn our attention to Japan and China. It goes without saying that space will not allow us to present a complete history of the reception of *Faust* in these three regions; we shall have to limit ourselves to the most striking features. Geographically and historically, the Middle East has been most involved with Europe, and we shall begin our study from there.

In spite of the multitude of cultures and countries in Asia, Asians in the modern age were, as a rule, first impressed by the military power of European countries and the success of their conquests in Asia and elsewhere in the world. This motivated Asian countries to use the European model to build up their armies and weaponry. Then they discovered that it was impossible to do so without having first developed science and technology. In its turn, they again had to realize that the technical aspects were a part of the modern culture thriving in Europe, including the arts. It was only then that attention was also turned to literature. Because the first and foremost attention had been on military strength, the Asian countries looked upon England and France, the superpowers in the nineteenth century, as their models. It was only toward the end of the century that Germany entered the picture rather dramatically. Because of this development, most Asian countries came into contact with German culture and literature through the intermediary of English and French. In the Near and Middle East (including Turkey), owing to historical development, French used to be the first foreign language. On the Indian subcontinent, however, it was English. Hence both the Arab countries and Turkey learned of Goethe in general and his *Faust* in particular through their intellectuals who had studied in France (Hilmi 1986: 8–10).

As in most countries, the first book by Goethe to be translated into Arabic was *Die Leiden des jungen Werthers* (*The Sufferings of Young Werther*). George Mutran translated it from the French into Arabic in 1905 (Hilmi 1986: 53). *Faust* was the second of Goethe's books to be rendered into Arabic. It was translated in 1911. However, it was not a real translation, as only the plot of the drama (Part I) was retold in prose. It was not until 1929 that *Faust I* was completely translated by Muhammad Awad Muhammad, who also gave a summary of Part II. The first translation of *Faust I* in Arabic verse was published in 1959. Ten years later, the same translator, Muhammad Abdel Halīm Karāra, also rendered *Faust II* into Arabic (Hilmi 1986: 55). It should be noted that Karāra was neither a professional translator nor writer; he had a Ph.D. in political science and economics. It is therefore small wonder that his rendition is less popular that Muhammad's. As a rule, Goethe was generally praised highly by his Arab translators and critics. As far as *Faust* is concerned, there are some factors which eased the reception and others which posed some problems.

The source of the Faust legend is Christian. Christianity is one of the three great monotheistic religions of the world. They share a creation myth, an omnipotent God, heaven and hell. Of the archangels, one had rebelled against God and become the devil. Because of these common tenets of belief, Goethe's *Faust* was readily accessible to Muslims. On the other hand, Goethe tempered the Christian elements in his drama. He presented God and the devil not as antagonistic, but as complementary entities. In addition, in the drama, Faust is redeemed not because of his faith, but because of his permanent striving for action. These items are unorthodox both in Christianity and Islam and are, therefore, unacceptable to the purists. However, in Islam there are two kinds of devils: the master of hell, known as Iblīs, and the devil who dwells on earth, shaytān. The first one is considered the incorporation of evil, as he disobeyed God.[1] The second kind, seemingly a remnant of pre-Islamic culture, has both positive and negative aspects. On the negative side, they seduce humans to evil deeds great and small, from greed and lust to murder and war. On the positive side, they can instill talent and creativity into artists, from writers to sculptors. Because of this ambiguity, the prophet Mohammed refused to be called a poet so that he would not be brought to the proximity of the shaytān. This quality of ambiguity seems to correspond more to Goethe's Mephistopheles (who describes himself as the force which intends evil, but achieves good) than to the traditional Satan of both faiths. Islamic culture was well-equipped to receive Goethe's drama.

Besides translations of Goethe's *Faust* into Arabic, there are also adaptations. One example is a play by Muhammad Farīd Abū Hadīd in Arabic, published in Cairo in 1945. The title, in English translation, is *The Slave of the Devil* (Hilmi 1986: 154–9). The protagonist is Tobuz, an impoverished writer. One of his books is entitled *The New Faust*. Because of his lack of success in life and his futile love for a girl from a rich family, he lives in utter despair. Before he is about to commit suicide, he calls upon the devil, who appears promptly. The devil assures Tobuz that he is the same one who signed a contract with Faust, even though his name is now Ahriman, that is, the spirit of darkness in Zoroasterism whose counterpart is Ahura Mazda. After negotiation, Tobuz agrees to sell himself. The signing of the contract now follows a different procedure. Ahriman uses his ring to make a cut on Tobuz' arm and put the ring on that wound. Immediately the words 'the slave of the devil' appear as if tattooed. Ahriman covers the mark with a bracelet. Then the protagonist is introduced to the highest society and with Ahriman's help he is able to seduce his former love, who has now become the wife of his best friend, and another woman, who abandons her children to be with him. In the meanwhile, Iblīs has been giving money to peasants and workers so that they do not work any more. Consequently, the economy breaks down and a coup d'état takes place. Eventually, Tobuz becomes the head of state. Because drinking and gambling are the order of the day, the entire country is now impoverished. Tobuz is not happy about the situation and there are often altercations between him and Ahriman. At this point two new characters are introduced, an economist who wishes to reform the economic system of the country and his daughter, who loves Tobuz and wishes to bring him back to the right path. Both plans are ruined by Ahriman. Again Tobuz loses his love. After his attempt to kill the devil has failed, he tries to flee from his clutches with a bag of gold. However, the gold, given by Iblīs, alias Ahriman, disappears into thin air, and the tattoo on his wound begins to multiply and covers his whole body. As the branded slave of the devil, he becomes the laughing stock of the country and despised by everybody. Ahriman does not answer Tobuz' appeal for help any more. He just enjoys his victory over Tobuz. Thus the play ends. The difference between this play and Goethe's drama is apparent. Whoever sells himself to the devil is not redeemable by his own efforts. The moral of the play is clear: do not ally yourself with the devil, as he will certainly abandon you to the vultures one day. This play also carries a political message. According to some critics, Ahriman stands for the British colonial power and Tobuz represents Mohammad Mahmud, the prime minister of Egypt of the 1940s, who collaborated with the British. It is not the unique case that the reception of *Faust* was linked with the political agenda of the day. We shall encounter similar cases in other cultures in Asia.

There are other instances of creative adaptation of *Faust*. In 1953, the Egyptian writer Tawfīq al-Hakīm published a short story in Arabic of which a German rendition appeared in 1970 translated by Horst Lothar Teweleit. Al-Hakīm was an old friend of *Faust*. Already in 1938, he published a story relating the fictional events that occurred while he was reading Goethe's drama around midnight. He identified himself with Faust as he also had been pursuing knowledge all his life without having the time and means to enjoy life. At this moment he sensed a presence in his room—the devil. They began to negotiate. In return for being transformed into the Arabic Faust, the protagonist agreed to surrender his youth. He enjoyed life for thirteen years, living the life of Faust. Then the moment of truth came. Looking into the mirror, he saw that he had become an old man. Now he regretted his dealing with the devil, but it was too late (Hilmi 1986: 159–60). We see this tale reverses the story of Faust who is rejuvenated by Mephistopheles. Also, it is clear that the devil is the winner.

In Tawfīq al-Hakīm's 1953 short story mentioned above, the devil is tricked by an ugly woman living in poverty and isolation. Their deal is beauty, love and all the pleasures of life for ten years, and afterward she would surrender her soul to the devil. During the period allotted to her, she experiences all the joys of life to her heart's content. When the end nears, the devil appears to remind her of their contract. She says she has indeed enjoyed every aspect of pleasure except the joy of the spirit which she now wishes to pursue in the last months of her life. Without suspecting a trick, the devil agrees. From this moment onward, the woman changes her life entirely. Overnight she becomes a pious woman. She puts on a pilgrim's attire and goes on a pilgrimage. She gives alms, does other good deeds and leads a chaste life. Thus she experiences spiritual happiness unbeknown to her until then. When the end comes, she waits for the arrival of the devil who comes to take her to hell. However, at its gate, angels intervene to take her soul to heaven. Both the devil and the woman point out their contract, and the devil accuses the angels of being unreasonable because the woman seems to follow him willingly to hell. The angels respond that because of the utter honesty of the woman and her willingness to keep her contract at all costs, she does not belong to hell. Thus there is a happy ending.

Even though there are two kinds of devils in Arabic culture, in the case of *Faust* adaptations, it is usually Iblīs who appears. Friendly conversations and bets between God and Satan as Goethe presented in his 'Prologue in Heaven' ('Prolog im Himmel') are not imaginable by devout Muslims and are usually avoided. With very few exceptions, people too involved with the devil are not able to extricate themselves and end miserably. Thus the ugly woman in al-Hakīm's story was quite rare. Moreover, she is unique in Islamic culture because she is a female Faust. It takes a woman to trick the devil and make him appear as some kind of clown. She would be of much interest to gender studies. But even she has to take the precaution of dealing with the devil in such a way so that she can still go to heaven legitimately. The author takes great care in preparing the scene. It is true that she is dissatisfied with her lot of being ugly, poor and unloved and calls on the devil to improve her fortune. However, when dealing with him, the author lets her appear to be in an unconscious state. This mitigates her dealing with the devil and makes her redeemable. Obviously, she is a very smart woman who has planned everything in advance. Besides pretending to be unconscious and therefore not really being responsible for her actions, even though the contract is signed in blood, she purposely becomes a pious woman just shortly before the contract ends. In addition, she appears to be ready to fulfill the contract by following the devil to hell. Certainly, she triumphs over the devil who has supplied her with beauty, wealth and pleasure for ten years. But it also appears that she also tricks God to send angels to intercept her soul at the gate of hell and lead her to heaven. It is a remarkable story indeed and should be entitled 'The woman who outsmarts God and the devil'.

This is more or less the space which we can allot to the Arabic reception of *Faust*.[2] We shall turn our attention to the reception of *Faust* in Hindi language. Before we go on, we should remind ourselves that one reason for the enthusiastic reception of Goethe's *Faust* by Islamic authors was that Arabic intellectuals made their first acquaintance with the German poet through the positive perception of their counterparts in France. This positive first impression was further reinforced when they learned of Goethe's lifelong interest in Islam and the orient.[3] For him, the Koran is 'the book of books'. Many Muslims, including the head of the Muslim community in Weimar (Al-Murabit 1995), regard him as a fellow believer. These favorable factors are not applicable in the Hindi reception, because Indians perceived Europe and its culture through British eyes. Throughout the British colonial empire, the primary concern of the masters was to promote the English language and the literature of the British Isles. Sisir Kumar Das, an Indian scholar from New Delhi, sums up the situation of India under British rule thus:

> The agenda of education . . . did not provide any space to accommodate any European literature other than English. The Indian understanding of Europe was monitored by the English language and the British perception of Europe. Indians were more familiar with classical European literature—Greek and Latin, than with medieval or modern European literature including great works like *The Divine Comedy* or *Don Quixote* . . . (Das 2000: 4–5)

The works of Goethe, including *Faust*, were not exempt from this situation. Apart from the politico-cultural factor, Goethe's relation with Indian culture is more ambivalent than it is with Islam. Hinduism knows no founder and no supreme leader like the pope, while Goethe's enthusiasm for Mohammed is reciprocated by practically all Muslims. As far as India is concerned, Goethe eulogized the Indian dramatist Kalidasa, whose drama *Shakuntala* he read in Georg Forster's translation. Today, it is well known that the 'Prelude in the Theatre' ('Vorspiel auf dem Theater') in *Faust I* was inspired by the Indian play. However, Goethe's praise of Kalidasa, deeply appreciated by Indian intellectuals since the nineteenth century,[4] is offset by his outspoken criticism of Hindu divinities and their representations in art. Sisir Kumar Das quotes Goethe's assessment (in English translation): 'I [Goethe] have been driving them out forever, those many-headed gods have been cursed by me—Vishnu, Kama, Brahma and also Hanuman'—and concludes that 'these words were not music to the Hindu ears' (Das 2000: 7). Goethe's judgment, Das believes, is a consequence of his superficial knowledge and understanding of Indian art and philosophy. The legacy of both factors, India's colonial past and Goethe's mixed feeling about Indian culture, makes Goethe's presence in India 'unfortunately only marginal' (Das 2000: 4). Das is convinced that Goethe, 'though certainly known, is hardly read' in India, except by Germanists (2000: 4). Consequently, translations of Goethe's major works are, again in Das' words, 'deplorably few' and academic discourses on his works 'almost non-existent in the Indian languages'. In addition, even the few existing works, discourses and translations 'remain in splendid isolation, yet to create a visible impact on our literary sensibility' (Das 2000: 4). Das' opinion is substantiated by the fact that the German cultural institute, which has a subsidiary in almost all major cities of the world and is known globally as the Goethe Institute, is called the Max Müller Institute in India. Goethe has to defer to the Indologue Max Müller.

India is a country of multiple languages and two major religions. The Urdu-speakers, because of historic reasons, are mostly Muslims. Consequently, their reception of Goethe is closer to the pattern of Islamic reception we have examined above.[5] Sisir Kumar Das is referring to the Hindu reception of Goethe. Another Indian scholar, Abhay Mishra (2003), who wrote on the Indian reception of Goethe's *Faust*, points out that the Hindi translation of *Faust* cannot fall back on the Hindu tradition (which, for example, does not have a concept of the devil) for support. Nevertheless, despite the rather gloomy historical background of reception described above, the circumstances and development of Hindi translation are very interesting. It is a classical example of how the recipient—the translator—uses a literary work for his or her own agenda. Our source regarding the background of Hindi translation is Anandita Sharma, a young Indian scholar who presented on the Hindu reception of *Faust I* at the symposium on non-Christian reception of *Faust* in 2006.[6] Sharma points out that even though the Hindi language includes Islamic and Persian concepts, the translator of the first Hindi rendition of the first part of *Faust*, Pandit Bholanath Sharma (1906–60), was not only a Hindu, but also intended his translation to help promote the Hindi language under British rule. When the rendition was published in 1939, colonial India still did not have its own national language; the language of administration and education was English. In addition, his translation should also help to promote Hindu tradition, for, unlike Islam, which has its canon of holy texts, a large part of Hindu tradition was handed down orally. It was through the efforts of German Indologues, who used philological methods to reconstruct texts from oral tradition, that Hinduism began to have a canon of authoritative holy texts. This may run against the grain of the Hindu tradition, but it is conducive to nation-building. The translation of *Faust* was part and parcel of this program and helped to establish the authority of Hinduism, because Pandit Bholanath Sharma declared in his introduction of his rendition that *Faust* was the proof that Goethe abandoned Christian tenets in favor of Hinduism. The evidence is, according to Sharma, when Faust retranslates the beginning of the *Gospel* according to John ('In the beginning was the Word . . . ') in his study and decides to substitute the 'Word' with something more appropriate. Sharma translates the German word 'Tat', which in English is 'deed' (Philip Wayne) or 'act' (Bayard Taylor), to the Hindu term 'karma'. His rendition would read in English translation thus: 'In the beginning was karma'. Then he asserts that the plot of Goethe's *Faust*, from the 'Prologue in Heaven' to the salvation of Faust at the end of Part II, follows the path of karma. According to Sharma, this is in agreement with the *Bhagavad Gita* when Krishna explains to Arjuna that all beginnings are sheathed in guilt, but whoever seeks refuge in him (Krishna), will be saved. Thus it is Faust's karma to sign his soul off to the devil in exchange for material gain and sexual pleasure; however, it is also his karma that he finally subscribes to selfless deeds to help mankind, which also saves him from damnation. Thus Goethe or at least his Faust is perceived as a covert Hindu. This interpretation enhanced the prestige of the Hindi language and the Hindu tradition, which was instrumental for the nation-building of India, which became independent in 1947.

Comparing the Islamic with the Hindu reception, it becomes evident that both the internal and external circumstances impact the reception of a product from an alien culture. There seems to be a closer affinity between Goethe's *Faust* and Islamic, rather than Hindu, culture. As far as Goethe and his *Faust* are concerned, it also seems that France is a more sympathetic intermediary than Great Britain. However, before we leave India and move on to East Asia, we should at least mention two facts. The first one is that in 1997, a Goethe Society of India was founded. Up to now, four issues of its yearbook have been published. The other matter is that there is also a stage reception of Goethe's drama in India, as discussed in Chapter 9 by the Canadian scholar, David John, who has done extensive research in this area.[7]

As cultural affinity plays an important role in the process of transcultural reception, this should be our first concern when we move on to East Asia. Comparable to the fact that the foundation of modern Europe, despite the national characteristics of each country, is built on the culture of ancient Greece and Rome as well as Christianity, East Asian countries also have common cultural roots of their own. These are Confucianism and Daoism of ancient China as well as Mahayana Buddhism.[8] Ever since Woldemar Freiherr von Biedermann's books at the end of the nineteenth century,[9] we know that Goethe was deeply appreciative of, in addition to Islam and the Indian theatre, the culture of Cathay, that is, ancient China. Katharina Mommsen (1985) has summarized this phenomenon in her essay 'Goethe und China in ihren Wechselbeziehungen' ('The interrelations between Goethe and China'). The observation of the Goethe-expert Mommsen is further elucidated by the Sinologist Richard Wilhelm, who wrote that, despite the poor quality of books on China in the early nineteenth century which Goethe read, he was able to capture the quintessence of the Chinese cultural heritage. Wilhelm further explained that Goethe was able to do so because of his innate congeniality to that culture (Hsia 2007: 12). It is, of course, impossible to explain the cultural foundation of East Asia, Daoism, Confucianism and Mahayana Buddhism adequately in this chapter. Therefore, we are forced to abbreviate Daoism as natural philosophy and Confucianism as interhuman moral tenets which shaped the mentality of the three countries of East Asia with which we are concerned. As for East Asian Mahayana Buddhism, with which Goethe was not really concerned, it evolved from individual to mass redemption through the merciful nature of Buddha. Their congeniality laid a solid foundation for the reception of Goethe's works in that region of the world.

The nineteenth and early twentieth centuries were times of extreme upheavals. The Western powers were expanding both militarily and commercially. Consequently, the non-European world was up for grabs. Even though none of the East Asian countries were really colonized by any Western power, their history and destiny were indelibly changed by the incursions of the West. China and Japan were forcibly opened up by warships and cannons, while Korea became a Japanese colony toward the end of the nineteenth century. Japan adapted itself to the new situation much faster than China by opening its political, commercial and cultural borders. Western ideas and ideals poured in along with less agreeable products. In the initial stage, Japan became the purveyor of Western culture for China and Korea. Then each went its own way. Japan's gate was pried opened by American warships; and Great Britain was the superpower of the day. It is, therefore, not surprising that English was the first foreign language of Japan. As a matter of fact, Goethe's name was first mentioned in the Japanese translation of John Stuart Mill's *On Liberty* in 1871 (Miyashita 1993: 82) and the first Japanese translation of Goethe's *Faust I* was done by a Japanese scholar of English literature, Takahashi Goro, who mainly used Bayard Taylor's English rendition. It was published in 1904 and by August 1913 it was reprinted five times (Kimura 1993a: 25–6). The first translation of both parts of *Faust* into Japanese was published in 1913. The translator was Mori Ogai, who became a legend, and his rendition enjoys an immortal status even today. However, after

Mori's work, twelve other translations of both parts of Goethe's *Faust* followed. This is a world record. The reason for this high number of translations is the rapid evolution of written Japanese. The written Japanese of Takahashi's translation, for example, was adapted from ancient China, which was only accessible to the highly educated stratum of Japan. When Mori planned to prepare his rendition from the original German, he was also thinking of a literary style fashioned according to traditional Chinese literature (Miyashita 1993: 88). Somewhere along the line, he changed his mind and rendered *Faust* into refined spoken Japanese.[10] In this way, his rendition helped to develop vernacular Japanese from vulgarity to a literary style, and his translation became a cultural monument.[11] Most of the later translations reflect a linguistic or sociolinguistic change or shift of later periods and the effort to make the work readable to new readers.

Consistent with the introduction of Western literature, Western plays and their stage productions were also introduced. The first part of Mori's *Faust* was published in January and the second in March. Nearly immediately afterward, *Faust I* was premiered on 27 March 1913, in the Imperial Theatre in Tokyo. It was adapted for the theatre by Iba Takashi, who divided the play into five acts with fifteen scenes altogether. Iba also played Mephistopheles, while Kamiyama Sojin assumed the role of Faust. Because the traditional Japanese theatre only used male actors, even for female roles, Iba asked a young woman without any stage experience whom he chanced to meet in a café to play Gretchen. After five nights in Tokyo, it was staged again in Osaka. It came as quite a surprise that the untrained Gretchen earned the highest praise, while Faust was generally disliked by the critics (Miyashita 1993: 90–2). In the thirties, the Marxist Kubo Sakae, who considered Faust and Mephistopheles as two different forms of resistance against feudalism, staged a simplified version of *Faust I*, adapted and translated by him.[12] In 1942, there was a short amateur production with which not even the translator-director himself was satisfied. However, in 1965, Senda Koreya, who became famous for his production of plays by Bertolt Brecht, staged the complete *Faust I* for the first time. His interpretation of Goethe's drama was socialist à la Brecht; for example, the night of Walpurgis, for him, is perceived as a reflection of the French Revolution (Miyashita 1993: 101). The text used was a prose version of the drama, rendered into Japanese by Tezuka Tomio. In Tokyo alone the performance ran from 4 to 29 September 1965, and it was then continued in other large cities such as Kyoto, Osaka, Kobe, etc. This was apparently the climax of the reception of *Faust* on the Japanese stage.

The academic reception was much earlier. Kimura Naoji, probably the best known Japanese Goethe-scholar of today, speaks of a cult of Goethe in the thirties, when *Faust* was actively promoted by the circle of Kimura Kinji (the two Kimuras are not related), the chair professor of German literature at the Imperial University Tokyo, and his students. It was also during this period that the most complete collected works of Goethe in Japanese, altogether thirty-six volumes, were published (Kimura 1993b: 73). Following the footsteps of one of the earliest interpretations, namely Anezaki Masaharu's essay on the fate of Gretchen published in 1895 (Ashizu 1990: 49–51), Kimura Kinji gave Goethe's drama a Buddhist interpretation. According to one school of Buddhist thought, the all merciful Amida Buddha helps all departing souls, no matter how sinful their lives have been, to be reborn in the Pure Land or paradise, one step before entering the stage of nirvana. Gretchen went there before Faust, and when he dies, she receives him into heaven. Thus the Christian foundation and Goethe's changes to the Faust material are all absorbed in the teaching of the Pure Land Sect of Buddhism. Accordingly, the question of quilt has become a nonissue. The Japanese version of Pure Land teaching, in particular, goes even further than the Chinese origin. It postulates that Buddha gives priority to redeem sinners. This is considered the Japanese reception of Goethe's *Faust* (Kimura 1993b: 70).

Even though Buddhism was introduced into Japan via China, the Chinese reception of Goethe's *Faust* is completely non-Buddhist, because it took place at a much later date than in Japan. The first translation of anything by Goethe happened in 1903. It was the song of Mignon by Ma Junwu, who studied chemical engineering in Japan and later in Germany. In comparison, Goethe's *Reineke Fuchs* was published in Japanese in 1884. The first part of *Faust* in Japanese was published in 1904, while the Chinese translation appeared only in 1928 in the translation of Guo Moruo. In Japanese, the complete drama was published in 1913; in Chinese only in 1935, translated by Zhou Xuepu. The Japanese stage production of *Faust* took place in 1913; in China, it had to wait until 1994. In addition, it was co-organized with the Goethe Institute in Beijing. Guo Moruo is one of the best known Chinese writers in the twentieth century. After the foundation of the People's Republic of China in 1949, he became the uncrowned pope of the Chinese literature sanctioned by the Chinese Communist Party. Goethe's *Faust I* was not his first translation of Goethe's works; it was *Werther* (1922). It goes without saying that Guo studied in Japan and was deeply influenced by the Goethe-cult, especially the 'Werther-fever', there. This period of his life in Japan, along with two other Chinese scholars, the famous playwright Tian Han and the philosopher Zong Baihua, is documented in the correspondence of these three and published in 1920.[13] In this exchange of letters, Guo compared Walt Whitman, Heinrich Heine and Goethe. He wrote that the poetry of Heine was beautiful but not great, that of Whitman was the reverse. Only the poems of Goethe were both beautiful and great. Based on Zhou's translation of the second part of *Faust* mentioned above, Guo rendered it again into Chinese in 1947. It took him, as he professed in the preface, only four weeks. It seems that what he did was more to rephrase Zhou's version than to translate directly from the original, as he used the former's book to write down his translation line by line (Hsia 1990: 38). By today's standards, both Zhou and Guo should be listed as translators of the version now still accredited to Guo.

After the Communist Party took over power in China in 1949 until the official end of the Proletarian Cultural Revolution in 1979, only the reprints of Guo's translations of Goethe's works were published. Perhaps one should say that only these were allowed to be published. In 1978, Zhou's rendition was reprinted in Taipei, and in 1982 a new Chinese translation of both parts was also published in Taipei, but it was translated from the English translation by Philip Wayne. In the same year, there were two new translations of the complete *Faust* published in Shanghai. The translators were Dong Wenqiao and Qian Chunqi. Dong was a professor of German in Shanghai and a party member of long-standing. Qian, however, was a rare specimen under the Communist rule. He was a dentist by training, but gave up his profession for love of poetry and became a freelancer. Before China accepted a market economy, anybody not working for the state had no regular income and no guaranteed housing. It meant living in permanent poverty. Qian, however, was ready to accept the risk in order to cultivate his lyrical talent. His translations were well accepted by his readers. In my opinion, his translation in verse (he tried to match Goethe's form) is very readable as well as accurate. With the new translations, Chinese readers have better access to Goethe's drama than ever before. However, as far as the appreciation and interpretation of Goethe's *Faust* is concerned, China is still lagging behind Japan, because the official ideology of the People's Republic of China is still socialist. Even though people can usually express their opinion privately without fear of retribution, whatever is disseminated within its boundaries, except in Hong Kong and Macao, must conform to the official ideology, including literary criticism. Consequently, the academic reception of *Faust* is both socialist and atheist in nature. Nevertheless, general readers can enjoy published translated foreign works without impediment.

As we have seen in this survey of the reception of Goethe's *Faust* in the three major cultures of Asia, the dynamics of reception depend on several factors. In the instance of Islamic reception, the favorable reception of Islam by Goethe as expressed in his works facilitates reception of his works in Islamic countries. Events and descriptions which do not conform to orthodox Islamic tenets are either glossed over or substituted. This is especially evident in the adaptation and further development of Faust material in Arabic. Judging from the fiction in Arabic based on the material, it seems to have acquired its own dynamic in development. In Hindu India, the reception of *Faust* was impeded by the country's colonial history. Because of the British agenda in the past, Christopher Marlowe's *Dr. Faustus* is better known than Goethe's *Faust*. In addition, for most Indian intellectuals, English is like a first language. Even among Indian Germanists, their conversation is usually conducted in English. The need for reading translations in an Indian language is only common among those less educated. This feature is quite unique in Asia. Even though there is a Goethe Society of India, its aim is to promote Goethe's works along with those of modern German literature. Even though established only in 1997, its yearbook appears only irregularly. In comparison, the first yearbook of the Japanese Goethe Society was published in 1932, and it is published on a regular basis, with the content of the essays focused on Goethe or at least related to his time. The reception of Goethe and *Faust* is really quite extraordinary in Japan. Goethe research is quite developed; much background material and research literature has been translated into Japanese. In addition, the social and industrial structure has developed beyond what Goethe envisioned in *Faust* so that in popular culture, such as in 'manga' or Japanese comics, Faust is perceived as an evil scientist. The Faustian spirit, that is, striving at all cost, which is really non-Goethean because the question of guilt is missing, has become congenial to the Japanese.

The reception of Goethe's *Faust* in China is again another matter. First of all, China is a socialist country with tight ideological control as far as dissemination of ideas is concerned. In addition, the translators, with the exception of Zhou Xuepu, were mostly convinced socialists. Moreover, from the beginning of the reception of Goethe, China was in a continued state of conflict. It overthrew the Manchu Dynasty and endured Western exploitation, invasion by Japan and civil war until it became a People's Republic in 1949. Up to this point, it received all Western literature, including Goethe's *Faust*, within this context, measuring each and every work in terms of how it could serve the development of China into a strong country. Consequently, it valued the Faustian element of striving in order to strengthen China. Even though reception there came more or less to a standstill during the years 1949–78, however, the instrumentation of the market economy reinstated this Faustian spirit. Of course, how this spirit agrees with Goethe's *Faust* is another problem. So far, we see that the intercultural reception of literature is mainly conditioned by the attitude of the author vis-à-vis the recipient culture as well as the perceived needs of the latter. With the interaction between the author and the recipient, a new work or spirit is created. The Japanese understanding of *Faust* is thus different from the Indian and, in turn, also different from the Arabic reception. Each reception or re-creation is unique in its own way.

Notes

1 According to the Koran, after the creation of Adam and Eve, God commanded all angels to acknowledge the superiority of humans by kneeling before the first couple. Iblīs, however, refused.
2 For further examples please see Hilmi (1986). For a complementary, but very sketchy list, see Radwan (1993: 303–12, especially 309).
3 See Mommsen (1988; 2001) for detailed discussion of Goethe's oriental studies.
4 Cf. Das (2000: 5–6): 'Every educated Indian in the nineteenth century knew Goethe's four-line verse on Sakuntala ... It is this verse which became the central spirit for Rabindranath Tagore's famous critique of the play by Kalidasa'.
5 Cf. Mishra (2003: 174). Regarding the reception in Urdu, Mishra emphasizes that the similarity between Satan and Iblīs gives a point of reference which helps interpreters to recognize that Faust is 'humanity individualized'.
6 The symposium, co-organized by Adrian Hsia and Jochen Golz, took place in Montreal, Canada, in October 2006. A selection of papers, including Sharma's, will be published by Böhlau-Verlag.
7 John's article 'Stage productions of Faust in India' will be published in the same volume as Sharma's.
8 We exclude Buddhism not because it originated in India, but because Goethe was not very concerned with it.
9 He analyzed Goethe's *Elpenor* in *Goethe-Forschungen* (1879), then 'Chinesisch-deutsche Jahres- und Tageszeiten', in *Goethe-Forschungen N. F.* (1886) and 'Goethe und das chinesische Schriftum' in *Zeitschrift für Vergleichende Litteraturgeschichte N. F.* (1894) and reprinted in *Goethe-Forschungen* v. 3 (1894).
10 This is a common phenomenon of East Asia. China and Korea also had to develop a new literary style from the vernacular.
11 It would be the ideal stage for the Hindi translation of Sharma.
12 From 7 to 14 January 1936 and then again from 22 February to 12 March 1939.
13 About the correspondence of these three persons, see the following articles in Debon and Hsia (1985): Wuneng Yang, 'Goethe und die chinesische Gegenwartsliteratur' (127–37) and Hsia, 'Zum Verständnis eines chinesischen Werther-Dramas' (183–93).

Bibliography

Al-Murabit, S. A. (1995), 'Goethe als Muslim', www.enfal.de/gote-fat.htm (retrieved 15 August 2007).
Ashizu, T. (1990), 'Buddhisdische *Faust*-Rezeption in Japan', *Studien des Instituts für die Kultur der deutschsprachigen Länder*, 8, 44–58.
Das, S. K. (2000), 'Goethe and India', *Yearbook of the Goethe Society of India*, 3–18.
Debon, G. and Hsia, A. (eds) (1985), *Goethe und China—China und Goethe*. Bern: Peter Lang.
Hilmi, A. (1986), *Die Rezeption Goethes in Ägypten*. Stuttgart: H.-D. Heinz.
Hsia, A. (1990), 'Zur Faust-Rezeption in China', *Studien des Instituts für die Kultur der deutschsprachigen Länder*, 8, 31–43.
— (ed.) (1993), *Zur Rezeption von Goethes 'Faust' in Ostasien*. Bern: Peter Lang.
— (2007), 'Goethes Affinitäten zur chinesischen Geisteswelt nach der Sicht Richard Wilhelms', in D. Wippermann and G. Ebertshäuser (eds), *Wege und Kreuzungen der China-Kunde an der J. W. Goethe-Universität, Frankfurt am Main*. Frankfurt: IKO-Verlag für Interkulturelle Kommunikation, pp. 9–21.
Kimura, N. (1993a), 'Probleme der japanischen *Faust*-Übersetzung', in A. Hsia (ed.), *Zur Rezeption von Goethes 'Faust' in Ostasien*. Bern: Peter Lang, pp. 23–43.
— (1993b), 'Probleme der *Faust*-Rezeption in Japan', in A. Hsia (ed.), *Zur Rezeption von Goethes 'Faust' in Ostasien*. Bern: Peter Lang, pp. 65–80.
Mishra, A. (2003), 'Die Rezeption von Goethes *Faust* in Indien', *Yearbook of the Goethe Society of India*, 171–81.
Miyashita, K. (1993), '"In diesem Sinne kannst du's wagen": Goethes *Faust* auf der japanischen Bühne', in A. Hsia (ed.), *Zur Rezeption von Goethes 'Faust' in Ostasien*. Bern: Peter Lang, pp. 81–104.
Mommsen, K. (1985), 'Goethe und China in ihren Wechselbeziehungen', in G. Debon and A. Hsia (eds), *Goethe und China—China und Goethe*. Bern: Peter Lang, pp. 15–33.
— (1988), *Goethe und die arabische Welt*. Frankfurt: Inselverlag.
— (2001), *Goethe und der Islam*. Frankfurt: Inselverlag.
Radwan, K. (1993), 'Die Rezeption der Faustgestalt in der arabischen Literatur', in H.-C. G. v. Nayhauss and K. A. Kuczyński (eds), *Im Dialog mit der interkulturellen Germanistik*. Wroclaw: Wydawn. Uniwersytetu Wroclawskiego, pp. 303–12.
Teweleit, H. L. (ed. and trans.) (1970), *Von Wundern und heller Verwunderung und von denen, die es mit Himmel und Hölle halten*. Berlin: Rütten and Loening, pp. 110–17.

9 Goethe's *Faust* in India: The Kathakali Adaptation*

David G. John

There has long been interest in *Faust* among scholars and educated persons in India who have read Goethe's tragedy in the original or English, one of the country's official languages. Many no doubt have also read it in Hindi or one of the six other Indian languages into which it has been translated: Bengali, Kannada, Malayalam, Marathi, Tamil and Urdu.[1] Despite that long-standing interest, there is no formal record of *Faust* performances in India, which in fact include renditions or adaptations in some of these and other Indian languages as well. In the course of my research I have found five such stagings: 1999 *Urfaust* in English, in Chennai, directed by A.V. Dhánushkodi; 1998 *Faust I* in Bengali, in Kolkata, directed by Santanu Bose; 1994 *Faust I* in Hindi, in Mumbai, directed by Fritz Bennewitz and Vijaya Mehta; 1993 *Faust I* in Malayalam, in Kerala, directed by Erin B. Mee; 1976 *Faust I and II*, in Malayalam and performed as a Kathakali dance, in Kerala, New Delhi and elsewhere, directed by Aymanam Krishna Kaimal.[2]

With the exceptions of my own overview of the subject, currently in press, and a short article by Annakutty Findeis, scholars have not addressed the topic of *Faust* stagings in this huge, varied and populous country. In my overview, I state that Kaimal's Kathakali *Faust* of 1976 is, in comparative cultural terms, by far the most important of these five stagings, a claim on which I intend to expand in detail now. There, I called the American director and theatre specialist Erin B. Mee's impressive 1993 staging a convincing runner-up. Mee used a Malayalam adaptation of *Faust* written by Kavalam Narayana Panikkar (1999), a renowned Indian playwright and director, and Indian actors. She placed Goethe's work into a naturalistic Indian folk setting with realistic costumes and included dialogue, music and dance. The most significant difference between this and Kaimal's 1976 production was that the latter was not just a stage work but an addition to the repertoire of an indigenous Indian dance form with a pedigree stretching over a half millennium. Kaimal's Kathakali, hence highly stylized narrative dance or 'Attakkadha' version of *Faust*, an adaptation rather than a translation of Goethe's text, has become part of the Kathakali canon.

---

* I wish to thank the Social Sciences and Humanities Research Council of Canada for financial assistance to help me conduct this research.

Because both Kathakali and Malayalam are almost impenetrable to Westerners, with the rare exception of scholars like Mee and Phillip Zarrilli, and also to Eastern, indeed most *Indian* people, the first intention of the following chapter is to provide access to an unknown and virtually unexplored adaptation of Goethe's text. To that end, I will present some background information on the Kathakali dance form and describe its main elements, then discuss the adaptation using four pieces of primary evidence, two playbills with plot summaries in English, the text of Kaimal's published adaptation in Malayalam, and a videotape of scenes from one performance. Further, I shall discuss Kaimal's Hindu and English sources and add comments by director Kaimal and his assistants, whom I interviewed on site in Kerala (January 2003). In all, I hope to show how Goethe's work was transformed into an expression of Indian culture, mores and Hindu philosophy.

The Kathakali Dance Form

Kathakali, the classical dance-drama of the southwestern coastal Indian province of Kerala, dates from the end of the sixteenth century and has roots in earlier dance forms. D. Appukuttan Nair and K. Ayyappa Paniker describe it thus:

> Among the various performing arts in India and, perhaps, even the world, Kathakali is unique in so far as it is one of the farthest from earthly reality and humanism. There is no attempt at representing the mundane world in any manner—whether by imitation or otherwise. Only epic non-human beings are chosen for the re-creation of a story for presentation on the stage. And that presentation, whether in form, color, behaviour, or sound, is deliberately made contra-human, to exist in another world: that of the imagination of the connoisseur. If any element in the dance bears even a remote resemblance to *ihaloka* (this world) it appears comic. Kathakali takes the connoisseur away from the transient worldly experience of pleasure to one of transcendental entrancement.[3]

The phrase 'farthest from earthly reality and humanism' prepares us for a highly stylized world in which every movement, detail of make-up and costume, every gesture, every interaction is symbolically codified.[4] Traditional Kathakali plays perform stories from the Indian epics and Puranas, especially the *Bhāgavata purana* which tells the story of the life of Krishna, revealer of sacred truths and one of the ten incarnations or avatars of benevolent Vishnu, who is, in turn, along with Brahma and Shiva, one member of Hinduism's highest trinity. The form has about 500 plays in its repertoire, composed by playwrights in Malayalam, the native language of Kerala.

The story, in which the dancers portray scenes of dramatic confrontations between gods and demons, is told through recitation and singing by narrators, accompanied by musicians who keep the rhythm with a variety of percussion instruments, the gong ('chenkala'), cymbals ('ilattalam'), vertical drum ('chenda'), barrel drum ('maddalam') and small side drum ('idakka'), and concurrently by the movements and gestures of the performers. Interspersed with the dances directly related to the story are 'kalasams', brief, set dances used in all plays, inserted after every dialogue and after particularly important scenes. They punctuate the story and link it to the overall Kathakali genre tradition. The actor/dancers are traditionally all male, though females are now accepted. While there are no rehearsals for a performance, the dancers undergo years of intensive training so that characters, associated choreography and performance scores become second nature to them. Intricate and complex hand gestures and facial expressions are of central importance to convey the narration. Eye movements express inner states of mind. The eyes are often opened wide to the extreme, and rolled up, down, sideways, often in rapid succession, communicating a large range of meanings. The eye whites are reddened with the juice of the 'chunda' flower to 'provide grace and elegance to the expressions of the character'.[5] There are twenty-four basic symbolic hand gestures and arrangements ('mudras'), with hundreds of different applications and combinations.[6] These convey objects, feelings and actions. An example of their complexity is the 'pataka mudra' in which the hand is held open except for the ring finger which is bent, and which has over forty uses. As a single-hand gesture, depending on context, it may denote a day, the tongue, a mirror, the forehead, the body, a messenger, sands on the beach, young leaves, or the act of departing, and while in a combined-hand gesture it may be used to depict the sun, a king, an elephant, a crocodile, an ox, an archway and many more things (Massey 1989: 49). There are nine basic facial expressions or moods ('navarasas'), discernible from the characters' mimicry and eye movement and positioning, each of which sets a tone to individual scenes or parts of scenes. They include love, contempt, sorrow, anger, valor, fear, the grotesque, wonder and detachment.[7] The dancers wear elaborate costumes, many of them multilayered skirts, tunics, breastplates, colorful jackets, scarves and headdresses, in addition to elaborately colorful and evocative make-up, as well as intricately designed painted masks. Costumes and make-up are locked in tradition and immediately signify to audiences a fundamental character type and hence a predictable behavior. The costume and make-up take several hours to put on. Kathakali dancers must also learn a set of unique postures and movements. They all perform barefoot and, with their weight on the outside part of the foot and with legs somewhat bowed, generally remain on one spot after entering until they break into action or elaborate 'kalasams'. They then engage in raising or lowering their legs in tempos from slow to fast, or resting, sometimes breaking into a frenzy of movement including whirls, jumps and rapid stamping along with extreme gestural and mimic activity to depict climactic portions of the scene and story. Dancers must also learn to perform the 'ragas', set rhythms, chanted melodies and texts which accompany the action as a narrated text, should they be needed to serve as accompanying musicians or narrators of the action. All of these elements, eye movement, make-up, digital signage, arm and body gestures, body movement, costume-sewing, 'raga' chanting and instrument playing are parts of the rigorous six-year full-time residential training of a Kathakali performer. The handful of professional training centers such as that in Kottayam is comparable to that of national ballet training academies throughout the world.

In contrast to the elaborate appearance, mimicry, gestures and movements of the dancers, the Kathakali performance space is a simple square at ground level, marked by four poles at the corners adorned with bright cloths, without scenery or props beyond a few basic necessities such as chairs and stools. A brightly colored silk curtain of concentric nested black, blue, green, yellow, red and white rectangles is raised or lowered by hand at the beginning and end of scenes. The performance space is lit traditionally by a single brass lamp 1 m high with kerosene flame at the front of the stage, the aura of which encapsulates the 'maya' or realm of magical illusion in which the performance comes to life. Kathakali performances traditionally occur at night, and last until dawn, though in recent times they may be shortened to a long evening, or a brief demonstration. The light at the front of the stage is the focal point of the performance, though supplementary lighting is used as well. It separates the audience which is seated on all three sides and creates an eerie mood. Dancers can approach the flame to enhance the striking features of their masks, or retreat from it to the shadows, and even make sudden startling appearances among the audience which sits in the darkness. Scene separations are indicated by two stage assistants raising or lowering the curtain at the front of the stage.[8]

There are five main character types in the Kathakali drama, the first of which is the heroic or virtuous beings, such as gods, kings or heroes. They wear what is known as the 'pacca' or light-green make-up with black eyebrows and under-lining, red lips and a stylized mark of Vishnu painted on the forehead. 'Chutti', or rice paste, is applied in rows to frame the cheeks and chin and appears as a white, stiff beard-like appendage. Second, the demon king types wear the 'katti' or knife make-up which also has a green base but the green is broken by red patches at the sides of the nose and above the eyebrow from the bridge of the nose there are drawn two broad, flat-ended curves in red and outlined in white. Above these are white lines across the forehead with an inverted capital 'A' between them and the bridge of the nose. Another red and white oval patch is painted on the nose. Above the upper lip is painted a stylized red moustache which curls over the cheeks, and which is also outlined in white. Finally, there are two, white pith knobs or bulbs on the tip of the nose and in the middle of the forehead, symbolic warts or disfigurations, the more wicked the character, the larger their size, and fangs are inserted under the upper lip. A third type, the wicked 'kari' characters, can be male or female. Their basic make-up and costume is black, including the lips, with bright red crescents on the cheeks and forehead, outlined with white, as is the whole face. A red and white pattern embellishes the chin and the tip of the nose. They have fangs and the females have large black breasts. A fourth type is comprised of the bearded, or 'tadi', characters, of which there are three kinds. White beards signify goodness; black, barbaric forest hunters and robbers; and red, demonic personalities. Beyond the characteristic beard, individual 'tadi' types, such as the monkey god Hanuman, have detailed distinctive costumes as well. The fifth type is the 'minukku'. These include all female characters, such as heavenly nymphs, queens, goddesses and heroines, and minor male characters such as holy men, Brahmins, charioteers and messengers. Their basic color is pale beige, with women's eyes outlined in black and eyebrows emphasized with a graceful curve. The red lips are given a distinctive shape, intended to suggest the figure's beauty, and sometimes the cheeks are adorned with a curved line of white dots which are repeated on the forehead and chin. A dusting of finely powdered mica imparts a soft glow to the skin. Unlike all other characters, the 'minnuku' wear simple costumes, males a simple long or short loin-cloth, females full-length skirts. In addition to these basic types are some characters who have their own particular make-up and costume, immediately recognizable by audiences familiar with the genre. Further symbolic significance of costumes, jewelry and headdresses could be explored in just as much detail for the various basic types.[9]

The videotape of excerpts from the production, given to me by Kaimal, shows a close adherence to the conventions of Kathakali make-up, costuming, staging and performance. In the first scene the Lord wears the green 'pacca' make-up and a large crown of an heroic type, indicating his goodness, and the details of his appearance indicate that he is in fact Lord Krishna, the hero of the epic *Bhagavad Gita*. Faust wears the heroic green make-up of the 'pacca' as well, but a crown of different style. Mephistopheles' black attire, and his alternation between turban and crown headdresses, denote a 'kari' type and signify his villainous duplicity. Lucifer's costume and his crown and sword make him immediately recognizable as a 'katti' type, an arch-evil figure, but of higher order than Mephistopheles. In scenes in which they are in their own domain, both he and Mephistopheles are adorned with white pith knobs—Mephistopheles' are enormous when he is in his true costume—denoting their ugliness and evil. They both exhibit fangs. There are three 'minukku' figures, first the two angels of the prologue with bare upper body, one with a gold, one a silver skirt and turban above the characteristic South Indian white 'lungi' (trousers); and then Margaret, whose costume is more modest, covering her entire body except her face and hands. All characters are played by males—in Margaret's case this is obvious from the performer's size and facial features.

The Hindu and English Sources

Kamail claimed that his adaptation was based partly on the legend of Rugmamgatha from Chapter 21 of the *Padma purana* and the Kathakali play *Rugmamgatha Caritam (King Rugmamgada's Law)*. The play, written in the second half of the eighteenth century, focuses on the significance of 'ekadasi', the eleventh day of every fortnight in a lunar month, which is sacred to Vishnu, and a day on which His devotees are supposed to fast and meditate. The action of the play involves the King, a follower of Vishnu, being led astray by his female consort Mohini, neglecting his 'ekadasi' duties, and being forced to sacrifice his son as penance. The son and Rugmamgatha are saved by Vishnu's direct intervention, receive His blessing and are taken to His heavenly abode.[10] The legend of Rugmamgatha and Goethe's *Faust* have in common themes surrounding the motifs of seduction, betrayal, conscience, redemption and divine intervention. Kaimal explained that he set his adaptation to accord with the prevailing beliefs of Hinduism. King Rugmamgatha's devotion to Vishnu, the Lord's charity to him and by extension Faust's relationship to the Christian God, would be in tune with the ethical sense of propriety of his almost exclusively Hindu audience, Hinduism being the faith of 85 per cent of India's approximately one billion people. But his orientation was not simply to Hinduism; his second source left a different religious stamp.

Kaimal made it clear that his adaptation also owed a debt to Christopher Marlowe's *Doctor Faustus*, and specifically its figure of Lucifer. Both major versions of Marlowe's text include the characters Mephistopheles, Lucifer and Beelzebub, as well as numerous other devils and even evil angels.[11] Lucifer, Satan and Beelzebub are all names used for chief devils, sometimes interchangeably, since their New Testament sources (Mt. 12.24–8; Mk. 3.22–6; Lk. 11.15–20) do the same. In demonology there are distinctions among these devils when they are tempting and overthrowing souls, but not when the souls face damnation.[12] The multiplicity of evil figures in Marlowe, and by extension in Kaimal, stands in contrast to the Christian dualism of goodness and evil represented in Goethe's debate between the Lord and Mephistopheles, and corresponds much more readily to Hinduism's diffuse cosmology and the common practice in Hindu belief and daily life to refer to a variety of devils at every turn. Kaimal's evocation of Lucifer's court is a fundamental change to Goethe's text and concept. Unlike his Christian model, in which Mephistopheles and Faust repeatedly discuss and debate the notions of good and evil, with the pendulum of judgment swinging back and forth, Kaimal drives to the foundations of evil in absolute terms, making philosophical debate on this point irrelevant. In Marlowe's play, which is also a much more visceral and absolute treatment of the protagonist than Goethe's, and which ends in the condemnation of Faust and an unequivocal victory for the forces of evil, Lucifer is particularly prominent. He is introduced in the first act through an invocation by Faust (127), mentioned repeatedly by Faust and Mephistopheles both, in the conjuration and pact scenes (I.iii.78–103; II.i.53–69), and finally appears with Beelzebub and Mephistopheles at the end to confront Faust, denounce his appeal to Christ for salvation and convince him to follow their course. As a result, and therewith sealing his fate, Faust vows:

> ... never to look to heaven,
> Never to name God or to pray to him,
> To burn his Scriptures, slay his ministers,
> And make my spirits pull his churches down.
> (II.iii.95–8)

It is Lucifer, not the Christian God, who takes the stage in Marlowe's final scene, leading Mephistopheles and the other devils to take Faust away, the Chorus concluding,

> Cut is the branch that might have grown full straight,
> And burnèd is Apollo's laurel bough
> That sometime grew within this learnèd man.
> Faustus is gone. Regard his hellish fall,
> Whose fiendful fortune may exhort the wise
> Only to wonder at unlawful things,
> Whose deepness doth entice such forward wits
> To practise more than heavenly power permits.
> (V [Epilogue])

Eternal damnation was the inevitable fate for a Reformation Christian who denied God as absolutely as Marlowe's Faust, and Lucifer the victor, but despite the fact that the multiplicity of Marlowe's devilish presences appealed to Kaimal's sense of what would appeal to his Hindu audience, that conclusion would certainly not.

Kaimal's adaptation is preceded by a foreword, also in Malayalam, by his theatre and academic colleague K. M. George, who begins by confessing to a 'mixed feeling of fascination and surprise' in discovering that the 'legendary Western character' of Goethe's *Faust* would be presented in Kathakali form.[13] Indeed, though Goethe's work was known to many educated Indians, it was understood as a representative of Western thought. George draws a deep furrow between that world view and his own, yet observes with pleasure that as he read the play he almost lost the Western origins and context of the story as it seemed to have become so integrated with the art form of 'Attakkadha' (v). He was reminded of its origins only from time to time by the names Faust, Lucifer, Mephistopheles and Margaret, and with appetite sets out to explain how a European story has been so successfully transformed into Kathakali. Faust and Faustus, he notes, are known worldwide as characters in plays by numerous celebrated authors, two of whom are Goethe and Marlowe, and that Faust is not just a literary figure, but indeed a sorcerer who lived in Germany in the sixteenth century and whose life and fate are documented in a dozen works of the time, most of which, he stressed, do not describe him as a person who yielded himself to Satan and his evil powers (vi). In this, George begins to describe the Hinduizing process, using historical and literary evidence to challenge the generally accepted Western notion that Faust's submission to the devil is inherent to the figure. Usually, he continues, literary works in English, German or other languages do not cross borders to far away lands or vice versa, but a few exceptions are accepted universally because they share some sort of similarity in either form and shape, or in approaches and aims, in contemporary or national perceptions, in social tastes, or in other areas. George claims that *Dr. Faust Attakkadha* bears evidence of such border crossing from Europe to India, and then, to reinforce the point, reverses the perspective to claim the same for the sixth-century Indian playwright Kalidasa's famous Sanskrit verse drama *Shakuntala* which he knew Goethe had read. *Shakuntala or The Recovered Ring* celebrates the loves and trials of King Dushyanta and the hermit girl Shakuntala, and the birth of their son Bharata, the mighty founder of the renowned Bharata dynasty of kings, whose final wars are the theme of the Hindu epic *Mahabharata*.[14] Indeed, Goethe not only read *Shakuntala* (in Georg Forster's German translation of the first English version of 1789 by William Jones), he lauded it to the heavens:

> Willst thou the blossoms, fruits of autumn time,
> Willst thou their charm, delight, be filled and nourished,
> Willst thou all heav'n and all earth comprehend,
> Then thou shall't be Shakuntala, and know all to the end.[15]

George further points out that Goethe used the *Shakuntala* Prologue as a model for his own 'Prelude in the Theatre' ('Vorspiel auf dem Theater') in *Faust* (vi). He didn't need to say as well, for every Indian reader or audience member would notice, that Kaimal was following the same convention by commencing his adaptation of *Faust* with such a prologue, or 'purappad'. There, Kaimal introduces his audience to the Faust legend and to Goethe.[16]

George goes no further about Goethe's connection to India, perhaps because there is little more to say, for Goethe's relationship with India and its civilization left only a slight trace in his writings. He did at times show a great deal of interest in the orient, as scholars such as David Bell (2002) have demonstrated, particularly the orientalism reflected in his *West-östlicher Divan* (*West-Eastern Divan*), but with regard to India specifically, we can only refer further to a trickle of poems, 'The God and the Bayadere', the 'The Pariah' trilogy and a few other allusions to Indian mythology, religion and society in his writings, certainly no focused or enduring presence. In fact some aspects of Indian life and culture were distasteful to him, particularly its circular philosophical foundation, grotesque deities and cruel social stratification.[17] Moreover, had he known the

Kathakali dance form, its exclusive concentration on 'epic non-human beings' and 'presentation, whether in form, color, behaviour, or sound, [that is] deliberately made contra-human' (Nair and Paniker's definition above), may not have appealed to his naturalistic sensibilities.

Although Goethe neither loved nor admired India, in the past century India has come to love and admire him, as George's further comments make clear. In sketching the German poet's biography, George suggests, as did Kaimal, that Goethe's Faust character is fundamentally autobiographical, both Faust and Goethe himself torn by inner conflict, drawn to mysticism, troubled by dualities, wrestling with the incessant inner conflict between emotion and reason, and split between conservative and radical political leanings. By creating the Faust figure, claims George, Goethe was seeking to free himself from the bondage of these contradictions (viii). George's biographical interpretation is common in Indian scholarship, and although not subscribing to it, I would point out that, phrased in Hindu terms, the process of freeing oneself from the bondage of contradictions would amount to finding one's karma, the Hindu or Buddhist notion of personal destiny or fate, which of course Goethe's Faust never does. We will see that the opposite is the case in Kaimal's version.

Kaimal's Adaptation and its Performance

In turning now to Kaimal's *Faust*, we must first make a clear delineation. As with most theatrical productions, we should expect differences between his published dramatic text and what was performed; in fact, because Kathakali productions are staged without rehearsal, relying on the long classical training of the performers, their knowledge of set roles, and certainly the impulse of artists and celebrities to rise to the occasion in different ways in different circumstances, there were almost certainly differences from night to night. Four primary documents provide insight into Kaimal's *Faust* adaptation, two playbills with plot summaries in English, *Dr. FAUST* [1976] and *Dr. Faust* (1983), distributed at performances in Kerala and New Delhi; his published text (Kaimal 1979); and a videotape of scenes recorded during a performance in Kerala (Kaimal 1976).

The Playbills

From Kaimal I received the original of a playbill, entitled *Dr. FAUST— KATHAKALI*, which was likely distributed at performances in Kerala in 1976. In the Fritz Bennewitz archive in Leipzig—Bennewitz (1926–95) was an East German director who visited and directed in India many times—I discovered a second playbill of a performance of Kaimal's Kathakali *Faust* in New Delhi on 22 October 1983, with the slightly different title *Dr. Faust in Kathakali*. Both playbills contain a very similar synopsis of the play in English, which I have paraphrased as follows:[18]

> *Scene I. Heavenly-Divine Assembly: The Battle of Words between Angels and Mephistopheles and the Ensuing Oath of the Devil*
> In the presence of the Almighty, the angels compliment man for his righteous living on earth and aspiration to be with God. The enemy of mankind, Mephistopheles,

who appears in disguise, asserts in contrast that mankind is suicidally greedy, callous, cruel and lustful. He questions Faust's claim to salvation and argues that his place is in hell, confidently affirming his intention to bring him there. God dissolves the assembly and directs the angels to do their work, assuring them that divine grace and ultimate salvation will ever be man's, despite succumbing to evil temptation along the way.

Scene II. The Study in Faust's Home—His Soliloquy—Divination—Philosophic Reflections

Faust, in his study, lost in thought, reviews his life and realizes that his search for higher values through intellectual and spiritual pursuits has been in vain. He resorts to necromancy, turns to a book on the black art and seeks truth through incantations. He evokes the Earth-Goddess whose mighty presence causes him to shrink back in terror, which brings him to an impasse in his search for truth.

Scene III. Hell—Infernal Court of Lucifer

Mephistopheles reports to Lucifer, who hatches a plot with him to bring Faust to damnation, beginning with a pact in blood to surrender his soul in return for sensual pleasures and supernatural gifts.

Scene IV. Faust's Home. Mephistopheles' Interview with Faust—Their Show of Might—the Final Pact

Mephistopheles, in disguise, follows Faust into his study, and assumes a horrible form, but is trapped by Faust's magical powers. Yet he entices Faust to slumber and escapes. Faust wakes and falls despondent, whereupon Mephistopheles returns with Lucifer who tempts him with promises and Faust signs in blood to exchange his soul in return for supreme knowledge and power. Mephistopheles leads him first to a tavern, then an elfin grotto where he drinks a rejuvenating potion. He feels a new man, sees an image of Helena and will thereafter see her beauty in all women. He encounters Margaret, falls in love, and Mephistopheles arranges a rendezvous.

Scene V. Faust and Margaret in the Enchanted Garden

Margaret counts petals on a lily and feels Faust's adoration. He approaches ardently and her modest claim of purity inflames his passion. She becomes pregnant but Mephistopheles contrives against their marriage. She bears a son, is shamed and shunned by society and attempts suicide by plunging from a cliff into the river below. The child dies and she is sentenced to death.

Scene VI. The Prison—Margaret's Lament—Reunion with Faust—the Separation

Faust visits the grief-stricken Margaret, confesses his guilt, asks forgiveness and breaks down in tears before being led away forcibly by Mephistopheles.

Scene VII.
a) *Faust's Home—His 'Samadhi'*[19]

Now removed, the experience with Margaret has left an indelible impression on Faust and the realization that it was caused by Mephistopheles' power. Yet, dejected and guilt-ridden, repentance and contrition purge his soul. He presages his paramour summoning him from the realms of eternity and feels his end near. The divine sound of heavenly bells rings in the air as if God's firmament is prepared to receive him. In a moment of sublimity his soul soars up to salvation.

b) *Conflict between the Angels and the Devils for the Soul of Faust—the Triumph of the Angels*

While Faust's soul is suspended in the air waiting for emancipation from the bondage of Lucifer, the devils argue vehemently to establish their claim that the contract remained valid only while Faust lived on earth. God dismisses this

170   *International Faust Studies*

outright and the angels carry Faust's soul to heaven. As the curtain falls, angelic hymns rise, praising the Omnipotent one and praying for His continued blessings.

The synopsis suggests that Kaimal included in adapted form Goethe's prologue, the core scenes of Faust's philosophical and metaphysical problems and the essential Gretchen tragedy of *Faust I*. He added an important new character in the person of Lucifer and some stronger social realism in the plight of Margaret and her child, variations to the tempting of Faust and a more confrontational conclusion. His prologue reinforces the supremacy of the Lord and his confidence in Faust, and prepares the final act which moves to a metaphysical sphere to parallel the final scene of Goethe's Part II, leaving no doubt that Lucifer will be defeated by the powers of good and that Faust will be saved, the conclusion already affirmed in the prologue, and the only one acceptable to almost all Hindu members of the audience. Lucifer's function then is more dramatic than substantive, for despite his forceful presence, there is no real debate with the Lord. Kaimal has Hinduized the outcome of the tragedy.

The Adaptation

The cover of Kaimal's adaptation bears a sketch of Tischbein's *Goethe in der Campagna* beside the head of a classic Kathakali heroic figure, which links his work to its German classical source. The publication occurred three years after his 1976 staging of the drama, upon the urging of others, as he wrote in the dedication.[20] Kaimal called it a 'translation', but its very length, thirty-two pages, makes it clear that it is not. The plot line is for the most part the same as the synopsis, in much more detail, but with some striking differences, the first being that the published version is divided into four acts. Act I covers the action of Goethe's *Faust I* up to the beginning of the Gretchen tragedy; Act II, the Gretchen tragedy from the encounter between Faust and Gretchen in the street to Faust's departure at the end of the prison scene; Act III, the first *four* acts of Goethe's *Faust II*, with emphasis on Act III, Faust's relationship with Helena, and IV, the Emperor's war; Act IV parallels Goethe's Act V, showing Faust's death, his spiritual release and the victory of the angels. It is striking that the adaptation *omits* the outline's *Scene III. Hell – Infernal Court of Lucifer*, in fact it makes no mention at all of Lucifer, not even in the final act. In contrast, it *adds* the Helena episode, to which there is only a fleeting reference in the playbill synopsis, and does this in considerable detail.[21]

Before looking at some scenes, it is worth remembering that when this play was performed, as any other Kathakali work, all of the fundamental production elements of the genre were in place: the clearly-defined quadratic theatre space with audience surrounding it closely on three sides; the lapping kerosene lamp on its brass stand defining the realm of illusion in the gloom of night; the gloriously colored silk curtain rising and falling to divide the scenes; the musicians performing a ceaselessly driving variety of 'ragas' with their cymbals, gong and drums; the narrators singing and chanting the story acted before our eyes; and the sudden, oft startling, oft frightening and always fantastic appearance and disappearance of the surrealistic Kathakali figures.

After the 'purappad', Act I commences with the *Heavenly Divine Assembly* and a dispute between Mephistopheles and the angels, and while the Lord takes part, His role is that of consoler. It is the angels, not He, who carry on the vigorous debate with Mephistopheles for most of the scene, and there are two of them, not three, as in Goethe's text. The Christian notion of an underlying trinity appears to have been disregarded, but Kaimal just smiled at that notion, explaining that he cast only two angels because the Kathakali stage was too small to accommodate more players.[22] This serves as a warning. While it can be argued that Kaimal Hinduized Goethe's *Faust* in some fundamental ways, and at the same time retained Christian underpinnings, which Hinduism, in its liberalism, could manage quite comfortably, many of his decisions were made simply for the practical purpose of effective staging. While it may carry a heavy load of gods, demons, heroes and moral absolutes, Kathakali must be, above all, a dramatic spectacle.

There are further interesting religious manipulations. In the study scene, the Lord does not have a Hindu designation. He is not Brahma, Vishnu, Shiva or another god from the plentiful Hindu cosmology, but referred to throughout the adaptation as 'Baghavan', 'Daivam' or 'Devan', alternate words in the Malayalam language for the general concept of the Almighty. By contrast, in the study scene, the intensity of the Earth Goddess is underscored. She appears as a bloody image in a blazing fire, causing Faust to cringe like a worm (6). Kaimal explained this figure as 'Bhumi Devi' ('Earth Goddess'), linking it to Hinduism's conceptions of the earth as a female, and the Hindu creation myth. This then becomes mixed with Christian allusions when in his depression Faust sees a bottle of poison and decides to take his life, but is saved by the sweet song of the gathering folk outside. As he listens, he realizes that it is Easter Day and that they are celebrating Christ's resurrection—the reference to Easter is explicit in the text. The song awakens his inner spirit and saves him from suicide, a sin unacceptable in Roman Catholicism and Hinduism both.

The romance with Margaret begins, but the videotape shows that at its midpoint a major digression from the text of Kaimal's adaptation occurs. Suddenly, Lucifer appears on stage, as he did in the synopsis, and indeed reappears with some force at the play's conclusion. As was pointed out above, there is no mention of Lucifer in the *published* adaptation. When asked about this aberration from his own work in the performance, Kaimal explained that since it is assumed in Goethe that Faust is fundamentally a good man, he can only be corrupted by deceptive and evil means. The Kathakali convention and its underlying Hinduism both demanded a stronger representative force of evil than Goethe's text provided, not to mention Lucifer's enormous visual and dramatic power; so Kaimal added him to the performance, but not the text. The scene of Lucifer's court is visually stunning, he and Mephistopheles immediately recognizable by their gloriously malevolent costumes, green and black make-up with red patches and designs, moustaches and pith knobs. They engage in extensive dialogue, each in turn performing a vigorous 'kalasam', stepping, twirling, springing, gesticulating and engaging in stunning digital play, with fluttering, bloodied eyes. Lucifer first sits, impassive, as did the Lord in the Prologue. Now the lord in his own realm, he watches and listens as his minion reports. Then, the Prince of Darkness stands, draws his menacing sword and gives his orders. He would return at the end to fight for Faust's soul. Kaimal could not put this character into Goethe's *Faust*, but to convince and to please his audience in both religious and theatrical terms, he had to include him in the Kathakali performance.

In Act II, Faust instructs Mephistopheles to use sorcery to bring Margaret to the magic garden where he will be waiting (16). She plucks a flower and plays with the petals as she waits while Faust, hiding behind a bush, cries with joy. He approaches her and describes the beauty of her body: her feet are like the petals of the lotus, her eyes beautiful, her skin like the scent of flowers that stir passion, her glance akin to Cupid's arrows, her bearing as though wearing a wreath, her voice sweet. Margaret insists that she is just an ordinary village girl, perhaps not a suitable match, that she must work hard for a living while he is rich and might abandon her. Faust will have none of that, calls her ideal and presses for their union (17). She is drawn in: 'An unknown power, like Cupid's arrow, attracts me to you and I fully surrender'. They embrace 'for quite some time' and later sit apart. Margaret queries once more, 'Will your kin, highly placed in society, accept me, an orphan, as your wife?' Again Faust replies that she is a goddess, beyond the censure of society. They pluck flowers, make garlands and wear them as royal appointments. She asks him to tie a chain around her neck as a symbol of marriage. They sing, dance, embrace and make love (18).

The videotape of these scenes shows the two lovers attired in highly stylized, elaborate costumes, Faust stiff in the heroic type's green 'pacca' make-up with elaborate eye, lip and forehead markings, large crown, decorated jacket, sash and wide-spreading buffeted skirt, with Margaret draped completely in her 'minukku' shawl, dress and head scarf. Since the Kathakali form rejects naturalism out of hand, there is no attempt to depict active love-making realistically. Yet through the smallest of gestures, lightest of touches and tiniest details of mimic exchange, subtleties of moving apart and together, the couple conveys a convincing sense of devotion, intimacy and union.

Although personal and intimate in essence, this love-making is associated principally with mythical and symbolic figures—Cupid is invoked repeatedly, Margaret carries herself as if bearing a crown. Faust describes her as he would describe the statue of a goddess, and calls her that repeatedly. The lotus flower carries symbolic meaning in Hindu lore, the flower that rises in beauty from the darkness of the swamp and which is always associated with Vishnu, the great preserver. Her reference to the symbolic nuptial flower chain refers to that practice among both Hindus and Christians in Kerala as part of the wedding ceremony. Although there is discussion of their social inequality, they emerge as a royal, heroic couple, preparing the way for Helena.

In Act III, Faust longs for the presence of Helena. To this point there has been just one small allusion to her. At Faust's first encounter with Margaret on the street he was enticed by her, thinking she was Helena (12). Now he commands Mephistopheles to conjure Helena up and bring her and her companions to his garden. The heroic women 'from the west'—the geographical orientation is specific in the text—dance and infatuate him. We are reminded of George's argument in the introduction that Kaimal's work is a model of transculturalism. Here, Kaimal alters the north-south polarity running through Goethe's version to east-west, an apposition meaningful to Southeast Asian people. Faust welcomes Helena, pleads for her love and uses the same European mythological imagery as he had with Margaret (25):

> I had spent days and nights searching the world for you as memories about you had been haunting me like the arrows of Cupid. O beautiful woman, you the gem of all ... You are a beautiful goddess, the whole world swoons by your magical powers. (26)

Helena reciprocates, likening Faust to the God of Love, using the Malayalam name 'Kamadisundaran' ('Kaamadev', in Hindi, is the God of Love; 'kaamad' means 'granting desires'; and 'sundaran' denotes male gender) instead of a name from Western mythology. She surrenders to him and together they make love, just like the Margaret scene. Suddenly then, she departs, returning with a baby boy who grows to become a youth before our eyes and then, to his parents' astonishment, disappears (27). A loud noise interrupts, and Faust gives orders to his commanders to fight against his enemy Menilass. The historical references become mixed, but remain European. Just as abruptly Faust returns to Helena and continues to make love, but again they are interrupted, this time by a loud cry from above. No more is said, the Euphorion episode is over, Helena vanishes, leaving a veil from her golden dress which Faust embraces in sorrow (27). Clearly Kaimal wanted to do justice to Goethe's motif of classical beauty and its links to the Gretchen figure.[23]

Still in Act III, Faust feels invigorated by the Helena episode and is taken by a new vision. Her garment spurns him on and wafts him to a mountain top as if possessed. He looks down to see two figures, bathed in bright light, and assumes them to be Margaret and Helena. He feels as if his soul is being lifted to a higher level, a clearer vision, and realizes that mankind is called to live a nobler life than worldly pleasures. He is attracted to the roaring ocean waves and envisions a grand plan to reclaim the land and convert it to arable pastures for the good of mankind. He visits the Emperor, convinces him and moves ahead (28). The land is cultivated, crops grow and the green fields resemble a silk carpet spread out over the countryside. Faust experiences a deep satisfaction at having done something useful for the world, his heart is overwhelmed with joy and filled with godly feelings (29).

With this interpretation of Goethe's fourth act, Kaimal turns away from the dualistic struggle of his source to prepare for his advaitic conclusion. As Faust surveys the territory, it is not Philemon and Baucis that he sees, but the remaining vision of Margaret and Helena. The apotheosis of his two heroic love affairs establishes in him a state of mind which continues into Kaimal's Act IV and results in his full command over mind and body. Feeling the favor of fate, joy and contentment, he is transformed, detached from worldly pleasures. He reflects on the past when he was under the spell of the Prince of Darkness, expresses regret for the suffering he caused Margaret, but, most importantly, realizes that it was the evil spirit that had been the cause of his misery (30). He hears a bell and feels the presence of death. He sees a bright light nearing as if to invite him. He thinks that it could be bringing his lovers' or God's blessings, and his face reflects heavenly bliss in the thought. Faust slowly falls back and draws his last breath (31), a curtain falls to cover him, the angels shower flowers on his soul and carry it away to heaven, while the devils are burned and tortured, remaining to mourn their defeat. A song of praise is raised by the angels to God Almighty who provides us with strength to live a truthful and useful life, for as long as the Lord's presence remains with us, the soul is everlastingly beautiful. When the body is alive and earthly, it may fall to lower levels, but upon death it remains with the earth and decays while the indestructible soul joins the Supreme Being (33). A Hindu drama has reached its typical conclusion.

The videotape shows Faust full face, stage front, eyes closed, apparently in a trance, sitting in the lotus position with hands on knees, then pressed together at his breast in prayer. His fingers move in silent, intricate digital gestures—the audience can, in effect, read the content of his mind. The camera moves to capture the lapping flame beside him, illuminating his face as if translucent, indicating that the 'maya', the illusion, has moved to a different world. The 'raga' tempo slows to a standstill, like a heart that has stopped, and Faust's fingers become motionless. His soul has begun the journey to another world and the struggle for possession begins. Mephistopheles and the golden angel rush to lay claim, as does Lucifer, brandishing the signed pact, but he is rebuked. Finally, Margaret appears in a pose of prayer and adoration, placid, dignified, ready to rise to Faust's side. For adapter and director Kaimal, Faust was a man in search of the advaitic ideal, an ideal which would grant him insight into the nondualism of absolute reality. In this he may be a universal model of personal fulfillment, completeness, contentedness and peace.

Conclusion

There are many reasons to argue that Krishna Kaimal's Kathakali *Faust* adaptation is an important text and drama for Goethe research. The heroic Krishna figure beside Tischbein's *Goethe in der Campagna* on the book's cover is an invitation to consider this as a meeting of two classical cultural traditions, East and West. In a world in which interculturalism and transculturalism are becoming not a curiosity but a necessity, Kaimal's scholarship and artistry are instructive. His *Faust*, three decades ago, crossed German and Indian, European and Asian, Western and Eastern cultural borders. Kaimal merged the classic European legend of Faust with the ancient Hindu legend of King Rugmamgatha and found profound commonalities between them. In grounding his adaptation in Marlowe's tragedy and Goethe's dramatic poem, and giving it expression through a Kathakali narrative, he recast Western poetic forms into an original contribution to the classical Indian dance canon. Kaimal reinterpreted Christian ethical problems in terms of India's Hinduism, making the heroic Faust understandable as a good man whose vile actions are explained in the end by the influence of external forces of evil, which releases him from responsibility and enables him to find his karma and peace in heaven. In portraying Helena as representative of the West, who finds her aesthetic and romantic completion in the Hindu Faustian Krishna figure, Kaimal recalibrates the structural and thematic north-south axis of Goethe's tragedy with an east-west apposition, and as a result provides a new orientation, outcome and interpretation of the work. As K. M. George understood, Kaimal's *Faust* is an outstanding example of crossing borders in both directions, of mutual intercultural, hence transcultural, enrichment. His adaptation is largely unknown to Goethe scholarship. Perhaps it deserves more attention.

Notes

1 The *Goethe-Bibliographie* lists all but the Hindi translation of 1939 (v. 1, 107–89), which was documented by Anandita Sharma at a recent conference (see John [forthcoming] in Bibliography).
2 Neither of the last two is the same as Narayama Kurup's (1972) Malayalam translation listed in the *Goethe-Bibliographie*. As published works, they need to be added to that list.

3 Nair and Paniker (1993: x). These scholars, along with Zarrilli, are the leading experts in Kathakali who publish in English. Their *Kathakali* includes detailed information on the form's background and performance, a bibliography of several hundred plays and their authors written from c. 1625 to c. 1938, an extensive glossary and list of technical terms in Malayalam and English and scores of black and white and color plates. Zarrilli's works are comparable. Kaimal is also an outstanding Kathakali scholar, as evidenced by his encyclopaedic reference work (2000), but since it is entirely in Malayalam it is inaccessible to most.
4 My sources for the following description of the Kathakali dance form include Chaturvedi, the *New Grove Dictionary of Music*, Nair and Paniker (1993), Zarrilli, other scholars as noted and my own viewing of Kathakali performances and instruction during visits to Cochin and the Kathakali academy Kerala Kalamandalam in Thrissur District where I was able to interview and observe the director, instructors, students and training (January 2003).
5 Balasubramanian (2001: 8–9).
6 Illustrations and designations in Malayalam and English in Nair and Paniker (1993: 113, 121–3) and Zarrilli (2000: 74–6).
7 Zarrilli (2000: 77–8).
8 Details of training and staging above are paraphrased from Chaturvedi (1998: 166–7).
9 Details of make-up and costume above are paraphrased from Massey (1989: 54–6), although such brief descriptions as these cannot do justice to their magnificence. See Nair and Paniker's color photographs and Boner's unique hand-drawn and painted illustrations.
10 Zarrilli (2000: 150–74) offers a translation of the play with commentary.
11 By 'major versions' I refer to what Marlowe scholarship has designated as the A (1604) and B (1616) versions, both of which are contained in Marlowe (1993). I cite from A since the editors privilege it; however, the spelling of Mephistopheles' name varies.
12 Marlowe (1993: 129 n. 58).
13 Kaimal (1979: v–x). I am grateful to native Malayalam speaker Susan Mathews for guiding me through this difficult text and have based much of my analysis on her paraphrasing and advice. Further references to the adaptation are in parentheses in the text.
14 Edgren's plot summary from *Shakuntala* (1894: v). Thapar's (2002) *Śakuntalā* volume offers a new, modern translation and interpretive materials.
15 Goethe (*WA*, 1, 4: 122): 'Willt du die Blüthen des frühen, die Früchte des späteren Jahres,/ Willt du was reizt und entzückt, willt du was sättigt und nährt,/Willt du den Himmel, die Erde mit Einem Namen begreifen.—/Nenn' ich Sakontala dich, und so ist alles gesagt' (translation mine). See also Mehlig (1998: 521–4).
16 In his argument, George anticipates essential elements of Bharucha's critique of the notion of interculturalism more than a decade later in *Theatre and the World*, and his insistence on mutual interchange and enrichment, or transculturalism.
17 Mehlig (1998: 523–4).
18 Cited with minor editing from an original playbill in my possession, received in Kerala from translator/director Kaimal. I have made minor editorial spelling changes.
19 'Samadhi' has two meanings. It is a Hindu and Buddhist term describing a state of high concentration and consciousness in which an individual becomes one with the focus of his experience. It is also the Hindi word for a structure remembering the dead, which may contain a body.
20 Kaimal (1979: xi–xii). Further references to the adaptation will appear in parentheses in the text.
21 This inclusion of Helena perhaps shows additional dependence on Marlowe, who also grants her an important role. Marlowe (1993: 33; II.iii.26–7;V.i.11–32;V.i.82–110).
22 Findeis (2002: 292) writes that Kaimal claimed to have modeled this scene on 'Harischandra' and other stories in Hindu mythology.
23 Unfortunately the videotape does not include this scene.

Bibliography

Balasubramanian, K. (2001), *Eye and Flower*. Thrissur: Kriya.
Bell, D. (2002), 'Goethe's orientalism', in N. Boyle and J. Guthrie (eds), *Goethe and the English-Speaking World. Essays from the Cambridge Symposium for His 250th Anniversary*. Rochester: Camden House, pp. 199–212.
Bharucha, R. (1992), *Theatre and the World. Essays on Performance and Politics of Culture*. New Delhi: Manohar.
Boner, G. and Soni, L. and J. (1996), *Alice Boner on Kathakali*. Mumbai: Alice Boner Foundation.
Chaturvedi, R. (1998), 'India', in D. Rubin (ed.), *The World Encyclopedia of Contemporary Theatre*, v. 5, Asia/Pacific. London and New York: Routledge, pp. 125–73.
Dr. FAUST – KATHAKALI [1976], Playbill and synopsis. Kerala, S. India: Kottayam Kaliyarangu.
Dr. Faust in Kathakali (1983), Playbill and synopsis. New Delhi: n.p.
Findeis, A. V. K. (2002), 'Grenze und Entgrenzung: Faust-Rezeption in Indien aus interkultureller Perspektive', in *Epochenbegriffe: Grenzen und Möglichkeiten*, U. Japp, R. Maeda and H. Pfotenhauer (eds). Bern: Lang, 2002. Akten des X. Internationalen Germanistenkongresses Wien 2000. *Zeitenwende – die Germanistik auf dem Weg vom 20. ins 21. Jahrhundert*, v. 6. *Jahrbuch für internationale Germanistik*, Reihe A, Kongressberichte, v. 58, pp. 289–96.
Goethe-Bibliographie 1950–1990 (2000), S. Seifert (ed.), 3 v. Munich: Saur.
Goethe, J. W. (1887–1919), *Goethes Werke*, 4 pts. in 133 [143] v. Weimar: Böhlau. 'Weimarer or Sophienausgabe' [*WA*].
John, D. G. (forthcoming), 'Stage productions of *Faust* in India', in J. Golz and A. Hsia (eds), a volume resulting from the conference 'The Reception of *Faust* in non-Christian Cultures', McGill University, Montreal, 4–7 October 2006. Böhlau Verlag.
Kaimal, A. K. (1976), *Doctor Faust*, videotape of scenes from a Kerala performance. Kerala, S. India, 72:30 min.
— (1979), *Doctor Faust*. Aymanam: M. S. Printers.
— (2000), *Kathakalivijnana Kosam Encyclopaedia* (rev. ed. in Malayalam). Kottayam: SPCS.
Kurup, N. (trans.) (1972), *Faust*. Kottayam: National Book Stall.
Marlowe, C. and his collaborator and revisers (1993), *Doctor Faustus. A- and B-texts (1604, 1616)*, D. Bevington and E. Rasmussen (eds). Manchester and New York: Manchester University Press.
Massey, R. and J. (1989), *The Dances of India. A General Survey and Dancers' Guide*. London: Tricolour Books.
Mehlig, J. (1998), 'Indien', in *Goethe Handbuch. Personen. Sachen. Begriffe*, v. 4/1, H-D. Dahnke and R. Otto (eds). Stuttgart: Metzler, pp. 521–4.
Nair, D. A. and Paniker, K. A. (eds) (1993), *Kathakali. The Art of the Non-Worldly*. New Delhi: Marg Publications.
New Grove Dictionary of Music and Musicians, The (1980), S. Sadie (ed.), v. 9. London: MacMillan.
Panikkar, K. N. (1999), *Faust*, in *Poranādi*. Kottayam: D. C. Books, pp. 76–95.
Shakuntala or The Recovered Ring: A Hindoo Drama by Kalidasa (1894), A. H. Edgren (trans.). New York: Holt.
Thapar, R. (2002), *Śakuntalā. Texts. Readings. Histories*. London: Anthem Press.
Zarrilli, P. B (1984), *The Kathakali Complex: Actor, Performance and Structure*. New Delhi: Abhinav.
— (2000), *Kathakali Dance-Drama: Where Gods and Demons Come to Play*. London and New York: Routledge.

10 Faust's Spectacular Travels through China: Recent *Faust* Productions and Their History

Antje Budde

Trans_actions—Goethe, *Faust*, Men, Nation, State Affairs

KAMIYAMA. *What kind of thing is 'Faust'?*
IBA. *It's a masterpiece. Germany would sacrifice its country for it.*
KAMIYAMA. *So it's a national treasure!*[1]
           A National Literary Treasure of the German State![2]

Goethe and other (male) representatives of European national cultures, such as Shakespeare and Ibsen, are obviously well known in Europe, and so are the cultural and historical references to which their works relate. This includes the dialectically interwoven (his)stories and dissident counter-histories of ancient Greek and Roman culture, its Renaissance perceptions, regional pagan cultures and Christianity, including traditions of ethics and the definitions of good and evil. All of them built an extraordinarily complex cultural system of reference, which can in many ways be decoded within this framework. But if one of its components (e.g., *Faust*) travels elsewhere, removed from its original system of reference, it will be recodified within the referential system (e.g., Chinese culture and history) it then meets. We then have to deal with three lines of history: a given work of art's original history, that of the receiving culture and the history of the interactions between them. This becomes particularly important when we try to understand the perception of Goethe's work in non-Christian cultures.[3] We must consider why cultural products travel outside their original system of reference, particularly in times of violence and aggression. We have to take into account the historicity of interest in foreign cultural and other products. Goethe himself was one of the last witnesses of a time when Chinese and European power relations were more or less balanced. Hence, a positive, sometimes romantic image of China could be established, especially by representatives of the European bourgeois Enlightenment. Goethe was one of them. For instance, he appreciated Neo-Confucianist ideas and was interested in Chinese culture and literature (Mommsen 1985: 15–33; Lee 1985: 37–50; Debon 1985: 51–62). Hegel had a quite different approach and so had Marx. They were attached to the idea of an unchanging, passive Chinese culture that needed to be awakened by the higher developed, more or less 'Faustian'West, be it capitalist/bourgeois or proletarian/Marxist (Hsia 1985a; Marx 1955).

Igniting Goethe

Apparently, on 29 November 1878 the Chinese diplomat in the German empire Li Fengbao (李凤苞, 1834–87), most likely a Confucianist official of the Chinese empire, considered Goethe important enough to be mentioned in his diaries. Li, who was born two years after Goethe's death, was attending the funeral of an American diplomat, who was an admirer of Goethe. According to Li's diary, what really impressed the Chinese diplomat was the fact that Goethe was the writer of *Werther*, but even more so, that he was first and foremost a brilliant statesman, who even was decorated with medals from the Russian and French Emperor (Piskol 2006: 9). Three aspects are interesting about this statement.

First, Li felt he had to find out who Goethe was so that he could understand why Goethe was so admired by an American diplomat. Since power relations between China and the West had shifted drastically in favor of the West (certainly after the two Opium Wars in the 1840s), it must have been most interesting to find out what caused these countries to become so strong and aggressive. Li knew he should be interested in someone who was part of the power that an American diplomat represented at the time.

Second, for Li, the idea of being both an official and a poet was not contradictory, but rather conformed to the concept of what an ideal Confucianist scholar-official in the traditional sense was all about.

Third, that Li was interested in other men reflects an aspect that German and Chinese discourses on Goethe—whether academic, literary or artistic—have in common until today: these are dominantly male discourses. There are, of course, a very slowly growing number of exceptions. However, if we look at the Western film history of *Faust* interpretations, we will find few female directors (Hedges 2005: 203–6), but many sweet, innocent and nicely tortured Gretchens. It looks not much better in the realm of theatre, especially concerning German state and municipal theatres (the ones with significant amounts of subsidies). If we take a look at two recent German publications on theatre productions with regard to Goethe's *Faust* and *Urfaust*, we find there are—with two exceptions—no female directors, although each publication provides us with one token female director, Gabriele Gysi and Marianne Weems, both of whom have a unique approach to *Faust*.[4] In German and Western literature, in distinction from theatrical practices, there seem to be more female attempts at their own interpretations, including creations of alternative female Faust figures. The latter also include male writers.[5]

In both the German and the Chinese context the icon Goethe is intricately connected to state affairs, nation-building projects, social prestige, power and state institutions (including universities, state theatres, state/nonprivate television, state opera and, in the German case, Goethe Institutes around the globe—the cultural arm of the Federal Republic of Germany foreign ministry and the Federal Press Office).[6] If it comes to intercultural exchange regarding Goethe 'products', then there is always a political aspect involved.[7]

Diplomat Li's entry in his diary foreshadows in many ways the later perception of Goethe, Goethe's work and specifically *Faust* in China. Yet, it is also a random comment, because the practical introduction of Goethe and his work eventually started in and was transmitted via Japan. All early Chinese attempts at *Faust* translations depended on Japanese forerunners (Kimura 1993: 23–43; Kobori 1993: 45–64; Hsia 1993c: 107–45). In addition, English versions and the original German text were also used. Japan started its 'modernization', which had strong tendencies toward 'westernization', earlier than China. The arrival of the United States (US) Commodore Matthew Perry, accompanied by war ships on 31 March 1854, forced Japan open to the world, with all its implications for the American idea of 'fair' trade. The following Boshin War of 1867–8 caused the ruling shogunate to collapse. The reinstalled Japanese Emperor ('tenno') Meiji opened the country to the West and to all the blessings that came with it, starting with the British parliamentary system, to *Faust* and the nuclear bomb. The reforms, which led to the opening and industrializing process, were called Meiji reforms. In a sense, they could have been called 'Faustian', too.

Trans_lations—Chinese Perceptions of *Faust*

Kirk A. Denton points out that modern literature in the West very soon took a critical approach to the challenges of the emerging capitalist society, industrialization, science and technology, while in developing, colonized or semicolonized countries (e.g., China) these developments were embraced. This was due to the fact that for those countries industrialization was first and foremost viewed as one possibility of social progress that would help to resist colonization and to regain equality on an international scale. Literature, or the arts in general, were therefore used to promote such progress and to support the anticolonialist struggle for modern nation-building (Denton 1996: 59).

During the second half of the nineteenth century many Chinese students went abroad, often to Japan. Their Japanese studies became a kind of transitional experience for the future intellectual elite in China in their dealing with their own country's weakness, industrialization and modernization and the strong invading imperialist powers. The latter included Russia and very soon Japan, which had already learned a great deal about 'Faustian' activism.

At first, literary translations of Western origin were meant to be a tool in modern nation-building processes in China, even after the Republic of China was founded in 1912. It was said, 'Chinese knowledge as (general) basis, Western knowledge as (specific) application' ('zhongxue wei ti, xixue wei yong', 中学为体、西学为用). That was meant for the use of technologies such as cars, trains and factories, as well as for the use of economic strategies, philosophical methods or artistic ideas.

The year 1919, when Chinese students protested at Tiananmen Square against the outcome of the Versailles Treaty, becomes particularly important. The May 4th movement of 1919 was followed by an active, patriotic/nationalist cultural and intellectual movement. This included, in the theatre, the important introduction of Ibsen and Ibsenism, but also an increasing number of literary translations and experimental adaptations. In 1920, under the influence of Goethe's *Die Leiden des jungen Werthers* (*The Sorrows of Young Werther*), Guo Moruo

(郭沫若, 1892–1978), Tian Han (田汉, 1898–1968) and Zong Baihua (宗白华, 1897–1986) published their conversation on Goethe, which they had exchanged in letters, as a book entitled *San ye ji* (*Cloverleaf*). At the time Guo and Tian were students in Japan, while Zong studied in Germany (Hu 1991: 395, 400, 402).

The publication of this booklet is important in so far as it standardized the Chinese translation of Goethe's name. Until then, there were more than fifteen different versions in use (Piskol 2006: 12). To translate Western names into Chinese characters is always a tricky undertaking. Often names are translated phonetically on the basis of how they sound in their original language and according to the phonetic and cultural specifics of the Chinese language. Goethe's name in Chinese is 'Gede' (歌德). Each Chinese character has a number of different meanings and can evoke certain feelings or associations. In Goethe's case, the name can be translated as 'the German poet/singer' or 'the virtuous poet/singer'.

In 1921 Guo and Tian founded the Chuangzao she ('Creation Society') (1921–9) and they became the driving forces behind the introduction of Goethe's work to China. Both were representatives of a romantic school among the rising modern literature in China (Budde 2001b: 99–102). Both translated texts by Goethe. While Guo's project was the first part of *Faust* and *Werther*, Tian was more concerned with *Wilhelm Meister*'s Mignon story (Kaulbach 1985: 195–204; Budde 2001b: 320–84). The translation of *Werther* was followed by a Chinese 'Werther-fever', leading to novels and plays modeled after *Werther* (Ascher 1985: 139–53; Kubin 1985: 155–81; Hsia 1985b: 183–93). Chinese youth started to be interested in the Western idea of romantic love and refused the Confucianist practice of arranged marriages. This had liberating effects on Chinese gender relations and sexuality, but caused huge social conflicts as well.

Tian Han also wrote plays such as *Nü fushide* (女浮士德) (*The Female Faust*). Guo Moruo was influenced by the historical dramas of Goethe and Schiller. Guo as well as Tian developed an interest in strong female characters. This had, in part, to do with the fact that the power relations between the overwhelming West and the weak East were looked upon in gendered terms, leading a number of patriotic young Chinese male intellectuals to identify with the most oppressed people in their own culture, women. But that certainly did not make them feminists. They were talking about themselves (Budde 2001a: 222–35).

Discourse and Analogies

Apart from translations of Goethe's work into Chinese language and artistic products, there were also serious attempts at an academic discourse on Goethe. Introductions and cultural comparative explanations were needed. In this regard the 1921 publication 'Gede de fushide' ('Goethe's Faust') by Zhang Wentian (张闻天, 1900–76), a comrade-in-arms of Guo and Tian, became very helpful. In it, Zhang explains for the first time to his Chinese audience the historical forerunners upon which the Faust character was based. He specifically discussed an aspect to which the Chinese could relate, magic (Piskol 2006: 108). His discussion of magic might have, much later in 1991, inspired Zhang Deming

(张德明), who tried to relate the Chinese understanding of Goethe's *Faust* to a classic of Chinese Literature. He did an extensive comparison between the novel *Xi you ji* (*The Journey to the West*, anonymously published around the 1590s) and *Faust*, showing a number of similarities as well as differences which could make it easier for the Chinese to understand and appreciate *Faust*. One of his assumptions is that in *Faust* we have a single, genial individual who goes on a journey, while in the Chinese novel the equivalent to the Western super-individual is the artfully collaborating Chinese super-collective, including the popular Monkey King Sun Wukong (Piskol 2006: 112). Analogies were also drawn in the early stages by Wang Guowei (王国维, 1877–1927). However, Wang compared Goethe's Faust with the leading character in *Hong lou meng* (*The Dream of the Red Chamber*) by Cao Xueqin (曹雪芹) (Piskol 2006: 9). The novel was written in the mid-eighteenth century and is considered one of the four masterpieces of Chinese fiction, to which *The Journey to the West* also belongs. By comparing *Faust* with these two novels, Chinese scholars put Goethe's work on the highest level of literary appreciation. The traditional Chinese scholar has in common with Goethe that he is usually also an official in the imperial administration. Goethe's drama was not compared to a Chinese drama, probably because dramatic texts in the Confucianist literary understanding range far below poetry and novels.

In terms of analogies, what applies to *Faust* in general can also be said for more specific aspects, such as the idea of the 'Faustian' or single characters in the drama. Regarding the 'Faustian', some Chinese scholars regret the lack of it in Chinese culture, while others believe it is a genuine Chinese feature, which over time got somehow lost and has to be revived. One scholar who looked at *Faust* within the realm of Confucianist virtues was the conservative Gu Hongming (辜鸿铭, 1856–1928), fluent in German and English. He is the first to mention the 'Faustian', which he found in accordance with Confucian belief in the constant striving for self-improvement ('zi qiang bu xi', 自强不息) (Piskol 2006: 86). Yet, Wang Guowei was not as optimistic. He defined the 'Faustian' as tragic and passive and attributes this to Goethe himself, in addition to his dramatic figure, Faust, and to Bao Yu, the hero from *The Dream of the Red Chamber*.

Adrian Hsia, the well-known Chinese-Canadian scholar of German studies, introduced the idea of an East-Asian 'Faust'. Playing with the word 'Faust', which in German—if not referring to a name—also means 'fist', Hsia suggests that the Asian version of *Faust* should be called 'Hand' instead. 'Hand', for Hsia, implicates the Confucianist and Daoist principle of 'mutuality' (ethics of interpersonal responsibility) and 'responsibility for future generations'. He hopes the Asian 'Hand' could avoid the Western 'dictatorship of natural science and technology', which, according to Hsia, is based on the enlightened principle of exploitation. His idea is that 'Hand' would avoid all the violent, despotic and destructive mistakes by Faust. 'Hand' ensures a perfect, peaceful world, based on Asian wisdom and could become the universal principle of the 'post-Faustian' era for all cultures (Hsia 1993b: 15–20). This is a very idealistic view of the historical outcome of Chinese philosophy and ethics. Chinese history, to my knowledge, was as brutal, exploitive and oppressive as Western history, in spite of the fact that the West also has a history of idealizing philosophical, religious thought and ethics. In both cultures, nature and people were/are exploited, ethnic minorities mistreated and women put on a lower rank than men. In response to these difficult societal contradictions, we find in both cultures ideas of utopian hopefulness. Maybe Hsia's suggestion can be read as such.

The Chinese did not translate the drama's title or the name Faust into Chinese as Faust = fist (which would be 'quan' 拳 in Chinese, as in 'taiji quan' or 'shadow boxing'). Hence, the meaning of 'fist' disappears in the Chinese translation as it does in the English. Instead, it was translated phonetically as 'fushide' (浮士德). As with the translation of 'Goethe', a sound satisfyingly similar to Faust was used. 'Fu', the first syllable, carries several meanings, such as 'to emerge/appear on the surface', 'superficial', 'arrogant', 'hollow'. 'Shi' can mean 'bachelor', 'scholar', 'professional staff', 'brave people', 'bodyguard' (figure in traditional Chinese chess). 'De', the last syllable, is the same as in 'Gede'/'Goethe' and can mean 'German' but also 'virtuous'. Again, these characters, apart from their phonetic value, ascribe certain interpretative characteristics to Faust as a dramatic character.

The most interesting other characters in Chinese discourse were, of course, Mephistopheles, Gretchen, Helena, Homunculus and Wagner (Piskol 2006: 129–57). All of these characters are puzzles in themselves. They act in ways, or represent ideas, which do not follow any familiar logic. For example, the submissiveness of Margarete/Gretchen is understood and appreciated by Chinese male scholars. The sacrificial part of martyrdom is very much appreciated as well. In this regard, Gretchen has many Chinese sisters. Yet, Gretchen's strange religious behavior irritates, and so, too, the fact that she refuses to be saved by Faust, which in these scholars' understanding puts Faust in an unpleasant position (Piskol 2006: 144–7). He is stripped of the possibility of saving her, becoming a hero and finally getting rid of his responsibilities. That it was Faust who produced the hopeless situation for Gretchen in the first place does not bother anyone.

Stages of Chinese Goethe and *Faust* Reception

In summary, one can distinguish several stages in the Chinese reception of Goethe's work and the translation of *Faust*. The first consisted of random notes on Goethe with some information on his work. The second, under the influence of Japanese perception, consisted of partial translations of several works, first and foremost *Werther*, scenes from the *Wilhelm Meister* novels, and two early *Faust* translations, which could not really decide how to deal with the formal and rhythmic problems of the verse drama. During Goethe celebrations in 1932 a selected number of *Faust* scenes were staged. This period ends with the fascist Japanese invasion around 1937. Third, the only figure utilized during the war was Mignon. The 1928 version of *Mignon* (later entitled *Put Down Your Whip*, *Fang xia ni de bianzi*) by Tian Han was transformed by several people first into an anti-feudalist and then an anti-fascist one-act play for street theatre. It served the political purpose of mobilizing the masses against feudal backwardness and later against the Japanese aggressors. Fourth, by the end of the Anti-Japanese war, the civil war and the establishment of the People's Republic of China (PR China), revised versions were published, including *Faust II*. The translation by Guo Moruo, who meanwhile held top political positions in China, became the exclusive, yet often incorrect, version that was published several times (Gálik 1993: 183–95). This period ends with the outbreak of the Great Proletarian Cultural Revolution (1966–76). Fifth, during the 1980s two new, more accurate translations were published. Sixth, the 1990s witness an ever-growing, sophisticated scholarship on Goethe and *Faust*. In 1994, for the first time, both parts of the play were mounted on stage in an extraordinarily professional way. By 1999, the sarcastic comic version of a self-assured younger generation, *Bootleg Faust*, became a popular hit for urban, young and educated audiences.

During all these stages, the Chinese discourse is dominated by male scholars, writers and theatre directors. Except for Li Jianming (李健鸣), the translator and dramaturge of the 1994 theatre production, I did not come across a single name of any woman who might have been involved. This is a little different in German publications on Goethe/*Faust* in China and vice versa, although not much.

Trans_ferences—The National Experimental Theatre

The Zhongyang shiyan huaju yuan ('National Experimental Theatre') was the place of origin for the first Chinese production of *Faust I and II* by Goethe and *Bootleg Faust*. Based in Beijing, the theatre has existed for forty-five years.[8] In fact, it was founded twice, or even three times, involving several changes of name. It was founded for the first time, in 1956, to be the practical laboratory for the Zhongyang xiju xueyuan ('Central Academy of Drama'), established in 1950 in Beijing. It still exists on the same spot today. Earlier in 1956—so the story goes—Ouyang Yuqian, the female director Sun Weishi (孙维世, 1921–68), and three other people suggested to the political party authorities and to the premier Zhou Enlai (周恩来, 1898–1976) that an experimental theatre should be established. Most of the petitioners were involved in experimental theatre activities and schools from the 1910s–1940s, be it in communist and/or nationalist regions of the country. In 1956, the theatre was not meant to be an independently acting, self-administrating institution, but a department of the school. The idea was to provide learning-by-doing practice, hence an 'experimental' space for the Academy's students. The professional staff and artists had the duty to teach as well as to run the theatre as such.

The first president of the Theatre Academy was Ouyang Yuqian (欧阳予倩, 1889–1962), one of the most famous and multitalented actors (in spoken drama as well as Beijing opera), directors, playwrights, scholars and teachers of mainland China at the time. He was also a founding member of the then all-male Chunliu she (春柳社) ('Spring Willow Theatre Group') which was founded in 1907 by Chinese students in Tokyo. The Chinese consider the founding of this group to be the first modern spoken drama group in Chinese theatre history—like the starting signal for something completely new. Ouyang's first deputy was the equally famous playwright Cao Yu (曹寓, 1910–96), who became the head of the prestigious Beijing renmin yishu juyuan ('Beijing People's Art Theatre'), founded in 1952. Forty-four years later, Lin Zhaohua (林兆华, 1936–), a director of this theatre company, directed in 1994 the first *Faust I and II* production in China. Yet, he did not do it in his home base company, but in the National Experimental Theatre instead. In addition, it was staged neither in the People's

Art Theatre nor the National Experimental Theatre, but in a theatre venue that links the histories of the Academy and the National Experimental Theatre.

Ouyang Yuqian, as the president of the Academy, was of course also in charge of its experimental theatre department. It stayed this way until 1960. By that time the experimental theatre department of the Academy gradually moved away from its home institution and finally, in 1962, it was removed from it in order to be turned into a state theatre company instead. The background for this decision was the fact that educational matters often interfered with artistic and organizational matters. From 1962 on it was known as the National Experimental Theatre. Ouyang Yuqian became its first head and Sun Weishi the artistic director.

The English translation of the theatre's name is, in a way, misleading. If one translated it directly, the meaning would be the 'central' ('zhongyang', 中央) 'experimental' ('shiyan', 实验) 'theatre' for 'spoken drama' ('huaju yuan', 话剧院). 'Zhongyang' refers to the fact that this theatre is in administrative terms directly subordinated to the Cultural Ministry of China. It does not mean 'national'. 'Shiyan', in this context, signifies first and foremost 'practically tried out'.[9] It is also connected to the concept of innovation but always in practical terms. The practical application, doing rather than talking, superimposes the idea of utopian artistic potential or transgression on a given avant-garde. That by no means indicates that the latter quality cannot be found in this theatre's history. 'Huaju' or 'spoken drama' refers to the Chinese term for the adaptation of this Western genre of drama and (realistic, naturalist) performance. The term 'spoken drama' made sense in the 1920s, in order to distinguish it from other Chinese forms, which at least had two things in common: their musicality and the actor's body (instead of his speaking text decoration) at the center of performance, both being aspects of what the European avant-garde was longing for.

For ideological reasons, in 1966 the National Experimental Theatre was first merged with the Zhongguo qingnian yishu yuan ('National Youth Art Theatre'), which, in 1973, was merged with the Zhongguo ertong yishu yuan ('Chinese Children's Art Theatre'), forming the Zhongguo huaju tuan ('China Troupe for Spoken Drama'). What exactly happened artwise between 1966–73 was not really documented. Many artists, however, found themselves in work camps, prisons or were under house arrest. Only in April 1978 was it decided to separate the three companies again. Their programmatic identity was returned to them by reestablishing their original company's names. When Premier Zhou Enlai died in January 1976, this became a turning point for the fate of the hardcore Maoists, who had initiated the Cultural Revolution. They tried to prohibit the people's spontaneous mourning activities for Zhou on Tiananmen Square[10] and thereby unwittingly ignited a successful protest movement, which ended this horrible period of history.

Today, the Theatre Academy's performance venue is still called the 'Experimental Theatre of the Central Academy of Drama'. It was the first theatre of its kind in PR China, equipped in 1983 with a revolving stage built by East German engineers. In 1994, Goethe's *Faust I and II* was performed at it.

When the theatre was founded in 1956, it operated on a three-pillar conceptual model. First, in order to create a truly national modern Chinese theatre, the earlier Chinese tradition of theatre had to be linked to the political-ideological framework of Mao's view of the social function of the arts supported by the practical implications of the Stanislavskian system. That was specifically hard for those Chinese artists who studied in places such as East Germany, like Xue Dianjie (薛殿杰, 1937–), a stage designer who was educated on the basis of Brecht's and Felsenstein's theatre practices. Only from the late 1970s on did he have the opportunity to apply his specific knowledge and design to many performances, including *Faust I and II*, on a non-Stanislavskian basis. The Stanislavskian system was challenged by culturally diverse and individual directing and acting concepts. The Maoist definition of the arts was not really officially rejected, but in practice had basically disappeared. What is left of this concept is the objective to strive for a national theatre and a unique combination of classical and modern theatre.

The two other objectives of the theatre were that it should serve as a combined place of artistic production and education for theatre students, and that plays from foreign countries should be introduced to the Chinese audience. *Faust I and II* is a direct result of the latter strategy. At least one third of the productions in the company's history were dedicated to foreign plays. In addition, a few foreign artists, male and female, including directors and actors, have also worked with this theatre from the 1950s onward. Since the 1990s there are also a growing number of productions coproduced or cofunded by foreign agencies or institutions.

Trans_mission—The Director Lin Zhaohua (林赵华)

Over the past thirty years, Lin Zhaohua became one of the most significant modern theatre directors in China, with important links to the international theatre world. He was born in 1936 in Tianjin, not far from Beijing. He began his career as an actor in 1951 and was transferred to the Bayi Film Studio in 1956. In 1957 he entered the prestigious Acting Department of the Central Academy of Drama in Beijing. From 1961 on, Lin worked as an actor at the well-known Beijing renmin yishu juyuan ('Beijing People's Art Theatre'). After the period of the Cultural Revolution he returned there, starting his career as a theatre director. Between 1984 and 1998 he was Vice President of the Beijing People's Art Theatre. Since 1993, he has also worked as the artistic director of this company.

From the end of the 1970s until 1988, Lin Zhaohua was a close collaborator of Gao Xingjian (高行健, 1940–), one of the most experimental playwrights and dramaturges in contemporary China. Gao left China at the end of the 1980s and did not return, because of the Tiananmen events in 1989. In the year 2000 he was awarded the Nobel Prize for Literature. Both Gao Xingjian and Lin Zhaohua made theoretically and artistically important contributions to the discourse on modern Chinese theatre.

Lin and Gao established a small studio theatre which they used as a laboratory for theatre experimentations. *Juedui xinhao (Alarm Signal)* (1982)[11] and *Che zhan (Bus Stop)* (1983),[12] both early plays by Gao Xingjian, tried to employ a kind of performance theatricality, stage design and dramaturgy that strove to emancipate itself from the Chinese understanding of Stanislavskian realism and the Maoist concept of revolutionary romanticism. Instead, they aimed at a more playful, liberating and imaginative style of theatre. However, Lin does not consider himself avant-garde. Claiming to 'have no style', he explains, 'I have always abided by the law of the Golden Mean ... I haven't been in the status of breaking from traditional dramas from the very beginning. I don't have the courage or thought'.[13]

The use Lin and Gao made of the stage as a sophisticated 'empty space' can still be seen as a hallmark for Lin Zhaohua's projects today, including his version of *Faust I and II*. Since the Stanislavskian model was the *official* one—slowly implemented as a result of Maoist cultural politics—Lin's and Gao's experimentations were controversial and sometimes suppressed. However, these plays as well as some reflections on them were not only published in the West, but in China too. Their impact on recent Chinese theatre history and performance practices should not be underestimated.

The theatre of the 1950s and 1960s was mainly concerned with the revolutionary past, the new socialist China, new interpretations of classical Chinese stories and plays from foreign countries, basically focusing on socialist, Western anti-imperialist themes or plays from the third world (India, Africa). Along with Stanislavskian concepts came an interest in Russian drama (Chekhov) and socialist realism from the Soviet Union (except, of course, for the non-Stalinist avant-garde, like Meyerhold and Mayakovsky). The period 1966–76 had a disastrous impact on the diversity and vividness of the cultural realm, due to the implications of the Cultural Revolution. The year 1976 brought about great hope for something completely new. Until 1984–5, when the Communist Party launched yet another campaign against Chinese intellectuals and artists, there was some space for artistic freedom. And even after 1985 and 1989 this spirit could never really be stopped—actually, quite the opposite. The early theatre productions by Lin Zhaohua and Gao Xingjian have to be seen in this context. The protagonist of *Alarm Signal*, for example, is an antihero and a black sheep among other more or less black sheep—with no communist deus ex machina in sight. In his later directorial work in modern Chinese drama, Lin always deals with social and cultural issues in modern Chinese society.

The second path of Lin's theatre work is concerned with the adaptation of foreign drama, mainly Western drama. Chinese spoken drama ('huaju') as a new genre is, of course, a cross-cultural product. It developed as a result of China's encounter with the modern West and China's transitional assimilation of early Japanese attempts to deal with Western cultural input in an Asian way. *Bus Stop* is a hybrid work, often discussed in the context of *Waiting for Godot* (Riley and Gissenwehrer 1989: 129–51). Gao's play tells of a number of deindividualized characters who wait for a never arriving bus and avoid taking on responsibility for their own lives. This passivity, or lack of 'Faustian' activism, is what the play critically attacks. I also understand it as a critical reflection on the effects of the so-called Chinese government's 'iron-bowl' politics which made people dependent on the state and did not really encourage individual responsibility. But, in contrast to Beckett's work, there was still some hope on the part of Gao and Lin in the early 1980s. Eventually, the characters understand that sometimes one cannot just wait for other people/institutions to come and solve problems.

The waiting/activism dialectic remains important in Lin Zhaohua's and Gao Xingjian's work for the following decades. On the part of Lin, this includes his 1990s productions such as his highly acclaimed *Hamlet*, his unique collage of

Three Sisters. Waiting for Godot, as well as his very fast *Faust I and II*, as antitheses to waiting. On the part of Gao, it leads to his concept of Zen theatre and is reflected in works such as *Shengsi jie (Life and Death)*.[14]

New Approaches to Chinese and Western Concepts of Theatre

As for the fusion of the East and West, Lin Zhaohua has stated, 'I think that East is East, and West is West, that cannot be changed'. But, he added, 'their meeting is important to the future development of Chinese dramas'.[15]

The end of the Cultural Revolution produced an explosion in the performing arts. This included experiments with Shakespeare, Brecht, French absurdist playwrights and a new evaluation and appreciation of Chinese theatre traditions—both modern as well as classical. Of great importance were Brecht's theoretical works, specifically the concept of epic theatre, the V-effect and his understanding of traditional Chinese theatre,[16] particularly the art of performance by the impersonator of female roles, Mei Lanfang (梅兰芳). These Western artists represented a nonnaturalistic, nonrepresentational, nonlinear narrated theatre. Lin Zhaohua and Gao Xingjian were greatly involved in these lively discourses. Most interestingly, Chinese theatre artists became aware of the similarities between their classical concepts of theatre (including the empty stage, a specific form of performative theatricality, rhythmic musicality as well as cross-gendered acting) and Western avant-garde theatre practices. That also indicated a new self-confidence in Chinese traditions, including theatrical innovations.

What we see in this period are stunning experiments using dramaturgical and performative means of classical Chinese theatre, the foreign (spoken) drama and vice versa. The ways in which Western theatre is incorporated into the contemporary Chinese theatre were quite unique, from spoken drama productions of *Hamlet* or *Galileo Galilei* to innovative adaptations of Western plays into traditional musical theatre styles, such as *The Good Person of Szechwan* in the style of 'chuanju' (Sichuan opera) or *Othello* in the style of 'yueju' (Shanghai opera). Lin Zhaohua's production of *Faust I and II* should be understood in this context. What makes this performance particularly interesting is the fact that Lin not only incorporated products of the 'established' Western classical theatre or 'high culture', but by mixing it with rock music and blues, he recognized products of Western (European and American) pop culture on an equal level as well. This was the first production in mainland China that employed a Chinese live rock and blues band to guide the audience through the theatrical event.

Lin Zhaohua's *Faust*, co-directed by Ren Ming (任鸣), is a hybrid product that produces a genuine quality in itself. It is neither pure Goethe nor pure Lin, but both. This is where the term 'Weltliteratur' ('world literature') starts to make practical sense, if the term literature is extended to the performance text. We do have the very same challenge the other way round in Germany. If there is something universal about theatre, then it is the problem of cultural and historical translation—the solutions to this problem can be as manifold as the cultural histories of the theatre are around the globe.

Trans_ceiver—*Faust I and II* (1994)

'I like to represent masterpieces, for they are valuable legacies, and enable artists to fully develop', Lin Zhaohua believes.

> So I made *Hamlet, Faust, Three Sisters. Waiting for Godot* and *Richard III*. I feel that my works are semi-finished products. I have just faithfully presented these masterpieces before my audience in the way the picture-books do. It makes people understand easily and it is beneficial to young drama fans.[17]

When I first looked at the printed program for *Faust I and II*, I was surprised to find it contained the image of Goethe's death mask. The production date missed the 160th anniversary of Goethe's death by just two years. Throughout the Chinese history of Goethe reception the anniversaries of Goethe's birth or death always renewed interest in his work, probably part of the state-affairs game. Goethe and his work continue to be regarded with so much respect that any attempt to deal with them playfully seems to become a sacrilege.

The main obstacle in the way of the reception of *Faust* in China, as described by Chinese scholars, was, first of all, that the drama's roots lie deeply in European culture and symbolic history, which is hard for others to decode. Chinese religious concepts are not monotheistic and are based on at least four different, interacting systems—popular religion, Daoism, Buddhism and the mixture of rationalized ethics and religious thought called Confucianism. None of them includes even remotely a figure like the devil/Mephistopheles. A second obstacle is posed, in *Faust II*, by the discontinuous narrative/dramaturgy (Piskol 2006: 82). The verse language, which is almost impossible to translate into Chinese verse forms, also poses a challenge (Piskol 2006: 154), as does the fact that there are many lyrical, descriptive parts that lack action. Since these parts are not sung/danced but spoken or even recited, they would be hard for a Chinese audience to follow.

Guo Moruo, for political reasons the most influential translator of both parts of Goethe's *Faust* in PR China until the early 1980s, found it 'unnatural' to write a drama in verse only. First attempts at the translation of *Faust*, in Japan as well as in China, were in prose or colloquial dialogue. Chinese classical drama always included lyrical and colloquial language, while the lyrical parts were usually sung/danced. Guo imagined that the old Chinese theatre form of 'zaju' (杂剧), which emerged during the Song Dynasty (960–1279), but flourished in the Yuan Dynasty (1271–1368), would be a perfect performance style for Goethe's play. Monologues would be sung in verse, with dialogue spoken in everyday language (Piskol 2006: 154). During the Yuan Dynasty, quite different from the later Beijing opera (eighteenth century), it was common that men and women would perform together on stage, either according to their biological sex or even cross-dressed (Chou 1997: 130–52; Tian 2000: 78–97). This is something that Chinese theatre lost over the following centuries due to restrictive Neo-Confucian ethics and politics. That women could perform on stage again was a result of modern social and theatrical developments in the twentieth century, leading to such cross-dressed roles as Mephistopheles in Lin's production of *Faust I and II*.

In 1885, Mori Ogai (1862–1922) discussed his intention to translate *Faust* into Japanese, but in Chinese-style language, with a companion who suggested that the famous Kabuki celebrity Kikugoro be cast for the Faust role (Miyashita

1993: 81–104). Women were eliminated from Kabuki centuries ago, although it was a woman who invented it. Goethe might have liked the practice of female impersonation by men. He was interested in the ancient Roman tradition of male actors performing female roles (Goethe 1973: 11–14). In a way I agree, in that men are the most suitable ones to show their own constructions of women and femininity. In my view, Margarete—if performed by a man—would become much more 'real' because then she would be shown as what she is, a male fantasy. However, the first Japanese production in 1913 was one of the early experiments of 'shingeki' ('new theatre'), spoken drama. The female roles were performed by women. The inexperienced performer of Gretchen was an eighteen-year-old girl from a café (Miyashita 1993: 81–104). Actresses who nowadays play Gretchen should keep in mind that their role is a male representation of a young girl.[18]

In China, the first, very likely amateur, attempt to stage selected scenes of *Faust* took place in 1932 as part of commemorative festivities for the 100th anniversary of Goethe's death (Piskol 2006: 82). The method of staging and acting was, to my knowledge, not handed down. Unfortunately, Goethe scholars, German or Chinese, are usually concerned with textual or literary problems only. Matters of artistic performance and social theatricality seem to be too multilayered and often are not considered.

In his study of the first Chinese efforts to stage *Faust*, Adrian Hsia discusses how these plans focused on the idea of staging it as 'kunqu' (Kunqu opera), which belongs to the most elegant music theatre styles and, at one time, became the sophisticated art form of the ruling class, long before 'jingju' (Beijing opera). Kunqu opera was also performed by both sexes. Hsia hoped that the use of this performance style could help to present the nonrealistic elements in *Faust* in an accessible way for the Chinese (1993d: 181). I do not think that this project was put into practice, but it was a beautiful thought.

Finally, in 1994, the first professional production of *Faust I and II* was mounted in Beijing as 'huaju', spoken drama. In 1999, the sarcastic comic version *Bootleg Faust* followed. Both were projects of the National Experimental Theatre, the first being produced in collaboration with the Goethe Institute, Beijing.

Faust I and II Production Details

The cast had more than twenty people, which is quite remarkable in times of tight funding. The program lists twenty-one roles for Part I and thirty-five for Part II. Some of the roles were double cast; others, like Faust, were performed by two different actors (young and old). Lin Zhaohua and the much younger Ren Ming directed alternately or together. Lin had the practical experience with German theatre. The dramaturgical adviser and translator of the script was Li Jianming, who worked at the Goethe Institute, Beijing, and also had practical experience with theatre production. There were three stage designers: Xue Dianjie, who studied Brechtian and Felsenstein theatre in the 1950s in Leipzig, and is probably the one who came closest to 'Auerbach's Cellar' ('Auerbachs Keller in Leipzig'), was assisted by Wang Yin (王音), who also designed the costumes, and Zeng Li (曾力). In addition, there were two light designers,

Yi Liming (易立明) and Hou Chunhua (候春华). The rest of the production team included twenty-six people. This enormous amount of manpower must have taken the company to its limits. For Chinese standards in the field of spoken drama theatre, this was an extraordinarily large project. It was co-organized and funded by the National Experimental Theatre, the Goethe Institute (Beijing) and the Zhongguo yishu yanjiu yuan huaju xiju gongzuo shi (中国艺术研究院话剧戏剧工作室, 'The Chinese Theatre Studio for Spoken Drama'). The budget amounted to 150,000 RMB (25,000 DM) on the part of the theatre company and an additional 160,000 RMB (30,000 DM) on the part of the Goethe Institute. At that time, this was the highest amount ever spent for a Chinese spoken drama production.

The rehearsal process started on 11 March 1994, with a short interruption of two weeks. The first run-through, which also finalized the first phase of rehearsals at the Studio Theatre of the National Experimental Theatre, took place on 5 May 1994. After that the entire collective moved over to the performance venue of the Central Academy of Drama, a 900-seat theatre. The revolving stage was not used for this production.

Opening night took place on 27 May 1994 and was followed by about six or seven more shows. The auditorium was packed. The performance was, in part, also broadcast on Central Chinese TV (CCTV), which extended the size of the audience significantly.

Dramaturgical Approach

The dramaturgical adaptation (Gede 1994) of the original text shows that the translator and dramaturge Li Jianming tried to balance the length of Part I (seventy-eight pages) and II (seventy-seven)—obviously a radically altered version. The performance was about 2.5 hours long, with an intermission; the audience was in the theatre about 3 hours. This is quite unusual for a spoken drama production, which is usually about 90 minutes. There are other features in the script that suggest it was streamlined to enhance audience comprehension. For example, the entire script was absolutely action-based. The dramaturgy followed the director's approach, which played with a concept of spectacle or 'picture book'. Classical Chinese theatre had its origins in spectacle, including acrobatics and martial arts. Modern Chinese theatre, since the 1980s, has been influenced by concepts of Artaud, Brecht and Meyerhold, as well as a growing competition with popular media. To convince the Chinese to go to the theatre at all becomes a more and more difficult task. Li Jianming and the two directors were, of course, very much aware of this situation.

How did the dramaturgical structure reflect this? Part I of the performance script contains sketches of almost all the scenes plus a short 'Prologue in Heaven' ('Prolog im Himmel'). One could count the spectacular opening of the show as a theatrically staged 'Prelude in the Theatre' ('Vorspiel auf dem Theater') without the actual text. The white front curtain of the stage served as a giant projection screen, on which the shadows of the steel construction behind it were visible. When the band started playing, the singer, as a large shadow figure, came down one of the stairs, moved toward the curtain from behind and then slipped through, breaking the conventional 'fourth wall' and thereby indicating that this is a theatrical setting, not a naturalist play. He then addressed the audience, like a storyteller. This opening scene is a fabulous aesthetic and conceptional introduction to the director's concept of theatre, applying classical Chinese, modern and Chinese-Brechtian means of theatre.

Some scenes, like 'Faust's Study I and II' ('Studierzimmer I', 'Studierzimmer II') or 'Promenade' ('Spaziergang'), 'At the Neighbour's House' ('Der Nachbarin Haus'), 'Street' ('Straße'), 'Garden' ('Garten') and 'Summerhouse' ('Ein Gartenhäuschen') were transitionally merged together. This created organic sequences of time and space. Although the basic storyline was kept, each scene was nonetheless drastically abridged. The language was colloquial, without verse. In Part II the alterations were even more severe. For instance, the sections dedicated to ancient Greek culture were basically omitted, except for a very short 'Helena-Story' ('Vor dem Palaste des Menelas zu Sparta', 'Innerer Burghof', 'Schattiger Hain/Der Schauplatz verwandelt sich durchaus'). The same applies to most of the 'Classical Walpurgis Night' ('Klassische Walpurgisnacht'). In the television version even more important scenes were cut, such as 'Imperial Palace' ('Kaiserliche Pfalz—Saal des Thrones') or 'Laboratory' ('Laboratorium'), perhaps due to their critical potential.

The way in which the script was altered could be read as some sort of infidelity regarding the original text. This production was not made for 'authenticity' reasons, however, but rather to give the audience a first taste of what it would be like to perform and watch a drama like *Faust* in China. The audience as well as the performers and producers were faced with similar problems as how to understand *Faust*. Something that was not really accomplished through the dramaturgical alterations or the performance was a critical and contemporary comment on *Faust* from a Chinese perspective. It was rather a very cautious attempt to somehow 'do it right' but not to disturb the audience. Spoken drama as a genre is still an unfamiliar form of theatre for most Chinese. One has either to be very careful, like Lin Zhaohua, or completely go over the top, like Meng Jinghui.

Stage Design, Costumes, Props

The stage was on three sides framed with a gigantic black steel construction in U-form, the center of which provided a huge empty performance space. The back section served as a high bridge between two impressive staircases, directed toward the front stage and the audience. Below the bridge a big screen showed video images or a shadow play. As in classical Chinese theatre, no curtains were used between the pictures/scenes. There was only a light curtain in the front, which also served as a projection screen.

The move from one scene to the next often happened in transitional action-based steps. One image or action was smoothly dissolved into the following one. Sometimes turning on or off the light or music would indicate the end or beginning of a scene. There was almost no scenery. The props were used in transformative ways. For example, the steel construction on the center bridge could be the place of God, while the ground, close to where the staircase leads up to the bridge, could be Mephistopheles' place. The staircases would also symbolically transform into Marthe's place. Faust and Gretchen, after they have just fallen in love, mount opposite sides of the staircase. The stage provided great opportunities for an image-driven and creative use of transformative spaces.

Some of the smaller props reflected the symbolic use of props in traditional Chinese theatre (e.g., a whip indicates riding a horse). For example, a single white pillow on the black center stage indicated Gretchen's tiny room, which seemed even smaller because of the staircases framing it. That reminds us very much of the 'essential ways' ('xieyi') in which traditional Chinese painting, poetry or calligraphy works.

In Part II, Faust is greeted by a strange bust sculpture with ridiculously huge breasts, representing Helena. On the screens, however, were images of the shadow play and the modern cinema (in Chinese, 'movie' is 'dianying', 'electrical shadows'). One of the more spectacular props was the fantastically made-up jeep which drove Faust and Mephistopheles to 'Auerbach's Cellar'. Cars are vehicles for the small world. When Faust enters the big world in Part II, a remote-controlled aircraft flew over the heads of the audience, indicating that Faust and Mephistopheles were on their way to something grander.

The costumes were kept in a westernized, more or less dehistoricized, *inconspicuous* look. They were not historical costumes based on Renaissance culture, which, of course, is not necessary, but neither were they modern in a contemporary sense. They were a product of imagination, which refers to a more or less essential idea of 'Westernness'.[19]

The costumes did indicate social position and gender, although sometimes in an ironic way. God, for example, was in a white gown, talking through a microphone as if in a Karaoke show. The men in 'Auerbach's Cellar' wore greyish shirts and trousers, black boots and black waistcoats or brown jackets, a casual look that one would expect from young handsome craftsmen or apprentices. However, these were not work clothes in the actual sense. Mephistopheles, performed by a woman, was dressed in a black shirt and black trousers, plus a dark, somewhat military-looking long coat. On the more trivial side was Gretchen, who wore a light, innocent-looking girl's dress. Faust's costume looked as unspectacular as the other costumes. As an old man he wore a white shirt, grey trousers and a long sleeveless coat. As a young man he was still in the same outfit, only the coat was missing. Over his shirt he wore a pair of suspenders. Suspenders entered the world of European fashion in the eighteenth century as a useful accessory for working men's and children's clothing, but for a Chinese audience suspenders are simply something 'Western'.

Actors, Action, Music

One of the impressive features of traditional Chinese theatre is its noisy live music and the fact that the musicians visibly sit on one side of the stage. *Faust I and II* starts with a live rock band. The shadow of a male singer stepped down the staircase, as if he were painted with animated black ink on a huge piece of paper. The actor approached the front of the stage and sang a blues tune which had the refrain, 'if you are a man you must know the blues'. Then the shadow of the band appeared and finally the curtain was raised. The musicians left the stage, and the music stopped. Mephistopheles then entered the stage and walked to the right side of the staircase. God was seen in a spotlight on the bridging center of the high steel construction. Meanwhile, the old Faust entered from below, through an iron grille in the floor, while the young Faust sat on the stairs to the left, reading a book. Then the dispute between God and Mephistopheles started.

This spectacular opening was followed by more beautifully arranged images throughout the evening. Musically the band did not provide the sound for the entire show, as there were also recorded parts. The actors did not engage in anything musical or experiment with bodily produced rhythms.

The creative team, according to their own statements, tried to apply Yin-and-Yang principles to their interpretation. Hence the dualism between light and dark, real stage and shadow stage, white-dressed God and dark-dressed Mephistopheles, male actor Faust and female impersonator Mephistopheles. At first I thought that the impersonator cast had to do with the principle of seduction, which Mephistopheles also represents. The seductive power was there, but it was not based on the sexual contradiction between Faust and his counterpart. It was rather platonic. Sex and the Chinese stage are often at odds with each other. I felt the interactions were rather asexual, not only between Faust and Mephistopheles but also between Faust and Gretchen, not to mention Faust and Helena.

In general it must be said that the acting style was more on the conservative side, although on a highly professional level. But the acting did by no means match the highly artistic theatrical level of traditional actors or the freely improvising actors of Meng Jinghui's productions. Scenes like 'Auerbach's Cellar' or 'Imperial Palace' did, however, give a glimpse of what could have been possible. Both scenes were performed in funny, satirical ways. The latter played superbly with the absurdity of what people in power and their advisers are about.

When Lin Zhaohua states that he wants to present the masterpieces of Western drama like picture books, this is exactly what he achieved with his version of *Faust*, no more and no less. He was faithful to *Faust* within his framework of the concept of a 'picture book', which, as he pointed out above, 'makes people understand easily'. 'Faithfulness' for Lin Zhaohua does not refer to literary fidelity, but to theatrical 'fidelity', if this word would make any sense in the performance context at all. Lin's understanding of performative 'faithfulness' is based on classical Chinese theatre traditions as well as on classical, modern and post-modern theatre practices in the West. Theatre cannot be faithful to literary texts/drama, because it simply is not literature, but rather transforms any given text—including telephone directories—into another medium. While literature is a fixed two-dimensional medium, theatre is always transitional, transformative and three-dimensional.

The pictures Lin created were often of great and stunning beauty. Yet, for people who like slightly more intellectually and politically sophisticated productions, it was a little too light.

Transgression—*Bootleg Faust* (盗版浮士德) and Meng Jinghui

To me, Faust is not a foreigner. He is me. He is all of us.

Meng Jinghui[20]

In 1990 I first met Meng Jinghui (孟京辉, 1965–), the director of *Bootleg Faust*, when we were postgraduate students at the Central Academy of Drama in Beijing, where he composed a thesis on Meyerhold (Meng 1991). After my return to Berlin in August 1991 I interested the Berlin House of World Cultures[21] in Meng's remarkable student production of *Dengdai geduo* (*Waiting for Godot*) (1991) (Budde 1993) and they invited him to take part in the 'China Avantgarde'[22] festival in 1993. In Beijing, Meng had witnessed the results of Jürgen Flimm's *Woyzeck* workshop, which was co-organized by Lin Zhaohua at the Beijing People's Art Theatre. He is also a big fan of Fassbinder's movies. Together, we developed the project called *Put Down Your Whip—Woyzeck*, the only truly transcultural theatre project of the National Experimental Theatre.[23]

On 5 December 1999 (Wang, Z. 2001: 80), the year of Goethe's 250th birthday, Meng's version of the play *Bootleg Faust* premiered in Beijing. The first run was shown until 4 January,[24] which is an unusually long period for a Beijing theatre production. But throughout the last decade, Meng managed to become both artistically and commercially successful. Both forms of success generated a continuing criticism around his work. This is especially true for the commercial success, which in the general discourse on Meng's work is often related to his work as pop-art and the continuous surprise that he manages to combine experimental and avant-garde qualities of his work with an ever-growing popularity.[25]

Meng's version of *Bootleg Faust* is, in terms of plot, dramaturgy and characters, only roughly based on Goethe's *Faust*. It was put together by Shen Lin (沈林). The piece is typical of Meng's productions, in that the text, as well as the actions, is very much influenced by a living rehearsal process. Much space is given to the creative input of the production crew including the dramaturge, stage designer, musical adviser and, of course, the very center of any performance, the actors. Shen Lin, who created the script based on his own ideas and the improvised material, is a professor at the Central Academy of Drama in Beijing and was educated at Birmingham University in England, where he studied with Martin Esslin. He originally planned to call his play *Faust. A Comedy*, while the darker tragic-comical and quite pessimistic aspects were already inscribed (Piskol 2006: 92). Later, probably as a result of the collaboration with Meng, the play was called *Bootleg Faust*.

The term 'bootleg', of course, has an ironic touch to it. It also plays with stereotypes of the Chinese in terms of brand piracy and ignorance of international copyright law. Meng and Shen satirize the issue in one of Mephistopheles' speeches:

> To own knowledge is not the same as living wisely. Common people got the highest level of intelligence. That's also true for today. For instance, where do the farmers in Shanxi province start in order to fake booze trademarks? They fake the label and the bottle! Or should they start with faking the manufacturing process? . . . The same with imitating America, right? Everyone has his own little tricks: dye your hair, get nose surgery! That's the economical, instant and practical way to learn about America. It's not an abstract hassle. (Piskol 2006: 94)

If there is a continuity in Meng's work, one aspect of it is that Meng directs his plays as if they were based on Chinese life. He is probably the first Chinese director who has the ability and the courage to focus radically on what is interesting for a Chinese audience. He did not try to 'copy' a Western work or pretend 'to do it right according to foreign cultural standards' for the sake of 'serving the author's' or philologists' standards, which simply were not part of his experience and socialization. This was a dramatic and revolutionary turn in Chinese theatre history regarding the perception of Western culture, very revealing of the self-confidence as well as the self-awareness of this generation of Chinese theatre artists. Instead of using false beards or long noses to represent the European, they have emancipated themselves from these stereotypes and treat them in a satiric way. Lin Zhaohua and Gao Xingjian were very important forerunners for this practice of radical cultural adaptation and cross-cultural transformation.

Meng basically follows two different lines in his work. One is concerned with the radical adaptation of Western classics or classical heroes, mainly of the historical avant-garde. The other is concerned with his own plays or adaptations of Chinese literary or dramatic materials. Meng tries to expand his means of performance by including more and more multimedia elements, performance art and composed music (sometimes live). After he graduated from the Theatre Academy he had trouble finding work due to his production of *Waiting for Godot*, which officials of the school considered too close to the traumatic events in Tiananmen Square in 1989. Therefore, he turned to Chinese television to make a living. Finally he was offered a job at the National Experimental Theatre. Since his trip to Germany in 1993, he and his productions have traveled the world quite a bit, including Japan, Singapore and the US. He is not only successful in Beijing but also in Shanghai, Shenzhen and Hong Kong.

Bootleg Faust—Plot, Collage, Music

Bootleg Faust tells the story of a contemporary Chinese professor who is forced by economic circumstances to deal with the practicalities of life. It is a speciality of Meng's to make sarcastic fun of 'non-Faustian' Chinese intellectuals, traditional or modern. In *Bootleg Faust* Faust meets Gretchen—a waitress apprentice in a bar—on the street. Mephistopheles appears in the disguise of a television producer, who, on the basis of his bet, promises to make Faust rich and famous. Mephistopheles is understood as the representation of mere materialism, which challenges the idealism of a proper, unworldly Chinese intellectual. Mephistopheles believes that television becomes culture simply due to its quality as mass media: 'Whoever reaches out most to the masses of the people, defines culture'. Faust argues, on the contrary, that television can only be the transmitter of culture, but not culture itself. In spite of that, Faust later promises Gretchen that he will make her a television star and then seduces her. Her mother dies from drug poisoning and her brother Valentin is killed by Faust. Gretchen kills her baby and Mephistopheles assists her. Apparently, the final prison scene of Goethe's Part I stayed more or less intact. Gretchen is executed—a light spot zooms in on her neck. That is unsettling, if one thinks of the public executions in China, which are aired on television. Then she appears as a storytelling figure and comments on the action. She makes Faust appear in the virtual world of television (instead of ancient Greek mythology), where he becomes a jury member for a beauty contest. He is confronted with three stereotypical representatives of (Western) woman: Hera, Helena and Aphrodite.

Helena wins and leaves with Faust. Faust argues with Wagner about how one could save the world from corruption. Wagner believes in ideological influences, while Faust wants to replace all bureaucrats with robots. Faust's life is threatened because of that, and he escapes to another planet in a NASA uniform. His spaceship Apollo crashes and he dies. Gretchen comments on the end of Faust and then leads his soul to heaven (Piskol 2006: 92–5).

The principle of collage is a very important artistic means in Meng's theatre. So it comes as no surprise that this is also the case in *Bootleg Faust*:

> The dialogue in Bootleg Faust [sic] incorporates diverse dramatic devices including passages from classical Chinese poetry, references to characters from Chinese history and literature, contemporary slang, parodies of Greek mythology, and spoofs of the absurd dialogue that clutters so many contemporary TV shows . . .[26]

The music was also arranged on a collage principle, including songs by the Chinese rock musician He Yong, Greek choruses, French ballad tunes (for Gretchen's seduction) and Cantopop-techno.[27]

Meng's work shows a remarkable, sharp sense of black humor, drastic satire and subtle irony mixed with a healthy portion of self-mockery. There is really not much that is 'holy' to him—neither Chinese nor foreign/Western habits, institutions or myths and certainly not himself. He is not afraid and always ready to challenge the (young, educated, urban) audience. I am among those who appreciate this quality, especially since Meng is able to work with the best talents. The obviously high educational level of the people involved creates an artistic quality that is easily able to outdo television.

Bootleg Faust—The Stage

Bootleg Faust was not performed in the theatre of the National Experimental Theatre but was presented in the Studio Theatre of the Beijing People's Art Theatre, where Lin Zhaohua and Gao Xingjian once started their groundbreaking experimentations. Meng typically plays with a significantly 'empty space', often responding to the space as he finds it and usually using minimalist, symbolically transformable and movable pieces of scenery. By so doing he attempts to provide a maximum of space for the actors' actions as well as for the audience's imagination.

> The 'stage' for Bootleg Faust [sic] is a ground-level brick floor featuring three simple wooden tables, surrounded by piles of sand forming the only barrier between the actors and their audience. This stark space functions, among other things, as a Spartan scholar's cell, a bar, a model's catwalk and the planet Mars. The intimate black-box feeling of the Small Stage of the People's Art Theatre, and the actors' innovative use of space—Mephistopheles first appears hanging from the ceiling—ensures that the audience is constantly involved in the drama unfolding before them.[28]

Meng had been interested in exploring the totality of space—the (official) stage, back stage, auditorium and higher platforms or balconies. With *Bootleg Faust* he takes his explorations a step further, this time aiming at the audience itself. By so doing, he sets up a new quality of actor-spectator relationship, which is innovative in the context of Chinese spoken drama, but of course, not so new with respect to the open-air settings of classical Chinese theatre.

BootlegBootlegBootleg

The perception of foreign cultures provides many conflicts and challenges. The theatre generation of the globalized world of today, and that includes artists as well as audiences, has the opportunity to explore other cultures. Their knowledge comes from their own experiences and not just from books (or indoctrinating ideologists). In the case of China, one has to recognize that China has been developing extremely well in terms of economics. On the one hand, that creates immense social contradictions within the country. This is exactly the kind of material with which critically minded artists fuel their work. On the other hand, the economic success changed the reputation of China worldwide. The Chinese are proud of that and they want to see themselves on an equal level with others and to leave the hierarchical, colonialist view of culture (high/West) (low/Other) behind.

Those who believe in a rigid concept of the unchangeable 'authenticity' of a given literary work and/or the superiority of white male genius might argue that neither Lin Zhaohua's nor Meng Jinghui's interpretation of *Faust* is what Goethe wrote his drama for. But for whom did he, who coined the word 'Weltliteratur', write it? Did he write it for the stage at all, since he did not really believe in a proper staging of this work himself? Did he write it for male directors (and consequently critics) only? Lin and Meng have given a Chinese answer of their own and others will follow, including women. But that is another story, for both the East and the West.

Notes

1   The dialogue is a conversation between the first Japanese actors of Faust (Kamiyama) and Mephistopheles (Iba) (Miyashita 1993: 91).
2   Ibid. The statement was on the poster that advertised the first Japanese production of *Faust* (Tokyo, 27 March 1913).
3   Probably the first systematic attempt to work around this topic was made by the conference 'The Reception of *Faust* in non-Christian Cultures' in 2006 at McGill University, Canada, organized by Adrian Hsia and Jochen Golz. However, the part that was dedicated to China was once more only dealing with the literary aspect of the problem.
4   Weems is mentioned among twenty-eight analyzed productions of the 1990s by male directors. See Bayerdörfer (2002). Gysi is mentioned among dozens of male directors over a period of 102 years. See Mahl (1998).
5   For a European history of female Faust figures, created by male and female authors, see Doering (2001). See also Hedges (2005: 96–155).
6   See the 'About us' ('Über uns') web page of the Goethe Institute (retrieved 2 August 2007).
7   A planned guest performance of *Faust I and II* in Munich in 1996 was cancelled for political reasons concerned with human rights issues (Budde 2001b: 33–5, 320–84)—one of the most hypocritical reasons in the West for cancelling a humanist play. That the invitation to Munich was withdrawn without any fault on the part of the Chinese theatre company made all the Chinese involved loose face.
8   Wang, Z. (2001: 1, 3). This applies to the English version of the introductory text. The Chinese text states 'more than 40 years' ('si shi duo nian lai').
9   A comprehensive summary of the Chinese history of this term can be found in Budde (2001b: 33–86). For a different approach see Zhao (2000: 1–66).

10 For more information on this unique square and its political performance history see Wu (1991: 90; 2005) and Budde (2002: 197–346).
11 Sometimes translated as 'Warning Signal' or 'Absolute Signal'.
12 For the English translations of these plays see Gao (1996a: 159–232) and Gao (1996b: 233–90). See also Gao (1998: 3–59).
13 'The Un-Style of Lin Zhaohua' (2004).
14 For translations and analysis see Gao (1999) and Zhao (2000).
15 'The Un-Style of Lin Zhaohua' (2004).
16 Brecht (2000: 15–22; Tian 1998: 86–97). The latter is a curious Chinese misinterpretation of Brecht's German misinterpretation of classical Chinese theatre and an interesting example for how we sometimes talk at cross purposes.
17 'The Un-Style of Lin Zhaohua' (2004).
18 One way for actresses to gain some control, being already in a vulnerable position given that most directors of *Faust* are men, would be a strong artistic interpretation, based on a grown-up spirit of resistance. Yet, that might jeopardize their careers.
19 I use the term 'essential' in reference to the Chinese concept of 'xieyi', discussed above, which is about catching the 'essence' of something and is not based on the Western naturalist idea of realistic representation ('xieshi').
20 'Bootleg Faust' (1999).
21 For more information see www.hkw.de/
22 Haus der Kulturen der Welt (1993). This catalogue is also available in English and Chinese. It includes short essays by Meng Jinghui and I.
23 I strongly disagree with the information Conceison (2001: 286) gives about this production. It was in equal parts funded, produced and created by Chinese and German institutions and artists. The originally cast German amateur actor did not pull out due to anxieties in the rehearsal process; rather, Meng Jinghui and I decided to replace him because of his inappropriate behavior. It was not my intention to play this role myself, but there was no other way to save the project. There are other inaccuracies in Conceison's discussion.
24 'Bootleg Faust' (1999).
25 'Meng's experimental drama a hit in Shenzhen' (2003); 'Sex and the Chinese cities' (2007); '*Magic Mountain* to present world's largest ice cream cake' (2005); Zhang (2000); Wang, J. (2001: 1–27); Ivana (2005).
26 'Bootleg Faust' (1999).
27 Ibid.
28 'Bootleg Faust' (2003).

Bibliography

Ascher, B. (1985), 'Aspekte der Werther-Rezeption in China', in G. Debon and A. Hsia (eds), *Goethe und China—China und Goethe*. Bern: Peter Lang, pp. 139–53.

Bartke, W. (1985), *Die großen Chinesen der Gegenwart*. Frankfurt/M.: Suhrkamp Verlag, pp. 310–13.

Bayerdörfer, H.-P. (2002), *Im Auftrieb. Grenzüberschreitungen mit Goethes 'Faust' in Inszenierungen der neunziger Jahre*. Tübingen: Niemeyer Verlag.

'Bootleg Faust' (1999), *Beijing Scene*, 6, (10), 17–23, www.beijingscene.com/v06i010/culture.html (retrieved 10 August 2007).

— (2003), (23 December), www.chinaculture.org/gb/en_top/2003-12/23/content_44933.htm (retrieved 10 August 2007).

Brecht, B. (2000), 'On Chinese acting', in C. Martin and H. Bial (eds), *Brecht Sourcebook*. London: Routledge, pp. 15–22.

Budde, A. (1993), Wer wartet in China auf Godot?—Worauf warten wir? Experiment und Krise. Die Kontinuität des Bruchs am Beispiel des Sprechtheaters in der VR China. M.A.Thesis, Humboldt-Universität zu Berlin.
— (2001a), 'Frauenrollen im Theater Chinas', in B. Engelhardt, T. Hörnigk and B. Masuch (eds), TheaterFrauenTheater. Berlin: Verlag Theater der Zeit, pp. 222–35.
— (2001b), Kulturhistorische Bedingungen, Begriff, Geschichte, Institution und Praxis des Experimentellen Theaters in der VR China. Ph.D. Dissertation, Humboldt-Universität zu Berlin, http://edoc.huberlin.de/dissertationen/budde-antje-1999-12-20/PDF/Budde.pdf.
— (2002), 'Der Tiananmen Platz. Die größte Bühne der Welt.—Eine historisch-komparatistische Studie zur Theatralität des Platzes vor dem Tor des Himmmlischen Friedens und der geführten Diskurse', in A. Budde and J. Fiebach (eds), Herrschaft des Symbolischen. Bewegungsformen gesellschaftlicher Theatralität. Europa. Asien. Afrika. Berlin: Vistas Verlag, pp. 197–346.
Chen, J. (2004), '"Toilet" drama flush with hutong humour', China Daily, (8 July), www.chinadaily.com.cn/english/doc/2004-07/08/content_346564.htm (retrieved 15 August 2007).
Chen, R. (2007), 'Lin Zhaohua: Theatre without boundaries', Beijing Review, (19 July), www.bjreview.com.cn/quotes/txt/2007-07/19/content_70039_2.htm (retrieved 28 July 2007).
Chou, H. (1997), 'Striking their own poses.—The history of cross-dressing on the Chinese stage', The Drama Review, 41, 130–52.
Conceison, C. (1998), 'The occidental other on the Chinese stage: Cultural cross-examination in Guo Shixing's "Bird Men"', Asian Theatre Journal, 15, (1), 87–101.
— (2001), 'International casting in Chinese plays: A tale of two cities', Theatre Journal, 53, (2), 277–90.
Debon, G. (1985), 'Goethe erklärt in Heidelberg einen chinesischen Roman', in G. Debon and A. Hsia (eds), Goethe und China—China und Goethe. Bern: Peter Lang, pp. 51–62.
Denton, K.A. (ed.) (1996), Modern Chinese Literary Thought—Writings on Literature 1893–1945. Stanford: Stanford University Press.
Doering, S. (2001), Die Schwestern des Doktor Faust. Eine Geschichte der weiblichen Faustgestalten. Göttingen: Wallstein Verlag.
Ferrari, R. (2005), 'Anarchy in the PRC: Meng Jinghui and his adaptation of Dario Fo's Accidental Death of an Anarchist', Modern Chinese Literature and Culture, 17, (2), 1–48.
Fushide (Faust) (1994), 'Program'. Beijing: Central Experimental Theatre.
Gálik, M. (1993), 'Rezeption und Wirkung von Goethes Faust in China. Der Fall Guo Moruo (1919–1947)', in A. Hsia (ed.), Zur Rezeption von Goethes 'Faust' in Ostasien. Bern: Peter Lang, pp. 183–95.
Gao, X. (1996a), Alarm Signal, in S-L. S.Yu (ed.), Chinese Drama after the Cultural Revolution, 1979–1989. Lewiston: The Edwin Mellen Press, pp. 159–232.
— (1996b), 'Bus Stop', in S-L. S. Yu (ed.), Chinese Drama after the Cultural Revolution, 1979–1989. Lewiston: The Edwin Mellen Press, pp. 233–90.
— (1998), Bus Stop, in H.Yan (ed.), Theater and Society: An Anthology of Contemporary Chinese Drama. Armond, NY: M. E. Sharpe, pp. 3–59.
— (1999), The Other Shore. Plays by Gao Xingjian, G. F. Fong (trans.). Hong Kong: The Chinese University Press.
Gede/Goethe (1994), Fushide (Faust), J. Li (trans.). Beijing: National Experimental Theatre.
Goethe Institute, 'Über uns', www.goethe.de/uun/deindex.htm (retrieved 2 August 2007).
Goethe, J.W. (1973), 'Frauenrollen auf dem Römischen Theater durch Männer gespielt', in Schriften zur Literatur, v. 3. Berlin: Akademie-Verlag, pp. 11–14.
— (1983a), Faust. Der Tragödie erster Teil. Leipzig: Reclam.
— (1983b), Faust. Der Tragödie zweiter Teil. Leipzig: Reclam.
— (2005a), Faust, Part 1, D. Constantine (trans.). London: Penguin.
— (2005b), Faust, Part 2, P. Wayne (trans.). London: Penguin.

Haus der Kulturen der Welt, Berlin (ed.) (1993), *China Avantgarde*. Heidelberg: Edition Braus.
Hedges, I. (2005), *Framing Faust: Twentieth-Century Cultural Struggles*. Carbondale: Southern Illinois University Press.
Hsia, A. (1985a), *Deutsche Denker über China*. Frankfurt/M.: Insel Verlag.
— (1985b), 'Zum Verständnis eines chinesische Werther-Dramas', in G. Debon and A. Hsia (eds), *Goethe und China-China und Goethe*. Bern: Peter Lang, pp. 183–93.
— (1987), 'Huang Zuolin's ideal of drama and Bertolt Brecht', in C. Mackerras (ed.), *Drama in the People's Republic of China*. Albany: State University of NewYork Press, pp. 151–62.
— (ed.) (1993a), *Zur Rezeption von Goethes 'Faust' in Ostasien*. Bern: Peter Lang.
— (1993b), 'Einführung oder Die Konstruktion einer "anderen" Faust-Gestalt', in A. Hsia (ed.), *Zur Rezeption von Goethes 'Faust' in Ostasien*. Bern: Peter Lang, pp. 15–20.
— (1993c), 'Goethes *Faust* in vier chinesischen Übersetzungen', in A. Hsia (ed.), *Zur Rezeption von Goethes 'Faust' in Ostasien*. Bern: Peter Lang, pp. 107–45.
— (1993d), 'Zur *Faust*-Rezeption in China', in A. Hsia (ed.), in *Zur Rezeption von Goethes 'Faust' in Ostasien*. Bern: Peter Lang, pp. 165–81.
Ivana (2005), 'Meng Jinghui: A prodigy of Chinese theater', (10 May), www.chinaculture.org/gb/en_artqa/2005–05/10/content_68470.htm (retrieved 7 July 2007).
Kaulbach, B. (1985), 'Mignon auf der chinesischen Bühne', in G. Debon and A. Hsia (eds), *Goethe und China—China und Goethe*. Bern: Peter Lang, pp. 195–204.
Kimura, N. (1993), 'Probleme der japanischen *Faust*-Übersetzung', in A. Hsia (ed.), *Zur Rezeption von Goethes 'Faust' in Ostasien*. Bern: Peter Lang, pp. 23–43.
Kobori, K. (1993), 'Goethe im Lichte der Mori Ogaischen Übersetzungskunst', in A. Hsia (ed.), *Zur Rezeption von Goethes 'Faust' in Ostasien*. Bern: Peter Lang, pp. 45–64.
Kubin, W. (1985), 'Yu Dafu (1896–1945): Werther und das Ende der Innerlichkeit', in G. Debon and A. Hsia (eds), *Goethe und China—China und Goethe*. Bern: Peter Lang, pp. 155–81.
Lee, M. (1985), 'Goethes Chinesisch-Deutsche Jahres- und Tageszeiten', in G. Debon and A. Hsia (eds), *Goethe und China—China und Goethe*. Bern: Peter Lang, pp. 37–50.
'*Magic Mountain* to present world's largest ice cream cake' (2005), (28 December), http://english.peopledaily.com.cn/200512/28/eng20051228_231285.html (retrieved 5 July 2007).
Mahl, B. (1998), *Goethes Faust auf der Bühne (1806–1998)*. Stuttgart and Weimar: Verlag J. B. Metzler.
Marx, K. (1955), *Über China*. Berlin: Dietz Verlag.
Meng, J. (1991), Lun mei'erhede de daoyan yishu ('On Meyerhold's Art of Directing'). M. A. Thesis, Central Academy of Drama Beijing.
'Meng's experimental drama a hit in Shenzhen' (2003), (18 November), http://news.xinhuanet.com/english/2003–11/18/content_1184364.htm (retrieved 7 July 2007).
Miyashita, K. (1993), '"In diesem Sinne kannst du's wagen": Goethes *Faust* auf der japanischen Bühne', in A. Hsia (ed.), *Zur Rezeption von Goethes 'Faust' in Ostasien*. Bern: Peter Lang, pp. 81–104.
Mommsen, K. (1985), 'Goethe und China in ihren Wechselbeziehungen', in G. Debon and A. Hsia (eds), *Goethe und China—China und Goethe*. Bern: Peter Lang, pp. 15–33.
Piskol, T. (2006), Die Entwicklung des Goethe-Verständnisses der chinesischen Intellektuellen im 20. Jahrhundert. Ph.D. Dissertation, Freie Universität Berlin, www.diss.fu-berlin.de/2006/212/
Riley, J. and Gissenwehrer, M. (1989), 'The myth of Gao Xingjian', in J. Riley and E. Unterrieder (eds), *Haishi zou hao. Chinese Poetry, Drama and Literature of the 1980's*. Bonn: Engelhardt-NG, pp. 129–51.
'Sex and the Chinese cities' (2007), (4 April), www.china.org.cn/english/culture/205971.htm (retrieved 8 July 2007).
Sun, W. H. (1987), 'Mei Lanfang, Stanislavsky and Brecht on China's stage and their aesthetic significance', in C. Mackerras (ed.), *Drama in the People's Republic of China*. Albany: State University of New York Press, pp. 137–50.

Tatlow, A. (1985), 'Goethe, Brecht und der chinesische Universalismus', in G. Debon and A. Hsia (eds), *Goethe und China—China und Goethe*. Bern: Peter Lang, pp. 95–114.
Tian, M. (1998), 'Who speaks and authorizes? The aftermath of Brecht's misinterpretation of the classical Chinese theatre', in S. V. Longman (ed.), *Crosscurrents in the Drama. East and West*. Tuscaloosa: Southeastern Theatre Conference, University of Alabama Press, pp. 86–97.
— (2000), 'Male dan: The paradox of sex, acting, and perception of female impersonation in traditional Chinese theatre', *Asian Theatre Journal*, 17, (1), 78–97.
'The Un-Style of Lin Zhaohua' (2004), *China Pictorial*, (17 December), www.china.org.cn/english/NM-e/115200.htm (retrieved 28 July 2007).
Wang, J. (2001), 'Guest editor's introduction', *positions*, 9, (1), 1–27.
Wang, Z. (ed.) (1996), *Zhongyang shiyan huaju yuan. 1956–1996*. Beijing: Zhongyang shiyan huaju yuan.
— (ed.) (2001), *Zhongyang shiyan huaju yuan. shuanzuo yanchu jinian ce. 1997–2001*. Beijing: Zhongyang shiyan huaju yuan.
Wenxue baike da cidian ('Compendium of Literature') (1991), J. Hu, F. Wang and Y. Chen (eds). Beijing: Hualing chuban she.
Wu, H. (1991), 'Tiananmen square: A political history of monuments', *Representations*, 35, 84–117.
— (2005), *Remaking Beijing: Tiananmen Square and the Creation of a Political Space*. Chicago: University of Chicago Press.
Xue, D. (ed.) (1986), *Zhongyang shiyan huaju yuan. 1956–1986. zhongyang shiyan huaju yuan*. Beijing: Zhongyang shiyan huaju yuan.
Zhang, Q. (2000), 'Opera battles to keep audiences', (11 June), www.china.org.cn/english/3603.htm (retrieved 7 July 2007).
Zhao, H. Y. H. (2000), *Towards a Modern Zen Theatre. Gao Xingjian and Chinese Theatre Experimentalism*. London: University of London.

Part V

The Americas, Europe, Africa and Britain

11 Faust and the Magus Tradition in Robertson Davies' *The Rebel Angels*

Richard Ilgner

The Faust theme in Canadian culture for the first time gained international prominence in the 1980s, with three Faust works that were to receive recognition well beyond the confines of Canada: the novel *The Rebel Angels* (1981), by the Ontario author Robertson Davies; *Neuromancer* (1984) by the Vancouver-based science fiction writer William Gibson; and the film *The Adventure of Faustus Bidgood* (1986), directed by the Newfoundland filmmaker Michael Jones.[1] This surrealistic film, the first feature film that was totally a Newfoundland production, deals with recent Newfoundland history, namely the belated entry of this distinct insular culture—St John's, the capital city of the province, is the oldest North American city—into the Dominion of Canada in 1949. Many Newfoundlanders regard this major turning-point of their cultural history as a contrived event which was not necessarily a turn for the better. The film expresses these sentiments, in that Bidgood, a member of a well-established family name in the region, becomes President of an independent Newfoundland, his fantasy sidekick being Bogue, a shadowy figure partly inspired by the extremely ambiguous devil figure, Woland, from the Russian Faust novel *The Master and Margarita*, by Mikhail Bulgakov (as well as being reminiscent of the word 'bogy', Bogue also references the Russian word for god). Bulgakov's surrealist anti-Stalinist novel, translated for the first time into English in the 1960s, and routed via Marianne Faithful through Mick Jagger's 'Sympathy for the Devil' into Jean-Luc Godard's film of the same name, also inspired the Jones Brothers.

A protest work of another kind was the widely acclaimed cyberspace novel *Neuromancer*, by William Gibson. The necromancer of the novel is a hacker by the name of Case who exists in a dehumanizing multinational hell-on-earth—'for thousands of years men dreamed of pacts with demons. Only now are such things possible' (Gibson 1984: 163). With the help of genetic engineering, this artificial intelligence world of virtual reality hankers after immortality. And in that ultimate immortality project the enemy is the human body, 'the meat', and its most severe contingency, our mortal condition: body loss here is also soul loss. This, of course, is also the great topic of the Goethe-inspired Faust novel *The Rebel Angels*, by Canada's preeminent twentieth-century author, Robertson Davies.

Davies' novel is a rarity in the field of Faust studies, in that it encompasses the whole range of the magus tradition of which the Faust story is an integral part; perhaps only Goethe's *Faust* achieved a similar breadth and depth of this theme. John Kenneth Galbraith in the *New York Times Book Review* ranked *The Rebel Angels* among the very best work of the twentieth century, and the novelist Anthony Burgess considered it and Davies undoubted Nobel material, lobbying the Swedish Academy to award the Nobel Prize in Literature to Davies. Robertson Davies died before such distinction could be bestowed upon his work.

Davies first encountered Goethe's *Faust* at the age of ten, when he read it because his parents had enthusiastically returned from an Ottawa performance of Gounod's opera, *Faust*, based on Part I of Goethe's *Faust*. Then, as a student at university, just like Goethe, he saw a puppet-play performance of the Faust story, but in his case it was Christopher Marlowe's *The Tragical History of Doctor Faustus* performed by the Munich Marionettes. He himself adapted the Marlowe version in 1953 as a forty-year-old father for a puppet performance that his own children put on. But the big breakthrough to the understanding of Goethe's drama and the whole magus tradition that was to inform his novel occurred in 1965, when Davies witnessed a complete performance of Parts I and II of Goethe's *Faust* in Salzburg, at the Kleines Festspielhaus. By this time he knew both parts well, but he considered this performance to be one of the two or three supreme theatre experiences of his life—quite a statement for someone so steeped in theatre as Robertson Davies: 'I shall always remember this lovely city as a place where I had an important revelation' (Grant 1994: 479). In *The Rebel Angels* this revelation is summed up by the title of the novel within the novel, originally a Paracelsus quote, *Be Not Another*, written by the 'Devil', John Parlabane, which affirms the 'Mephistophelean' side of humanity as part of the holistic project of the magus tradition.

Since for Robertson Davies, as for Goethe, Faust is part of the magus tradition going back to shamanistic times, this first and archetypal Faust story needs to be reviewed. Clement Hollier, the Faust figure in *The Rebel Angels*, referred to as one of 'these ... wizards ... [and] shape-shifters' (using shamanistic terminology), states in the novel 'that people don't by any means all live in what we call the present; the psychic structure of modern man lurches and yaws over a span of at least ten thousand years' (Davies 1981: 4, 32). Goethe, too, by referring to his Faust as a second Orpheus, taps directly into the shamanistic paradigm, since his mentor, Johann Gottfried Herder, had always insisted that 'Orpheus ... was originally nothing else but the most noble shaman' (Herder 1990–3, 3: 63).[2] The central paradigmatic story of shamanism, varied in many cultures and over great extents of time, concerns the shaman's assertion 'that spirits would help him, with whom he had made a pact out there in the great solitude' (Hoffman 1967: 108–9). Among these helping spirits, with whom the wizard/shaman makes a pact, predominates the figure of an underground smith, who takes the shaman psychologically/existentially apart, only to then realign him/her in accord with holistic principles dictated by the goddess of complete being. In other words, the underworld smith serves the goddess, the good of the whole, by ensuring that two important principles are adequately integrated into the shaman's personality structure and the earthly nature of which he is a part, namely human mortality and technology. By Goethe's time the development of the monotheistic immortality ideologies had split off the smith figure from the goddess of complete being, and demonized both, the reason being that in any immortality project death is the arch enemy, and death is associated primarily with human corporeality, which also draws sex and anything feminine into this negative evaluation. Warren Shapiro, Professor of Anthropology at Rutgers University, has drawn attention to this central existential human dimension in an article entitled 'Thanatophobic Man' in *Anthropology Today* (1989):

> I unabashedly acknowledge Becker's *The Denial of Death* as the most profound analysis of human affairs I have ever come across ... Religious traditions ... have some set of notions that are readily rendered as an 'afterlife'. From such notions we can conclude—from common sense, in the matter of 'functionalist social science'—that such notions ameliorate death-fear ...

Now consider the following:

> ... Carnality—the body and its eliminations—bothers people ... Decaying organic material ... forges a link with death ... But there is even more evidence that the most bothersome of all aspects of carnality is the female reproductive tract and its emissions. St. Tertullian ... called the vagina the 'Devil's Gateway' ... These are patently sexist formulations. (1989: 1)

It is from this fateful cultural nexus that both Goethe's and Davies' Faust works take their genesis in an effort to undo this patriarchal assessment.

Robertson Davies' novel is constructed along the double helix of two intertwined narrations, that of the Anglican priest, Simon Darcourt, whose area of academic specialization is the Gnostic Apocrypha, and that of the only major female character in the novel, Maria Magdalena Theotoky, whose name symbolically unites the fateful split of the patriarchal vision of the female—Theotoky being an epithet of the Madonna and Magdalena referring to the biblical 'prostitute'. Both narrators are concerned with the restoration to wholeness of an entire range of aspects that were rejected by culture.

Goethe's *Faust*, too, deals with the restoration of the feminine, along the lines of one of his trenchant *Maximen und Reflexionen* (*Maxims and Reflections*): 'It requires no great art to turn a goddess into a witch, a virgin into a whore; but for the reverse operation, to give dignity to the despised, to make desirable the cast aside, that requires either art or character' (Goethe 1949: 131). In fact, according to Goethe's own admission, stated only a few years before his death, and summing up his life's work, it had ever been his 'intention ... to portray and concretize what women with their excellent propensities have desired and sought to actualize in and for themselves under every condition' (1975, 41: 58–60). Before, therefore, proceeding to *The Rebel Angels* and its project of cultural restitution, a brief overview of Goethe's similar concerns as evinced in his *Faust* is also in order.

Goethe insisted that it was the 'peak' of Helena from which alone a proper understanding of the entire play could be glimpsed (1975, 108: 112), 'since the whole drama was actually written because of this character' (1975, 134: 209). When he therefore calls 'Classical Walpurgis Night' ('Klassische Walpurgisnacht') the 'antecedents' (1975, 18: 224) of Helena, the female characters of both Walpurgis Nights assume much greater importance than is normally accorded to them. In the first 'Walpurgis Night' ('Walpurgisnacht') there are, tellingly enough, many nameless witches, but of the only three named, none are, tellingly enough again, given a voice. The three female characters open and conclude the witches' Sabbath and belong without exception to three separate myth complexes that deal with the abuse of formerly powerful female mythic characters. Baubo, as part of the Persephone myth, leads the witches' procession, and Lilith and Medusa conclude the satanic tableau. Moreover all three myths are usually associated with great dangers: Mephistopheles warns Faust about Lilith's sole treasure, her hair; Medusa's snake hair is, of course, also dangerous; and Persephone's name also originally means in Sanskrit 'crowned by snakes'. That the major female character of Part I, Gretchen, with her loosened hair is here also identified by Mephistopheles with Medusa, gives this particular symbolism great weight (in eighteenth-century German the term 'snakes' significantly enough refers to the disorderly, loosened hair of females). Goethe no doubt read in his Hederich, the source for him of all things mythological, that Medusa had become a poor old woman after 'her head, which had been her treasure' (Hederich 1967: 1550), had been cut off, just as Gretchen was slated to be decapitated. The rest of Goethe's drama is to take up the restitution of this 'treasure', the female head and its intelligence—Medusa, after all, means the thinking one, the mediator.

To achieve this, Mephistopheles has to be truly recognized for what he is. He is referred to as Woland, that is, Weland, the smith, in the first 'Walpurgis Night', where the chief subterranean ruler is Mammon, or Vulcan/Hephaestus, the limping smith god, according to Milton. For Goethe, not only here, but in other of his works, has created a mythology of smith figures and their rigid products, which have everywhere usurped power: 'The smiths have all power in their hand; they possess the monopoly on power' (Buck 1996: 337). Ranged against their rigidity, which is due to their fear of the fluidity of life, Goethe extols the creativity of Medusa's snake-crowned head. For Goethe, the snake represents the genius, exemplified by the snake monument near his garden house in Weimar with the inscription 'to the genius of the place', 'genio huius loci'—Goethe here restores an older more positive mythology, in which every child, male or female, had a native genius in the form of a snake as his/her personal demon. It is this symbol of female genius that Goethe resuscitates in the second 'Walpurgis Night', the classical one, and finally also in the last scene of the drama, the 'heavenly' 'Mountain Gorges' ('Bergschluchten'). In the 'Classical Walpurgis Night' the three questers all encounter the varied forms of Medusa and her sisters: Faust, in his search for Helena, must descend into the underworld, where he meets with Medusa and Persephone; Homunculus joins the snake-tailed retinue of Galatea's mermaids and mermen in the Festival of Eros in the Aegean—the name of the ocean etymologically related to the term aegis, referring to the Medusa-embossed shield of Athene; and Mephisto seeks out the cousins of Galatea's mermaids, the Phorkyades, among whom are also numbered the three Gorgons, that is, Medusa, and her two sisters. Then in the drama's culminating scene, after Faust's death, the four female figures in attendance to the Mater Gloriosa are, beside Gretchen and Helena (Mulier Samaritana), the formerly debased long-haired Mary Magdalen (Magna Peccatrix) and the Godiva-like, hair-adorned Gypsy Mary (Maria Egyptiaca). In other words, neither the Festival of Eros, which is the prerequisite for the appearance of Helena, nor the 'heavenly' conclusion of the drama, is complete without a reciprocal egalitarian depiction of the otherness of the sexes, from their geniality to their corporeality—Goethe and his wife, Christiane, who referred to the coming of the menses as the arrival of a mermaid, would have read this most rejected aspect of female biology positively into the portrayal of the mermaid procession of the 'Classical Walpurgis Night' celebration of Eros. Ultimately this acceptance of the corporeal means what it portended in the shamanistic narrative, namely the acceptance and integration into the whole of that archetypal other, mortality, as Sylvelie Adamzik rightly concludes: 'With Goethe the 'Eternal-Feminine' preserves the negative in death ... Under her garment the Madonna of the Protective Mantel gives refuge to the chthonic heaven, which encompasses the ground of death' (1985: 134). This, however, means that the rigid response to the fluidities of the life of the universe by the smiths—consider, for instance, the damming up of the ocean waves by Faust/Mephistopheles' megaproject as being the most egregious—has to be loosened in the course of the drama, from its initial position of Mephistopheles as the Medusa slayer in the first 'Walpurgis Night' (he still seeks out, at the beginning of the second 'Walpurgis Night', Perseus-like the Graiae).

Goethe already suggests the beginning of this transformation in the 'Walpurgis Night's Dream'('Walpurgisnachtstraum'), immediately following the first 'Walpurgis Night', when Oberon, the Germanic smith figure Alberich, and Titania, the goddess Diana, undo their erstwhile alienation and separation, and plight their troth once more. Thus the Helena Act and its 'antecedents', the 'Classical Walpurgis Night', is framed by the Athenian artisan/smith clan of the Erechtheans, descendants of Hephaestus, stepping aside as Erichtho at the beginning, to let life appear, and usurping life at the end with the death of Icarus/Euphorion, Icarus and Daedalus also being artisans/smiths of that same Athenian clan. To this general loosening of the rigidities of the smiths belongs also the central myth of these scenes, the artisan Pygmalion and his statue that comes alive as Galatea, as does the rigid product of the smiths/alchemists Wagner/Mephistopheles, Homunculus. In fact, all smith figures are now reintegrated into the living pageant of the goddess—see, for instance, also the Dactyls and Telchines, as the first archetypes of the smith figure, and their 'dead works' (*F*, 8305)—and are subsumed by the wavy lines of the Aegean and its snake-like denizens, because cosmologically, epistemologically and methodologically, Goethe's 'delicate empiricism' and his 'wave' aesthetics and poetics approximate life much better than the 'rigid aperçus' (Adamzik 1985: 22) of Newton's brave new world:

> The wave suits life much better;
> ...
> Ocean, grant your eternal reign.
> ...
> You sustain the freshest life.
> ...
> You're the source of freshest life.
> ...
> Hail to ocean! Hail to waves.
>
> (Dem Leben frommt die Welle besser;
> ...
> Ozean gönn' uns Dein ewiges Walten.
> ...

> Du bist's der das frischeste Leben erhält.
> ...
> Du bists dem das frischeste Leben entquellt.
> ...
> Heil dem Meere! Heil den Wogen!)
> (*F*, 8315, 8437, 8443–4, 8480)

Finally in the last scene of the drama comes to pass what Goethe had periodically intimated, namely the reintegration and reconciliation of Mephistopheles/ Weland as the church father, Origen, had heretically suggested in his belief in the 'apokatastasis panton'.

In the figure of Pater Profundus, whose epithet was usually associated with St Aegidius, patron Saint of Smiths, the Medusa aspect of his name (etymologically recalling the Medusa aegis) blends harmoniously with his smith function—indeed, the vita of St Aegidius speaks of his self-sacrifice in the service of the goddess. With that tour-de-force Goethe has concluded his drama by undoing all the cultural exclusions, and a closer look at Robertson Davies' Faust novel is now facilitated, since he also examines the whole spectrum of cultural exclusions and reintegrates them into a more holistically oriented vision of culture.

For Davies, the Faust theme is first of all represented by 'the continuity of the Prospero figure' (Brydon 1989: 117) in his works, Shakespeare's contribution to the Faust/magus tradition. So the reach extends from the first novel, *Tempest-Tost* (1951), of the first trilogy, *The Salterton Trilogy*, through the three novels of the second trilogy, *The Deptford Trilogy* (1970–5)—Deptford being the place where Christopher Marlowe, the first Faust dramatist, was murdered in 1593— where 'the Faust myth . . . [is] implicitly present . . . [and] the centre of gravity' (Monk 1976: 370), to the explicit exposition of the theme in its entirety—from shamanism to Goethe—in the first novel of the third and last trilogy in Davies' oeuvre, *The Cornish Trilogy* (1981–8). That Faust novel, *The Rebel Angels* (1981), was to become 'a celebration of what is great in universities' and 'a great paean to the learned life' (Grant 1994: 524). However, Davies 'anticipated that some aspects of the portrait would give offense' (Grant 1994: 524), since it would have as its extensive subtext the most taboo aspects of the human story, and also because he was to represent the university not as a 'city of youth', but quite as much 'a city of wisdom', showing that 'intelligent societies have always preserved their Wise Men' (Grant 1994: 526), and finally, and equally disturbingly, that 'many of its members pursue knowledge at the expense of wisdom' (Grant 1994: 525).

In the cast of its six major characters, one graduate student and five professors, there is one professor, Urquhart McVarish (Urky), who pursues only 'knowledge at the expense of wisdom'. Needless to say he is neither Faust nor devil, but only a 'gadjo' foil for the other four Wise Men or magi—'gadjo' being a term that the graduate student, Maria Magdalena Theotoky, employs from her gypsy background for the exclusionary mainstream world of Canadian bourgeois life. But the four Faust or magus figures—Simon Darcourt, professor of Classics specializing in early Christian apocryphal texts; Clement Hollier, a paleo-psychologist; John Parlabane, a philosophy instructor; and Ozias Froats, a biologist—were also at the same time designated Rebel Angels, not the ones made famous by Lucifer/Satan, although there is some overlap, but the ones from the book of Enoch, who came down to earth to teach the secrets of the arts to mankind. Apparently, at first, no condemnation is intended, and the shamanic origins of this tale are hinted at in the *Midrashim*. The leader of the rebel angels was Samahazai, a name which Simon Darcourt appropriates for himself. However, an even more important appropriation doubly accrues to him by way of his name and vocational specialty: by concentrating his research and teaching activities on those scriptures 'that didn't make it into the accepted canon of Holy Writ' (Davies 1981: 87), since they were 'not thought suitable for inclusion in the reputed Word of God', mainly because they made up for 'the lack of a feminine presence in Christianity' (Davies 1981: 235), and by stipulating a feminine half of God, the Sophia, Simon Darcourt moves himself into that dark arch-heretical identity represented by the father of all heresies, the Samaritan Gnostic, Simon Magus, designated Faustus, with his Sophia, named Helena. This is the first magus, in reference to whom the Renaissance magus, Johann Georg Faust, speaks of himself as magus 'secundus' (Tille 1900: 2). But the deepest and most taboo exclusion that the Anglican priest, Simon Darcourt, brings into his own brand of heresy, his holistic 'imitatio Christi', is the principle of mortality, which, just as for the shaman figure, becomes the rejected cornerstone, upon which to build the proper Solomonic temple of wisdom: 'My job as a priest is to look human frailty in the face and call it by its right name' (Davies 1981: 313), and realize that

> perhaps what was imitable about Christ was his firm acceptance of his destiny, and his adherence to it even when it led to shameful death. It was the wholeness of Christ that had illuminated so many millions of lives, and it was my job to seek and make manifest the wholeness of Simon Darcourt. (Davies 1981: 56)

So just like the archetypal Faust, the shaman figure, as well as Goethe's Faust, Simon recognizes that the gift of creativity and wholeness rests squarely on accepting the mortality principle, for the shaman represented by the 'dismemberment' given to him by the underworld demonic smith figure, for Goethe's Faust by the necessary shamanic soul journey to the underworld of Medusa/Persephone, the 'kathodos' (descent), that will restore the Helena figure to the upper world. Simon therefore fully supports the quest of the Sophia, Maria Magdalena Theotoky, to unite her gypsy roots with her crown—Davies uses this shamanic tree symbolism of the world tree or 'axis mundi' throughout the novel, to indicate that the wells of wisdom and creativity at the root feed the crown, whether in Maria's case or in that of John Parlabane, the 'devil', who has an extensive chthonic root system that does nevertheless in the end produce his crown—or to use the Jungian terms, whose psychology appealed so much to Robertson Davies—the golden shadow as the creative source lodged in the dark unconscious.

The second magus figure, Clement Hollier, 'one of the most brilliant men in this university and a man of international reputation' (Davies 1981: 101), and Maria's thesis advisor, is not only a shamanistic 'wizard', but one of 'the holy men who serve the forces of nature' (Davies 1981: 112), a Renaissance magus. Hollier is specifically identified with the rebel angel, Azazel, who gave the divine secrets to Eve, thus bringing about the enlightenment of humanity. Jung in his

Answer to Job (1954) mentions that these 'angels, among whom Azazel particularly excelled, taught mankind the arts and sciences. They proved to be extraordinarily progressive elements who broadened and developed man's consciousness' (Grant 1994: 519). Hollier, however, is not just Azazel, the Rebel Angel, but he is the only one of the magi professors who is also specifically identified as Doctor Faustus. His immediate research area is the work of the Renaissance magus, Paracelsus, and like him he is interested in the rejected agents of an old wisdom that has much to do with nature, alchemy, Gnosticism (like Simon). And so it comes as no surprise that Hollier values the gypsy lore of Maria's family and ancestors. Like a latter-day alchemist Hollier sees the golden potential in the barest most humble 'materia nigra'. His all-inclusive truly liberal and humanistic arts vision therefore also reeks with the stench of mortality: he has opened up his innermost sanctum and given domicile to a typically smelly 'devil', John Parlabane, as well as pursuing the so-called filth therapy of Paracelsus and the Middle Ages, to which he adds Mammusia's secret, the 'bomari'. Mammusia, Maria's gypsy mother, revivifies valuable stringed instruments by means of a horse-dung 'bath' derived ultimately from an Egyptian alchemist, Maria Prophetissa, hence the 'bath of Mary' ('balneus mariae'), 'bain-marie', or 'bomari' in the Roma language of the gypsies.

Robertson Davies also extends this search for high value in the totally valueless to the field of Science. Ozias Froats is also a latter-day alchemist and Paracelsian magus, whose philosopher's stone is human fecal matter, which he investigates in his laboratory experiments. Here too Davies shows that the acceptance of and integration of Thanatos is of the essence: 'The body is the inescapable factor' (Davies 1981: 249), and the death of the body is represented most aptly by its eliminations. By the end of the novel Froats, on top of the list for the Nobel Prize, has 'come to disturb the sleep of the world. We shall all have to revise our thinking' (Davies 1981: 326). That is because both Christianity and Science are immortality ideologies that wage war on Nature because mortality is a natural part of a holistically conceived universe: 'The pride of science encourages us to this terrible folly ... [and] Christianity is not helpful about Nature. None the less, Nature will have her say, and even that Human Nature that Christianity so often deplores' (Davies 1981: 179).

Urquhart McVarish is the one professor who represents the narrow, exclusionary mainstream: 'Urky ignores death' (Davies 1981: 85), and jibes at Froats, and demeans Maria to a sex object. He is therefore 'bogus' (Davies 1981: 92) and not a magus. In fact,

> one of the more thought-provoking aspects of the novel is its exploration of how the McVarish attitude, when writ large, can constitute a menace to society. Urky's sneering jibes take a greater force as they are echoed from a political platform by Murray Brown ... [who] seeks to turn ignorance and prejudice to his own profit ...This reductive attitude is infectious ... It is a lesson as old as the Faust tale, but it bears repetition in the nuclear age ... It is a serious piece of writing of vital concern to any civilized society. (Cude 1982–3: 191–2, 198–9)

The anthropological study that has explored scientifically what Davies has presented in *The Rebel Angels* is *Purity and Danger* (1966) by Mary Douglas: in an effort to shore up the purity of their immortality ideologies, fundamentalists both secular and religious declare any deviations from their dogmas as dangerous and impure. Davies alludes in a poignant way in his novel to the 'theories' of racial purity that produced the holocaust in which, in the inhuman jargon of the Nazis, the 'impure', such as 'dirty' gypsies and Jews, were eradicated. Davies himself has spoken of a sense of personal loss when, in 1945, he heard about the holocaust (Grant 1994: 533). The breakthrough for Maria, on the other hand, comes when she breaks down in tears on hearing the gypsy strains during a Liszt Concert, and she suddenly realizes that she almost eliminated her gypsy root in the same manner as the 'gadjo' mainstream, a root that is the source of her wisdom and creativity as a woman as well:

> Sophia: the feminine personification of Wisdom; that companion figure to God who urged Him on to create the Universe; God's female counterpart whom the Christians and the Jews have agreed to hush up, to the great disadvantage of women for so many hundreds of years. (Davies 1981: 279)

And it is the Mephistopheles figure of Parlabane, with whom in a sense she has made a pact like a latter-day 'shamanka', whose *baneful* talk turns out to be the most *bene*ficial after all: 'His talk about the need to recognize your root and your crown as of equal importance has made me understand that my Gypsy part is inescapable . . . I am much more serious, much more real, for having accepted my Gypsy root' (Davies 1981: 310), a root that includes as a prominent heritage her uncle, 'Yerko, who was a brilliant metalsmith' (Davies 1981: 125), and together with Mammusia brought new art into the life of musician artists in their underground basement laboratory thanks to their filth therapy, a therapy that also includes, Goethe-like, the reclaiming of the glory of Maria's long black gypsy hair from the usual epithet of 'filthy', as well as Mammusia's use of Maria's menses in an aphrodisiac, and most astoundingly Yerko's rendering of that other 'bomari', the Bebby Jesus in his lowly stable setting. Truly Thanatos is integrated in Eros by Davies on all levels from the diurnal to the sublime, the corporeal to the spiritual, just as in the shaman's story and in Goethe's latter-day recapitulation of it in *Faust*.

To sum up then, Robertson Davies in his Faust novel *The Rebel Angels*, just like Goethe before him and the original shaman's story, is concerned with the recovery of the holistic, which entails first and foremost a recovery of nature and the feminine from their devalued status in patriarchal cultures. For the shaman's story, the symbolism involved has to do with the primary identifications of the world tree, the 'axis mundi', as goddess, and the world snake as goddess. For Goethe, the restitution of the feminine and nature stretches from the demonized snake symbolism of the Medusa figures to the Eternal-Feminine—the recent book *Die Ketzermythologie in Goethes Faust* (*Heretical Mythology in Goethe's Faust*) (Ilgner 2001) is the first study in the history of Faust research that has discerned that extensive subtext of the double helix of the Medusa snake and the smith mythologies and their connections to shamanism. For the Davies novel, finally, the tree symbolism of root and crown, and the reclaiming of the Sophia aspect of the divine by Maria Magdalena Theotoky, revisits the same ground. The keystone figure, without which this central human recovery fails, is the demonic subterranean smith figure and the successful pact negotiations with its thanato-chthonic aspects. Thus the shaman can only become identified with the holistic—a precondition for his/her healing potential—by honestly facing his/her own dismemberment and death at the hands of the smith figure. Goethe's Faust can only recover Helena, the embodiment of the complete feminine, the 'Eternal-Feminine', by undergoing 'the Aesculapian cure' (*F*, 7487)—the presence of snakes at the healing sites of Aesculapius was a major part of achieving wellness, hence the Classical Walpurgis Night teeming with snake figures. And Maria Magdalena Theotoky can only arrive at the full stature of her being by integrating the various split-off parts of herself in a multi-layered course of so-called 'filth therapy', filth being associated by the narrow 'gadjo' mainstream with anything not profitable, useful, death being the utmost dirty secret of humanity's various immortality projects. In other words, Goethe's snake therapy and Davies' filth therapy are one and the same symbolism, behind which stands the frightful other of death. And both for Goethe and Davies the rigid ideologies of Christianity and Science are inappropriate responses to the holistic that includes Thanatos. Goethe in his own life and views went back behind the orthodoxies of the Church of Newton and the Church of Rome and called himself a latter-day Pelagian, since Pelagius, the Celtic church father, was the last proponent of a naturalization of the Thanatos principle—the Council of Ephesus in AD 429 not only branded his teaching heretical but also eradicated the last shreds of the divine feminine, the temple of Diana at Ephesus, from the consciousness of Western culture, a hard blow indeed for Goethe, who was to call himself in a credo-like statement of 1812 'one of the Ephesian goldsmiths' (Goethe 1958: 665) in the service of the goddess. For Davies, the rigid orthodoxies of Christianity and Science, which make up our 'gadjo' world, were to culminate in the holocaust, where the purity fundamentalisms of the 'gadjos' were to attempt the utmost in wiping out the 'filth' that was the wondrous and creative culture of the Sinti and Roma.

Notes

1 Having taught a course on the Faust theme from Russia to Argentina and much of everything in between every year of my university teaching career, I was called in by Michael Jones and his brother Andy Jones (who had been cast in the role of Faustus Bidgood) as part of the editing process—Robert Joy, one of the film's producers, who also acted in the film, gave me two early versions of the film script for the *Faustus Bidgood* movie.
2 All quotes from German texts are translations by the author. *F* references are to lines in Goethe's *Faust*.

Bibliography

Adamzik, S. (1985), *Subversion und Substruktion—Zu einer Phänomenologie des Todes im Werk Goethes*. Berlin: Walter de Gruyter.
Brydon, D. (1989), *English Studies in Canada*. Downsview: University of Toronto Press.
Buck, T. (1996), *Goethe-Handbuch—Dramen*. Stuttgart: Metzler.
Cude, W. (1982–3), *Studies in Canadian Literature*. Fredericton: University of New Brunswick, Department of English.
Davies, R. (1981), *The Rebel Angels*. Toronto: Macmillan.
Gibson, W. (1984), *Neuromancer*. New York: Ace Science Fiction Books.
Goethe, J. W. (1949), *Maximen und Reflexionen*. Stuttgart: Alfred Kröner Verlag.
— (1958), *Briefe*. Munich: Carl Hanser Verlag.
— (1975), *Werke*. Tübingen: Niemeyer.

Grant, J. S. (1994), *Robertson Davies—Man of Myth*. Toronto: Penguin.
Hederich, B. (1967), *Gründliches mythologisches Lexikon*. Darmstadt: Wissenschaftliche Buchgesellschaft.
Herder, J. G. (1990–3), *Werke*. Frankfurt: Deutscher Klassiker Verlag.
Hoffman, H. (1967), *Symbolik der tibetischen Religionen und des Schamanismus*. Stuttgart: Hiersemann.
Ilgner, R. (2001), *Die Ketzermythologie in Goethes Faust*. Herbolzheim: Centaurus Verlag.
Monk, P. (1976), 'Confessions of a sorcerer's apprentice: *World of Wonders* and the *Deptford Trilogy* of Robertson Davies', *Dalhousie Review*, 56, 369–81.
Shapiro, W. (1989), 'Thanatophobic man', *Anthropology Today*, 5, (2), 11–14.
Tille, A. (1900), *Die Faustsplitter in der Literatur des sechzehnten bis achtzehnten Jahrhunderts nach den ältesten Quellen*. Berlin: Verlag von Emil Felber.

12 They Sold Their Soul for Rock'n'Roll: Faustian Rock Musicals*

Paul M. Malone

From its birth, rock had a reputation as 'the devil's music'. The old blues musicians, the rockers' forerunners, had reveled in and contributed to this reputation: Robert Johnson, for example, sang the Faustian tall tale of selling his soul for musical prowess at the 'Crossroads' (Lipsitz 1997: 47). But the blues had also been demonized by its critics, often white observers disturbed by what they saw as a 'black' form of entertainment laden with dangerous sexuality (Maddock 1996: 183; Tucker 1989: 289–90). When white musicians began taking up a form of upbeat blues, fear of racist backlash impelled promoters to avoid the established term 'rhythm and blues', which was tied to black culture; in its place the label 'rock and roll', a little-known euphemism for sexual intercourse, became current (Barnard 1986: 11–12; Szatmary 1991: 21–2). Not surprisingly, the newborn musical form remained as suspect as its precursor. As a result, few rock artists of the first generation dared lay claim to demonic associations: the first great white rocker, Elvis Presley, undercut criticism of his racially and sexually loaded performance style by cultivating a reassuringly conservative private image, singing Gospel songs and willingly accepting the draft (Sullivan 1987: 316; Tucker 1989: 292–3).

The next generation was less circumspect. In the 1960s, for instance, Mick Jagger's devilish swagger in 'Sympathy for the Devil' and the Rolling Stones' corresponding image as 'Their Satanic Majesties' came close to following Robert Johnson's example (Wells 1983: 22–3), but their provocative posing never drew the furor unintentionally aroused by John Lennon when he remarked in 1966 that the relatively innocuous Beatles were 'bigger than Jesus' (Sullivan 1987: 315–6); and the Stones' pretensions to evil were shattered by their helplessness when violence broke out at the 1969 Altamont festival. Between these two dates lay the birth of heavy metal rock, which would update Johnson's basic blues with a mixture of extreme volume and, often, 'outright Satanism' (Hinds 1992: 156).

Common as the devilish undercurrents of rock music have been, however, and despite the frequency with which the devil has popped up in rock songs,

---

* I would like to thank Osman Durrani, David G. John and Bernd Mahl for giving me access to various materials in the course of researching the current chapter.

whether as protagonist, antagonist, prop or mere metaphor for hard times, it has been uncommon for rock music to make any concrete, explicit reference to the Faust theme specifically. The following study describes in brief four exceptions to this generalization.

These examples, all musicals rather than single songs, have been chosen on the basis of two criteria: first, because they contain three elements key to the Faust plot as configured by Goethe—namely, a Faust figure, a Mephistopheles figure and a Gretchen figure (the last a Goethean innovation); and second, because they all by some means set these elements within a rock music environment: the protagonist, so to speak, sells his soul for rock'n'roll. This criterion has eliminated a work that might otherwise be given pride of place in such a study, namely, the Austrian *Fäustling: Spiel in G* (*Fäustling: Play in G*). *Fäustling* was produced for the Vienna Festival of 1973, with text and direction by Josef Prokopets and music by Wolfgang Ambros (Mahl 2005: 206). As the diminutive form of the title indicates, the work shrinks the characters of Goethe's play to fit contemporary Vienna: civil servant Heinrich Fäustling, bored with his middle-class life, is introduced by the devil (a figure as much from the 'underground' as the underworld) to a looser, more hedonistic lifestyle. As a result, Fäustling feels more alive, even forgetting his infatuation with his secretary Grete; but in the end he is no more certain that he is happy.

Composer Ambros would go on to become the father of 'Austropop' (Larkey 1992: 158), a localized manifestation of the 'Liedermacher' (literally, 'song maker') or 'New Song' movement of the late 1960s and early 1970s. The 'Liedermacher' grafted social consciousness and Anglo-American rock tropes onto French-style 'chansons' to create a modern indigenous German-language popular music scene to rival imported rock (Schmidt 1979: 145–6). Austropop sought to use the same methods to counter not only Anglophone, but also (West) German, cultural hegemony (Larkey 1992: 153–4), particularly through its programmatic use of local Austrian dialects rather than Standard German (164–5). *Fäustling*, for example, is likewise characterized by its use of strong Viennese dialect: Ambros, as the devil, proclaims, 'I'm the devil and I say, "No!"' ('I bin da Teife und i sog, "Na!"'), *Fäustling*'s version of Goethe's 'I am the spirit that denies forever!' ('Ich bin der Geist der stets verneint') (*F*, 1338).[1]

Despite *Fäustling*'s initial success, the script was never published and the original 1973 vinyl cast album has never been reissued. Moreover, although the cover notes to the album boast of the use of the 'progressive pop music' idiom—the music ranges from orchestral to folk-tinged rock—they avoid the use of the word 'rock', and music itself plays no role in the plot, which remains firmly in a 'petit-bourgeois' milieu.

If *Fäustling* is eliminated, the pioneering work in this field is Brian De Palma's 1974 horror-comedy film *The Phantom of the Paradise*, with songs by actor turned singer-songwriter Paul Williams. Essentially a retelling of Gaston Leroux's *The Phantom of the Opera*, De Palma's script also includes elements of both Oscar Wilde's *The Picture of Dorian Gray* and *Faust*. The last-named story, however, is the only influence explicitly referred to in the dialogue.

Phantom's protagonist is Winslow Leach, composer of a 'pop cantata' entitled *Faust* (the original Phantom of the Opera's composition was called *Don Juan Triumphant*, but Faust and Don Juan have regularly been linked as thematically related figures). Leach tries out his material between acts at a rock club; early in the film he performs the title ballad, 'Faust', with its agitated rolling piano ostinato. Although the plot of Leach's cantata never becomes clear, the sentiments expressed might not be out of place in Faust's reveries in Gretchen's bedchamber (*F*, 2687–728): complaining of being miscast as a 'cryin' clown', Leach as Faust sings that he would sell his soul for one true love, in a fantasy of endless happiness and laughter (Williams 1998).

As luck would have it, the club where Leach is playing is owned by the reclusive record mogul Swan, who is in attendance. Impressed, Swan sends his lackey Philbin to obtain more of Leach's music, but Leach explains that he cannot hand over just a couple of upbeat excerpts, since the work is an organic whole telling the Faust story. The philistine Philbin has never heard of Faust, of course, and can only ask what label he is on. Leach's pedantic reply describing the historical/legendary Faust selling the devil his soul for 'worldly experience and power' fails to impress Philbin (*Phantom* 2003).

Appalled, Leach insists that his 'magnum opus' must be performed in its entirety, by Leach himself; otherwise he refuses to do business. Swan, however, is looking for fodder for his stable of acts to open his new concert venue, the Paradise. Philbin steals Leach's music and Swan frames the composer for drug pushing, ensuring that he is sentenced to life in prison. There Leach hears a mutilated version of 'Faust' on the radio, covered by one of Swan's bands, the Beach Bums: his ballad has become a surf-rock song about street racing. Enraged, the composer breaks prison and tries to destroy the albums at Swan's Death Records pressing plant, but he falls into a record press and is scarred horribly, his face and voice destroyed.

Soon, the Paradise is being haunted by a masked madman determined to prevent *Faust* from being staged. Swan quickly realizes that the Phantom is Leach; he also discovers the Phantom's weakness, when a young woman named Phoenix auditions with an organ- and guitar-based rhythm and blues song, 'Special to Me', fitting the Gretchen character's failure to understand Faust and his motivation (the singer sees the addressee as senselessly spellbound by ambition), even ending with a 'Gretchen question' (*F*, 3414–68): despite her love, Phoenix doesn't see where the lovers will go once they 'arrive' at success (Williams 1998).

Leach had fallen in love with Phoenix before his incarceration; now he cannot terrorize her as he has previous performers. Swan offers Leach a production of *Faust* with Phoenix in the lead as his 'voice', if Leach will rewrite the cantata for her—and sell Swan his soul. Leach agrees, and feverishly revises his work in a montage set to 'The Phantom's Theme', describing the famous Faustian inner conflict ('Two souls, alas, dwell in my breast' ['Zwei Seelen wohnen, ach! in meiner Brust'] [*F*, 1112]) as a tale in which 'All the devils that disturbed me and the angels that defeated them somehow' are bid to unite in the singer (in a distant, rather coy echo of the Beatles' 'Come Together') (Williams 1998).

Once Leach's work is done, however, Swan attempts to seal him up alive in his workroom, relegates Phoenix to backup vocals and casts the effeminate glam-rock star Beef in the lead. When Leach escapes and kills Beef onstage, Phoenix quells the crowd with the ballad 'Old Souls' and becomes a star herself—something she wants so badly that she will even sleep with Swan to keep it. In despair, Leach tries to kill himself, but his body refuses to die; it seems his contract, and thus his life, 'terminate with Swan'. An attempt on Swan's life proves equally fruitless, since, as the impresario explains, he is similarly 'under contract'.

Swan now plans to conclude 'his' *Faust* by marrying Phoenix on live television; but Leach discovers Swan's cache of surveillance videotapes, including a reel from 1953 that shows Swan selling his soul to the devil for eternal youth: now only Swan's video image ages. Leach also learns that Swan plans to have Phoenix killed during the wedding ceremony as a publicity stunt. Setting the video room alight, Leach rushes to the Paradise, foils the murder and rips off Swan's mask to reveal his true, aged visage. As the crowd carries off the dying Swan, Leach too expires, unmasked and horribly scarred, but redeemed in Phoenix's arms.

The song best suited to expressing the devil's cynical attitude, 'The Hell of It', with its heavy bass intro riff and boogie-flavored chorus, is displaced out of the plot and plays under the closing credits. Originally, the song had been written to be played as a back-handed 'tribute' at Beef's funeral, but this scene was never filmed (De Palma 2003: 22); as a closing title theme, 'The Hell of It' now seems to paraphrase Mephisto's pessimistic summary of human existence itself (*F*, 279–92): life is a game rigged against you and time is nothing more than a cheat, Williams sings as an omniscient narrator to the departed (who now, at film's end, seems more likely to be Swan and/or Leach than Beef). The 'hell of it' mentioned in the title and chorus is the fact that even this empty life is wasted by humanity, and particularly by the worthless addressee, whose demise is unmourned and whose damnation is certain (Williams 1998).

Phantom of the Paradise successfully satirizes both rock opera and theatrical rock of the era, but its melange of elements from several sources finally devolves into chaos rather than building to a climax. Perhaps the film's most interesting aspect is its warped reinterpretation of the 'double wager', another Goethean innovation to the Faust story. Although there is no wager between God and the devil in *Phantom*, there are two devilish pacts: on the one hand, Swan acts as Mephistopheles to Leach's Faust, but we later discover that this recapitulates the original contract between Swan and the devil himself. This doubling is made even more resonant by the fact that Swan, plagiarist of Leach's compositions, is played by Paul Williams, the songs' actual composer; and the devil appears to Swan as his own reflection—Williams again. This joke is underlined when Swan uses his knowledge of recording technology to restore Leach's destroyed voice temporarily, allowing Leach to perform the ballad 'Faust' again—this time with Paul Williams' singing voice. Although Williams had supposedly originally wanted to play the Phantom, identifying with 'the sensitive artist who has had his music commercialized to the point of its being unrecognizable to him but is, of course, fabulously successful by it' (De Palma 2003: 18), he is a more interesting choice as Swan. The diminutive Williams is well over a foot shorter than William Finley, the actor playing Leach, and even shorter than Jessica Harper, who plays Phoenix; with his teddy-bear face, long blond hair and adolescent voice, his childlike androgyny makes his ruthlessness even more disturbing.

Unfortunately, most of the film is less clever, with the exception of Williams' own witty songs, which stray well beyond his usual mild rhythm-and-blues musical style; although *Phantom* earned an Oscar nomination for its music, Williams would have greater success as composer of children's songs for *The Muppet Movie* (1979) and several of its sequels. As for the film itself, although *Phantom of the Paradise* eventually garnered a small cult following, at the time it was a critical and commercial failure (De Palma 2003: 43–4).

Nine years later, the Canadian stage musical *Starboy*, written by Randall Paris Dark, with additional lyrics by Cary Dark and music by Ian Crowley, was first produced in Calgary at the Loose Moose Theatre in 1983. The unpaginated published playscript describes *Starboy* as 'a fantasy based on the Faust tale of selling one's soul to achieve one's goal' (Dark 1983). The Mephistopheles role here is displaced onto the devil's daughter Satina, who introduces herself, and invites the listener to 'burn', in the play's opening number, 'My Place is Hot'. As the heavy dance beat proclaims, the portion of hell under Satina's sway is obviously a kind of disco inferno, where 'you won't be the first and you won't be the last' to end up (Dark et al. 1984) (compare Mephistopheles' remark to Faust, after the 'Walpurgis Night's Dream' ['Walpurgisnachtstraum'], that Gretchen 'is not the first' to 'perish without help and without hope' ['Sie ist die erste nicht'; 'lässest sie hülflos verderben'] [*F*, 'Trüber Tag—Feld' 12–13]). Satina is saddled with two incompetent assistants, the bubble-headed Rita and her bisexual brother Lucius. Rita, sent scouting for prospects, comes upon the hero, Jimmy Paul Beadley, reading *Rolling Stone* in his bedroom and wishing that he could become a rock star, not merely singing for huge audiences, but actually fronting for no less than the Rolling Stones. He sings 'Rock Star', a power ballad with overtones of the 1980s bands Styx and Toto in its music-box piano introduction, and faint echoes of Faust's craving for 'corrosive joy and dissipation' (*F*, 1766): Jimmy wants to be like his idols, traveling the world and leading a life of debauchery, a goal for which he is prepared even to deal with the devil, though apparently not to work hard, practice an instrument and pay his dues on the road. From outside, Rita asks if this means he would be willing to sell his soul, to which Jimmy replies that he would indeed go that far (Dark et al. 1984).

This is an implicit invitation that Jimmy does not need to utter three times. Seizing the opportunity once the song ends, Rita enters through the window and offers Jimmy the fulfillment of his desires in return for his soul; since he believes that she is no more than a dream, he ultimately agrees only to get rid of her. As Rita exits, Jimmy's girlfriend Christine enters; she wants him to quit living on unemployment insurance ('UIC') and find a job, so that they can get married. Jimmy wants to make her happy, but he also wants to live out his fantasy, and his conflict is sung out in the show-tune style duet 'Get a Job', another example of the Gretchen and Faust characters' failure to communicate on the same level (*F*, 3414–68). In this case, Christine, rather than Jimmy, seems the wiser and more practical partner. Christine offers Jimmy work at her father's car wash, which would allow them to marry and set up house in a condominium; her dreams of broadloom carpet, a linoleum kitchen and hall mirrors are contrasted with Jimmy's preference for mirrors in the bedroom and obvious disinterest in raising a family, given his sarcastic response to her suggestion of raising children.

Exasperated, Christine finally avers that there is no power on earth that can make Jimmy a rock star. By this point, however, there are two opposing unearthly forces at work on Jimmy's behalf: in heaven, gay fairy godfather Burt and his handsome son Steen have picked Jimmy's name at random to help him. Meanwhile, Rita has communicated Jimmy's agreement to Satina, who—since she only collects female souls—is willing to grant Jimmy's wish in return for Christine's soul as well. She has no intention of telling him the real price, of course, until it is too late. Satina brings a contract to earth and gets Jimmy's signature, tempting him via the duet 'Star Boy' [sic]; he will open his own rock show the very next evening in Las Vegas. Christine enters just as the contract is signed—sealed with a kiss—and jumps to the wrong conclusion; she immediately leaves him, singing her feelings of betrayal in the ballad 'Hollow at the Heart', a watered-down echo of Gretchen's sentiments before the shrine of the Mater Dolorosa ('How they rage/Deep in my marrow,/The pangs of my heart!' [*F*, 3596–8]). The bluesy sound of the saxophone and piano comes to the fore as Christine laments remaining for so long with Jimmy to no purpose but to be left with the feeling of hollowness described in the song's title (Dark et al. 1984).

Satina now informs Jimmy that he owes her Christine's soul, to be paid by burning a lock of her hair at midnight; his stardom will cost him all of his human relationships, for he will become vain and self-obsessed as Satina's first victim did, described in the song 'Sacrifice'. Jimmy and Christine reconcile, however, and with Burt and Steen's aid, outwit the devil's daughter. The lock of hair Satina burns turns out to come from one of Burt's wigs, and the contract is thus void. Jimmy can now defeat Satina by means of the power ballad 'Flashing Lights'. To add further insult, Satina loses both of her assistants, since Steen and Rita have fallen in love and Lucius pairs off with Burt. Satina disappears, swearing revenge; but Jimmy still gets his rock show, thanks to Burt and Steen—because he believed in himself and because he expresses proper remorse in the song 'Lost and Confused'—and at the end of the final number, the doo-wop inflected 'After the Battle', he and Christine fly up, apparently to heaven, on a glittering Las Vegas-style star (Dark 1983).

By contrast with *Phantom of the Paradise*, in *Starboy* the hero not only survives, but also gets to keep both his love and the goal for which he was willing to sell his soul in the first place. Moreover, there is another interesting revision of the double wager, since Satina is willing to purchase Jimmy's soul only if he will also sign away Christine's—though once again these are pacts, rather than bets. Despite some strong arrangements of the songs, however, which vary in style from Broadway through lounge and reggae to synthesizer-laden rock (complete with Eddie Van Halen-style guitar solos), the simplistic level of the plot, and particularly of its comic elements, reduce *Starboy* to a mediocre situation comedy: the script's mawkish handling of Burt's homosexuality and transvestitism, for example, has aged far more badly than the music.

More than another decade later, in 1995, *Randy Newman's Faust* appeared as an album. Like Paul Williams, Newman was originally a songwriter who had taken to recording his own material; the classically trained intellectual Newman, however, had seldom been hit-parade material. His dark and caustically witty songs, set to music less influenced by rock than by a combination of barbershop, gospel/blues, nineteenth- and early twentieth-century popular parlor music and Hollywood film scores (Winkler 1988), tend to be 'dramatic monologues' akin to Victorian poetry, featuring '"reprehensible" (grotesque) narrators' (Dunne 1992: 53–4). Moreover, Newman as performer totally subsumes himself into his narrators: 'no matter how depraved Newman's characters are, they are portrayed without condescension, and often with outright affection—the songs seem to ask, "are you and I really any better?"' (Winkler 1988: 24). Newman's version of *Faust*, however, does not necessarily display the same affection for its model: '. . . there's something so wise about [Goethe's *Faust*] that it made me want to try to destroy it, in a way . . . and have all its wisdom frustrated by the nature of *real* human beings' (Willman 2003: iv).

Where God seems to be completely absent in *Phantom* and works only through intermediaries in *Starboy*, he appears in person at the very top of Newman's *Faust*, as the angels back him up in a gospel number, 'Glory Train'. Their jubilation is dampened—and straight 4/4 time changes to jagged 7/8 (Lucchesi 2003: 113)—when Lucifer interrupts to point out loudly that neither God nor he himself actually exists, as they were both only invented by superstitious fools (Newman 2003a).

Newman's rude interruption here updates Boito's famous whistle aria in *Mefistofele*, while the scene as a whole mimics much of Goethe's 'Prologue in Heaven' ('Prolog im Himmel') (*F*, 243–98). As Kevin Courrier points out, however, 'Since the musical is built on the assumption that God and the Devil *do* indeed exist, Newman's claims that they are figments of our imagination [are] incongruous, and the Devil's barbed points have no sting' (2005: 273).

As a parody, Newman's *Faust* parallels Goethe's basic plot and character constellation; however, Newman substantially alters the protagonist. His Henry Faust is no wise and wizened scholar, but a lazy Notre Dame undergraduate, picked almost at random, whose inner conflict is outright schizophrenia, as displayed in his introductory song 'Bless the Children'. This song is both textually and musically bipolar, swinging from a driving hard rock section in which Faust complains of murderous insanity encroaching upon his consciousness and fantasizes the bloody murder of 'little piggies' to a Michael Jackson-style choral pop refrain, pleading for the 'children of the world' who only need understanding and support (Newman 2003a).

Despite this opening display of both violent aggression and sugary compassion, Faust's real ambition is to acquire 'money, power, control' with as little effort as possible, because he believes 'money, power, control equals love'. Even the devil finds him repulsive, but Lucifer nonetheless outstrips the original Mephistopheles' double-edged promise that 'still what you are, you always must remain' (*F*, 1809) in the rousing song 'The Man', whose gospel inflections indicate not religiosity, but rather the devil's pandering to Faust's megalomania by repeating to him that he is, in fact, 'the man', entitled to bodyguards and special treatment despite the lack of any real achievement on his part. Once Faust himself begins repeating 'I'm the man!' in awestruck tones, Lucifer's work would seem to be done (Newman 2003a).

This has been all too easy, however. Even before the devil has gone to work in earnest, Newman's Faust has already attained the soulless self-absorption that Satina had predicted as Jimmy Paul Beadley's fate. God is ultimately forced to make Faust fall in love with the waitress Margaret, via Cupid's arrow (no doubt inspired by Mephistopheles' mention of that cherub [*F*, 2598]), in order to render him relatively bearable. In response, in 'My Hero' Newman provides Margaret an apparently optimistic love song that is undercut by its own romantic naïveté and by its musical arrangement. As she sings, Margaret infantilizes Faust, describing him as a 'momma's boy' with a 'lazy little smile', and summing up with the simple statement that she likes him and hopes that he likes her (Newman 2003a).

Under the lyrics, however, the orchestra takes a minor turn in the second chorus, as if they know already that Margaret will kill her mother, her brother and finally her child (Willman 2003: vii, viii)—a series of deaths that Newman has retained from Goethe's original, though now it is God Himself who is indirectly responsible for them. Unfortunately, this 'rather bland cry of love' not only 'sound[s] like something found in a fortune cookie' (Courrier 2003: 278), it also seems to have no connection to the power-hungry character who sings 'The Man' immediately preceding this. As a result, Margaret appears worse than naïve.

The remainder of the plot diverges from Goethe's original most obviously in that, in Newman's version, the devil actually falls in love with Margaret's friend Martha, and has his heart broken when she leaves him. Moreover, at the end, when Margaret is taken up to heaven, Newman's Faust poisons himself in remorse and expires noisily, forestalling any possibility of a second part. Surprisingly, after his suicide Faust too is redeemed, to the devil's chagrin. The superficial romanticism of this ending is deflated by the realization that except for the love laid upon him artificially, the cowardly, lazy and venal Faust has undergone no psychological development whatsoever. Given such poor raw material to work with, neither God nor the devil could have won without cheating—and God, having outcheated the devil, is sympathetic enough to cheer up his opponent by joining him in a reprise of an earlier song, 'Can't Keep a Good Man Down'.

The original album, twelve years in the composition, is loaded with rock stars—James Taylor is God, the Eagles' Don Henley plays Faust, and Linda Ronstadt sings Margaret, with Elton John and Bonnie Raitt in supporting roles and Newman himself playing the devil. Unfortunately, as with many concept albums, including the landmark *Tommy* by The Who (1969), the overall dramaturgy is incoherent. Almost half of the songs on the album are digressions from the main storyline; in fact, the eponymous protagonist appears in only two songs out of seventeen, compared to three for Margaret and eight for the devil (who thus becomes by default another of Newman's reprehensible narrator figures). Only by means of a plot synopsis inserted into the album notes by Newman is it possible to re-create any story from the songs—and yet the synopsis places the songs in a different order from the sequence in which they appear on the album. Finally, as Kevin Courrier sums up,

> Newman, who thinks dramatically in his popular songs because he gets to play *all* the characters, doesn't know how to write dramatically for actors. He may have cast performers who best embodied the qualities of the part he'd written, but they did not have the acting skills to develop the characters they were given. (2005: 275)

In 1996 Newman's *Faust* was transformed into the stage musical he had always intended, playing first in San Diego and then in Chicago, and an attempt was made to redress these deficiencies. Several of the original songs were scrapped or reassigned, and others added, in the reworking, while the story was restructured with the aid of playwright David Mamet. Nonetheless, the plot still failed to cohere; the ongoing by-play between God and Lucifer, and the now expanded subplot of the devil's love for Martha, continued to detract from the main plot. In addition, the substitution of talented actor-singers for rock stars—though Henry Faust was now introduced singing his first song while playing electric guitar and dancing on his bed—only made even more apparent how unsympathetic most of the characters were (Brantley 1996; Courrier 2005: 283–4). The *New York Times* declared *Faust* 'an unwitting commentary on the banality of crowd-pandering musicals' (Brantley 1996). A projected move to Broadway was never realized; at the same time, the original album was proving a commercial failure (Courrier 2005: 284).

Because Newman's is the first adaptation to include God, it is also in a position to reproduce the double wager of Goethe's original directly; however, in this version, while the stakes of the wager with God are raised to allow the devil back into heaven if he wins, the agreement with Faust falls flat. In the original album, the devil 'proffers a contract that Faust signs without reading. The Devil is astonished. Henry explains that he doesn't like to read on his own time' (Newman 2003b: x). Thus there is no wager, but rather a perfunctory pact. In the stage version, Faust's reaction to the devil's demand for his soul becomes one of more active disbelief and suspicion—'What's the catch?' (Lucchesi 2005–6: 43). Moreover, the devil's offer of a recording contract leaves Faust cold: the real money is in video games, and so Faust resists signing until after Valentine's murder, when he needs Lucifer's aid to escape justice (Lucchesi 2003: 115; 2005–6: 38).

Randy Newman's Faust ultimately falls between two stools: attempting a backhanded parodic fidelity to Goethe's plot while continually being derailed by Newman's own sympathy for the devil. Kevin Courrier, in fact, compares Newman's work unfavorably to De Palma's *Phantom of the Paradise*, which in Courrier's opinion 'integrates, with shrewdness and bold imagination, Goethe's themes of damnation and salvation into a contemporary setting. By contrast, Newman's *Faust* is a lethargic piece of craftsmanship with no soul to sell' (2005: 282).

Finally, *Faust: Die Rockoper* (*Faust: The Rock Opera*), Rudolf Volz's 1999 recording of Goethe's *Faust I*, not only remains faithful to Goethe's plot, but also exclusively uses Goethe's own German text, though much abridged and transposed, set to rock music. As the work's original website proclaimed, 'Like the Hegelian principle of creating a synthesis from thesis and antithesis, . . . from these hitherto independent and unconnected elements a new product is created' (*Faust: Die Rockoper* 2004)—a product that, by virtue of its alleged fidelity to Goethe's original and its inclusion of Part II (which Volz released as an album in 2004), trumps the loosely adapted 'high-culture' operas of Spohr, Berlioz, Gounod, Boito, etc. At the same time, to be sure, this 'fidelity' has been bought at the price of the majority of Goethe's actual text: Bernd Mahl reckons that 75 per cent of *Faust I* and a full 95 per cent of *Faust II* have had to be cut in Volz's versions (2005: 205–6).

The concept behind Volz's *Faust* is straightforward: Goethe's work is 'one of the most significant in German literature', yet it remains 'for most readers not particularly easily digestible', and so Volz's rock adaptation serves as 'an easy introduction':

> The production takes the form of a contemporary rock concert. This is stylistically appropriate, because in recent years such diabolical variants as black metal and death metal have become popular. Mephisto is also a 'devilish fiddler', who indeed sounds more like Jimi Hendrix than Pagganini [sic]. (*Faust: Die Rockoper* 2007)

Volz in fact greatly exaggerates the links between his compositions and genuine 'death metal'. The majority of the songs in *Faust I* are solidly in the more melodic mold of so-called 'classic' hard rock/heavy metal; on the original website Volz declared his models to be Deep Purple and the Scorpions, whose heyday fell in the 1970s and 1980s respectively (*Faust: Die Rockoper* 2004).

Mephistopheles' introduction, for example, 'More Bestial than the Beasts' ('Tierischer als jedes Tier', sung to God in the Prologue; abridged from *F*, 271–90), like most of the devil's songs, is a skillfully executed song based on a solid guitar riff, employing the hard rock technique of using electric guitar and lead vocal as joint solo instruments, and conveying Mephisto's confrontational attitude toward God by means of musical aggression, undercutting the apparently tactful form of address:

> Because, O Lord, you show yourself and ask
> about conditions here with us,
> and you were glad in former days to have me near,
> you see me now as one among your servants.
>
> (*F*, 271–4)

Similar musical stylings are used in Faust's opening monologue, which provides two songs: in 'Turned to Magic' ('Der Magie ergeben', based on *F*, 354–85), a ponderous organ and guitar rhythm creates the musical image of the scholar's life as a tough slog before the open anguish of 'Moonlight' ('Mondenschein', derived from *F*, 385–409), an emotional 'heavy ballad' in which the reverb on the lead guitar reinforces the sense of despair and isolation ('Alas! Am I still wedged within this prison cell?' [*F*, 398]), while the blues-based call-and-response structure foreshadows the fact that Faust is indeed about to be answered from the infernal regions (Malone 2004: 270).

Like his precursors, Volz attempts to use different musical genres to aid characterization: 'While the songs of Faust and Mephisto range from heavy metal to death metal [sic], Gretchen's songs are ordinary pop songs' (*Faust: Die Rockoper* 2007). However, ongoing revisions to the work have altered this relationship somewhat. 'My Peace is Gone' ('Meine Ruh ist hin'), for example, is one of the few songs that can use Goethe's words virtually unchanged (though rearranged from *F*, 3373–413). In Volz's original version, this became a dreary country-pop waltz (Malone 2004: 270–1); the musical effect was a conservative interpretation of Gretchen as an ineffectual and passive character. In more recent recordings, however, 'My Peace is Gone' has become a slow rhythm-and-blues torch song. Several other of Gretchen's songs have also been rewritten, so that she is more of a match vocally for the male characters than she was—though her final number, 'I Killed My Mother' ('Ich hab' meine Mutter umgebracht', based on *F*, 4427–40; 4507–9), remains overly bombastic.

Perhaps the most notable alteration to Volz's work from its initial form is the complete revision of the song 'Still What You Are, You Always Must Remain' ('Du bleibst doch immer'; from the pact scene: *F*, 1806–9); originally, this number was the keystone of Volz's 'Hegelian synthesis':

> This synthesis reaches its climax in the song 'Still What You Are, You Always Must Remain', which uses the same music as [Steppenwolf's 1968 hit] 'Born to be Wild'. At first glance it seems impossible that a classic text by Goethe could be reconciled with a classic motorcycle song. (*Faust: Die Rockoper* 2004)

Indeed, one of the triumphs of Volz's work was that this appropriation of an authentic piece of rock history (legally authorized by the original composer, Mars Bonfire) did not stand out musically from the rest of the work as anachronistic, nor did it make the other songs seem amateurish. In more recent versions of *Faust*, however, this song too has been completely reworked, with lyrics partially rearranged and a completely original melody and musical arrangement. The new version, however, like the rest of Volz's *Faust I*, remains beholden to musical styles three decades old.

This sense of nostalgia is only intensified in Volz's setting of *Faust II*, in which the musical palette is broadened to include art-rock and progressive rock styles in the spirit of Emerson, Lake and Palmer and David Bowie, with musical quotations from Mussorgsky and Chopin (Malone 2004: 272). These styles were originally contemporaries of hard rock; during the 1970s, some bands moved from one style into the other, including Deep Purple, who had been a keyboard-dominated art-rock band before pushing the guitar sound to the fore (Nicholls 2004: 122).

This nostalgia also has another effect, however: Volz declares that 'the Faust theme is independent of historical period, since it deals with crossing the border between ignorance and knowledge, and the automatically associated question of good vs. evil' (*Faust: Die Rockoper* 2007). By synthesizing Goethe's classic text with 'classic' rock, Volz's version updates the text, yet keeps the opera at a vaguely defined historical remove. As a result, the action occurs in an alternate medieval/modern reality, where Faust and Mephistopheles use bicycles, computers, electric violins, cell phones and space shuttles made of CDs while interacting with witches, Greek mythological figures and Holy Roman Emperors. The fact that many of these juxtapositions have a humorous effect, of course, only adds to the show's entertainment value and further sweetens the difficult pill of the text.

Indeed, it is striking that all three of the other Faustian musicals described here are explicitly intended as comedies (and *Fäustling*, too, is hardly dour)— which does not mean that they cannot be seriously intended, but it certainly does not conform to the conventional view of Goethe's masterwork. In fact, both *Starboy* and Volz's *Faust* owe some inspiration to Richard O'Brien's 1973 musical comedy *The Rocky Horror Show*, as is clear from the instrumental and vocal arrangements in *Starboy*, and as openly acknowledged by Volz on the original *Faust: Die Rockoper* website (Malone 2004: 271). These influences show up most obviously in the songs for the 'Erdgeist' or 'Earth-Spirit' (adapted from *F*, 481–513) and in the Walpurgis Night scene (based on *F*, 4128–43).

Volz's *Faust* is most intriguing because it remains a work in progress, still undergoing revision—and in the case of Part I, expansion as well—and appearing in new forms. Where a few years ago Volz seemed focused on international success, with a Spanish-language touring company and an English version available for interested parties (Malone 2004: 272–3), these offshoots have now disappeared from the show's website. Instead, having established regular stagings of the original show on the Brocken, site of Goethe's Walpurgis Night, Volz is attempting to disseminate his work in other German-language media: a DVD version of *Faust I* appeared in 2007, while the original independently distributed single-CD recording of Part I and double-CD version of Part II, after a brief life as a now-deleted triple-CD set from Sony BMG (2005), have expanded into a four-CD set (*Faust: Die Rockoper* 2007). In any case, there appears to be no end in sight for *Faust: The Rock Opera*.

It is notable that all of these productions are essentially the work of figures marginal to the mainstream rock music industry. This does not mean, however, that their attitudes toward rock music are the same; and in fact, it is the variance in the dynamic between the various creators' attitude toward rock and their attitude toward the Faust theme that makes for the notable differences in tone among the four works.

Despite Paul Williams' obvious affection for the musical styles he parodies, for example, Brian De Palma expresses open disdain for much rock music, and little regard for fans who prefer the Rolling Stones to the music from his film (2003: 18–19). In *Phantom*, rock is truly the devil's music: everyone in the business—Swan, his employees, his entourage and his musicians—is dishonest, if not absurdly evil. Even Phoenix becomes more pliable with every taste of success, until she is finally prepared to sleep with and marry Swan. As for Leach, his appreciation for the Faust legend in the face of Philbin's ignorance demonstrates the gulf between 'real' culture and rock music; at the same time, the diabolical subject of Leach's 'pop cantata' reverses and mocks the messianic themes of the most successful rock operas of the late 1960s and early 1970s, *Godspell, Jesus Christ Superstar* and *Tommy*, all of which De Palma despises (2003: 43–4). This does not make Leach a mere mouthpiece of the director, however; on the contrary, he is a pretentious pedant who naïvely thinks that there will be an audience for his solo performance of a 300-page cantata. Moreover, as it is for the other main characters, Leach's mere ambition to become a rock star is itself the first step to damnation since, in De Palma's opinion, rock culture is 'obsessed with death, with destroying yourself, burning yourself up, consuming yourself for entertainment and amusement' (2003: 19). Accordingly, all of the principals die at the film's end, except for Phoenix, whose sanity appears to hang by a thread.

In *Starboy*, by contrast, Randall Paris Dark treats rock music as a positive force, but with no more connection to the realities of the musical genre or to show business: he has Jimmy worship the Rolling Stones, but then gives him stardom in the form of a concert in Las Vegas. In rock music terms, Las Vegas is the home of crooners, not rockers, and iconic only as the locus of Elvis Presley's self-trivializing decline into a 'bloated, pathetic figure' (Tucker 1989: 282, 292–3); but at the same time, Presley's move to Vegas, 'the definitive symbol of affluent middle America, and the global capital of the marriage between show business and gambling' (Inglis 1996: 63–4) marked rock's move into mainstream respectability. And despite his desire to 'live in sin', Jimmy's music is correspondingly relatively bland and nonthreatening, ersatz corporate rock, to match the second-rate devils that disturb him and the counterfeit 'angels' that defeat them. Thus it appears natural that his desire to become a star—bizarrely unconnected to any desire for money—should in the end be happily fulfilled with the same aid from above that allows him to cheat the devil, regain his love and attain a final onstage apotheosis.

If in *Phantom* rock music is the highway to hell and in *Starboy* it turns out to be the stairway to heaven, by the mid-1990s, in *Randy Newman's Faust*, rock is simply the road to nowhere. Newman, a musician's musician, has always been an outsider to the mainstream rock world (Courrier 2005: xiv). His slacker Henry Faust may grab an electric guitar to express himself, but he lusts for a CEO's office, not a star dressing room. Faced with this Faust, God and the devil are equally at a loss. They would have known what to do with Winslow Leach or Jimmy Paul Beadley—or, for that matter, with any of the stars who sing on Newman's original album, all a good fifteen years past their peak. Ironically, the real wit of Newman's *Faust* lay in these erstwhile giants willingly singing in the service of a musical gadfly who had never had a fraction of their commercial success (Courrier 2005: 271–2); as a mere musical, without their charisma, the joke fell flat.

No wonder, then, that at the turn of the twenty-first century Rudolf Volz's grand design for a rock *Faust* is essentially a nostalgic vision, based on the music of the late 1970s and early 1980s—music of the period between *Phantom* and *Starboy*, when the diabolical forces that De Palma saw in the music emerged to be tamed into familiarity by heavy rotation on radio, and ultimately video, but before ubiquity had reduced them to the utter inconsequence Newman describes. In the 'timeless' context of Volz's production, there is no such thing as wanting to be a rock star; yet at the same time, as Faust's guitar playing and duets with Mephisto demonstrate, in the parallel world constructed by the production's premise, everybody's a rock star already.

Nonetheless, it is rather unsettling to see, in this admittedly limited survey, that a progression nearer to Goethe's actual work has been countered by an odd musical regression back to the era of the first attempts to mix the Faust theme with contemporary popular music; the sounds of *Faust: The Rock Opera* may still be popular—and I admit to liking them too—but they are certainly no longer contemporary. Volz's production is supposedly geared to appeal to students (*Faust: Die Rockoper* 2007), but surely that would be better suited to a techno *Faust*; or a hip-hop *Faust*, mixing and rapping; or even the death metal *Faust* that he promises but fails to deliver. One wonders, in fact, whether the real objects of Volz's appeal are not the teachers and parents who are old enough to share his—undoubtedly sincere—affection for music from three decades ago. Of course, such nostalgia can be extremely lucrative, as demonstrated by the licensing of countless classic rock songs, once emblems of a supposed counter-culture, for corporate advertising campaigns.

Volz's music may be inspired by Deep Purple and the Scorpions, but as he himself points out (*Faust: Die Rockoper* 2007), Mephisto's black-and-white makeup is intended to recall not Gustaf Gründgens, but rather the rock band KISS, whose painted faces—Gene Simmons was the Demon, Paul Stanley was the Starchild—masked the 1970s most brazenly successful marketing machine. Randy Newman had satirized this machine long before he wrote his *Faust*: on the cover of his 1979 album *Born Again*, Newman wears a business suit and whiteface, with green dollar signs painted around his eyes in deliberate imitation of KISS; the album's opening song was 'It's Money That I Love' (Courrier 2005: 187–8). De Palma's *Phantom* also parodies KISS, in the form of Swan's band the Undeads; the joke is that all of his bands—the heavy-metal Undeads, the surf-rock Beach Bums and the 1950s-style Juicy Fruits—are the same three singers. KISS, the ultimate hard rock party band, gave new meaning to the idea of the faceless corporation.

In the end, Volz's reverence for Goethe's classic text and his reverence for rock's classic sounds seem just as calculated as KISS' shrewd self-promotion: skilful and sincere, indeed, but ultimately rather hollow—already in its conception, his rock opera is even more a museum piece than Goethe's original. One need not share Brian De Palma's obvious distaste for rock music to ask whether, in Volz's work, *Faust*—not the character, but the little remaining of the text—has indeed sold its soul for rock'n'roll.

Notes

1   All references to Goethe's *Faust*, abbreviated as *F*, are to Salm's translation (Goethe 1985) and Goethe (2005).

Bibliography

Ambros, W. and Prokopets, J. (1973), *Fäustling: Spiel in G*, original cast. Metronome [sound recording: vinyl].
Barnard, S. (1986), *Rock: An Illustrated History*. New York: Schirmer.
Brantley, B. (1996), 'Two takes on the devil: The charms of the seedy give way to Sunday best', *The New York Times*, (26 October), http://theater2.nytimes.com/mem/theater/treview.html?_+2&res=9D01E4DA1E30F93 (retrieved 23 May 2007).
Courrier, K. (2005), *Randy Newman's American Dreams*. Toronto: ECW Press.
Dark, R. P. (1983), *Starboy*. Toronto: Playwrights Guild of Canada.
Dark, R. P., Dark, C. and Crowley, I. (1984), *Starboy*, original cast. Ariel [sound recording: vinyl].
De Palma, B. (2003), *Interviews*, L. F. Knapp (ed.). Jackson: University Press of Mississippi.
Dunne, S. (1992), 'Randy Newman and the extraordinary moral position', *Popular Music and Society*, 16, (3), 53–62.
Faust: Die Rockoper (2004), original version, www.faust.cc (retrieved 24 September 2004).
Faust: Die Rockoper (2007), www.faust.cc (retrieved 18 July 2007).
Goethe, J. W. (1985), *Faust, Part I*, P. Salm (trans.). New York: Bantam.
— (2005), *Faust*, A. Schöne (ed.). Frankfurt/Main: Deutscher Klassiker Verlag.
Hinds, E. J. W. (1992), 'The devil sings the *blues*: Heavy metal, gothic *fiction* and "postmodern" discourse', *Journal of Popular Culture*, 26, (3), 151–63.
Inglis, I. (1996), 'Ideology, trajectory & stardom: Elvis Presley & The Beatles', *International Review of the Aesthetics and Sociology of Music*, 27, (1), 53–78.
Larkey, E. (1992), 'Austropop: Popular music and national identity in Austria', *Popular Music*, 11, (2), 151–85.
Lipsitz, G. (1997), 'Remembering Robert Johnson: Romance and reality', *Popular Music and Society*, 21, (4), 39–50.
Lucchesi, J. (2003), 'Das Spiel von Nintendo und deutscher Misere: Randy Newmans und Hanns Eislers "Faust"', *Peter Weiss Jahrbuch*, 12, 102–16.
— (2005–6), '"Wir lesen die Klassiker fünfmal": Hanns Eislers und Randy Newmans *Faust*', *Faust-Jahrbuch*, 2, 35–47.
Maddock, S. (1996), '"Whole lotta shakin' goin' on": Racism and early opposition to rock music', *Mid-America: An Historical Review*, 78, (2), 181–202.
Mahl, B. (2005), '"Faust. Die Rockoper". Rudolf Volz setzt erstmals beide Teile in Töne—ohne Textveränderungen', *Faust-Jahrbuch*, 1, 205–9.
Malone, P. M. (2004), '"You'll always be the one you are". Faust as rock opera', in O. Durrani, *Faust: Icon of Modern Culture*. London: Helm Information, pp. 263–73.
Newman, R. (2003a), *Randy Newman's Faust*, expanded reissue. Reprise/Rhino [sound recording: CD].
— (2003b), Plot synopsis, in *Randy Newman's Faust*, expanded reissue. Reprise/Rhino [sound recording: CD].
Nicholls, D. (2004), 'Virtual opera, or opera between the ears', *Journal of the Royal Musical Association*, 129, (1), 100–42.
Phantom of the Paradise (2003), B. De Palma (dir.). Beverly Hills, 20th Century Fox [video: DVD].
Schmidt, M. H. (1979), 'The German song-writing movement of the late 1960s and 1970's', *Journal of Popular Culture*, 13, (1), 44–54.

Sullivan, M. (1987) '"More popular than Jesus": The Beatles and the religious far right', *Popular Music*, 6, (3), 313–26.

Szatmary, D. P. (1991), *Rockin' in Time: A Social History of Rock-and-Roll*. Englewood Cliffs, NJ: Prentice Hall.

Tucker, B. (1989), '"Tell Tchaikovsky the news": Postmodernism, popular culture, and the emergence of rock'n'roll', *Black Music Research Journal*, 9, (2), 271–95.

Volz, R. (1999), *Faust I*, Beelzebuben-Ensemble. Xdra Productions [sound recording: CD].

— (2004), *Faust II*, Beelzebuben-Ensemble. Xdra Productions [sound recording: CD].

Wells, J. D. (1983), 'Me and the devil blues: A study of Robert Johnson and the music of the Rolling Stones', *Popular Music and Society*, 9, (3), 17–24.

Williams, P. (1998), *Phantom of the Paradise*, original soundtrack. A & M [sound recording: CD].

Willman, C. (2003), 'Randy Newman's Faust: A New Musical Comedy'. Liner notes in *Randy Newman's Faust*, expanded reissue. Reprise/Rhino [sound recording: CD].

Winkler, P. (1988), 'Randy Newman's Americana', *Popular Music*, 7, (1), 1–26.

13 The Faustian Disguise of Edoardo Sanguineti and Luca Lombardi

Gabriele Becheri

Revisiting *Faust*

Goethe's *Faust* has caught the attention of many musicians from the Romantic period to today. An aspect of Goethe's *Faust* that still fascinates us today is, as philosopher Carlo Sini suggests, the fact that *Faust* is a great myth of modernity and, like all myths and legends, it is intrinsic to 'an inexorable abundance of the senses' that it 'can trigger an inexorable avalanche of interpretations and disguises' (1995: 267). One of the reasons why *Faust* has been so successful, not only among composers, is its very myth, which offers us such a large number of interpretative possibilities and a plethora of nuances. This, of course, is a typical characteristic of all great literature and of all art forms in general. Sini observes, a 'myth is literally what we may call, with the words of Thomas Mann, a *mise-en-scène* of time: something that is given as an origin that is not an origin but that indeed seems a *mise-en-scène*, a theatrical scenery that veils another one and yet another one. At every instance the legend has already begun and what we see is the mere disguise of something else' (1995: 267).[1] But what happens if this kaleidoscopic multiplicity passes from the sphere of fruition and interpretation to the sphere of creation? What happens, in other words, when the 'avalanche of interpretations and disguises' becomes one of the poetic motifs? During the spring and summer of 1985, Edoardo Sanguineti finished a theatrical opera called *Faust. Un Travestimento* (*Faust. A Disguise*) upon the request of Marialuisa and Mario Santella's theatre company Alfred Jarry. Based on Goethe's *Faust*, this subject had been taken up by Sanguineti more than once during his long career as critic, poet, essayist, novelist and theatrical author. Sanguineti's career cannot be entirely understood without considering his numerous collaborations with musicians and composers, particularly the texts he wrote for Luciano Berio and Vinko Globokar. The musical aspect of his activity inevitably grew with time, as far as manifoldness and quantity are concerned. Today there are approximately fifty composers who have put Sanguineti's works into music, which is almost unique in the contemporary panorama. There is no all-inclusive definition that may describe Sanguineti's collaboration with the musical world if not in the sense of an absolute diversity to be scrutinized case by case, author by author, composition by composition. Unique, and in certain respects unitary, has been the liberty that the poet has granted musicians when collaborating with them. Unlike many writers or theatrical authors, Sanguineti does not jealously cling to his work because he has well understood the musicians' differing structural necessities in order to adapt the poetic text to their musical needs. Sanguineti's collaborations with musicians can be looked at in a threefold way: on the one hand, there are texts deliberately written for musical performance, while, on the other hand, there are texts originally written not for musical purposes but later chosen for such by the author himself, and, finally, there are those works that were not originally written for musical performances but later chosen by the poet and entrusted to the musicians who had requested them. Besides Berio and Globokar we must immediately mention such names as Fausto Razzi, Andrea Liberovici, Stefano Scodanibbio and Luca Lombardi who have most often made use of poems and literary works by Sanguineti. More sporadic but no less interesting have been collaborations with artists such as Armando Gentilucci, Giacomo Manzoni and Fernando Mencherini.

This chapter focuses on Luca Lombardi's operatic version of Sanguineti's *Faust. A Disguise* as a crucial work both within the composer's career as well as seen in the light of music history. *Faust. A Disguise*, which was composed by Lombardi in 1986 and first performed in 1990, is indeed an emblematic example of that multiplicity that we have become so used to and that would have caused a lot of criticism and perplexity only a few decades earlier, mainly due to avant-garde preconceptions that were still rather firm at the time. We must thus necessarily begin with Sanguineti's *Faust. A Disguise*, which, in a way, introduced or gave way to the establishment of disguise as an independent category that later on became of such importance in the development of his poetry.

The Disguise in Sanguineti

As author and essayist, Sanguineti continues to consider his activity as avant-garde, that is, as an activity that constantly analyzes and questions the world surrounding him. Over time, this 'tension' has obviously found different ways of expression. Here we are urged to remember that the erratic aspect of Sanguineti's first poetic works from the late 1950s onward was characterized by the central image of the labyrinth that manifested itself in a rather unstable linguistic style. In 1985, when the poet talks of his own activity, we notice a general tendency toward a 'lightening up' because he uses expressions that often make us think again of a sort of game, a concealment ('make-believe'), of disguise (Sanguineti 1985a). Even though we come across these expressions repeatedly in the oeuvre of Sanguineti, disguise is the category that has won major importance over time. It is this category that has, in the eyes of the poet, brought together a series of procedures, from theatre to translation, that has furthermore characterized the rest of his work. In a literal sense, disguise is a peculiar characteristic of the theatre, that is, the pretence of dressing up, moving around and speaking in a personality different from one's own. An appropriate dimension of disguise may thus appear to be the theatrical dimension, and it is not by accident that *Faust. Un Travestimento* was one of the first works in which the term, which is also part of the main title, became a poetical category. At first glance, the phenomenon of disguise may seem perfectly comprehensive and linear but if we take a closer look, we will soon realize that often a disguise is intrinsically connected to a series of different procedures that are not always easy to distinguish. Sanguineti has discussed his *Faust* as exemplifying a complex level of disguise:

> [W]e not only find a rather informal yet solid way of translating, for there are whole passages from Goethe. We also find procedures of modernizing, of connecting to our modern world. All this brings with it conspicuous procedures of alienation to be realized in the theatre. Sometimes a parody is created compared to the original. Goethe was perfect because he himself was always very uninhibited as far as the variety of themes and styles is concerned. He is already Brecht. (Sanguineti and Buonaccorsi 2001: 8)

Translation, modernization, parody: a disguise is all this and a lot more, meaning that these different procedures do not occur all at the same time and with the same intensity, but they are often put together like a puzzle and are never present in a continuous mode. This way, elements such as translation, modernization or parody that are normally reassuring for the audience when presented on a singular base, become continuously illusive to the listener, who will never be able to recognize perfectly where parody ends and where translation or modernization begins. The audience will never clearly understand up to which point Sanguineti has intermixed these elements into a perfectly functioning mechanism that has become inseparable. The consequences of disguise for the adopted language are not be taken too lightly, for they never continuously tend to be either trivial or sublime, but are characterized by constant alternation of the two with a plethora of infinite intermediary possibilities. Sanguineti explains:

> I realized that I was rewriting 'Faust', which was the initial idea when commissioned, a modern version that was in part translation, addition, in part modernization and parody. All these elements were present together oscillating between seriousness and persiflage, between ancientness and modernism with the citation clearly recognizable and the doubt *do we find that in Goethe or not?*, realizing that in Goethe there were parts that, even though translated in a real, literal way, seemed like they had been written by myself. Somebody who does not know Goethe too well might have said: 'This one was put in by Sanguineti'. (Sanguineti and Liberovici 1998: 113–14)

In order to obscure yet at the same time to render the category of disguise richer, one must add that during the phase of translation, Sanguineti has naturally left his own authorial and poetical imprint, having other 'voices' converge where necessary. One of these voices, which Niva Lorenzini (2003) mentions in her study on *Faust. A Disguise*, is Giacomo Leopardi (1798–1837), an Italian poet whom we remember above all for his nocturnal invocations to the moon. Some elegiac suggestions in certain parts are joined by moments of linguistic playfulness, the use of nursery rhymes, simple rhymes or clearly melodramatic influences in Neapolitan style. The category of disguise, due especially to the importance it has assumed over time, has been applied retrospectively by Sanguineti to many of his formerly written theatrical works. Let us look at an example: *Orlando furioso*, a poem Sanguineti arranged for director Luca Ronconi from the homonymous epic poem by Ludovico Ariosto (1474–1533). Even though at the time the poem was thought to be a simple 'reduction' of the original, in Sanguineti's *Orlando furioso* we already find some features of disguise that were to become typical of his further production. It is not by accident that in the introduction of *Orlando furioso*, the term 'masquerade' ('mascheratura') was used, which in a certain way already insinuates the element of disguise, though in this case the main focus lies on the text and is understood as 'Ready-Made', that is, the original text was rewritten in a way that rendered it functional in a theatrical environment.

> Orlando works because, even though it is a classic, it is also a *masquerade* and it allows us to play around with a *pre-text* (in the literal sense of the word), with an already existing text that doesn't present problems of invention but rather of *mechanism*, i.e., to make something work that was already there. (Sanguineti and Ronconi 1970: 14)

The changes made by Sanguineti to Ariosto's and Goethe's poems are undoubtedly very different from each other, especially since the two works were written in two different languages (and, as a consequence, Sanguineti had to adapt the kind of changes to be made). The term disguise has been, even though not exclusively, more and more connected to the category of translation, to which Sanguineti has repeatedly dedicated himself and which allowed him to give voice, by means of other voices, to more or less ancient texts with an identical tendency toward costuming and masquerading. He states,

> [a]ll true translations are false documents, the more so true than false, made to disappoint the literary police and censorial strategy. And a mask is a mask and there is no mask that is more true or more false than another one . . . Because a translation, being 'imitation', is nothing else but the art of honest simulation and dissimulation. (Sanguineti 1993a: 174)

Every critique of Sanguineti's oeuvre must necessarily begin with a discussion of disguise. His success with many composers cannot be understood without considering the opportunities the poet has opened up. These opportunities naturally include the category of disguise, in terms of intermingling languages, superimposing and interlacing narrative levels and continuous linguistic changes.

Some Thoughts on Lombardi's Music

Faust. A Disguise was the first but not the only collaboration between Sanguineti and Lombardi. Others were to follow throughout the years, including the most recent, *Lucrezio. Un oratorio materialistico* (*Lucretius. A Materialistic Oratory*) in three parts of which only two are as yet completed. However, compared to the other compositions, *Faust. A Disguise* was written during a period of important changes for the composer. His musical language became freer and he started reacting to incentives from different directions. At the same time, the heterogeneity of Lombardi's compositions has been a typical trait of his activity as a composer from the very beginning. We only need to take a look at the terminology Lombardi uses. Ever since the 1970s he has been trying to define his proper compositional activity, thus coining, above all, a series of word pairs: 'gestural' and 'planning out' in 1979 (Lombardi 1979); 'inclusive' and 'exclusive' in the first half of the 1980s (Lombardi 1983, 1985a; Galliano 1995; Maggi 1988); 'figurative' (and, as an opposite, we could add 'non-figurative') in 1986 (Lombardi 1986). For the purposes of this chapter, it is important to take a closer look at what 'inclusive' and 'exclusive' really mean.

With the word 'inclusive', Lombardi indicates a style that is compositionally plural and that includes or considers different cultures and traditions. From a constructive point of view, this is reflected in a variety of materials, styles and ways of expression. In Lombardi's inclusive realm, the musical spelling is marked by a tendency to absorb or to assimilate different compositional techniques, different sounds (serious and comic, tragic and burlesque) and links to both educated and popular ambiences, to classical as well as commercial music.

Lombardi's 'exclusive' element is concerned with the development of a composition as a whole or with one of its parts, with a single chord or musical figure (a scale, a sequence of sounds, etc.), an event, musically outlined. Inclusiveness has with time become more important in the thought and production of Lombardi because, being synonymous with plurality, it comprises the exclusive mode on its inside and thus forms a subset.

Even though *Faust. A Disguise* may be considered a moment of crucial transformation in the career of Luca Lombardi, it is, on the other hand, nothing less than the result of a convergence of the two different aspects of Lombardi's expressiveness, the inclusive and the exclusive aspect that have been fused in an opera apparently centrifugal from a stylistic point of view, but really altogether uniform as far as structure is concerned.

The Opera Libretto

We have seen that Sanguineti's *Faust. A Disguise* constitutes a complex operation of disguise of Goethe's original version, embracing elements of translation, parody, modernization and alienation but also a series of major and minor removal of parts, changes and montages that are really not easy (and maybe even useless) to list here in all their detail because they are to be found all over the entire text. Lombardi realized that Sanguineti's text had very strong musical 'possibilities' but had, however, not been written for musical realization. These strong musical possibilities depended on the fact that some parts of the text had already been thought of for an autonomous musical treatment, namely as arias or romances. Nevertheless, the length of Sanguineti's *Faust* would not have permitted use of the entire text because it is a known fact to composers that a text with music lasts much longer than the same text without musical rendering. Therefore, Lombardi turned to a final elimination of verses and sections. In my estimate, this elimination amounts to approximately 1120 verses Lombardi took out as compared to the original version by Sanguineti. Eliminations may spread from a single verse to entire scenes. Every single elimination is naturally a consequence of a number of different necessities: long and voluminous sections had to be cut down to the main plot and deviations and embellishments had to be deleted. On the other hand, single verses had to be adapted to rhythmic and musical needs. It is immediately clear that Sanguineti divided Goethe's *Faust* into two 'parts' (as in a film) without further scenes. Lombardi, on the other hand, divided the opera into three parts and twelve scenes. Compared to Sanguineti's text, the only scene Lombardi eliminated entirely is that between Greta and Lisa.

The 'Materials' of *Faust. A Disguise*

Sanguineti's text, which is extremely diverse and full of stimuli, seems to cause Lombardi to take a twofold approach: on the one hand, he wants to maintain musically the multiplicity of the text-libretto; on the other hand, he is searching for coherent musical material that may guarantee the homogeneity of the opera as a whole. In order to obtain this homogeneity, he attributes specific musical material to each of the main characters (Faust, Mefistofele, Greta), such as chords or sounds that characterize them throughout the entire opera. This way, Lombardi is able to confer a constructive density on the opera, at the same time rendering the characters musically concrete and well-defined. This procedure is not new in music but is here being used with a richness of references that is worth dwelling on to understand the intense preparatory work that lies behind *Faust. A Disguise*. This is illustrated by numerous sketchbooks and notebooks in which the main characters of *Faust. A Disguise* were associated with chords and sound sequences that can be transposed to different degrees of the scale in order to obtain a series of possible mutations. For Faust, Lombardi used two chords (one minor triad and one major triad) built around a note they have in common: for example, *C-E flat-G/B-D sharp-F sharp* (the note they both have in common is *E flat/D sharp*). Mefistofele, on the other hand, is musically characterized by the crossing of two tritone-intervals (augmented fourth): for example, *E-A sharp+A flat-D=E-A flat-A sharp-D*. Greta is attributed with three tones that were obtained by superimposing two intervals of major thirds: for example, *D flat-F-A*. The chords for the individual characters have not only a structural but also a symbolic value for the composer: the minor-major oscillation in Faust delineates a complex and unstable personality that is consequently subject to intense transformations in the course of the opera; the tritone, that is, the 'diabolus in musica' of medieval tracts, is the interval that is musically most suited for the diabolic Mefistofele; the two major third-intervals give Greta an air of humbleness or meekness that is a lot more static than the other two major characters, even though the augmented fifth of the two extreme tones (*D flat-A*) creates, according to the composer, a rather characteristic effect. Personal and traditional motifs have surely determined the choice of the musical material for each single character. However, in order to understand the symbolism of the chosen chords for the single characters, we must remember that the sounds of Faust, Mefistofele and Greta, once they are crossed, use up the entire chromatic scale, that is, they cover the entire gamut of an octave's sounds. This way, Lombardi suggests that the destinies of the three main characters are indissolubly and musically combined. This brings us back to Lombardi's terminology. So far we have talked about the exclusive and inclusive aspects of his opera. Every character is attributed specific musical material. They are subject to transformations, which often does not allow an immediate and clear perception. A vast opera like *Faust. A Disguise* certainly necessitates a strong structural foundation but at the same time needs the possibility of a gamut of materials in order to guarantee a variety of sounds. For this reason, every chord can be transposed onto the various degrees of the scale so that we obtain twelve possible permutations for Faust, six for Mefistofele and four for Greta:

FAUST (in parenthesis, the extended forms of the chords are listed, that is, the single notes of each chord)
1) C-E flat-G/B-D sharp-F sharp (B-C-E flat-F sharp-G)
2) C sharp-E-G sharp/C-E-G (C-C sharp-E-G-G sharp)
3) D-F-A/C sharp-E sharp-G sharp (C sharp-D-F-A flat-A)
4) E flat-G flat-B flat/D-F sharp-A (D-E flat-G flat-A-B flat)
5) E-G-B/E flat-G-B flat (E flat-E-G-B flat-B)
6) F-A flat-C/E-G sharp-B (E-F-A flat-B-C)
7) F sharp-A-C sharp/F-A-C (F-F sharp-A-C-C sharp)
8) G-B flat-D/F sharp-A sharp-C sharp (F sharp-G-B flat-C sharp-D)
9) A flat-C flat-E flat/G-B-D (G-A flat-C flat-D-E flat)
10) A-C-E/A flat-C-E flat (A flat-A-C-E flat-E)
11) B flat-D flat-F/A-C sharp-E (A-B flat-D flat-E-F)
12) B-D-F sharp/B flat-D-F (B flat-B-D-F-F sharp)

MEFISTOFELE
1) C-E-F sharp-A sharp
2) C sharp-F-G-B
3) D-F sharp-G sharp-C
4) E flat-G-A-C sharp
5) E-G sharp-A sharp-D
6) F-A-B-E flat

GRETA
1) C-E-G sharp
2) C sharp-F-A
3) D-F sharp-B flat
4) E flat-G-B

If we look at Faust's chords in their extended form and put them in order (1–8–3–10–5–12–7–2–9–4–11–6), we obtain a chain of sounds with the following intervals: one half step, three half steps, three half steps, one half step, three half steps, three half steps, one half step, etc. (1–3–3–1–3–3–1–3–3–1 etc.). The chords for Mefistofele were opportunely combined and thus caused a dodecaphonic series, that is, a more complex sequence in respect to the simple one of the chords. From a musical point of view, the least changeable character is Greta, whose musical rendering, however, is supposed to maintain complex relations of affinity with the other characters and their musical representations: the three notes of the first chord (*C-E-G sharp*), for example, can be found again in the 2, 6 and 10 sequences of Faust. In the 1, 3 and 5 sequence of Mefistofele two notes of the first Greta chord are present (*C-E, C-G sharp, E-G sharp*). Besides the three main characters, there are a number of secondary roles with specific musical material. Wagner (I.i–I.ii), Faust's assistant, for example, is characterized by simple major triads to express his closed-minded mentality. The same accounts for Valentino (III.i), the arrogant and soldierly brother of Greta, or for the students at the cellar (I.iv), who are blitheful and light-hearted. The character of Valentino is interesting because it supplies us with some more detail about the way Lombardi composes. The following observations are based on my analysis of the preparatory drafts. Even though Lombardi uses major triads for the character of Valentino, he is trying to avoid any possible tonal attraction due to a combined system that externally establishes the triad sequences. For this purpose, he numbered all major triads built on the different degrees of the chromatic scale from 1 to 12. The twelve chords thus obtained have been used by Lombardi in a sequence given in a permutation table. The first line consists of the numbers 1 to 12 read from left to right. Each following line is the result of a combination of its previous line based on two different mechanisms: by jumping from the first position to the twelfth, from the second position to the eleventh, from the third to the tenth and so on and by jumping from the twelfth position to the first, from the eleventh to the second, from the tenth to the third, etc.

The table allows Lombardi to use a sequence of previously numbered triads, which does not, however, determine any kind of tonal attraction. Again, this is not a new procedure in music and was especially popular in serialism right after World War II. *Structures I* (1951–2) for two pianos by Pierre Boulez comes to mind immediately. The motifs and mechanisms are obviously different for both composers, even though the effort to attain spontaneity of the musical material by means of a preestablished mechanism is characteristic for both. In the scene with Valentino as protagonist (III.iii), Lombardi arranges the twelve major triads based on the permutation table and its numerical sequences to avoid any possible tonal attractions that would relapse to a traditional use of the triads. In this way, that is, by arranging and choosing the chords on a numerical basis, he runs no risk of rendering tonally functional triads, which are being used as traditional musical material even though utilized in an altogether different way. Here one may also almost think of some sort of musical 'disguise', using materials (in this case, the major triads) that tradition has passed down to our modern days.

The Multiplicity of *Faust. A Disguise*

So far, we have examined the numerous elements that impart on *Faust. A Disguise* a structural continuity guaranteed by an intense preparation, which is shown by the many notes and drafts that I was able to read and analyze. The draft analyses show that Lombardi has worked intensely on the possibility of expanding the materials for each individual character (by combining more chords, building different tone sequences and so on) and on the 'musical affinity' of the different characters. *Faust. A Disguise* is an opera that contains an inexhaustible stylistic multiplicity. On the one hand, this multiplicity is created by Sanguineti's text, which alternates episodes that can show a variety of stylistic nuances. On the other hand, this stylistic manifoldness depends on Lombardi's development as a composer: an inclusion and mixture of musical material and styles of different origins has always been important in the compositions of Lombardi, and in *Faust. A Disguise* he oftentimes uses citations and musical disguise to attain the desired multiple effects. To illustrate this multiplicity further, we shall take a look at the musical score. In scene I.iv, Sanguineti alludes to the Rolling Stones. Lombardi musically relates to this moment by composing a version for orchestra of 'Sympathy for the Devil'. He duly abstracts and parodies the song of the English rock band and evidently creates the incentive for an extensive song of the diabolic Mefistofele (bars 1295–364). The song is utilized in the style of an aria, that is, well defined and distinguished from the rest. On other occasions we find citations that are much shorter, for example, in bars 1127–30 of scene I.iv, where Lombardi alludes to the anthems of West Germany and former East Germany. In this case, the citations were inserted in relation to the text by Sanguineti, who utilizes the image of a divided Germany instead of the Holy Roman Empire in Goethe's original.

There is no use in listing all of the citations (sometimes literal, sometimes stylistic) that can be found in *Faust. A Disguise*. Instead, we shall look at just one episode that may serve as a general example to understand how the citation works and how it can assume a structural importance. This example shall be scene II.iv, which is also called *Canzone di Greta* (*Greta's Song*), which is also an independent piece for soprano and string quartet. In this example, the text written by Sanguineti is a case of 'light' disguise. First, the poet maintains the structure of the original text, which now becomes a poem of ten stanzas with four septenarii each (the first three are trochaics and the last one is a catalectic). The second reason why we can talk about a 'light' disguise is the fact that Sanguineti makes an almost literal translation of the original—almost literal because in some parts he uses a more 'modern' linguistic style, that is, a more colloquial language. This seems to give Greta the characteristics of a modern-day teenager in love with Faust. Sanguineti chose Goethe's *Faust* because it is a great myth of modernity but also because the original version is already a 'disguise' of traditional tales. In order to illustrate this layering or 'domino effect', Sanguineti refers to the field of fine arts. He explains how Pablo Picasso repainted Edouard Manet's *Déjeuner sur l'herbe* (*Luncheon on the Grass*) and at the same time took the previous models of Marcantonio Raimondi, Palma il Vecchio and Gustave Courbet into consideration (Sanguineti 1993b: 232). Sanguineti seems to be fascinated by the possibility of multiplying images with different styles and voices, and he is driven by a kind of challenge: to write the ultimate *Faust* (Sanguineti 1993b: 232–3). Lombardi, on his part, tries to find an adequate musical solution to the multiplicity of the text, thus protracting Sanguineti's disguise in the musical ambience. It is a disguise that Lombardi describes as follows in relation to *Greta's Song*:

> I start with the piano accompaniment in the *Lied* of Schubert, which becomes a minimalist *ante litteram*. Another part from Schubert's *Lied*, a chord, gives way to other chords by means of some inversions. Those chords are different both harmonically but also as far as their meaning is concerned (the Schubert-chords are being changed into late-romantic and expressionist chords). (Sanguineti 1993b: 231–2)

Lombardi's starting point, one may also call it 'his Goethe', is in this case 'Gretchen am Spinnrade' ('Gretchen at the Spinning Wheel') (1814), a 'Lied' by Franz Schubert, in which the same passage from Goethe's *Faust* is being used that underlies Sanguineti's disguise for *Greta's Song*. Lombardi contents himself with just a few elements from the 'Lied' by Schubert to compose the major part of scene II.iv. At the same time, he uses citations as an inclusive method and then elaborates them as an exclusive component. With this in mind one might take a look at the beginning of Schubert's 'Lied', bars 1–2.

At the beginning of Lombardi's *Greta's Song*, all four instruments of the string quartet play a melodic line that reflects the piano accompaniment (right hand) of Schubert's 'Lied'. A first disguise, if one may call it thus, occurs with the change of meter from 6/8 to 3/4. Lombardi himself notes that the passage assumes minimalist traits due to a progressive shifting between the instruments of the quartet: in bar 5, violin I abandons the figuration of semiquavers in favor of semiquaver quintuplets; in bar 6, the cello changes to quaver triplets and the viola to semiquaver sextuplets in bar 7. This allows the shifting to happen and then, in bar 11, a counter-shifting takes place with all instruments returning to alignment, even though for a short time. The other element, that is, the chord, to which Lombardi refers above, has been identified with the one in bar 8 of 'Gretchen at the Spinning Wheel', to be more precise with B-D-F-A flat-C. This chord can be found for the first time in bar 136 of *Greta's Song* and then, immediately following, in bar 143. The chord in its root position, even though without any tonal functions, is made of three intervals of minor thirds and of one interval of major third. The very same structure can be found in all chords in bars 137–48, except some sporadic cases.

However, there are to be found other similarities between Schubert's 'Lied' and *Greta's Song* by Lombardi: the melodic line of the soprano in *Greta's Song* is evidently inspired by the one in 'Gretchen at the Spinning Wheel'. Naturally, Schubert's 'Lied' does not constitute the only foundation of *Greta's Song*. In the seventh bar, for example, Lombardi inserts an episode 'a mo' di rock' (i.e., 'in the style of a rock song'), or in bars 229–32, he takes on an evidently emphatic and theatrical style. Furthermore, citations are being used as comments and critiques, as, for example, in *Greta's Song* where Lombardi tries to liken Greta to other characters, here to Isolde from Richard Wagner's *Tristan und Isolde* (*Tristan and Isolde*) and to Marie from Alban Berg's *Wozzeck*. In bars 150–3 of *Greta's Song* we can find citations from Berg's *Wozzeck* (I.iii, bars 372–5, melodic line of Marie) and from Wagner's *Tristan and Isolde* (Prelude, bars 1–4). One can observe that the melodic line of Marie is being reproduced in bars 150–1 (cello), 151 (violin I) and 152 (violin II) of *Greta's Song*. Furthermore, the ascending chromatic line of the oboe that may be reassociated with the character of Isolde, of the Wagnerian passage, may be found in bar 150 (violin I) of Lombardi's disguise.

In Sanguineti's text, Lombardi seems to have found a solution to his own expressive needs, which seem to be more and more concerned with the inclusive element as a fundamental and essential compositional category. Sanguineti's text is filled with a plethora of incentives and possibilities that welcome montages and combinations of different musical realities.

Conclusions and Observations

As has been shown in this chapter, Sanguineti's and Lombardi's *Faust* is the result of a sort of twofold disguise. The first one was undertaken by the poet and based on the original text by Goethe. The second disguise is the opera of Lombardi, which was based on multiple incentives in the musical field. Even though *Greta's Song* is a specific episode of the opera, it constitutes a good example in this regard. However, one must not think of Lombardi's *Faust. A Disguise* as a fragmented opera because, first of all, there are so many elements that contribute to an overall structure (from the chords of the individual characters to a number of musical instruments and figures that stand in relation to those chords). Secondly, from a dramaturgical point of view, the opera shows a tendency of becoming charged with more and more tension in the course of its own development. The comical and carefree nuances that characterize the initial part of the opera start to fade and toward the end become rather rare.

It has already been said that *Faust. A Disguise* is an essential opera in Lombardi's *oeuvre*. However, this must not be understood in terms of a 'turning point'. On the contrary, *Faust. A Disguise* can be seen as a moment of convergence where many typical elements of Lombardi's former production become more evident and fuse together. It may be more opportune to think of *Faust. A Disguise* as a 'starting point'. As a matter of fact, it is exactly with this opera that Lombardi begins his career as opera composer, which is becoming more and more his principal activity. After *Faust. A Disguise*, he composed *Dmitri oder der Künstler und die Macht* (*Dmitri, or the Artist and Power*) (1994–9), *Prospero* (2005) and *Il re nudo* (*The Naked King*) (first performance: March 2009). These operas not only manifest Lombardi's interest in the theatrical stage as a means of expression, but also his interest in the representation of power, an interest that is taking on more and more significance in his work as opera composer. In *Faust*, one crucial point revolves around the pact with the devil, in other words around the possibility of having control over the surrounding reality. In *Dmitri*, the central topic is the relationship between power and the arts, illustrated in the life of Dmitri Šostakovič and his connection to Stalin. *Prospero*, which is based on Shakespeare's drama, deals with the subject of real power and supernatural power (Prospero practices the art of magic and is exiled to an island after his brother and the king of Naples usurp his duchy). Lombardi's latest opera in preparation, *The Naked King*, is a chamber opera freely inspired by a comedy by Evgenij Schwarz, who has rewritten three narratives by Hans Christian Andersen ('The Princess and the Pea', 'The Emperor's New Suit' and 'The Swineherd'). Here again, we find that the element of power is the central subject.

We shall thus conclude that, in this respect, *Faust. A Disguise* is a synthesis of the political dimension that characterized the musical production of Luca Lombardi rather explicitly during the 1960s and 1970s. It is transformed into a series of questions on power that he now seems to ask himself in front of his audience and on the theatrical stage.

(Translation from Italian to English by Anja Gräfe)

Notes

1 Translations by Anja Gräfe, unless otherwise indicated.

Bibliography

Baccarani, E. (2002), *La Poesia nel Labirinto. Razionalismo e Istanza 'Antiletteraria' nell'Opera e nella Cultura di Edoardo Sanguineti*. Bologna: Il mulino.

Becheri, G. (2005), *Catalogo delle Opere di Luca Lombardi. Composizioni, Scritti, Bibliografia, Discografia*. Rome: Rai Trade.

Bramani, L. (1991), 'Faust, un travestimento', *Ricordi Oggi*, 2, n.p.

De Meijer, P. (2003), 'Goethe, Faust e Sanguineti', in E. Sanguineti, *Faust. Un Travestimento*, N. Lorenzini (ed.). Rome: Carocci, pp. 127–140.

Galliano, L. (1995), 'Note sull'opera di Luca Lombardi (1967–1985)', *Nuova Rivista Musicale Italiana*, 2, 253–65.

Gambaro, F. (1993a), *Colloquio con Edoardo Sanguineti. Quarant'Anni di Cultura Italiana attraverso i Ricordi di un Poeta Intellettuale*. Milan: Anabasi.

— (1993b), *Invito a Conoscere la Neoavanguardia*. Milan: Mursia.

Heister, W.-H. (1991), 'Nachklassische Walpurgisnacht und posttonale Idiomatik-zu Luca Lombardi Oper "Faust, un travestimento"', *Dissonanz-Dissonance*, 30, 19–23.

Lombardi, L. (1979), [Interview without title], in M. Mollia (ed.), *Autobiografia della Musica Contemporanea*. Cosenza: Lerici, pp. 132–48.

— (1980), 'Sul rapporto tra musica popolare e musica colta', *Chigiana. Rassegna Annuale di Studi Musicologici*, 17 (new series), 113–17.

— (1983), 'Costruzione della libertà', *Musica/Realtà*, 10, 190–8.

— (1985a), 'Per una musica "ex-clusiva"', *1985. La Musica*, 4, 38.

— (1985b), '(Ipo)tesi su avanguardia e tradizione', *1985. La Musica*, 1, 5–6.

— (1985c), '(Ipo)tesi su avanguardia e tradizione', *1985. La Musica*, 2, 47–8.

— (1985d), 'Sisifo come autoritratto?', *1985. La Musica*, 9, 17–18.

— (1986), 'Materiali per un'indagine sul concetto di figura', *I Quaderni della Civica Scuola di Musica*, 13, 86–91.

— (1988a), '(Note di) diario (di note)', *Eunomio*, 8, 22.

— (1988b), 'Tra preistoria e postmoderno', in D. Tortora (ed.), *Molteplicità di Poetiche e Linguaggi nella Musica d'Oggi*. Milan: Unicopli, pp. 27–42.

— (1988c), 'Tre testi', *Eunomio*, 9–10, 23–6.

— (1991), 'Su Faust, un travestimento', *Ricordi Oggi*, 2, n.p.

Lombardi, L. and Thym, J. (2006), *Construction of Freedom and Other Writings*. Baden-Baden: Verlag Valentin Korner.

Lorenzini, N. (2003), 'Introduzione. Il *Faust* di Sanguineti: la parola all'inferno', in E. Sanguineti, *Faust. Un Travestimento*, N. Lorenzini (ed.). Rome: Carocci, pp. 7–47.

Lorenzini, N. and Risso, E. (eds) (2002), *Album Sanguineti*. Lecce: Manni.

Maggi, D. (1988), 'Molteplicità di poetiche e linguaggi nella musica d'oggi', in D. Tortora (ed.), *Molteplicità di Poetiche e Linguaggi nella Musica d'Oggi*. Milan: Unicopli, pp. 140–55.

Mazzoni, G. (1998), 'Elogio dell'antitesi. Il significato dell'avanguardia oggi. Intervista a Edoardo Sanguineti', *Allegoria*, 29–30, 219–29.

Pietropaoli, A. (1991), *Unità e Trinità di Edoardo Sanguineti. Poesie e Poetica*. Naples: Edizioni Scientifiche Italiane.

— (2002), *Per Edoardo Sanguineti: 'Good Luck (and Look)'*. Naples: Edizioni Scientifiche Italiane.

Sanguineti, E. (1974), 'La macchina narrativa dell'Ariosto', in L. Ariosto, *Orlando Furioso*, M. Turchi (ed.). Turin: Garzanti, pp. li–lvii.

— (1985a), 'Un giuoco sociale', *Alfabeta*, 69, 5.

— (1985b), 'Notizia', in E. Sanguineti, *Faust. Un Travestimento*. Genoa: Costa & Nolan, pp. 67–8.

— (1986), 'L'atto di scrittura oggi, per me', *Alfabeta*, 84, 4.

— (1987), 'Teatro con musica, senza musica', in E. Sanguineti, *La Missione del Critico*. Genoa: Marietti, pp. 189–201.

— (1988a), 'Parole e musica', in B. Gallo (ed.), *Forme del Melodrammatico. Parole e Musica (1700–1800). Contributi per la Storia di un Genere*. Milan: Guerini e Associati, pp. 339–42.

— (1988b), 'Parole per musica', in E. Sanguineti, *Ghirigori*. Genoa: Marietti, pp. 127–8.

— (1988c), 'Per la storia di un'imitazione', in G. Leopardi, *La Batracomiomachia*, G. Binni (ed.). Macerata: Cassa di Risparmio della Provincia di Macerata, pp. ix–xviii.

— (1993a), 'Il traduttore, nostro contemporaneo', in *Edoardo Sanguineti. Opere e Introduzione Critica*. Verona: Anterem, pp. 171–6.

— (1993b), *Per Musica*, L. Pestalozza (ed.). Milan-Modena: Ricordi-Mucchi.

— (1996), 'Rap e poesia', in E. Sanguineti, *Rap*. Bologna: Fuori Thema, pp. 5–9.
— (1999), 'Avanguardia e coscienza del passato. A colloquio con Fausto Razzi', *Nuova Rivista Musicale Italiana*, 1, 71–91.
— (2001a), *Ideologia e Linguaggio*, E. Risso (ed.). Milan: Feltrinelli.
— (2001b), 'La maschera e la fiaba', E. Sanguineti, *L'amore delle Tre Melarance. Un Travestimento Fiabesco dal Canovaccio di Carlo Gozzi*. Genoa: Il Melangolo, pp. 7–14.
— (2001c), *Verdi in Technicolor*. Genoa: Il Melangolo.
Sanguineti, E. and Buonaccorsi, E. (2001), 'Il grande teatro è solo hard', in E. Sanguineti, *Sei Personaggi.com. Un Travestimento Pirandelliano*. Genoa: Il nuovo melangolo, pp. 7–21.
Sanguineti, E. and Liberovici, A. (1998), 'Intervista a Edoardo Sanguineti', in E. Sanguineti and A. Liberovici, *Il Mio Amore è Come una Febbre e Mi Rovescio*. Milan: Bompiani, pp. 103–22.
Sanguineti, E. and Ronconi, L. (1970), 'Un teatro dell'ironia (a colloquio con Luca Ronconi ed Edoardo Sanguineti)', in G. Bartolucci (ed.), *Orlando Furioso di Ludovico Ariosto*. Rome: Bulzoni, pp. 11–23.
Sica, G. (1974), *Sanguineti*. Florence: La Nuova Italia.
Sini, C. (1995), '"Faust" mito della modernità', *Nuova Rivista Musicale Italiana*, 2, 267–72.
Wiesmann, S. (1993), '"Mi fai orrore". Einige Bemerkungen zu Henri Pousseurs *Votre Faust* und Luca Lombardis *Faust. Un travestimento*', *Wort und Musik. Salzburger Akademische Beiträge*, 18, v. 2, 573–81.
Wohlthat, M. (1991), 'Doktor Faust als pluralista: ein Briefwechsel mit Luca Lombardi über seine erste Oper', *Neue Zeitschrift für Musik*, 12, 15–22.
Zàccaro, G. (1987), 'Luca Lombardi ovvero l'identità politica della musica', *Eunomio*, 7, 21–5.
Zurletti, M. (1990), 'Intervista a Luca Lombardi', *Ricordi Oggi*, 2, n.p.

14 Contemporary African and Brazilian Adaptations of Goethe's *Faust* in Postcolonial Context

Katharina Keim

Undoubtedly there is no play that embodies German identity and its historical past more than Goethe's *Faust*. But it was only in the mid-nineteenth century that Goethe's main character became an example for German culture. In particular, the last act of Part II—Faust's colonization of the shore conferred to him by the Emperor after the victorious war—played a crucial role in the building of German nationhood and accompanied nearly every important step in German history. The foundation of the German state in 1871, as well as the proclamation of the Weimar Republic in Goethe's Theatre in Weimar in 1919, referred to *Faust*'s heritage. However, the fascists also used the text in order to legitimize their politics: it was Joseph Goebbels who justified his race policy with the famous lines from the pact between Faust and Mephistopheles, 'Blood is a very special juice' ('Blut ist ein ganz besondrer Saft') (*F*, 1740).[1] This abuse of Goethe's play by the fascists was one of the main reasons which led theatre directors—such as Gustaf Gründgens, Klaus-Michael Grüber or Peter Stein—to stage mostly apolitical versions of *Faust* from the mid-twentieth century to the 1990s (Mahl 1998). But since the fin de siècle, one can observe a marked increase in interest in the political and postcolonial aspects of the play, especially in a more international context.

This development was, of course, supported strongly throughout the Goethe year in 1999—the author's 250th birthday—and by the various activities of the Goethe Institutes abroad. From the many Faust productions that resulted, two will be treated here as exemplary of the attempt to adapt *Faust* from the perspective of the indigenous or at least the local syncretic cultural tradition, thus breathing new life into older material. The productions concerned were given in South Africa in 1995 and the Brazilian city of Salvador da Bahia in 1999.

Both regions share a colonial past that continues to overshadow present day-to-day life. Despite the end of the apartheid regime in South Africa in 1994, and despite the freedom granted to slaves in Bahia in 1888 (where, in contrast to all other provinces in Brazil, two thirds of the region's population are black), the underprivileged situation of black people has changed but a little. In religious and cultural areas too, traces of European dominance can still be made out; as colonization and decolonization took their course, imported West European and African or autochthonous elements mingled with each other. In these cultures, a theatrical tradition comparable with the Western is missing. This gave rise to a special form of theatrical syncretism, one which combines structures of presentation and of organization drawn from the traditional European theatre with local or African aesthetic positions, especially in the areas of dance and music (Balme 1995: 1–46).

The South African and Bahian productions stake their claim on a search for a national and cultural identity as articulated in the *Faust* text itself. Faust's subjective desire for recognition—to 'learn what, deep within it,/binds the universe together' ('Dass ich erkenne was die Welt/im Innersten zusammenhält') (*F*, 382)—is understood in both cases as a collective amnesia of the indigenous cultural history acting as a precondition for a fresh orientation.

Since Aimé Césaire's *Une Tempête* (*A Tempest*) (1969), Shakespeare's works have been the principal model for postcolonial adaptations of classical plays in many areas around the world. In contrast, German-speaking theatre is represented at the most by the didactic plays and epic theatre of Bertolt Brecht or social dramas such as Büchner's *Woyzeck* (Orkin 1987; 1991). The colonial and postcolonial impact not only of *Faust* but also of German literature in general has only a relatively marginal existence in the public imagination. Literary postcolonial research is still primarily an anglo- or francophile domain. The neglect of this domain within German literary research can no doubt, in the first instance, be traced back to German colonial history itself. This era extended, as is well known, for only two decades, from 1884 to 1918–19 and affected, along with the important colonies of Namibia and Tanzania in southern Africa, a small number of strategic locations in the Far East too.

Colonial Discourse in Goethe's *Faust*

The possible point of convergence between the most renowned German drama and postcolonial ways of seeing the world is not readily identifiable in historical events, but can be glimpsed in the history of ideas, just as is the case with Faust's colonialization project in Act V of Part II. As Michael Jaeger argues in *Fausts Kolonie* (*Faust's Colony*) (2004), we are confronted here with the central tenet of 'Goethe's critical phenomenology of modernity', the subtitle of the study. With a view of images of a paradisiacal future the radical campaigner Faust negates, in these scenes, the tradition as well as the historical being of the present in favor of a technocratic subjugation of nature (Jaeger 2004: 25). But that which the blinded Faust believes he can see in the large outer courtyard of the palace is just a mere vision: 'If I can furnish space for many millions/to live—not safe, I know, but free to work' ('Eröffn' ich Räume vielen Millionen,/Nicht sicher zwar, doch tätig-frei zu wohnen') (*F*, 11563–4). Here the protagonist declaims a quasi-religious promise of redemption, that is to say, the prophecy of a possible identity of daily tasks and existence.

> To this idea I am committed wholly,
> it is the final wisdom we can reach:
> he, only, merits freedom and existence
> who wins them every day anew.
>
> (Ja diesem Sinne bin ich ganz ergeben,
> Das ist der Weisheit letzter Schluß:
> Nur der verdient sich Freiheit wie das Leben,
> Der täglich sie erobern muß.)
>
> (F, 11574–6)

Faust's 'megalomaniac project' (Jaeger 2004: 25) calls nonetheless for the eradication of previous societal and traditional norms, just as is demonstrated in the previous scene—represented as a 'teichoscopia'—in which Philemon and Baucis are destroyed along with the wanderer who shares their lodgings. Faust's ownership is thus based not on the foundation of productive work, but on a partial confiscation and on goods gained by war. In his treatment of the workers, too, there exists an atmosphere of exploitation, seen in his brutal, commandeering manner exhibited toward Mephistopheles:

> Use every means you can
> and get a plentiful supply of laborers,
> use benefits and discipline to spur them on,
> make payments, offer bonuses, conscript them!
>
> (Wie es auch möglich sei
> Arbeiter schaffe Meng' auf Menge,
> Ermuntere durch Genuß und Strenge,
> Bezahle, locke, presse bei!)
>
> (F, 11551–4)

Faust's project is not only viewed with skepticism by Philemon and Baucis but also by Mephistopheles himself. In an aside, he evinces sarcastic disbelief with regard to the continual attempt to defeat the force of natural violence, and foresees that the water—personified in the god of the ocean Neptune—will sweep across the land that has recently been won:

> And yet with all your dams and levees
> your striving serves no one but us;
> in fact, you're now preparing a grand feast
> for the water-daemon, Neptune.
> All of your kind are doomed already;—
> the elements have sworn to help us;
> the end will be annihilation.
>
> (Du bist doch nur für uns bemüht
> Mit deinen Dämmen deinen Buhnen;
> Denn du bereitest schon Neptunen,
> Dem Wasserteufel, großen Schmaus.
> In jeder Art seid ihr verloren,
> Die Elemente sind mit uns verschworen,
> Und auf Vernichtung läufts hinaus.)
>
> (F, 11544–50)

The moral reflections that Faust has only recently opined in 'Midnight' ('Palast—Mitternacht'), which have already characterized his lengthy 'Night' ('Nacht') monologue in Part I, give way here to a carrying out of tasks without regard for the consequences in the name of an optimistic view of technological progress and the domination of the forces of nature which themselves do not shy away from the loss of human life. Thus, the final redemption of Faust is hardly to be legitimatized through the concept of the 'act', but only on religious grounds. Albrecht Schöne has proven that Faust's salvation is based on an idea of the Greek Church Father Origen, namely that of 'apokatastasis panton', which is radically different from any other eschatological concept. The theory of the 'apokatastasis panton', that is, the notion that all spirits will return to God eventually, is based on the concept of the world as a divine and all-embracing pedagogical process in which, as a basic principle, all—including the evil one—are destined to return to God as true angels (Goethe 1994a, 7/2: 787ff).

Just as the salvation cannot be justified by any secular argument, dramaturgically it works only by getting back to the initial Baroque 'theatrum mundi' metaphor as the only possible framework for the triumph of divine grace over mundane and historical justice. The angels' sentence at the end of Part II, 'for him whose striving never ceases/we can provide redemption' ('"Wer immer strebend sich bemüht,/Den können wir erlösen"') (*F*, 11936–7), echoes and amplifies the Lord's initial statement in the 'Prologue in Heaven' ('Prolog im Himmel'): 'men err as long as they keep striving' ('Es irrt der Mensch so lang' er strebt') (*F*, 317).

Reception History of the Faustian Colonization Project

While Goethe's *Faust* takes a highly critical view of the 'project of the modern age' and demonstrates its darker sides, an ideologically guided stylization of the Faust figure as a 'Tatmensch', a 'man of action' or 'doer', did not set in before reception history of Goethe's protagonist as someone with whom German people striving for national unification could identify took root during the nineteenth and twentieth centuries (Schwerte 1962). This tendency reached a highpoint in the era bounded by the Wilhelmenian Empire and World War II, that is, from 1871 onward.

Thus it is that the editor of the Weimar edition from 1887–8, Erich Schmitt, allows the 'Faustian' character of modern times to slip into the navigable waters of that Wilhelmenian era that see their culmination in the avowed historical attitude to progress. In *Decline of the West*, Oswald Spengler (1988: 136) interprets the Faust figure as a 'portrait of an entire culture'—the 'Faustian occident' that marks the transition from culture (in Part I) to civilization (at the end of Part II).

Along with such culturally pessimistic readings of *Faust*, there were nevertheless simultaneous attempts in Germany to design a colonization project of Faustian dimensions which would benefit mankind. We are dealing here with a geopolitical project initiated by the architect Herman Sörgel (1885–1952) and other renowned colleagues in 1929 that went by the name of 'Atlantropa' (Voigt 1998). This notion envisaged a gaining of new living space ('Lebensraum') through the winning of incredibly large land masses in the Mediterranean. The sea level was to be reduced by up to 200 m, whereby new areas of land could be colonized. At the same time, gigantic dams and hydraulic works would provide, for times to come, enough energy for the whole of Europe, as well as providing irrigation systems that would transform arid terrains in North Africa into fruitful areas of cultivation. Further, a railway network was planned to extend from Europe to Cape Town with the aim of opening up the African continent.

The overall aim of 'Atlantropa' remained—after the model of the Monroe Doctrine—the creation of a European hegemonial power diametrically opposed to the antipodes of America and Asia. Hereby, the African hinterland was to act as a joint European reservoir for raw materials and cheap labor. This racist vision of Africa as a 'beast of burden' for complacent civilized Europe is represented by the cartoonist Heinrich Kley, in the mid-1930s, as an African elephant on which sits Europe under a canopy, surrounded by barbed wire (Voigt 1998).

Plans and charts pertaining to Sörgel's 'Atlantropa' project were on view during a traveling exhibition at the beginning of the 1930s in Germany and Switzerland. The press saw in these exhibits a veritable 'Faust at work', as the *Münchner Post* described it on 7 March 1933. For his part, Sörgel placed a *Faust* quote at the beginning of the first edition of his project: 'I love the man who wants what cannot be' ('Den lieb' ich der Unmögliches begehrt') (*F*, 7488).

Although this winning of new 'living space' seems at first glance to conform to the geopolitical principles of the fascist party who had recently taken power, they do not shore up the project, because it is based on pacifistic, pan-European thoughts and constructs as opposed to being infiltrated with specifically German attitudes to power. The national socialists were, as is well known, directing their military efforts to expansion in the east. They did not ignore, however, the legitimacy propounded by the rhetoric of Faust's colonization project which crystallizes in the words, 'If only I might see that people's teeming life,/share their autonomy on unencumbered soil' ('Auf freiem Grund mit freiem Volke stehn') (*F*, 11580) (Mandelkow 1980/1989, 2: 9).

Faust from Postcolonial Perspectives

These tenets relating to Faust's colonization project may have made clear that, first of all, reception history of the *Faust* subject matter, textually laden with ambiguities, gives rise to postcolonial readings. The modification of the Faustian impetus of enlightenment to an imperialistic attitude is portrayed somewhat critically and in a rather aloof manner by its author Goethe himself. Moreover, hardly has a classical author explored oriental cultures in such extended literary 'travels' on Persian, Arabian and Indian poetry (Bobzin 1998: 53ff). The most convincing poetical and metrical rapprochement of the two main strands of European culture, namely the North-Germanic and the ancient Hellenistic, is undoubtedly realized in the Helena act of Part II.

It should rather be assumed that Goethe's work in all its openness, especially due to the profound analysis of various cultural traditions, offers itself up to a great extent, again and again casting out extremely varied transcultural starting points, while at the same time making the terms 'source culture' and 'target culture' obsolete. Thus, for the analysis of postcolonial stage adaptations of *Faust* it proves useful not to assume the model of transformation from one culture into another, but rather one of cultural interaction between text and theatrical production, where the latter can also render new semantic potentials of the dramatic text productive. The intercultural contact situation as a space for translation is highly problematic in any case (Bhabha 2007: 51) and is subject to a string of not always comprehensible, and therefore elusive, premises, prejudices and possible misunderstandings. Moreover, theatre productions of foreign-language classical texts often pass through a number of transformational processes such as linguistic translation, reception of the work through adaptations by other authors, special semiotic generation of meaning through a specific performance code of practice, the cultural or local context or simply through the casting of a role with a specific performer.

For the following discussion of these postcolonial theatrical *Faust* productions it is key to note that—besides the intercultural literary inspirations—Goethe's play should be considered also as a (textual) intermedial journey through European theatre history with its different forms of scenic representation. As is well known, the very young Goethe became familiar with the Faust myth by admiring a puppet theatre version at a fair. This unforgettable experience led him to write his own *Faust*, inspired by Spies' chapbook and several adaptations of the legend, including various popular puppeteer versions. The enormous popularity of the puppeteer stage until the seventeenth century has left its marks in the dramatic text itself. In Part I of Goethe's drama, the transformation of the poodle into Mephistopheles, the rejuvenation of Faust in 'Witch's Kitchen' ('Hexenküche') and the juxtaposition, in 'A Garden' ('Garten'), of Faust and Gretchen's romantic dialogue, on the one hand, and Mephistopheles and Marthe Schwerdtlein's comic conversation, on the other hand, recall devices of puppetry. Other scenes, such as the miraculous wine fountains in 'Auerbach's Cellar' ('Auerbachs Keller in Leipzig'), or 'Walpurgis Night' ('Walpurgisnacht'), are partly inspired by the spectacularity of the Renaissance and Baroque theatre, even though the representational or religious impact of these theatrical forms has been totally inverted by Goethe. This is actually the case in the masquerade which nearly seems to get out of control in Act I of Part II, alluding to the Roman and Italian 'trionfi', as opposed to the German medieval carnival and theatre:

> Imagine that you're not in Germany—
> instead of Dance of Death or dancing fools and demons
> expect a cheerful entertainment.
> When in your interest and his own
> our Emperor traversed the lofty Alps
> and traveled down to Rome ...
>
> (Denkt nicht ihr seid in deutschen Grenzen
> Von Teufels- Narren- und Totentänzen;
> Ein heitres Fest erwartet euch.
> Der Herr, auf seinen Römerzügen,
> Hat, sich zu Nutz, euch zum Vergnügen,
> Die hohen Alpen überstiegen ...)
>
> (F, 5065–70)

This parade culminates at the end of Act I in the apparition of Helen of Troy ('Kaiserliche Pfalz—Rittersaal'). The phantasmagorical character of this scene—anchored thematically in the myth of the Egyptian Helen and technically based on the 'laterna magica' effect—also reflects on a metatheatrical level the essence of theatre with its faculty to visualize the fictional world in a way that it becomes even more real than the actual world (Lehmann 1998: 206ff, 413ff). Thus Goethe not only anticipates Baudrillard's theory of the 'simulacra' but also appeals to the miraculous feature of the scenae to generate new ideas at a prelogical and preverbal stage by creating their 'eidos' on stage. This literary and presentational complexion of Goethe's text allows the postcolonial adaptation to use it—according to the theatrical aesthetics of Brecht—as (raw) 'material' for the artistic reflection of the region's specific cultural and historical problems. It also gives reason to deal with various modes of indigenous paratheatrical presentation and to combine these with traditional, new or syncretic forms of the visual and the performing arts.

Faust's stations in the mundane as well as the wider world shall serve as examples of how in both productions the cultural interaction is being achieved.

Faust and the Mundane World: *Fausto Zero*

The Bahian production by director Márcio Meirelles was produced at the Teatro Vila Velha by the Teatro dos Novos company in Salvador, the provincial capital of Bahia. In the eighteenth century it was one of the main centers of the slave trade and still today more than two thirds of the region's population are black. The director Meirelles is renowned in the country of his birth, and since 1990 he has been the leading light of the company Bando de Teatro Olodum, a group also counting the Teatro Vila Velha as its premises. The aim of this theatrical troupe, which started out as a carnival organization, was and remains the achievement of a contemporary theatrical aesthetics within the traditional Bahian, Afro-Brazilian performance practice, thus engendering a local theatre for the nonprivileged black population of Salvador (Schaeber 2003: 272). In the beginning, the members of the troupe wrote their own plays, but quite soon, they moved on to producing dramas by playwrights such as Shakespeare, Büchner and Brecht. Meirelles' work is oriented to that of Augusto Boal's 'theatre of the oppressed'. He favors the principle of 'création collective', the collective process of creation, based on the development of characters by acting improvisations and operating strongly with musical elements and dance. This artistic approach is present, too, in his version of *Urfaust* (*Fausto Zero*) with the group Teatro dos Novos, a production that in the Goethe year 1999 was premiered in the new translation by Christine Röhrig (Goethe 2001).

Meirelles deliberately chose *Urfaust*, for it is this early version in which the director sees all the typical elements of folk theatre, ones which are relevant for his theatrical aesthetics and the local audience as well. Although this production adheres very closely to the original text, the director has fundamentally revised the connotations associated with the dramatis personae and their motifs in the European cultural context. Harro Müller-Michaels has pointed out that the pact between Faust and Mephistopheles is finally based on a mutual misunderstanding of the central term of enjoyment ('Genuss'). Whereas Faust strives for a concept of holistic knowledge and cognition, Mephistopheles comprehends only the physical aspects of the term (Müller-Michaels 1998: 11). This apparent opposition between overestimated mind and subordinated 'physis' can be considered a legacy of Christian religion and the Cartesian concept of perceiving the world. Meirelles tries to subvert this antagonism by revaluating the stereotypes of vitality and sensual revels, habitually projected on to a black population.

The performance of Mephistopheles, played by the black actor Gustavo Melo, is, in particular, dominated by these principles. Faust, on the other hand, appears as a dreamer who is completely cut off from the world, a figure who discovers his other side on meeting the devil: 'Two souls, alas! reside within my breast' ('Zwei Seelen wohnen, ach! in meiner Brust') (*F*, 1112). The appreciation of Mephistopheles' character is strengthened in this context by the highly popular Afro-Brazilian Candomblé ritual practiced in the Bahia region. This religion of African origin was in colonial times mingled with a plethora of spiritualist and American Indian traditions, but mainly, however, with Catholic dogma, the result taking on the appearance of a syncretic assemblage. Characteristic for the Candomblé is the worship of multiple gods and the belief that the gods themselves are, for a short time, at least, present in the corporeal husk, entering the body of a chosen few adherents in order to make revelations. The god of nature Exu is of especial relevance here. He was, in colonial religious syncretism, associated with the devil of Christian belief. However, the Christian dichotomy of good and evil does not exist in the cult of the Candomblé. Exu is the messenger between mankind and the other gods, ensuring the communication between both and thus easily comparable to the Greek herald Hermes. Simultaneously he is also the god associated with the fulfillment of human wishes. Thus the role of Exu lends itself to that of Mephistopheles as a spirit who mediates Faust's hidden longings and aspirations, both physical and intellectual.

The pact between Mephistopheles and Faust is represented in Meirelles' production by the contextualization of the Candomblé rite as engendered by the harmonious balance of opposites and the positive principle of vitality represented by the god Exu. This renders explicable the similar simple white costumes worn by the actors playing Faust and Mephisto, their physiognomic differences rendered virtually null and void. In contrast to this, the previous appearance of the Earth-Spirit is presented by a wild and vivid ritual dance of Exu wearing a colored costume and a herald's staff, thus establishing the contact to the gods according to Candomblé rite. Also the subsequent chanted interlude in 'Auerbach's Cellar' stresses the abundant sexual allusions of the scene by an offensive and, at the same time, comic choreography.

The character of Gretchen, portrayed by a black actress, is obviously influenced by Bertolt Brecht and Egon Monk's production of *Urfaust* with the Berliner Ensemble in 1952–3 (Mahl 1986). We are comparably concerned here with a member of the petty bourgeoisie deliberately displaying her sexual charms and dreaming of social advancement through the relationship with Faust. In an interview, the actress, Rita Santana, characterizes in quite an explicit manner the inner workings of her character as to the 'Gretchen question' as follows:

> When Gretchen asks Heinrich about religion, she basically means whether he will marry her. What has remained of religion today is moralistic. The woman is tied to customs and ways of life, and to free herself from them, as Gretchen does, is still a problem for the women [in Bahia] today. (Jeshel and Kramer 1999)[2]

Regarding the Gretchen tragedy, the production simply relies on the contemporary relevance of the moral conventions of the Goethe era. These may appear for a European audience to be traditional or outdated; however, in Bahian society this is still by no means the case. Thus, in the performance itself, society, along with its questionable moral codex based on Christian religion and the idol of female virginity, is naturally also jointly responsible for the tragic end of the events. On stage, this societal framework is embodied by a chorus of singers and dancers surrounding the protagonists and commenting on their actions like the chorus in Greek tragedy. Sometimes they even intermingle with the audience so that the borderline between actors and spectators gets blurred, both becoming at the same time accessories and witnesses to Gretchen's destiny, which could easily be their own fate.

This harsh critique of dubious Christian ethics is especially accentuated in the scene 'By the Ramparts' ('Zwinger'). In front of a stabbed living Mater Dolorosa statue, Gretchen, weeping at her mother's coffin, is haunted by the evil spirit. The latter is portrayed as a combination of a debauchee and the crucified Christ, wearing a crown of thorns and a loincloth. This equation of the good and the bad, of victim and doer, leads the whole dichotomic system of European knowledge and religion ad absurdum by demonstrating the relevance of both aspects for the human being. Thus the postcolonial theatre practice decolonizes the stage (and hopefully also the society) by creating new visions going beyond the dualistic logic. The performative act of overcoming oppositions is realized first and foremost as a corporal one. By this means the production scenically transforms the idea and the need of somatic and mental metamorphosis as a central theme of *Faust* into a visual and physical demonstration of the power and strengths of the syncretic Bahian theatre culture.

Faust in the Wider World: *Faustus in Africa!*

Faustus in Africa!, by the white South African director William Kentridge and the Handspring Puppet Company, was first given on stage in 1995 and is deeply influenced by the attempts to cope with the country's racist past after the African National Congress (ANC) victory in 1994. Since his schooldays Kentridge, who later became famous in visual arts, worked on many theatrical productions directed against the apartheid system. As a descendant of a Jewish family that emigrated from the Baltic States to South Africa at the beginning of the twentieth century, he became familiar with middle and Eastern European culture at a very early age:

> When I was twelve years old, in a *Time Life* book on the mind, I came across a chart of great geniuses of all time . . . Heading the list . . . was Goethe, a name quite unknown to me amongst the Einsteins (position 6th I think) and Mozart's 3rd.
>
> A few months later I was given, among the atlases, dictionaries, and fountain pens that constituted the typical presents for a Bar Mitzvah, a two volume translation of Parts One and Two of Goethe's *Faust*. For approximately twenty-five years the books stood unopened on my bookshelf.
>
> The production *Faustus in Africa!* has a number of starting points. One of which was the silent rebuke of the Goethe on the bookshelf. During the period of

stalking or avoiding the text, I tried to find other versions, other less daunting tellings of the story and considered at different times everything from Marlowe, to George Sand, to Gertrude Stein, to Lunarcharsky's pre-revolutionary *Faust*, to Bulgakov's marvellous version, *The Master and Margerita* [sic]. (The Hyena in our production gives a nod and cocked leg to Bulgakov's cat.) But in the end there was no avoiding the power and strangeness of the two volumes. The play we finally ended up with uses sections of Part One, fragments of Part Two, and new material written by the South African poet Lesego Rampolokeng . . . All this with the aim of finding the place where the play ceases to be a daunting other— the weight of Europe leaning on the Southern tip of Africa—and becomes our own work. (Kentridge 1999: 45)

Besides this extended literary and dramaturgical adaptation work another striking characteristic of productions by the Handspring Puppet Company is the method of theatrical presentation. The characters are represented by large rod puppets akin to the Bunraku tradition, in which the puppeteers remain visible to the audience. Most puppets are designed by the puppeteer Adrian Kohler himself. One exception remains the character of Mephistopheles (Leslie Fong). This reference to the folkloristic tradition of *Faust* as a puppet play may feel distracting to the Western audience at first, but the production indeed manages to present on stage an abridged version of both parts of the drama within a mere 2 hours. The text is based on a translation by the Glaswegian writer Robert David MacDonald which was produced by the dramaturge and translator himself at the Citizen's Theatre as the very first English production of both parts of the drama in 1986 (Goethe 2002). Additional texts and further adaptations for the South African stage were written by Kentridge himself and local rap poet Lesego Rampolokeng, whose poetry is a hybrid composition of the traditional 'dithoko' with contemporary rap or dub. Its rhythm is actually quite close to the Goethean doggerel ('Knittelvers') (Dreymüller 1999).

The adaptation takes the Faustian project of colonization as a starting point in order to display the colonial history of the African continent with all its negative results as a kind of collective amnesia. Despite the scenery's dislocation to Africa, the first part of the drama is still strongly geared to the flow of Goethe's drama. In the second part the production gradually departs from the Eurocentric perspective of the text. The plot starts off with the end of German colonialism at the beginning of the 1920s. Faust, a light-skinned rod puppet, is characterized as colonial master, explorer and missionary who keeps the pot boiling as a deedless, homeless and melancholic figure, void of property, sticking around in a hotel room in East Africa.

By deleting those parts of the text that raise Faust's connection with magic forces as a central theme, the Faust figure is stripped of its metaphysical components. Faustian striving is from the very first catered to material gain and carnal enjoyment which the disguise of humanitarian ideals barely manages to cover. Mephistopheles, in contrast, is played by a colored performer. He acts as a clerk in a telegraph office and—on a metatheatrical level—as master of ceremony of the whole performance, thus taking over God's position in the 'theatrum mundi' metaphor. At the beginning, in the shortened 'Prologue in Heaven', he establishes contact via telephone with God, his master, who is presented only by a female voice and the projection of a gramophone at the rear wall, imitating the disc label 'His Master's Voice'. After the pact between Mephistopheles and

Faust is made by a mosquito bite (this refers to Mephistopheles being named 'God of the Flies'), the two go on a journey across the mundane and the wider world that is Africa. The topographical and historical expansion of events, which is contrary to the simplistic and uniform stage setting representing Mephisto's telegraph office, is effected by black and white animation film sequences drawn by Kentridge, which are continuously interwoven. Faust meets and seduces his black Gretchen, a nurse in the Lambaréné Albert Schweitzer Hospital taking care of lepers as well as of natives mutilated by colonial masters. Afterward he goes on a safari, an ironic allusion to the Swahili translation of the word 'journey'. This trip—presented as an animated panopticon—turns out to be the exploitation of the treasures the African continent once offered and is interspersed with ironic illusions to Goethe: Faust shoots not only exotic animals but also a statue of the German author, in what appears to be an amusement arcade. He buys the legendary 'Ife' heads from Sotheby's in London and has delightful meals during which he literally 'consumes' Africa by digging down a spoon into the stratified earth of the continent.[3]

After the intermission, at the beginning of Part II, Faust finally ends up at the bankrupt Abyssinian imperial court where he meets and becomes desirous of Helen, a concubine of the Emperor. There he also meets his black ex-servant Johnston again. While Faust devotes himself to Helen, it is up to Wagner's modern double to do postcolonial battle. Becoming first a black general and finally the Emperor, Johnston appears as bloodthirsty as the white colonial masters before him. The 'Classical Walpurgis Night' ('Klassische Walpurgisnacht') may be seen in the tributes to the victims of the South African apartheid regime and those who fell in the postcolonial wars, accompanied by Zulu songs of lament.

At the close, as the aging figure of Faust looks back at his life of guilt, he does not experience God's grace, a redemptive act that Goethe's Faust would have experienced. More to the point, Gretchen and Helen take on the appearance of two equally viable positions of dealing with the guilt of the past: Helen's pleading is not rooted in the temporal, because she has not been involved in tragic events, in contradistinction to Gretchen. Her desire is to forget completely that which has gone before in order to create a new beginning. Gretchen, for her part, has suffered intimate wounds and takes up the position that remembering horrific events is a vital necessity because forgiveness is never ruled out:

>HELEN. Greenery closes off where a conflagration once blazed.
>All in its path is razed
>by the wind blowing over trace and track.
>And dust fills every crack
>of man inflicted friction.
>
>GRETCHEN. Long after the wound's gone
>the lines of each blow and cut can still be read.
>
>HELEN. The scar itself
>is subject to the plastic surgeon's blade and thread.
>
>GRETCHEN. The skin growing back is mere trick to the eye.
>The missing limb still itches through the night,
>and memory lives further than sight.
>
>HELEN. You are what you forget
>And the living feed on the dead.

GRETCHEN. The hardest struggle is against forgetting.

HELEN. Let us welcome the strands
shutting us off from regretting.
>   (Kentridge and Rampolokeng 1995: xxxi)

These positions present ways forward, especially in the country of South Africa, where the Truth Commission has declared indemnity in exoneration for acts and events during the apartheid era. A tool which may be used to understand the racist past has been created, one which might just be useful for other nations.

Prompted by Gretchen and Helen's uttering, Faust is eventually forced to exclaim the fateful words, 'Then to this fleeting moment/I can say you are so beautiful!' In contradistinction to Goethe's blinded protagonist, there takes place a process of recognition, and Faust comprehends just why his project is destined to fail:

> The discourse is lost
> but the sound of those voices of paradise and hell
> brings on such a satisfying chill.
> This is where my life is gone
> and yet its sense is born.
>   (Kentridge and Rampolokeng 1995: xxxi)

Alas, in the end the events take a surprising turn. Emperor Johnston appears as a deus ex machina and decrees a general amnesty. Faust's redemption, however, follows purely pragmatic motives, because Johnston requires Faust and Mephisto to serve as model citizens for the construction of his new postcolonial state. The new state promises nonetheless hardly a change in the exploitative political conditions.

At a dramaturgical level, however, there follows a symbolic discharge of authority that up to now has ruled the plot. Contrary to the original text, the master's (female) voice now wishes once more to be heard, although (s)he does not manage to regain his subjects' attention. His or her plea to Mephisto to adapt to the divine order and to return to his hereditary place in hell now meets with resistance. The voice of the master is simply switched off. With this final dramaturgical intention, based as it is on the ironic treatment of the metaphor of the world as theatre, the protagonists step out of the drama's constellation of characters. They become emancipated from preconceived behavior and directed toward a self-governed existence. Mephistopheles, the black, has learnt his lesson and, laughing, frees himself from the cultural artifacts of Eurocentric structures of power and ideas. Accompanied by the sound of a puppet brass band, he grasps the playing cards and reshuffles the pack, preparing a new game with an uncertain outcome.

Kentridge's production is an excellent example of theatrical syncretism combining Far Eastern style puppetry with cinematographic elements from epic theatre, traditional Western realistic acting and indigenous African speech rhythm and music. This aesthetic allows not only a distant sight of the scenic action but also draws the spectator's attention from Faust to the other characters, especially Mephistopheles, who eventually acts out the emancipation of people of color. Here the theatrical presentation with its innovative arrangement symbolically enacts the historical process of coming into power of the non-white South African population.

Conclusions

Just as Meirelles scrutinizes the pact between Faust and Mephistopheles in a completely different light, and blames societal moral and religious conditions for Gretchen's doom, so does Kentridge go against the grain in his reading of *Faust*. In stripping the Faust figure of its idealistic raiment, and presenting the protagonist as a former colonialist pursuing only material interest, he focuses on the dark sides of the European Enlightenment without ever glorifying a mythical past of the black continent. One key aspect pertaining to this anti-idealistic concept is, according to Kentridge, '[t]o see if a riposte could be given to Hegel's high-handed dictum (written at the same time Goethe was writing his *Faust*) that "after the pyramids, World Spirit leaves Africa, never to return"' (Kentridge 1999: 46).

Hegel's rebarbative assertation of the inferiority and ineptitude of the central African people culminates in his study *The Philosophy of History*, in which he reduces the relationship between Europeans and black people to one defined purely in terms of slavery:

> Another characteristic fact in reference to the Negroes is Slavery. Negroes are enslaved by the Europeans and sold to America. But as this may be, their lot in their own land is even worse, since there a slavery quite as absolute exists; for it is the essential principle of slavery, that man has not yet attained a consciousness of his freedom, and consequently sinks down to a mere Thing—an object of no value ... Slavery is in and for itself *injustice*, for the essence of humanity is *Freedom*, but for this man must be matured. (Hegel 2001: 113, 117)

Slavery is conceived by Hegel as an understanding of black people's precivilized state of mind, primarily oriented toward the primal senses. This concept provides ample legitimacy for slavery up to the point where these individuals finally conquer their natural state. In relation to Hegel's captious argumentation, both productions, each in its own way, revise the enlightened conception of freedom and sentience which negates the sensual aspects of existence. In the case of Meirelles, this takes place in *Fausto Zero* through the positive evaluation of sensual pleasure on the part of Faust himself. Kentridge, for his part, contrasts Mephistopheles' symbolic declaration of independence with the voluntary acceptance of guilt by his master Faust.

Although both productions appear to revise markedly the traditional European reading of *Faust*, it is, finally, the incredible validity of Goethe's work—one that understands the various concepts of enjoyment as the basis for the pact between Mephistopheles and Faust as well as the duplicity of Faust's unjustifiable redemption—which affords an appropriation of the old text from the radically new perspective of African and Afro-Brazilian cultural contexts.

Notes

1   *F* references are to Goethe's *Faust* translated by Atkins (Goethe 1994b), unless otherwise indicated. All German quotations of *Faust* refer to Goethe (1994a).

2   My translation.
3   For drawings, descriptions and photos of the production see Christov-Bakargiev (1998: 101ff); for additional information and visual material, consult also the Handspring Puppet Company's homepage: www.handspringpuppet.co.za/ (retrieved 23 October 2007).

Bibliography

Balme, C. (1995), *Theater im postkolonialen Zeitalter. Studien zum Theatersynkretismus im englischsprachigen Raum.* Tübingen: Theatron.
Bhabha, H. (1994), *The Location of Culture*. London and New York: Routledge. [(2007), *Die Verortung der Kultur*, M. Schiffmann and J. Freudl (trans.). Tübingen: Stauffenberg.]
Bobzin, H. (1998), 'Zwischen "Mahomets" Gesang und "Faust": Goethes Lesereisen in den Orient', in Evangelische Akademie Iserlohn, '*Faust*' *auf der Seidenstrasse. Die Sehnsucht nach dem West-östlichen Divan. Interkulturalität und Interreligiösität bei Goethe*. Iserlohn: Evangelische Akademie, 116, pp. 53–60.
Christov-Bakargiev, C. (1998), *William Kentridge*. Brussels: Palais des Beaux Arts.
Dreymüller, C. (1999), 'Aus den Poren der Straße. Entfesselter Rap aus Südafrika: der Lyriker Lesego Rampolokeng', *Süddeutsche Zeitung*, (20 April), 10.
Faustus in Africa (1999), *Contemporary Theatre Review*, 9, (4), 45–82.
Goethe, J. W. (1994a), *Sämtliche Werke*, v. 7/1: *Faust. Texte*; v. 7/2: *Faust. Kommentare*, A. Schöne (ed.). Frankfurt/Main: Deutscher Klassiker Verlag.
— (1994b), *Faust I and II*, S. Atkins (ed. and trans.). Princeton: Princeton University Press.
— (2001), *Fausto Zero (Urfaust)*, C. Röhrig (trans.). Sao Paolo: Cosac and Naify.
— (2002), *Faust Parts One and Two*, R. D. MacDonald (trans.). London: Oberon.
Hegel, G. W. F. (2001), *The Philosophy of History*, J. Sibree (trans.). Kitchener, Ontario: Batoche Books, http://socserv2.mcmaster.ca/~econ/ugcm/3ll3/hegel/history.pdf (retrieved 25 October 2007).
Jaeger, M. (2004), *Fausts Kolonie. Goethes kritische Phänomenologie der Moderne*. Würzburg: Königshausen and Neumann.
Jeshel, J. and Kramer, B. (dirs) (1999), *Gute Reise Faust*. Nachtaktiv Production, with ZDF/3 Sat/Goethe Institute [video].
Kentridge, W. (1999), 'Director's Note: *Faustus in Africa*', *Contemporary Theatre Review*, 9, (4), 45–6.
Kentridge, W. and Rampolokeng, L. (1995), *Faustus in Africa!* Promptbook (typescript), by courtesy of A. Kohler.
Lehmann, H.-T. (1998), *Postdramatisches Theater*. Frankfurt/Main: Verlag der Autoren. [(2006), *Postdramatic Theatre*, K. Jürs-Munby (trans.). London: Routledge.]
Mahl, B. (1986), *Brecht und Monks Urfaust-Inszenierung mit dem Berliner Ensemble 1952/53*. Stuttgart: Belser.
— (1998), *Goethes Faust auf der Bühne (1806–1998)*. Stuttgart: Metzler.
Mandelkow, K. R. (1980/1989), *Goethe in Deutschland. Rezeptionsgeschichte eines Klassikers*, 2 v. Munich: Beck.
Müller-Michaels, H. (1998), 'Goethe, "Faust I"', in Evangelische Akademie Iserlohn, '*Faust*' *auf der Seidenstrasse. Die Sehnsucht nach dem West-östlichen Divan. Interkulturalität und Interreligiösität bei Goethe*. Iserlohn: Evangelische Akademie, 116, pp. 9–18.
Orkin, M. (1987), *Shakespeare against Apartheid*. Craighall: Donker.
— (1991), *Drama and the South African State*. Manchester: Manchester University Press.
Schaeber, P. (2003), Die Macht der Trommeln. Die kulturelle Bewegung der schwarzen Karnevalsgruppen aus Salvador/Bahia in Brasilien. Das Beispiel der Grupo Cultural Olodum, Doctoral thesis, Freie Universität Berlin, www.diss.fu-berlin.de/2003/211/index.html (retrieved 22 October 2007).
Schwerte, H. (Schneider, H.) (1962), *Faust und das Faustische. Ein Kapitel deutscher Ideologie*. Stuttgart: Klett.

Spengler, O. (1988), *Der Untergang des Abendlandes, Umrisse einer Morphologie der Weltgeschichte*. Munich: dtv.
Voigt, W. (1998), *Atlantropa: Weltbauten am Mittelmeer; ein Architektentraum der Moderne*. Hamburg: Dölling und Galitz.

15 Reality Just Arrived—Mark Ravenhill's *Faust is Dead*

Bree Hadley

In *Faust is Dead* (1997), Mark Ravenhill retells the Faust legend for the end of the twentieth century. One of Ravenhill's first plays, *Faust is Dead* is firmly grounded in the cruel, confrontational nihilistic spirit of the in-yer-face theatre with which he is frequently associated. It recontextualizes the Faust tale as the road trip of a postmodern philosopher, a selfish protagonist whose sadistic acts and stilted attempts at human interaction highlight his inability to access the 'real' in a world where CNN, MTV and cyberspace hold more substance than science or religion. *Faust is Dead* combines Ravenhill's distinctive theatrical sensibility with a plethora of American pop cultural references to contemporize its representation of the Faustian thinker's quest to get past word, image and idea to something really real. In the process, it complicates some of the ideas that are, for Ravenhill, iconic of postmodern philosophy—including a tendency to relinquish social responsibility and celebrate a simulated, commodified reality. The play provides a strange—and, for all its depraved absurdities, some say strangely moral—tale which shifts the Faustian dilemma to society as a whole, instead of dismissing it as one man's doomed quest to discover things he is not meant to know.

In this chapter, I consider what Ravenhill's radical reinterpretation of *Faust* contributes to understanding of the Faustian impulse in the early twenty-first century. I start by contextualizing Ravenhill's work in the scope of so-called in-yer-face theatre in Britain in the 1990s. I then provide a detailed description of the play, and the devices it uses to take the Faust thematic in new directions. I conclude with discussion of the way in which *Faust is Dead* extends the thematic and theatrical terrain established in Goethe's *Faust*, and where it sits in the landscape of several recent reexaminations of the Faust tale by ensembles as diverse as Théâtre du Soleil, The Wooster Group and La Fura dels Baus. I suggest the combination of philosophical, pop cultural and theatrical frames deployed in *Faust is Dead* draws on a legacy of intertextual, intermedial adaptations since Goethe's day to construct an image of the Faustian impulse in modern society. It invites spectators to think about modern culture, and about the (im)possibility of accessing the 'real' in a media-saturated world.

In-Yer-Face Theatre

After his first play premiered at the Royal Court in 1996, Mark Ravenhill was rapidly identified with what critic Aleks Sierz (2001) calls 'in-yer-face' theatre in Britain in the 1990s, along with writers like Sarah Kane and Anthony Nielsen. Sierz coined the term in-yer-face theatre to convey the confrontational spirit characteristic of what he saw as a new breed of British writing in the 1990s. 'In the nineties', he contends, 'in-yer-face theatre injected a dose of blatant extremism into British theatre and changed the theatrical sensibility' (Sierz 2001: 10). 'Never before had so many plays been so blatant, aggressive or emotionally dark' (Sierz 2001: 30).

Sierz's term did not necessarily sit well with the writers themselves, who approached their work in different ways. Accordingly, Sierz, and later commentators such as Ken Urban (2004: 354), stressed the fact that in-yer-face theatre was not a movement with a shared aesthetic, purpose or manifesto of the sort seen with its modernist predecessors. The writers drew on theatrical legacies as diverse as Edward Bond's social realism, Harold Pinter's comedy of menace, and Peter Brook's experiments with the work of Antonin Artaud and Bertolt Brecht, and in some cases also developed contemporary inflections of classical and Shakespearean themes. Their work ranged from the brutal experience of extreme behavior in small spaces through to full estrangement, from gritty realism to alienation and absurdity, from violence to comedy and corny sentimentality (Sierz 2001: 5–6).

In spite of these stylistic differences, what so-called in-yer-face plays seemed to have in common was a theatrical sensibility that converged around a concern with confrontation, shock, cruelty and nihilism. In-yer-face theatre experimented with content and conventional theatrical form to shake spectators free from their comfort zones, cross theatrical and moral boundaries, and challenge moral norms (Sierz 2001: 4).

The cause of this distinctive convergence of cruelty, shock and violence in British theatre in the 1990s has since been debated by many commentators. 'England was', as Urban suggests, 'in the midst of a period of economic certainty and cultural renaissance' (2004: 354–5). A creative, vital, swinging British style was back with a vengeance with Tony Blair's New Labour after the political strife and privations of the Thatcher years. 'Things can only get better' (Philippou 2007) became the positivist catch-cry of the time. But young British writers were cynical about the shallow consumerist prosperity of the 1990s, and the social and ideological systems implicit to it. They saw Blair's New Labour as 'little more than Thatcherism lite' (Urban 2004: 356), recycling 1960s pop culture through the lens of late consumer capitalism into something that seemed cool, funky and potentially subversive of the staid old Tory systems. 'New Labour used coolness as the means by which to reconcile the basic contradictions of capitalism: the need to work and the desire of the individual', Urban argues (2004: 358). Influenced by the negativist philosophies of continental Europe, the writers' concerns recalled Guy Debord's situationalist anxiety about an accumulation of representations in today's 'society of the spectacle', representations that mediate reality, mediate social relationships and position people as passive spectators isolated and alienated from reality by their participation in this meaningless cacophony of images (Debord 1994: 12).[1] In-yer-face writers tried in their different ways to get beneath the 'cool' to an increasingly fragmented and uncertain world. They forced themselves and their spectators to cut through the numbingly superficial façade of contemporary culture, the way a self-harmer cuts him/herself, submitting to the cruelest chastisements, in order to have any sensation at all. Accordingly, cruelty, as the motivating aesthetic force behind British in-yer-face theatre in the 1990s (Urban 2004: 361–3), was not simply a shock tactic. This was a means of awakening audiences to the pain and horror born of, and hidden behind, the gloss of a superficial, self-indulgent capitalist world. With its desire to disrupt moral and theatrical orthodoxies, to do something real through debased action, in-yer-face theatre could be a particularly apt form for delving into the Faustian impulse in contemporary society, as Ravenhill would in *Faust is Dead*.

Ravenhill and the In-Yer-Face Critique of Consumer Capitalism

Mark Ravenhill has consistently probed the way commerce and consumer culture drive Western social relationships (Svich 2003). In his words,

> [p]lenty of commentators, mainly journalists, but a few people who should know better, have chosen only to report the 'shocking' moments in my plays: the 'bloody rimming' moments. But other commentators have spotted another, bigger project in my plays to date: something which may even report upon, maybe even critique, a world of globalised capitalism. I'd like to think that's there . . . I'd like to think that the best bits of my writing have captured some of the weightless, soulless, emptiness of contemporary, global capitalism and in doing so opened up a space for some of the audience to think more critically about The Way We Live Now than they might have done before. (2006: 132)

Ravenhill's project is, of course, a critique that comes from inside this very culture—what Hal Foster would call an act of resistance rather than an act of transgression (1985: 139–55). Ravenhill's plays provide a cynical, ironic take on the morality of a generation for whom '[t]he market ha[s] filtered into every aspect of their lives' (Ravenhill cit. in Sierz 2001: 123). As Rebellato observes, 'Ravenhill shows us our society, the state of our communal bonds, ripped and tattered by transcontinental economic forces' (2001: x). The central characters in Ravenhill's early plays are overgrown children, concerned only with gratifying their own financial, social and sexual desires (Svich 2003: 86). Self-centered consumerism has replaced the revolutionary zeal that may once have driven some of Britain's disaffected youth. As a result, Ravenhill observes,

> [n]obody in these plays is fully adult. They are all needy, greedy, wounded, only fleetingly able to connect with the world around them. Consumerism, late capitalism—whatever we call it—has created an environment of the infant 'me' where it is difficult to grow into the adult 'us'. (2004: 311–12)

The communal social structures that might have given these characters the capacity to live together have been destroyed, as Rebellato argues (2001: xi). Pathetic, childlike creatures, '[t]heir primary relationships are with consumer goods, and they seem barely able to form any kind of connection with one another' (Rebellato 2001: xi). New media technology further compounds the disconnection, creating a McLuhanian dystopia, in which technology determines the thoughts and feelings possible for people as well as recording and reporting on them (Ravenhill 2006: 131).

Faust is Dead

In *Faust is Dead*,[2] Ravenhill uses the complex cultural referencing, cruelty and absurdity characteristic of in-yer-face theatre to explore how the Faust thematic speaks to us at the end of the millennium. The play was conceived when Ravenhill was commissioned by Nick Philippou to write a contemporary version of *Faust* for the Actors Touring Company, a British company specializing in radical reinterpretations of classic plays (Svich 2003: 83). The commission was unconventional, insofar as it was prefigured by another work, a piece called *Brainy*, in which Philippou had collaborated with designer Stewart Laing to produce 'a kind of avant-garde biopic of Foucault' (Philippou 2007; cf. Sierz 2001:134–5), whose negativist philosophies had begun to interest them. They depicted Foucault as a disembodied head upside-down in a dark space,[3] a thinker with a desire to discover more about his body through experiences with drugs and sex in the United States (US), in a performance art piece already related to the Faustian thematic which they would take further in *Faust is Dead*.

With this as its starting point, Ravenhill's *Faust is Dead* is indeed a radical retelling of the Faust story. The central motif of the key Faust texts—including the *Historia von D. Johann Fausten* (1587), Marlowe's *The Tragical History of Doctor Faustus* (1604) and Goethe's *Faust I* and *II* (1808 and 1832)—is one man's willingness to make a pact with the devil in the pursuit of knowledge and power, and the price he pays. Ravenhill, however, is suspicious of black-and-white ideas about good and evil. He tends to a worldview in which 'evil', or what we call 'evil', is a product of society, not something absolute (Ravenhill 2004: 306). Accordingly, he baulks at the notion that his plays are a meditation on the metaphysics of evil. 'Look at the way my plays happen within a specific world of late capitalism. This is not a world of metaphysical absolutes', Ravenhill states, recalling his comments on hearing an academic argue the centrality of evil in his work (2004: 313). This worldview is perhaps why Ravenhill did not want, in Sierz's words, 'to simply update the notion of a pact with the Devil, by substituting a drug dealer or a company executive for Mephistopheles' (2001: 135), setting him up as an all-powerful seducer who draws Faust forward toward debased action. Instead, Ravenhill wanted to explore the possibilities the Faust legend holds 'in a world that has lost the ability to separate good from evil, reality from simulation' (D'Cruz 1999: 187). In *Faust is Dead*, good and evil are no longer clearly distinguished (Sierz 2001: 136; Svich 2003: 85). Instead, the two central characters—Pete, the software developer's son, and Alain, the philosopher (named after the actors who created them, but textually and intertextually referenced to Bill Gates and an 'incongruous amalgam of Foucault, Lacan, Fukuyama and Baudrillard') (D'Cruz 1999: 187; cf. Callens 2003: 63; cf. Rebellato 2001: 36)—both display a postmodern changeability or uncertainty in their subjectivity (Sierz 2001: 136). In effect, Ravenhill's characterizations emphasize and extend the inconsistency already seen in Mephistopheles as he moves from fiend to servant to friend down the ages, and in Faust as he moves from arrogance to altruism and nobility (Durrani 2004: 4, 94–5). According to *Faust is Dead* director Philippou,

> [i]t was important to us to say that being Faust doesn't just mean being tempted ... In a sense, what we were suggesting was that there is great strength in being Faust and great weakness in being Faust, and there is also great strength in being Mephistopheles and great weakness in being Mephistopheles. (2007)

This indeterminacy leads commentators like Sierz (2001: 136) and Svich (2003: 85) to suggest that the notable thing about *Faust is Dead* is that it seems to abandon the devil-follower dyad, or at least complicate it beyond all recognition. Although Ravenhill and Philippou may have had a clear conception while producing the play (Philippou 2007), these critics see it as constructing a narrative in which no single character serves as a Faust figure, and, more importantly, no single character serves as a Mephistopheles. Alain, in particular, oscillates between the two roles. This indeterminacy is critical in setting up the idea that it is not the characters but the world itself that has sold its soul. *Faust is Dead* in fact depicts a whole society that has sold its soul to consumer capitalism, all the characters bearing the cost of the death of God, progress, man, humanity and reality. The text serves, Svich contends, 'as the ultimate comment on the Faustian bargain the world has made for itself in the name of progress ... The Faustian bargain has been made before the play begins; it is the bargain Western culture has inherited' (Svich 2003: 85).

This concern with the consequences of the Western pursuit of progress at all costs made it seem imperative that the play be set in the United States. While workshopping *Faust is Dead*, neither Ravenhill nor Philippou had much experience of the US beyond that which, in their view, all the world has of the cultural and economic changes it has wrought on a global scale (Philippou 2007; Sierz 2001: 137; Urban 2004: 363). Nevertheless, it existed for them, through this influence, as '[t]he great society of progress', bound to the positivist ideals of the Enlightenment, particularly the idea that '[e]verything will get better, and we will understand more, and the more we understand the better we will become as a society' (Philippou 2007). In Philippou's words, this idea was 'kind of profoundly disturbing' (2007). The US existed as a society of extremes—extreme sex, drugs, rock'n'roll, religion, politics and war—and of extreme mediation, an idea encapsulated in Baudrillard's book *America* (1989), which argues that because everything in America is framed, mediated and media manipulated, 'nothing is real' (Philippou 2007). In Baudrillard's theorization, America is not real, it is more real than real—hyperreal—an idea raised again and again in *Faust is Dead*.

According to Ravenhill (2006: 133), this image of the US meant that, from early in his career, the impulse to write about capitalism, globalization and a society completely mediated by images has always been accompanied by the impulse to situate the work in the US, much the way Brecht did when critiquing a previous phase of capitalism via the fugitives, gangsters and corrupt city officials found in plays like *The Resistible Rise of Arturo Ui* or *The Rise and Fall of the City of Mahagonny*. In *Faust is Dead* Ravenhill attempts this with what he has since described as 'mixed results' (2006: 133), feeling, as I will shortly indicate, that this has allowed the United States to circumscribe his narrative, confirming rather than challenging its global dominance.

The first production of *Faust is Dead* developed a sense of the US as a setting for the action, and as a simulated, hyperreal space, by combining sometimes brutal interactions on a dark, claustrophobic set with mediatized images on bodies and screens (Megson 2004: 26). The video art of Alain Pelletier was projected across a television and two L-shaped screens that came together to create a labyrinth with a bed and other furniture, the screens covered with scrims that provided different effects with front and rear projection (Philippou 2007). The projections on these screens included images of talk shows, cyberspace, hotels and desert, interspersed with images of the televised violence of the 1992 Los Angeles riots, which Callens (2003: 63) calls America's political 'unconscious', and images of a chorus of American students recounting '[b]leak, but also very funny' (Ravenhill cit. in Sierz 2001: 137) tales of Los Angeles life.[4] This made the America of Ravenhill's play 'a recognisable world of webcams, mobiles, CCTV, and pagers' (Rebellato 2001: ix). The projections were designed to intensify and multiply the pop cultural references of the piece, rather than further the plot, creating, through the confluence of Ravenhill, Philippou and Pelletier's influences, a sense of the different, more mediated, level of reality referred to in the play (Philippou 2007). Recalling the process, Ravenhill explains that,

> [w]hat I engage with is narrative. But when we all worked together I became excited by the way [multimedia] could be used more thematically. To what extent are we living in a bubble of images and news? So then the use of video seemed to be integral to the whole theme of the piece—then it became exciting. (Ravenhill cit. in Callens 2003: 63)

Ravenhill has recently expressed concern that setting a play in the United States in this way is in some sense dishonest. He admits, 'I can't help feeling that to write plays set in America is to have one's narrative defined by America, however critical the play might be of American globalisation' (2006: 133). Critical reception of the play tends to suggest, however, that while the play is set in America, this is not viewed in the traditional sense of limiting the action (Callens 2003: 64). Rather, as Svich suggests, '*Faust* (*Faust is Dead*) presents California as a virtual Baudrillard-like world whose topography is flattened by transitory experience' (Svich 2003: 85). This flattened topography becomes a core and defining feature of the play.

Set in this flattened, simulated world, the play's plot caricatures the icons of postmodernity. The French postmodernist philosopher Alain has come to America to promote his book *The Death of Man* on the US talk show circuit. Like the historical Faust, Alain is the detached, solitary figure frequently associated with the scientist in Western literature (Haynes 1994: 1)—the dissociated spectator, as Debord might have it. Limited by the academy, and by the academy's attitude to the power of word and act, Alain displays a Faustian desire to escape entrapment in what Hamlin (2002: 123) calls the 'prisonhouse' of learning. After Alain has a falling out with the university's director of studies (Ravenhill 2001: 99), a Faustian desire to experience life more fully drives him to flee both the university and the US chat shows. 'The idea of shaking off academic life and setting off on an adventure became', as Sierz observes, 'one of the play's motifs' (2001: 135). But precisely what Alain wants from this adventure is perhaps less clear in *Faust is Dead* than in previous Faust plays. Alain is not an Enlightenment scholar interested in progress, improvement or the pursuit of knowledge, be it to benefit society or himself. He, in fact, displays a distinctively postmodern disdain for such concepts, and for the grand narrative of man's continued social and scientific progress. For Alain, History, as many human beings have for centuries known it, has ended. Echoing Baudrillard, he declares that Man, humanity and progress are dead, and that human beings have entered an age of simulation (Ravenhill 2001: 117, 132). Alain's is not a situationalist lament over a society losing touch with reality. It is, rather, a recognition that we live in what Baudrillard would call a hyperreal world, in which signs, symbols and simulations have replaced reality (Ravenhill 2001: 133). Though he does want to experience the real world, and escape the restrictions of the university, Alain, like Baudrillard, believes we are only deluding ourselves when we try to posit an original reality beyond the signs, symbols and simulations that populate our world (Callens 2003: 61). This is where Alain differs from many previous Faust figures in important ways. Previous Fausts wanted to break through language, image and mediation to touch life, and Alain, too, has aspirations in this regard. But, paradoxically, Alain's postmodernist stance also leads him to believe language is life. In a society overrun by simulation, the word is in fact the world, and the expression is in fact the event (Ravenhill 2001: 133). This means people have to embrace the chaos of an existence in which God, man, progress, humanity and reality are but empty concepts. Alain suggests, as Baudrillard does in *Fatal Strategies* (1990), that the path beyond suffering and existential despair in a postmodern world is not the opposite of cruelty and suffering; it is the intensification of cruelty and suffering (Ravenhill 2001: 121). Throughout the play he recounts riddles from Baudrillard's *Fatal Strategies* book.[5] He speaks of precisely the sort of absurdly literal attempts at human interaction and seduction, that, for Baudrillard, complicate the relationship between seducer and seduced—a cannibalistic businessman who literally has a woman for dinner, or a seductress who offers her lover the eyes that most arouse him in a bloody little box, for instance (Ravenhill 2001: 98–9, 103–4).

Seeking further examples of cruelty and seduction, Alain sets off on a road trip into the California desert, into the very heart of the America where children born of the twentieth century most belong (Ravenhill 2001: 101). In a bar one night he hooks up with the teenager Pete. Pete, it transpires, is on the run from his software developer dad Bill ('flirtatiously suggested to be the cyberpatriarch Bill Gates' [Rebellato 2001: xiv]), with the only copy of the Chaos program, ready to be released on the market to give the company the lead for centuries to come. The two travel to the vast, desolate space of Death Valley desert, and a concrete reference to Foucault's physical, psychological and philosophical travels during his time in America starts to form a palimpsest over the Faust myth (Philippou 2007). As Ravenhill tells Sierz, '[w]hen Foucault was in the States . . . he drove to Death Valley with a student and they took LSD and had sex' (Ravenhill cit. in Sierz 2001: 135). And that is precisely the scenario that plays out here. What is most apparent in this scenario, though, is the way both remain alienated from the world around them, wittingly or unwittingly finding ways to filter their interaction with this world and with one another— Alain through the lens of his theory, and Pete through the lens of his camcorder and his drugs (cf. Megson 2004: 26). In one scene, for instance, Pete looks through the camcorder, and provides commentary to frame his sexual encounter with Alain, so he does not have to feel it directly (Ravenhill 2001: 116).

The play's commentary on the mediated consumption of sensuality, suffering and cruelty in a postmodern world comes to a head when Alain and Pete meet Donny, the catalyst for the play's climax, via an internet community of self-cutters. The reference to cutting in *Faust is Dead* comes from at least two sources—a Faust play by Lenau first published in 1836, shortly after Goethe's classic, and from a critique of the so-called self-mutilation 'chic' among American teens (Sierz 2001: 135–7).

Philippou, who introduced Ravenhill to Lenau's *Faust* (Sierz 2001: 135), comments on the way in which it went to the core of what he and Ravenhill wanted to explore with the cutting motif in *Faust is Dead*. 'All I remember about Lenau's Faust', he observes, 'is that he begins the piece walking and thinking, and he doesn't do anything, he just thinks' (Philippou 2007). Trapped in his thoughts, Lenau's Faust seeks an authentic experience of the embodied self through a constant dialogue on dissection, stabbing and cutting.

> Lenau says at one point . . . I paraphrase, but something like I wish I could understand what it would feel like to have a knife go in my heart, and of course that experience is mirrored in the play, where kids really want to have that 'true' experience of cutting . . . In a sense the supposition from Lenau, who killed himself, was that the closer you are to death, the closer you are to the only real authentic act any human being can actually experience. Death being the only unmediated, unfiltered experience we could ever have . . . It goes back to something Edward Bond said, that you prove the world real by dying in it. (Philippou 2007)

For Ravenhill and Philippou, Lenau's *Faust* captured the depressive, negativist tradition they wanted to pursue in their *Faust*. It countered the positive glorification of 'humanity' and 'progress' that comes through in other Romantic reincarnations of the legend. Even in Goethe, Philippou (2007) suggests, there is a tendency to place man at the top of the Enlightenment pyramid, achieving something through debased actions that became but a tool in the pursuit of power, knowledge and progress. In *Faust is Dead*, however, the characters pursue death and depravity not as a path to a higher truth, but as a path to the experience of unmediated existence, the debased desires that for philosophers like Foucault may be the most defining elements of man (Philippou 2007). Philippou links this emphasis on the depraved to his memories of Foucault's writing about man's descent into the Labyrinth to meet the Minotaur, only to discover that the Minotaur is a facet of himself that cannot be defeated or destroyed. '[W]e have constantly said to ourselves the more we understand, the more we know, the better as a race we will be', Philippou argues, 'but it has not been true' (Philippou 2007). Instead, 'many of our discoveries really match the image of getting deeper into the Labyrinth, knowing less and less. And the less we know, the more we become true as human beings' (Philippou 2007).

In *Faust is Dead*, this philosophical desire to touch the darker, baser impulses in human beings, to truly understand what it means to be alive in a world where man's primacy can no longer be assured, is laid against the cutting culture of the Los Angeles kids. Donny cuts himself—just as other kids take drugs, drink or diet—because he has grown up in a culture that denies any chance at accessing an unmediated reality. The cutting is, as Rebellato suggests, 'a desperate way of making contact with reality, pain stimulating a body numbed by the delirium of consumer pseudo-choice and mediation on every level' (2001: xvi).

It helps Donny have a sense of who and what he is in the isolating, media-saturated, market-saturated space that is contemporary society.

The pivotal moment of the play comes when Donny comes out of the cyber world to cut himself to death on Alain and Pete's hotel room floor.[6] At this point, Alain's faith in postmodernism's defeat of the real, his desire to embrace chaos, suffering and cruelty, and Pete's faith in the camera as a way to frame rather than feel social and sexual encounters collide violently with Donny's faith in blades and broken bottles as a way to access a pain that is truly real. Alain talks, thinks and philosophizes, but his fashionably postmodernist stance leaves him with no power to act in a situation where, as Pete puts it, '[r]eality just arrived' (Ravenhill 2001: 132). All he can do is talk. He cannot do anything for Donny, who, for Ravenhill, represents the victim, the 'poor bastard' (Ravenhill cit. in Sierz 2001:136) whose real-life suffering complicates the intellectual puzzles with which academics like Alain concern themselves.

What the play shows, in this moment, is '[t]he breathtaking abdication of responsibility these ideas entail' (Rebellato 2001: xv). The Faustian impulse in Alain means he is fascinated by the cutting, and the celebratory intensification of cruelty it involves. But he immediately brings the physical act of cutting back into a conceptual terrain (Sierz 2001: 137), intellectualizing it as a form of control, a form of self-creation (Ravenhill 2001: 124). He ignores Pete's derisive counter that Donny is simply an emotionally scarred teenager who slashes his body to exteriorize his psychic pain (Ravenhill 2001: 124). When the logical climax of this cutting ritual comes, all Alain can do is frame it, mediate it, strip it of its reality. 'Alain discourses with the utmost seriousness about the death of reality, while Donny lies at his feet, really dying', as Rebellato puts it (2001: xv). In this respect, Donny's death becomes but one more Baudrillardian fatal strategy for Alain's collection. He reads it as an affirmation of his philosophy, rather than dealing with it. He takes the spectatorial position again, intellectualizing the act, turning it into precisely the abstract, symbolic idea he had (at least in part, if paradoxically) sought to escape on his adventure in America.

The play's climax means that, like previous Fausts, the characters—and, perhaps, the audience—start to feel the consequences of pushing the different forms of 'knowledge' Alain, Pete and Donny prefer to their limits in an effort to engage the real in a postmodern world. But this flirtation with the real is brief. The play ends with another absurdly literal gesture of 'blind folly' as Pete visits Alain, whom he has shot, in hospital, to offer him Donny's eyes as a parting gift before rejoining his father.

The Faustian Thematic in *Faust is Dead*

Ravenhill's *Faust is Dead* is one of many adaptations of the Faust thematic for the twentieth-century stage. There has, in fact, been what Osman Durrani describes as 'an explosion of Faust-derivatives' (2004: 220).[7] Goethe's *Faust* remains the touchstone for some theatre-makers. Over 12,000 lines in length, the play has had two extensive productions—the first was Rudolf and Marie Steiner's (which started rehearsals in 1913), the second Peter Stein's for the Hanover Expo in 2000 (Fischer-Lichte 2001: 488; Hamlin 2002: 118; Durrani

2004: 208). There have also been several other lengthy productions, including Max Reinhardt's productions for the revolving stage in Berlin in 1909 and 1911, Gustaf Gründgens' production in Hamburg in 1958 and Claus Peymann's production in Stuttgart in 1977 (Hamlin 2002: 118). The adaptations, readaptations and recontextualizations of the tale have, however, been far more numerous. The temptation to adapt the Faust tale is perhaps not surprising if we follow the transitions from the *Historia von D. Johann Fausten* to Marlowe's *The Tragical History of Doctor Faustus* to Goethe's *Faust* and beyond. It is clear that every age finds its own relevance in the Faust tale. There is a constant shift in emphasis, which, according to Ravenhill, has less to do with a search for eternal verities than with an exploration of the way in which we change as our world changes.

> Why do some stories—Oedipus, Hamlet, Don Juan, Faust—
> seem to have a hold on generation after generation?
>
> Some would say 'Ah, that's the eternal verities, the never
> changing essential truths of human nature'.
>
> And I would say: 'Bollocks'.
>
> What I think is fascinating about human beings is the way
> our whole identity changes as we change, and are in turn
> changed by society and the economy we create.
> (Ravenhill cit. in D'Cruz 1999: 187)

Goethe's *Faust* is already grounded in the fascination/frustration with words, images and ideas, and their power to mediate reality, which will reappear in Ravenhill's play nearly two centuries later. Goethe's Faust wants, as Westfall (2004: 52) argues, to get beyond the books and words that trap him. Unwilling to grant the word 'such high worth' (*F*, 1226, cit. in Westfall 2004: 52), Faust wants to get to the deeds, the acts, that will allow him to know all reality at once—'the intellect, the emotions, and transcendent experience' (Haynes 1994: 78). It is this passionate desire to transcend the impoverished reality of the word that allows him to reconcile his depraved actions. It is a theme pursued, and further complicated, in Ravenhill's postmodern rendering. The Faustian impulse in Alain does lead him past the word to the act, the deed, the adventure. But, paradoxically, his postmodern stance means he also believes the word is the deed, with a 'worth' all its own in a media-simulated world, meaning it no longer needs to reference the pale shadow of a 'real-er' reality beyond itself. It is this paradox that is, as I have suggested, a critical progression in Ravenhill's construction of a late-twentieth-century Faust.

Also interesting is the fact that Goethe's Faust's desire to transcend the impoverished reality of the word is reflected in the theatrical structure of Goethe's play, as it is in postmodern adaptations like Ravenhill's. As many critics have noted, Goethe's *Faust* is deeply bound up in the politics of representation both thematically and theatrically. The play's theme captured the imagination of Romantic audiences, but its theatrical structure seemed undramatic and unstageable to many commentators well into the twentieth century. '*Faust*, if it is a drama, is scarcely a stage-drama', as Barker Fairley (1953: 2) puts it in one fairly representative reading. The short scenes, disjunctive transitions and social satire of *Faust I* were already a challenge to theatrical conventions of the day

(Hamlin 2002: 117; Fischer-Lichte 2001: 488). But the vast leaps across space, time and context in *Faust II*, combined with its 'ragout' (Hamlin 2002: 120) of theatrical styles, landscapes and characters, and its complex intertextuality, completely defied theatrical convention (Durrani 2004: 142). The characters, including Faust, were based on symbol or impulse, functioning as personifications of philosophic themes (Fairley 1953: 8, 13, 31–2). The desire for knowledge faded as Faust traveled time, space and history surrounded by a deceptive cascade of characters and images, dying at the mercy of his delusions while Mephistopheles was denied his prize (Durrani 2004: 142, 151–2).[8]

Though nineteenth-century critics struggled with the theatricalization of *Faust*'s themes—the fragmentation, the experimentation and the exploitation of all the resources of the theatre at a time before technological mediation was available—contemporary practitioners revel in it (Hamlin 2002: 118). For them, Hamlin contends, '*Faust* in its entirety proves to be theatrical through and through' (2002: 118). And it is these theatrical qualities that capture and concretize the play's central conflict and metaphysical crisis. This is why many of the most compelling contemporary interpretations continue the formal experimentation. Like Ravenhill's in-yer-face interpretation, they juxtapose plots, theatrical forms, images and intertextual references to literalize the issues central to the Faust thematic in their staging.

Ravenhill's *Faust is Dead* does this primarily through a sparse plot, intertextuality, intermediality and what the creators saw as a switching between linguistic, imagistic and embodied layers of reality in the staging of the piece. They tried, Philippou argues, to dramatize the difficulty of moving between intellectual and embodied terrains in an extremely mediated reality by separating the two in the staging.

> [T]here were points at which the characters spoke and there were points at which they did, and it was important to keep those two things separate. And in a sense that is what we wanted the audience to see.[9] We wanted the audience to see this talking head, which is how the piece begins, and then we wanted them to witness the death of the body at the end. And in a sense, that was Foucault's quest, as it is Faust's quest. To get into his body. (Philippou 2007)

As I have suggested, Ravenhill's *Faust is Dead* is not alone in using these sorts of strategies to construct a late twentieth-century Faust. It sits in the context of several landmark recontextualizations of the Faust tale by contemporary theatre-makers worth mentioning here. Ariane Mnouchkine's *Mephisto* (1979), for instance, combines a retelling of Klaus Mann's controversial novel with Gustaf Gründgens' Nazi production of *Faust* (Durrani 2004: 176). It also counterposes two stages, played in conventional realist and physical styles, to reveal how these styles were implicated in the contrasting political ideologies of communism and fascism.[10] Elizabeth LeCompte's *House/Lights* for The Wooster Group (1998) also constructs a highly intertextual take on the Faust tale, counterposing Gertrude Stein's representation of Faust as polymath, alchemist and misogynist in *Dr Faustus Lights the Lights* with the plot of a B movie, Joseph Mawra's *Olga's House of Shame* (1964), in order to draw attention to the representation of women (Gendrich 1998: 380–2). Gustav Ernst's *Faust*, staged in tandem with the Het Theatre Festival (1995), sets the Faust tale against a backdrop of contemporary atrocities (McKernie 1996: 232–3). Faust is a crude, scatological performance artist, undulating naked before news images of suffering, cruelty and violence, taunting spectators. Realizing his shows lack real-life impact, he is led by Mephisto to commit actual atrocities, including cannibalizing his child with Somali refugee Gretje (McKernie 1996: 233). This Faust challenges us, Grant McKernie argues, to think about 'our own complicity with the violence of contemporary society' (233). *F@usto: Version 3.0* (1998), Pablo Ley's adaptation for the Spanish company La Fura dels Baus, is similarly extreme in its depiction of the violence of the postmodern world (Baker 1998: 511). Here, Faust is a middle-aged Catalan whose violent sexual and intellectual awakening is played against lurid projections of cyberspace, splatterpunk, soft porn and kinky relationships on a metal screen at the rear of the stage. In *F@usto: Version 3.0*, Kit Baker claims, the characters become 'ciphers', 'extension[s] of Faust's private cyberspace' (Baker 1998: 511–12), manipulated and violated in a way that amplifies the sexual subtexts of Goethe's *Faust*, stressing the duality of self in its unstable juxtaposition of Faust and Mephisto, live and virtual, sensual and cruel.[11]

These productions all deal with suffering, sexualized violence and oppressions of one sort or another, whether it is Nazis, the prostitution of women or the internet. They speak to our power to intervene in a world with its priorities out of whack. They try to get beyond the prisonhouse of representations, beyond the words, images and ideas that mediate reality, and really do something. And Goethe's legacy of unconventional theatricality and cipher-like characters informs the intertextual, intermedial ways in which they choose to stage Faust's debased acts in the pursuit of knowledge, power and worldly impact.

Each of these productions could be argued to have a point of difference that contributes to contemporization of the Faust thematic toward the end of the twentieth century in important ways. The point of difference with Ravenhill's *Faust is Dead* is, of course, the particular set of frames it uses to fragment, intensify and formally concretize the thematic terrain. Ravenhill's frames focus not just on debased acts, or on pop cultural representations of debased acts, but on the philosophers who, in his opinion, romanticize the power of these debased acts as responses to contemporary realities.

Undoubtedly, it is the philosophical frames and referents that give Ravenhill's *Faust is Dead* much of its power. It is important to recognize, though, that for all these frames and referents, *Faust is Dead* does not function as an enactment, or a critical staging, of poststructuralist philosophy (D'Cruz 1999: 188). It is an incongruous text, seemingly based more on memories of engagement with poststructuralist philosophy, or moments of excitement while engaging with poststructuralist philosophy, than on a consistent critical reading of it. It glosses the complex relationship between Baudrillard's and Foucault's theories. Baudrillard, after all, wrote a book called *Forget Foucault* (1988) in which he deconstructs or reverses Foucault's own discourse on sexuality, power, production and repression, suggesting Foucault's ideas should not be ascribed truth value on their seductive force alone. It also glosses Baudrillard's complex relationship with the situationalist movement. And there is a slide between Foucault's writing and Foucault as writer that might trouble those with an interest in Foucault's theories about the Western need to construct author figures for specific sets of ideas. What, then, is the value of the play in the face of these incongruities in its representation of the postmodern philosopher as Faust figure?

The value comes, I think, from recognition that the play is not enacting philosophy so much as engaging a particular cultural moment via the philosophy so characteristic of it, and via the Faust myth, as carriers of textual and intertextual meaning. The incongruous philosophical referents make sense because they serve the critique of a self-indulgent, individualistic society that Ravenhill attempts with so much of his work.

The theatrical and theoretical foundations of *Faust is Dead* leave it in a typically precarious position in relation to Ravenhill's critical project—the critique of postmodern culture's fascination with consumerism and violence, and its denial of a fundamental reality beyond the constructed world. On the one hand, the content of *Faust is Dead* does leave it open to the charge of an empty reverence of cruelty sometimes leveled at in-yer-face theatre—the suggestion that this sort of theatre, like the philosopher Alain, romanticizes violence and cruelty without recognizing the real-life suffering going on all around it. This reading fits with Ravenhill's 'reputation amongst some critics as a theatrical *enfant terrible* purveying a sexually explicit, sensationalist, shock-loaded drama' (Rebellato 2001: x). On the other hand, the critical readings of *Faust is Dead* I have referred to in this chapter all argue that the shock factor should not be allowed to conceal the play's critical force. Spectators should not, Rebellato suggests, let the plethora of recognizably postmodern slogans and posturings they see in a play like *Faust is Dead* conceal 'the fact that Ravenhill's use of their ideas is fiercely sceptical' (Rebellato 2001: xiv). Ravenhill applies in-yer-face theatre conventions—including the pastiche of pop cultural references, the unexpected content and consequences of their interactions and the absurd forms of dismemberment and death the characters describe, encounter or create in the course of their search for 'real' in a mediated world—with an alienatory intent characteristic of his work. This satirical, alienatory dimension means Ravenhill is not advocating the dissociation we see in Alain in *Faust is Dead* any more than he is advocating the horrific acts we see in some of his other plays (Ravenhill 2004: 313). Ravenhill is, rather, constructing his own version of a Brechtian 'Verfremdungseffekt', the cruelty and suffering designed to make people think.[12] Read this way, Ravenhill is writing against the tendency of philosophers like Alain to gloss over issues of responsibility, agency and the human cost of cruelty and violence (Callens 2003: 74). He is writing against the tendency to give way to moral relativism (Ravenhill 2004: 313; Sierz 2001: 151). He remarks,

> [c]ertainly I've always written against moral relativism. I want audiences to make moral choices: to decide moment by moment—intellectually and emotionally—whether what the characters are doing and the choices they are making are right or wrong. I find this dramatic. It makes good theatre. A constant shift, dialectic, between empathy and judgment, sympathy and criticism, makes for a rich evening. To write against our ironic, easygoing times, where any hierarchy of values has melted away. (Ravenhill 2004: 313)

What Ravenhill's *Faust is Dead* wants to challenge, according to commentators like Rebellato (2001) and Sierz (2001), is the philosophical problematization of a core reality which—for all that it has political valence when it comes to shifting gender and racial stereotypes—can leave us without concern for the real personal and social consequences of the constructed world we share. 'For Ravenhill', Sierz puts it, 'philosophy's retreat from social responsibility is deeply reactionary. His play dramatizes the "meeting of somebody with a very chic notion of violence with people for whom violence is real'" (Sierz 2001: 135). He wants spectators to work, moment by moment, to make moral choices about what these people do. So, while there is a shock factor at play in *Faust is Dead*, there is also a set of choices for spectators to consider, choices that come primarily from what commentators who have discussed the work to date see as the possibility of redemption for the philosopher in the play's climax. According to Sierz, 'Ravenhill's feeling was that "the international capitalist is irredeemable, but the academic, if he connects with reality," can find redemption' (2001: 137). In other words, the academic, if he can react to the reassertion of the real that comes in the climatic moment of the play, can achieve what Callens calls 'a renewed social agency amidst the rampant simulation' (2003: 64). This interpretation of the play comes full circle back to situationalism, to lament the loss of agency, subjectivity and reality. It suggests that redemption for Alain lies in the possibility of returning from the distanced, scientific, 'spectatorial' position—the Faustian position—to touch base with the real. It is an interpretation commentators like Sierz (2001) favor, but, as I will shortly suggest, for me a bit too firmly delineated in its reading of the play. Yes, redemption for Alain does lie in the possibility of a return to the real. But, because the play's philosophical discourse also makes it apparent that there is no true reality for Alain to come back to, no true comfort in accessing the absurd reality of Donny's death, the choice for spectators also remains unclear, unresolved. The bleak ending means the death of reality is no longer lauded. But the return of reality is not really lauded either. The spectator is, in this sense, left without a firm position from which to read and react to the possibility of redemption raised in the play.

Commentators who focus their analysis primarily on the possibility of redemption for the philosopher in *Faust is Dead* talk about an almost classical moralism in the play, connected to what they see as a leftist sentimentality in all of Ravenhill's writings (Svich 2003: 82). 'Ravenhill is profoundly moral in his portraiture of contemporary society', Rebellato observes. 'His vision is elliptically but recognisably social, even socialist' (Rebellato 2001: x). 'His motive is always moral, his politics leftist', Sierz concurs (2001: 151). For these critics, Ravenhill's *Faust is Dead* is trying to remind spectators that humans are social beings, and that we should not allow the shallow consumer culture that surrounds us to conceal our need for social interaction (Svich 2003: 82; Rebellato 2001: xviii). Read this way, Ravenhill's *Faust is Dead* is not showing the consequences of a shallow, spectatorial connection with life for a single person. Instead, it shifts the Faustian dilemma to society as a whole, creating a critical take that cannot be dismissed as one man's folly.

That this redemptive reading of *Faust is Dead* prevails among the commentators who have so far considered the work makes it difficult to ignore. Certainly, *Faust is Dead* does shift the Faustian dilemma to society as a whole, and does agitate for a less individualist, isolationist approach to social life, and this is one of its strengths. But my own analysis suggests that commentaries that stop here may be delineating the moral position in *Faust is Dead* too cleanly. After all, Alain in *Faust is Dead* misses his moment. He does not find redemption, only the blind folly of that final fatal strategy, the gift of Donny's eyes. And there is little sense that it could or should have been different. So, as I have argued, while the play does advocate pulling back from the isolated, spectatorial position, it does not necessarily suggest a return to the real is possible, a solution of which any poststructuralist commentator on the play might rightly be suspicious. What is interesting about *Faust is Dead* is, in fact, the irresolvability. Alain needs to pull back from the Faustian position to find the human bonds lost to him in his hyperreal world. But, at the same time, Alain was right when his postmodern stance led him to suggest that it is implausible, impossible, to return to the real in this way. With Pete gone, Alain is left on his own, with only the pathetic figure of the dead, eyeless Donny for comfort. The (im)possibility of a comforting return to the real for Alain makes the alienatory force of *Faust is Dead* more unstable than some commentators suggest. *Faust is Dead* does not necessarily open up a clear set of alternatives, a coherent moral line, to the degree that Brecht or Bond might have done (Philippou 2007). It can, in fact, be taken as an unresolved reading of the Faustian impulse in contemporary society, which highlights Alain's at times simplistic mode of engagement with the 'simulated' world without cleansing him of it, solving it or ending it. Dead, but not dead, Alain as a late-twentieth-century Faust figure continues to problematize the complex range of ideas in play in the Faust thematic.

Conclusion

In *Faust is Dead*, the desire to disrupt moral orthodoxies that characterizes Faust tales down the centuries is drawn together with the desire to disrupt moral and theatrical orthodoxies in in-yer-face theatre. The Faust tale is played out against a landscape of textual and intertextual references to philosophy, pop culture and the shallow, self-indulgent consumer culture of the late twentieth century—the new orthodoxies of the postmodern world. The twin legacies provide a context for Ravenhill's examination of the Faustian thinker's efforts to get past the rampant simulation to something real, while at the same time, paradoxically, finding power in the simulation itself.

It is fair to say that *Faust is Dead* has not been the most noted, popular or produced of Ravenhill's plays (cf. Ravenhill cit. in Sierz 2001: 138). Moreover, some critics thought it could have gone further with its critique of power, sexuality and stereotypical identity categories, particularly in the dramaturgical structure and staging (D'Cruz 1999: 188). After all, the play does, but at the same time manifestly does not, get past the orthodoxies of the modern Western world.

Even if *Faust is Dead* is not a great play, though, the problems spectators face in forming a pointed, productive, resolved reading of it only make it more intriguing as a twentieth-century consumer culture mobilization of the Faust thematic. It consolidates Ravenhill's reputation for social critique, for rallying against the rampant simulation and the self-indulgent individualism that stunt people's capacity to engage their world at intuitive, emotional and intellectual levels, as much as Faust's narrow-minded academy ever did. It shows how Ravenhill shifts the Faustian dilemma to modern society as a whole, as Alain, Pete and Donny all find themselves in a fraught relation both to the simulations and to the suspected reality beyond them. The play, it turns out, fails to provide a path past this crisis of the 'real' postmodern culture. Instead of providing philosophical redemption, it prompts spectators to think about the ways in which this crisis is manifested, the stakes, and about the permutations of their own impossible cravings for contact with the real in a media-saturated world.

Notes

1. For a fuller analysis of the way Ravenhill's *Faust is Dead* is linked to the situationalist legacy in British theatre see Megson (2004).
2. I reference my analysis to the published playtext, which differs from the first production in some of its details, including the inclusion of the character Donny in person as well as in the cyberworld in a way that was not possible in the first production (cf. Sierz 2001: 136).
3. According to Philippou (2007), 'a riff on Beckett', as well as a reference to the relationship between thought and body.
4. Live actors were used in a later Los Angeles production of *Faust is Dead* (Sierz 2001: 137).
5. "'I read a lot'" while writing the play, Ravenhill says, "'starting with the *Baudrillard for Beginners* book'" (Ravenhill cit. in Sierz 2001: 135).
6. An important difference between the first production and the published playtext. In an interview with Sierz, Ravenhill indicates the issue that drove him to include Donny in the flesh in the published playtext. "'Because Donny only appears on video [in the first production], you don't really connect with him, so audiences missed the fact that he's the real victim," says Ravenhill. "By the end of the play's London run, I thought that Donny was the most important character'" (Sierz 2001: 136).
7. Durrani's *Faust* (2004) does an impressive job of the 'well-nigh impossible task' (4) of tracing Faust's influence down the centuries in books, music, plays, films and other media.
8. Anticipating the reaction of critics and audiences of his day, and the difficulty they would have staging *Faust II*, Goethe did not publish it during his lifetime (Fischer-Lichte 2001: 488; Durrani 2004: 153).
9. This switching between the dialogue and the physical dimension of the piece was not necessarily perceived by spectators, at least one suggesting that '[g]iven its subject matter, [*Faust is Dead*] is an unexpectedly wordy, conventional two-hander, which relies on naturalistic dialogue to illustrate its "theory"' (D'Cruz 1999:187).
10. The play was later translated into English by Timberlake Wertenbaker and performed by Tim Robbins' The Actor's Gang in 2001 (Case 2002: 298–9).
11. Isidro Ortiz and La Fura dels Baus later collaborated on *Fausto 5.0*, a dystopic horror film in which Dr Faust, at a conference to speak on terminal medicine, is drawn into the city's fetid underworld (cf. Durrani 2004: 8).
12. On the whole, Ravenhill's is a Brechtian approach, compared to the Artaudian approach characteristic of other in-yer-face writers like Sarah Kane (Philippou 2007).

Bibliography

Baker, K. (1998), 'Review—*F@usto: Version 3.0*', *Theatre Journal*, 50, (4), 511–13.
Baudrillard, J. (1988), *Forget Foucault*, N. Dufresne (trans.). New York: Semiotext(e).
— (1989), *America*, C. Turner (trans.). London: Verso.
— (1990), *Fatal Strategies: Crystal Revenge*, P. Beitchman and W. G. J. Niesluchowski (trans.). New York: Semiotext(e).
Callens, J. (2003), 'Staging the televised (nation)', *Theatre Research International*, 28, (1), 61–78.

Case, S. (2002), 'Review—*Mephisto*', *Theatre Journal*, 54, (2), 298–9.
D'Cruz, G. (1999), 'Theory, theatre and the West (End): Or talking to the tax man about theatre', in R. Fensham and P. Eckersall (eds), *Dis/orientations: Cultural Praxis in Theatre: Asia, Pacific, Australia*. Melbourne: Monash University, pp. 175–94.
Debord, G. (1994), *The Society of the Spectacle*, D. Nicholson-Smith (trans.). New York: Zone Books.
Durrani, O. (2004), *Faust: Icon of Modern Culture*. East Sussex: Helm.
Fairley, B. (1953), *Goethe's Faust: Six Essays*. Oxford: Clarendon Press.
Fischer-Lichte, E. (2001), 'Review—*Faust I und II*', *Theatre Journal*, 53, (3), 488–9.
Foster, H. (1985), 'For a concept of the political in contemporary art', in H. Foster (ed.). *Recodings: Art, Spectacle, Cultural Politics*. Port Townsend: Bay Press, pp. 139–55.
Gendrich, C. (1998), 'Review—*House/Lights*', *Theatre Journal*, 50, (3), 380–2.
Goethe, J.W. (1976), *Faust I and II*, C. Hamlin (ed.), W. Arndt (trans.). New York: Norton.
Hamlin, C. (2002), 'Faust in performance: Peter Stein's production of Goethe's *Faust*, Parts 1 and 2', *Theater*, 32, (1), 117–36.
Haynes, R. (1994), *From Faust to Strangelove: Representations of the Scientist in Western Literature*. Baltimore and London: The Johns Hopkins University Press.
McKernie, G. (1996), 'Review—Het Theatre Festival', *Theatre Journal*, 48, (2), 232–4.
Megson, C. (2004), '"The spectacle is everywhere": Tracing the situationalist legacy in British playwriting since 1968', *Contemporary Theatre Review*, 14, (2), 17–28.
Philippou, N. (2007), Telephone interview, 25 May and 22 June.
Ravenhill, M. (2001), '*Faust (Faust is Dead)*', in *Mark Ravenhill, Plays: One*. London: Methuen, pp. 93–140.
— (2004), 'A tear in the fabric: The James Bulger murder and new theatre writing in the "nineties"', *New Theatre Quarterly*, 20, 305–14.
— (2006), 'Me, my iBook, and writing in America', *Contemporary Theatre Review*, 16, (1), 131–8.
Rebellato, D. (2001), 'Introduction', in *Mark Ravenhill, Plays: One*. London: Methuen, pp. ix–xx.
Sierz, A. (2001), *In-Yer-Face Theatre: British Drama Today*. London: Faber and Faber.
Svich, C. (2003), 'Commerce and morality in the theatre of Mark Ravenhill', *Contemporary Theatre Review*, 13, (1), 81–95.
Urban, K. (2004), 'Towards a theory of Cruel Britannica: Coolness, cruelty and the "nineties"', *New Theatre Quarterly*, 20, (4), 354–72.
Westfall, J. (2004), 'Zarathustra's Germanity: Luther, Goethe, Nietzsche', *Journal of Nietzsche Studies*, 27, 42–63.

Index

absolutism 74, 75
absurdism 187
Abū Hadīd, Muhammad Farīd, *Abd al-Shaytān* (*The Slave of the Devil*) 150–1
Abyssinia 254
Academy of Motion Picture Arts and Sciences, Award nomination 219
accompaniment, orchestral 65, 239
Achilles 26
acoustics 55, 56, 57, 66
acrobatics 190
acting 185, 187, 189, 193
action 18, 23, 37, 43, 44, 47, 49, 50, 62, 70, 71, 72, 78, 82, 89, 91, 95, 118, 130, 135, 138, 149, 150, 152, 188, 190, 191, 192, 194, 195, 196, 226, 247, 252, 255, 261, 262, 264, 266, 267, 268
activism 179, 186
adaptation
  Faust theme:
    Arabic 149, 150–3
    Chinese 149, 155, 157, 177–201
    Dutch 269–70
    English 107–23, 126, 132, 133, 161, 178, 205–15, 216–17, 218–24, 227, 228, 238, 253, 259–75
    'fidelity' 126, 188, 191, 193, 224
    French 206, 217, 224, 253, 259, 269
    German 37, 65–6, 178, 217, 224–6, 228, 239–40, 244, 247–8, 251, 266, 268, 269
    Italian 66, 222, 224, 231–43

    Japanese 149, 155–7, 158, 189
    Malayalam 154–5, 161–76
    Portuguese 244–5, 248–52, 256
    Russian 205, 253
    sound effects 55, 65–6
    Spanish 259, 270
    see also Faust Books; legend; Marlowe, Christopher, *Doctor Faustus*; Goethe, Johann Wolfgang von, *Faust, ein Fragment, Faust. Eine Tragödie* and *Urfaust*; puppet theatre *see* Beckett, Samuel; Brecht, Bertolt; Büchner, Georg; China; Goethe, Johann Wolfgang von, *Die Leiden des jungen Werthers* and *Wilhelm Meisters Lehrjahre*; Ibsen, Henrik; Shakespeare, William
aegis 208, 210
Aesculapius 213–14
Africa 23, 186, 244, 245, 248, 252, 253, 254, 255, 256
  African National Congress 252
aging 107
Ahriman 151
aircraft 192
Alberich 209
alchemy 58–9, 209, 212, 269
Alexander the Great 17–35
  'Epistola Alexandri ad Aristotelem' ('Letter to Aristotle') 18
Al-Hakīm, Tawfīq
  'Ahd al-Shaytān' ('Era of the Devil') 151
  'Imra'at ghalibat al-Shaytān' ('The Woman Who Beat the Devil') 152

Index

alienation 74, 114, 117, 209, 235, 260
  'Verfremdungseffekt' 65, 66, 187, 233, 271
allegory 23, 44, 45, 58, 62, 71, 100, 127
Alps 249
alter ego 46, 95
altruism 263
Amadis 23
Amazons 18
ambiguity 113, 116, 119, 150
ambition 17, 18, 19, 21, 23, 26, 27, 28, 29, 71, 76, 218, 222, 227
ambivalence 111
Ambros, Wolfgang, *Fäustling: Spiel in G (Fäustling: Play in G)* 217, 226
Amida 156
amnesia 245, 253
amnesty 255
Amsterdam, Het Theatre Festival 269
ancien régime 66
Andersen, Hans Christian 241
androgyny 219
Anezaki, Masaharu 156
angel 24, 38, 56, 57, 58, 88, 89, 90, 91, 96, 97, 98, 115, 150, 152, 165, 168, 169, 170, 171, 173, 174, 205, 206, 207, 210, 211, 212, 213, 218, 222, 227, 247
animation 254
anonymity 28, 90, 97, 100, 124, 125, 126, 127, 131, 137, 138, 181
Anster, John 124, 133
anthem 239
anthropology 207, 212
apartheid 244, 252, 254, 255
Aphrodite 195
Apollo
  god 166
  spaceship 196
apotheosis 173, 227
appropriation 56, 79, 211, 225, 256
architectonics 73, 75, 80
architecture 73, 80
Ariosto, Ludovico, *Orlando furioso* 233, 234
Aristophanes 40
Aristotle 18, 19, 57, 60
Arrian 18, 22, 24
  Anabasis Alexandri (Anabasis of Alexander) 18
  Indica 18

art 79, 80, 153, 231, 264
  Chinese 192
  classical 63
Artaud, Antonin 190, 260
Arthur 23
artificial intelligence 205
ascension 115
asceticism 22
Asia 19, 149–60, 161–76, 177–201, 248
astronomy 111
  Ptolemaic 56
atheism 158
Athene 208
attraction, sexual 93
audibility 57
Auschwitz 81 (n.1)
Austria 217
autobiography 37, 63, 90, 99, 168
automaton 67 (n.16)
avant-garde 65, 184, 186, 187, 194, 195, 232, 262
avatar 162
Azazel 211, 212

Baader, Franz von 58
Babylon 28, 89
Bacon, Francis, *Novum Organum (The New Organon)* 23
Bahia 244, 245, 250, 251, 252
ballet 163
Bancroft, George 133
Barcelona, La Fura dels Baus 259, 270
Bar Mitzvah 252
Baroque 48, 247, 249
bathos 109, 110, 119, 120, 121
Baudrillard, Jean 250, 262, 263, 264, 265, 267, 270
  Amérique (America) 263
  Oublier Foucault (Forget Foucault) 270
  Les Stratégies fatales (Fatal Strategies) 265
The Beatles 216, 218
beauty 26, 39, 58, 60, 89, 111, 115, 118, 127, 137, 138, 152, 157, 164, 169, 172, 173, 193, 195
Becker, Ernest, *The Denial of Death* 207
Beckett, Samuel, *En attendant Godot (Waiting for Godot)* 186, 187, 188, 194, 195

Beijing
  Bayi Film Studio 185
  Beijing People's Art Theatre 183–4, 185, 194, 196
  Central Academy of Drama 183, 184, 185, 190, 194
  National Experimental Theatre 183, 184, 189, 190, 194, 195, 196
  see also opera
benediction 89
Bennewitz, Fritz 161, 168
Berg, Alban, *Wozzeck* 240
Berio, Luciano 231
Berlin 268
  Academy 59
  Berliner Ensemble 251
  House of World Cultures 194
Berlioz, Hector 224
Berman, Marshall 70
Bhagavad Gita 154, 165
Bible
  Abel 113, 114
  Adam 60, 89, 112
  Beelzebub 165, 166
  Cain 100, 111–15
  Eden 60, 93
  Eve 89, 112, 211
  Genesis 40, 55–6, 58, 93, 113
  Isaiah 89
  Job 38, 88, 89, 91, 98, 100, 115, 116, 130, 212
  John 56, 63
  Mary Magdalen 208
  Matthew 130, 131
  Satan 20, 38, 64, 88, 89, 90, 91, 93, 96, 97, 100, 108, 110, 112, 115, 116, 117, 118, 150, 152, 165, 167, 211
  Virgin Mary 49
  Yahweh 56, 88
bicycle 226
Biedermann, Woldemar Freiherr von 155
Big Bang theory 56
biographical criticism 108, 168
biography 18, 88, 89, 91, 92, 168
  saint's 17
biopic 262
Birmingham, University 194
Black Mass 96
Blair, Tony 260

blank verse 124, 125, 126, 128, 129, 132, 133, 135, 136
Boal, Augusto 250
Böhme, Jakob 56
Bohte, Johann Heinrich 124, 125, 126, 131, 133, 134, 138
Boileau, Daniel 124, 131, 132
Boito, Arrigo, *Mefistofele* 222, 224
Bond, Edward 260, 266, 273
Boosey, Thomas 124, 125, 126, 131, 132, 135, 136, 138
Bose, Santanu 161
Boshin War 179
bowdlerization 43
Bowie, David 226
Brahma 153, 162, 171
brand piracy 194
Braunschweig 65
Brazil 244, 245, 250, 251, 252
Brecht, Bertolt 65, 156, 185, 187, 189, 190, 191, 233, 245, 250, 251, 260, 263, 271, 273
  Der aufhaltsame Aufstieg des Arturo Ui (*The Resistible Rise of Arturo Ui*) 263
  Aufstieg und Fall der Stadt Mahagonny (*The Rise and Fall of the City of Mahagonny*) 263
  epic theatre 187, 245, 255
  Der gute Mensch von Sezuan (*The Good Person of Szechwan*) 187
  Leben des Galilei (*Galileo Galilei*) 187
  Urfaust 251
Brion, Friederike 109
Brook, Peter 260
Büchner, Georg 250
  Woyzeck 194, 240, 245
Buddhism 188
  Mahayana 155, 157
    Pure Land Sect 156–7
budget, production 190
buffoonery 43
Bulgakov, Mikhail, *Master i Margarita* (*The Master and Margarita*) 205, 253
Bunraku 253
bureaucrat 196
Burgess, Anthony 206
Burke, Edmund 63
burlesque 97, 98, 121, 235
Burney, James 135

Byron, Lord 107–23, 135
  Cain 111–15
  The Deformed Transformed 121
  Don Juan 107, 108, 111, 118, 119, 121, 122
  Manfred 108–11, 121, 129
  The Vision of Judgment 115, 118, 120, 135
  Werner 107

Caesar, Julius 17, 23
caesura 80
Cairo 150
Calderón de la Barca, Pedro 37
Calgary, Loose Moose Theatre 220
California 264, 265
calligraphy 192
Calvinism 30 (n.18)
Campbell, Thomas 127, 128
Canada 205, 220
Candomblé 251
cannibalism 265, 270
canon 154, 161, 174, 211
Cao, Xueqin (曹雪芹)
  Hong lou meng (红楼梦) (*The Dream of the Red Chamber*) 181
    Bao Yu, Faust comparison 181
Cao, Yu (曹寓) 183
Cape Town 248
capitalism 74, 178, 179, 260, 261, 262, 263, 271, 272, 273
caricature 264
Carlyle, Thomas 128, 129, 136, 137
  Life of Schiller 128
  Wilhelm Meister 128
carnality 207
carnival 40, 96, 249
Caroline, Queen, divorce 133
Carthaginians 19
Catalan 270
Catholicism
  iconography 98, 99
  liturgy 61
  see also Christianity
cellular phone 226
Cervantes, Miguel de, *Don Quixote* 108, 153
Césaire, Aimé, *Une Tempête* (*A Tempest*) 245
Chaos 92
chapbook *see* Faust Books

Charles V, Emperor 20, 21
Chekhov, Anton 186
Chicago 223
China 149, 155, 157, 158, 159, 177, 178, 179, 180, 181, 182, 183, 184, 185, 186, 187, 188, 189, 190, 191, 192, 193, 194, 195, 197
  Maoist aesthetics 184–5
    politics 184, 186
  theatre 180, 182–97
    adaptation 179, 180, 182, 184, 186, 187, 188, 195
    musicality 184, 187
    spoken drama 183, 184, 186, 187, 189, 190, 191, 196
    'xieyi' ('essential ways') 192
  see also adaptation, Faust theme; music; opera; philosophy
Chladni, Ernst Florens Friedrich 57
Chopin, Frédéric 226
choreography 163, 251
chorus 57, 62, 63, 66, 121, 127, 137, 166, 264
  Greek 196, 252
Christ 24, 30 (n.26), 97, 166, 171, 211, 216, 227, 252
Christianity 19, 24, 38, 89, 90, 91, 92, 96, 98, 99, 100, 149, 150, 154, 155, 157, 165, 171, 174, 177, 211, 212, 213, 214, 227, 251, 252
  see also Calvinism; Catholicism; Luther, Martin; Methodism; Reformation
Chunliu she (春柳社) (Spring Willow Theatre Group) 183
Clarke, William Barnard, *Faust* 138
Cleitus 25, 29
Colburn, Henry 127
Coleridge, Samuel Taylor 124–45
  Biographia Literaria 134
  Christabel 125, 126
  Christabel, Kubla Khan, and The Pains of Sleep 132
  Confessions of an Inquiring Spirit 128
  Death of Wallenstein 124, 127, 128, 130, 132, 138
  'The Eolian Harp' 130
  The Fall of Robespierre 130
  'Fire, Famine, and Slaughter' 135
  The Friend 134
  'Glycine's Song' 127

'Know'st thou the land' 128
'Love' 135
'Monody on the Death of Chatterton' 130
'Ode to the Departing Year' 130
Poetical Works 134
Remorse 130, 131, 132, 135
Rime of the Ancient Mariner 131
Sibylline Leaves 134
'Song of the Pixies' 130
Table Talk 137
The Three Graves 131
'To a Gentleman' 134
'To William Wordsworth. Composed on the Night after his recitation of a Poem on the Growth of an Individual Mind' 134
Zapolya 127, 132
collaboration 189, 194, 231, 234
collage 186, 196
Cologny, Villa Diodati 107
colonialism 151, 153, 154, 155, 158, 179, 197, 244, 245–8, 251, 252, 253, 254, 255, 256
comedy 36, 38, 40, 43, 44, 97, 116, 194, 217, 221, 226, 241, 251, 260
commedia dell'arte 43
computer 65, 226
concubine 254
Condillac, Étienne Bonnot de 78
Confucianism 155, 178, 180, 181, 188
conjury 25, 46, 60, 109, 166
  formula 46
conqueror 18, 20, 29
Constantinople 47
containment 76, 78
conumdrum 47
copyright 194
cosmology 55, 166, 171
costumes 44, 189, 192, 251
  see also Kathakali
coup d'état 151
Courbet, Gustave 239
court jester 41
courtship 94
Crabb Robinson, Henry 118, 124, 135, 137
creation 55, 56, 58, 59, 60, 90, 91, 92, 99, 100, 108, 114, 121, 149, 150, 171, 208, 211

Croly, George 133
cross-dressing 187, 188, 189, 193, 221
Crowley, Ian, *Starboy* 220–1, 222, 226, 227, 228
cruelty 260, 261, 262, 265, 266, 267, 269, 271
cult 219
Cupid 172, 222
curiosity 19, 20, 21, 131, 132
curse 127, 129, 130, 131
Cuvier, Georges 111
cyberspace 205, 259, 264, 270
cynic 113, 120

Daedalus 209
damnation 23, 64, 116, 117, 118, 138, 154, 166, 169, 219, 224, 227
dance 42, 63, 96, 188, 245, 249, 250, 251, 252
  see also Kathakali
Daniel, Samuel, *The Tragedy of Philotas* 23
Dante 37
  La divina commedia (The Divine Comedy) 56, 68 (n.26), 153
Daoism 155, 181, 188
Darius 19, 21, 22, 25, 29
Dark, Cary, *Starboy* 220
Dark, Randall Paris, *Starboy* 220–1, 222, 226, 227, 228
Davies, Robertson 205–15
  The Cornish Trilogy 210
  The Deptford Trilogy 210
  The Rebel Angels 205–15
  The Salterton Trilogy 210
  Tempest-Tost 210
Death Valley 265
Debord, Guy 260, 264
decolonization 245
decontextualization 78
Deep Purple 225, 226, 228
dehumanization 75
demonology 165
De Palma, Brian, *The Phantom of the Paradise* 217–19, 221, 222, 224, 227, 228
Deptford 210
desert 58, 264, 265
detachment 108, 113, 163
deus ex machina 186, 255

devil 20, 42, 60, 88–103, 108, 110, 112,
    113, 114, 115, 116, 117, 119,
    120, 121, 149, 150, 151, 152,
    154, 165, 166, 167, 168, 169,
    173, 188, 205, 206, 207, 210,
    211, 212, 216, 217, 218, 219,
    220, 221, 222, 223, 224, 225,
    227, 238, 241, 251, 262, 263
Dhánushkodi, A.V. 161
dialectic 50, 55, 59, 70, 121, 177, 186, 224,
    225, 271
Diana 209, 214
diction 128
Diderot, Denis 78
disclaimer 136
discontinuity 188
disguise 169, 195, 231, 232, 233, 234, 235,
    236, 238, 239, 240, 241, 253
disillusionment 122
dismemberment 24, 211, 213, 271
divinity 19, 22, 39, 90, 109
    Hindu 153, 171
Dong, Wenqiao (董问樵) 157
Don Juan 217, 268
    see also Byron, Lord; Mozart, Wolfgang
    Amadeus
dramaturgy 65, 185, 188, 190–1, 194, 223,
    241, 255
Dresden 66, 141
drugs 218, 262, 263, 265, 266
dualism 91, 96, 166, 168, 173, 174, 193, 252
duel 95
dystopia 262

The Eagles 223
earthquake 58
Easter 63, 64, 130, 171
Eckermann, Johann Peter 59, 98
education, colonial 153
egotism 110
Egypt 22, 151
Einstein, Albert 252
electricity 77
elephant 163, 248
'eloquentia' 62
Elton John 223
emancipation 169, 255
Emerson, Lake and Palmer 226
emission, solar 56

empire
    Alexandrian 26
    British 153
    Chinese 178
    German 178, 247
    Holy Roman 21, 226, 239
    Roman 76
empiricism 209
'empty space' 186, 191, 196
energy 56, 71, 74, 76, 77, 78, 79, 80,
    90, 98, 248
'enfant terrible' 271
Engel, Wolfgang 66
England 42, 132, 149, 194, 260
Enlightenment 78, 92, 112, 113, 114, 149,
    177, 256, 263, 264, 266
Enoch 211
entelechy 59, 98, 99
Ephesus, Council 214
    Temple of Diana 214
epic 162, 165, 167, 168, 233
epilogue 97, 166
Ernst, Gustav, *Faust* 269–70
Eros 213
    see also Goethe, Johann Wolfgang von,
    Faust. Eine Tragödie
eschatology 247
Eschenbach, Wolfram von, *Parzival*
    (*Parsifal*) 37
Esslin, Martin 194
eternity 90, 169
ether 58
etymology 61, 90
Europe 21, 22, 127, 149, 153, 155, 167,
    177, 248, 253, 260
evil 38, 60, 90, 91, 92, 93, 95, 96, 97, 100,
    108, 110, 111, 112, 113, 114, 116,
    117, 119, 135, 136, 150, 158, 165,
    166, 167, 169, 171, 173, 174, 177,
    216, 226, 227, 247, 251, 252, 262
excess 19, 107, 108, 118
execution 64, 96
    Chinese 195
exile 108
exorcist 64
experimental theatre 65, 179, 183, 184,
    185, 187, 190, 194, 195, 196, 269
Exu 251
eye movement 163

fable 112
fairground 43
Faithful, Marianne 205
farce 43, 97, 119
fascism 182
   see also National Socialism
Fassbinder, Rainer Werner 194
Faust see adaptation; Faust Books;
      Goethe, Johann Wolfgang von,
      Faust. Eine Tragödie and *Urfaust*;
      legend; magus tradition; puppet
      theatre
Faust Books 17, 18, 20–2, 25, 26, 27, 37,
      38, 40, 46, 90, 91, 99, 100, 149,
      249, 262, 268
   Faustus 18, 20, 21, 22, 91, 99, 100
   Mephostophiles 22, 38, 90
   Old Man 100
Faustus, historical 17, 20, 167, 180, 211
Felsenstein, Walter 185, 189
female directors 178
female Faust 152, 178
   Nü fushide (女浮士德) (*The Female Faust*) 180
female reproduction 207
fetus 59
feudalism 156, 182
Fichte, Johann Gottlieb, 'Von der
      Sprachfähigkeit und dem
      Ursprung der Sprache' ('On the
      linguistic capacity and the origin
      of language') 59, 60
film 65, 66, 178, 192, 205, 214 (n.1),
      217–19, 221, 222, 224, 227, 228,
      254, 255, 269, 274 (n.11)
final judgment 97, 116, 122
fin de siècle 244
Finlay, George 107
Finley, William 219
flight 18, 19, 21, 27
   balloon 27
Flimm, Jürgen, *Woyzeck* 194
foil 46, 210
folklore 38, 50, 63
folk setting, Indian 161
Fong, Leslie 253
Fool 41, 43, 45
forgetting 81 (n.1), 109, 255
Forster, Georg 167

Fortunatus 20
Foucault, Michel 262, 265, 266, 270
France 149, 150, 152, 154
   classical theatre 36, 43
   Revolution 93, 156
Frankfurt 36
Franklin, Benjamin 67 (n.11)
frequency, electronic 66
Frere, John Hookham 137
Fukuyama, Francis 262
fundamentalism 212, 214

Galbraith, John Kenneth 206
gangster 263
Gao, Xingjian (高行健) 185, 186, 187, 195, 196
   Che zhan (*Bus Stop*) 185, 186
   Juedui xinhao (*Alarm Signal*) 185, 186
   Shengsi jie (*Life and Death*) 187
Gates, Bill 262, 265
Gaugamela 28
gender 152, 173, 180, 192, 231
genetic engineering 205
genius 120, 135, 197, 208
Gentilucci, Armando 232
geology 57
George III 115
George, K. M. 166–8, 172, 174
Germany 24, 36, 45, 127, 149, 157,
      167, 177, 178, 180, 184, 185,
      187, 195, 239, 244, 245, 247–8,
      249
ghost 109
Gibson, William, *Neuromancer* 205
Glasgow, Citizen's Theatre 253
globalization 263, 264
Globokar, Vinko 231
Gnosticism 207, 211, 212
Godard, Jean-Luc, *One Plus One* (*Sympathy for the Devil*) 205
goddess 71, 164, 169, 171, 172, 206, 207,
      209, 210, 213, 214
Godiva 208
Godspell 227
Goebbels, Joseph 244
Goethe, August von 124, 132
Goethe, Christiane von 209
Goethe Institute 153, 178, 244
   Beijing 157, 189, 190

Goethe, Johann Wolfgang von 17, 27, 28, 29, 36, 37, 38, 39, 40, 41, 42, 45, 46, 47, 48, 49, 50, 55, 56, 57, 58, 59, 60, 61, 62, 63, 65, 66, 70, 72, 74, 76, 81, 88, 89, 90, 91, 92, 96, 97, 98, 99, 100, 107, 108, 109, 110, 112, 115, 116, 118, 120, 121, 122, 124, 125, 126, 127, 128, 129, 130, 131, 132, 133, 134, 135, 136, 137, 138, 149, 150, 151, 152, 153, 154, 155, 156, 157, 158, 159, 161, 162, 165, 166, 167, 168, 170, 171, 172, 173, 174, 177, 178, 179, 180, 181, 182, 183, 184, 187, 188, 189, 190, 194, 197, 205, 206, 207, 208, 209, 210, 211, 213, 214, 217, 222, 223, 224, 225, 226, 228, 231, 233, 234, 235, 239, 240, 244, 245, 247, 248, 249, 250, 252, 253, 254, 255, 256, 259, 262, 266, 267, 268, 270

Dichtung und Wahrheit (*Poetry and Truth*) 36, 45, 50, 59, 90, 99

Epimenides Erwachen (*Epimenides' Awakening*) 45

Faust, ein Fragment (*Faust, a Fragment*) 88, 121, 135

Faust. Eine Tragödie (*Faust. A Tragedy*) 26–9, 36, 37, 38, 39, 40, 41, 45–50, 55–69, 70–87, 88–103, 107, 108, 109, 110, 111, 112, 113, 115, 116, 117, 118, 119, 121, 124, 125, 126, 127, 128, 129, 130, 131, 133, 134, 135, 136, 137, 138, 149, 150, 151, 152, 153, 154, 155, 156, 157, 158, 159, 161, 162, 165, 166, 167, 168, 170, 171, 173, 174, 177, 178, 179, 180, 181, 182, 183, 184, 185, 186, 187, 188, 189, 190, 191, 192, 193, 194, 195, 196, 197, 205, 206, 207, 208, 209, 210, 211, 213, 214, 217, 218, 219, 220, 221, 222, 223, 224, 225, 226, 228, 231, 233, 234, 235, 239, 240, 244, 245, 246, 247, 248, 249, 250, 251, 252, 253, 254, 255, 256, 259, 262, 265, 266, 267, 268, 269, 270

'Abend' ('Evening') 218
'Anaxagoras' 57, 58
'Andrer Bürger' (Second Burgher) 27
'Anmutige Gegend' ('Pleasing Landscape') 57, 63, 66
Ariel 57
'Astrolog' (Astrologer) 60
'Auerbachs Keller in Leipzig' ('Auerbach's Cellar in Leipzig') 46, 50, 63, 93, 137, 138, 189, 192, 193, 249, 251
Baubo 208
bell 64, 65, 130, 169, 173
'Bergschluchten' ('Mountain Gorges') 97, 98, 99, 100, 208, 247
boils 98
'Daktyle' (Dactyls) 209
'Dom' ('Cathedral') 60, 135
Erichtho 209
Eros 208, 209
Euphorion 62, 66, 173, 209
'Ewig-Weibliche' ('Eternal-Feminine') 70, 207, 209, 213
Faust 26, 27, 28, 29, 38, 39, 40, 46, 47, 48, 50, 56, 57, 60, 61, 62, 63, 64, 65, 70, 71, 72, 73, 74, 75, 76, 80, 81, 88, 90, 91, 92, 93, 94, 95, 96, 97, 98, 99, 100, 109, 110, 111, 112, 113, 116, 117, 118, 119, 120, 121, 122, 127, 129, 130, 135, 136, 137, 138, 149, 150, 151, 152, 154, 156, 158, 159, 165, 166, 167, 168, 169, 170, 171, 172, 173, 174, 178, 179, 180, 181, 182, 186, 188, 189, 191, 192, 193, 195, 196, 206, 208, 209, 210, 211, 213, 217, 218, 219, 220, 222, 223, 224, 225, 226, 227, 228, 236, 237, 239, 244, 245, 246, 247, 248, 249, 250, 251, 253, 254, 255, 256, 261, 262, 263, 264, 265, 268, 269, 270, 272, 273
Gabriel 56
'Galatee' (Galatea) 58, 208, 209
'Garten' ('Garden') 94, 191, 249
'Ein Gartenhäuschen' ('Summerhouse') 191
'Des Gegenkaisers Zelt' ('The Rival Emperor's Tent') 29
'Geist' (Earth-Spirit) 109, 110, 111, 120, 121, 136, 169, 171, 226, 251

'Graien' (Graiae) 209
'Graue Weiber' (Grey Women) 61, 66, 100
'Greif' (Griffin) 61
'Gretchens Stube' ('Gretchen's Room') 62, 125, 225, 239
Helena 26, 27, 40, 49, 60, 62, 63, 71, 76, 118, 169, 170, 172, 173, 174, 182, 191, 192, 193, 195, 196, 207, 208, 209, 211, 213, 248, 249, 250, 254, 255
'Der Herr' (The Lord) 38, 50, 56, 88, 89, 90, 91, 96, 97, 108, 116, 117, 121, 150, 152, 165, 166, 168, 169, 170–1, 173, 191, 192, 193, 219, 222, 223, 224, 225, 227, 253
'Die Hexe' (Witch) 93, 94, 135, 137
'Hexenküche' ('Witch's Kitchen') 49, 61, 65, 66, 93–4, 112, 118, 136, 249
'Hochgebirg' ('High Mountains') 27–8, 70, 71
'Hochgewölbtes, enges, gotisches Zimmer' ('High-Vaulted Gothic Chamber') 65
'Homunkulus' (Homunculus) 47, 58, 59, 60, 66, 182, 208, 209
Incubus 64
infanticide 95, 96, 136
'Innerer Burghof' ('Inner Courtyard of a Castle') 62, 191
'Irrlicht' (will-o'-the-wisp) 58, 96
'Kaiser' (Emperor) 26, 28, 29, 49, 170, 173, 244, 249, 254, 255
'Kaiserliche Pfalz – Finstere Galerie' ('Imperial Palace – Dark Gallery') 26, 61
'Kaiserliche Pfalz – Lustgarten' ('Imperial Palace – A Pleasure Garden') 50
'Kaiserliche Pfalz – Rittersaal' ('Imperial Palace – Baronial Hall') 60, 249
'Kaiserliche Pfalz – Saal des Thrones' ('Imperial Palace – Throne Room') 49, 191, 193
'Kaiserliche Pfalz – Weitläufiger Saal' ('Imperial Palace – Great Hall') 249

'Kerker' ('Prison') 62, 64, 95, 96, 135, 137, 169, 170, 195, 225
'Klassische Walpurgisnacht' ('Classical Walpurgis Night') 191, 207, 208, 209, 214, 254
'Klassische Walpurgisnacht – Am obern Peneios' ('Classical Walpurgis Night – Again on the Upper Peneus') 57–8
'Klassische Walpurgisnacht – Felsbuchten des Ägäischen Meers' ('Classical Walpurgis Night – Rocky Inlets of the Aegean Sea') 60
'Klassische Walpurgisnacht – Peneios' ('Classical Walpurgis Night – Peneus') 213–14, 248
'Klassische Walpurgisnacht – Pharsalische Felder' ('Classical Walpurgis Night – The Pharsalian Fields') 61
'Klassische Walpurgisnacht – Telchinen von Rhodus' ('Classical Walpurgis Night – Telchines of Rhodes') 58, 209–10
'Laboratorium' ('Laboratory') 47, 58, 60, 65, 191
land reclamation 64–5, 70–87, 173, 209, 245–8, 253, 255
'Lemuren' (Lemures) 29, 65, 66
Lilith 208
'Lustige Person' (Clown) 45, 46, 50
'Luzifer' (Lucifer) 90, 98
Lynceus 64, 97
Magna Peccatrix 208
Mammon 129, 208
'Margarete'/'Gretchen' (Margaret) 49, 60, 62, 64, 71, 74, 90, 94, 95, 96, 97, 109, 112, 113, 125, 136, 137, 138, 156, 157, 165, 167, 169, 170, 171, 172, 173, 174, 178, 182, 189, 191, 192, 193, 195, 196, 208, 217, 218, 220, 221, 222, 223, 225, 236, 237, 239, 240, 249, 254, 255, 256, 270
Maria Egyptiaca 208
'Marthe' (Martha) 46, 47, 94, 191, 223, 249

Goethe, Johann Wolfgang von (*Cont'd*)
   'Marthens Garten' ('Martha's
     Garden') 61, 95, 218
   Mater Gloriosa 97, 99, 208
   Medusa 208, 209, 210, 211, 213
   Mephistopheles 27, 28, 38, 40, 46, 47,
     48, 49, 50, 59, 60, 61, 62, 64, 65,
     66, 70, 74, 76, 88–103, 107, 108,
     109, 110, 111, 112, 113, 115, 116,
     117, 118, 119, 120, 121, 122, 130,
     135, 136, 137, 138, 149, 150, 151,
     156, 165, 166, 167, 168, 169, 170,
     171, 172, 174, 182, 188, 191, 192,
     193, 194, 195, 196, 206, 208, 209,
     210, 213, 217, 219, 220, 222, 225,
     226, 228, 236, 237, 238, 244, 246,
     249, 250, 251, 253, 254, 255, 256,
     262, 263, 269, 270
   Michael 56, 58
   monkeys 61
   Mulier Samaritana 208
   'Die Mütter' (The Mothers) 60, 61
   'Der Nachbarin Haus' ('At the
     Neighbor's House') 47, 94,
     191
   'Nacht' ('Night') 36, 39, 47, 48, 62,
     64, 71, 109, 130, 137, 225, 226,
     245, 247
   'Narr' (Fool) 50
   'Neptunus' (Neptune) 246
   Oberon 209
   'Offene Gegend' ('Open
     Country') 64, 75
   'Palast – Grablegung' ('Interment') 29,
     97–8
   'Palast – Großer Vorhof des Palasts'
     ('The Great Outer-Court of the
     Palace') 65, 72, 76, 81, 97, 245,
     246, 248
   'Palast – Mitternacht' ('Midnight') 61,
     63, 65, 66, 73, 100, 247
   'Palast – Tiefe Nacht' ('Deep
     Night') 64, 97
   'Palast – Weiter Ziergarten'
     ('Palace') 64, 74, 75
   Panthalis 63
   Paris 26, 49, 60
   Pater Profundus 210
   'Persephoneia' (Persephone) 208, 211

Philemon and Baucis 29, 64, 65, 70,
   74, 75, 79, 97, 173, 246
'Phorkyaden' (Phorkyades) 208
Phorkyas 62, 63
poodle 63, 249
potion 95, 118, 119, 136, 169, 195
'Prolog im Himmel' ('Prologue in
   Heaven') 37, 38, 46, 50, 56, 57,
   65, 66, 88–9, 90, 91, 92, 96, 97,
   100, 108, 115, 116, 117, 121, 137,
   152, 154, 190, 222, 225, 247, 253
Proteus 60
Raphael 56
reception:
   Austria 37, 66, 206, 217, 226,
     239–40, 266, 267, 268, 269–70
   Brazil *see Urfaust*
   Canada 205–15, 220–1, 222, 226,
     227, 228
   China 149, 155, 157–9, 177–201
   France 150, 152, 154, 206, 217, 224,
     253, 259, 269
   Germany 40, 55, 65–6, 178, 189,
     190, 224–6, 228, 244, 245, 247–8,
     251, 267, 268, 269
   India 149, 152–5, 158, 159, 161–76
   Italy 66, 222, 224, 231–43
   Japan 149, 155–7, 158, 159, 179,
     180, 182, 188–9
   Middle East 149–53, 154, 158, 159
   The Netherlands 269–70
   Russia 205, 253
   South Africa 244–5, 252–6
   Spain 259, 270
   Switzerland 107, 248, 267
   United Kingdom 107–23, 124–45,
     154, 253, 259–75
   United States of America 161, 178,
     217–19, 221–4, 227, 228, 253, 269
Salamander 63
'Schattiger Hain' ('Shaded Grove') 62,
   63, 191
'Schüler' (Student) 46, 93, 137
Seismos 58
'Silphe' (Sylphide) 64
'Sirenen' (Sirens) 58
'Sorge' (Care) 63, 65, 100
'Spaziergang' ('Promenade') 94, 191
'Sphinxe' (Sphinxes) 58

'Straße I' ('Street') 94, 170, 172
'Straße II' ('Street') 191
striving 27, 73, 98, 99, 116, 121, 149, 150, 158, 159, 181, 246, 247, 253
'Studierzimmer I' ('Study') 56, 64, 90, 91–2, 110, 116, 119, 136, 154, 191, 217
'Studierzimmer II' ('Study') 46, 61, 64, 71, 90, 93, 127, 129, 130, 138, 191, 222, 225, 244
'Telchinen' (Telchines) 209
Thales 57, 58, 60
Titania 209
translation:
  Arabic 149–50
  Bengali 161
  Chinese 157–8, 159, 179–80, 181, 182, 183, 188, 189, 191
  English 107, 108, 115, 117, 121, 124–45, 155, 157, 161, 226, 253
  French 150
  Hindi 153–4, 161
  Italian 232, 233, 234, 235, 239
  Japanese 155–7, 179, 182, 188
  Kannada 161
  Malayalam 161, 170
  Marathi 161
  Portuguese *see Urfaust*
  Spanish 226
  Tamil 161
  Urdu 161
'Trüber Tag – Feld' ('An Expanse of Open Country') 96, 112, 220
Undine 64
'Valentin' (Valentine) 60, 64, 95, 195, 224, 237–8
'Vor dem Palaste des Menelas zu Sparta' ('Before the Palace of Menelaus at Sparta') 191
'Vor dem Tor' ('Outside the City Gate') 27, 50, 63, 64, 71, 136, 138, 218, 251
'Vorspiel auf dem Theater' ('Prelude in the Theatre') 45–6, 62, 137, 153, 167, 190
Wagner 40, 46, 47, 58, 59, 62, 63, 64, 70, 109, 137, 182, 196, 209, 237, 254
'Wald und Höhle' ('Forest and Cave') 63, 94–5, 110, 136
'Walpurgisnacht' ('Walpurgis Night') 49, 58, 63, 65, 66, 93, 96, 115, 136, 137, 138, 156, 207, 209, 226, 249
'Walpurgisnachtstraum' ('Walpurgis Night's Dream') 209, 220
'Zueignung' ('Dedication') 66
'Zwinger' ('By the Ramparts') 221, 252
'Der Gott und die Bajadere' ('The God and the Bayadere') 167
Hanswursts Hochzeit oder der Lauf der Welt (*Hanswurst's Wedding or the Way of the World*) 45, 50
Jahrmarktsfest zu Plundersweilen (*Market Festival at Plundersweilen*) 45
Die Leiden des jungen Werthers (*The Sufferings of Young Werther*) 107, 150, 157, 178, 180, 182
Maximen und Reflexionen (*Maxims and Reflections*) 207
mythology 90, 99
'Paria' ('The Pariah') 167
Reineke Fuchs (*Reynard the Fox*) 157
Tagebuch (*Diary*) 134
Über Kunst und Altertum (*On Art and Antiquity*) 134
Urfaust 47, 48, 50, 96, 161, 178, 250–2, 256
  Faust 250, 251
  Mephistopheles 250, 251
  'Margarethe'/'Margrete'/'Gretgen' (Margaret/Gretchen) 251, 252
  translation 161, 250
'Urworte, Orphisch' ('Orphic Utterances') 134
Die Wahlverwandtschaften (*Elective Affinities*) 74
West-östlicher Divan (*West-Eastern Divan*) 29, 167
Wilhelm Meisters Lehrjahre (*Wilhelm Meister's Apprenticeship*) 37, 128, 157, 180, 182
Zur Farbenlehre (*Theory of Colors*) 55, 57, 58
Goethe Society
  India 154, 158
  Japan 158
gong 66

Gottsched, Johann Christoph 36, 39, 43, 44, 45, 48, 49, 50
  Versuch einer critischen Dichtkunst vor die Deutschen (*Essay on a German Critical Poetic Theory*) 39, 43, 44
Gounod, Charles, *Faust* 206, 224
gramophone 253
grand narrative 265
Great Britain 153, 154, 155, 259, 260, 261
Greece 107, 149, 155, 177, 191
  drama 36, 37, 43, 48, 110
  see also chorus
griffin 18, 27, 61
Grüber, Klaus-Michael 244
Gründgens, Gustaf, *Faust* 65, 228, 244, 268, 269
Gu, Hongming (辜鸿铭) 181
Guo, Moruo (郭沫若) 157, 179, 180, 182, 188
  Tian Han and Zong Baihua, *San ye ji* (*Cloverleaf*) 179–80
Gymnosophists 24, 25
gypsy 208, 210, 211, 212, 213
Gysi, Gabriele 178

hair 59, 194, 208, 213, 219, 221
Hamann, Johann Georg 59
Hamburg 65, 268
Handspring Puppet Company 252, 253
Hanover, World Expo 55, 267
Hanuman 153, 164
harem 21
Harlequin 43, 45
Hartlieb, Johann, *Alexander* 18
hatred 107, 108, 111, 120
Hazlitt, William 125
heaven 26, 37, 38, 46, 50, 56, 57, 65, 88, 89, 90, 91, 92, 96, 97, 99, 100, 108, 115, 116, 118, 120, 121, 137, 150, 152, 154, 157, 166, 168, 170, 173, 174, 190, 196, 209, 220, 221, 222, 223, 224, 227
Hederich, Benjamin 208
Hegel, Georg Wilhelm Friedrich 177, 224, 225, 256
Heidegger, Martin
  'Die Frage nach der Technik' ('The question concerning technology') 70, 76–81
  'Der Ursprung des Kunstwerkes' ('The origin of the work of art') 79–80
Heine, Heinrich 157
  Der Doktor Faust. Ein Tanzpoem nebst kuriosen Berichten über Teufel, Hexen und Dichtkunst (*Dr Faust, a Dance Poem, with Interesting Reports on Devils, Witches and the Art of Poetry*) 42–3
  Reisebilder (*Travel Pictures*) 40
Helen 76
  see also Goethe, Johann Wolfgang von, *Faust. Eine Tragödie* and *Urfaust*; Marlowe, Christopher, *Doctor Faustus*; puppet theatre; Simon Magus
hell 18, 19, 39, 42, 47, 49, 64, 90, 91, 93, 95, 96, 97, 98, 110, 118, 121, 150, 152, 169, 170, 205, 219, 220, 227, 255
hell-mouth 97
Hendrix, Jimi 224
Henley, Don 223
Hephaestion 23
Hephaestus 208, 209
Hera 195
Hercules, Pillars of 19, 21
Herder, Johann Gottfried 206
  Abhandlung über den Ursprung der Sprache (*Treatise on the Origin of Language*) 59
Hermes 251
heroism, classical 27
He, Yong (何勇) 196
hierarchy, satanic 90, 93
Hinduism 153, 154, 162, 165, 171, 174
Hinduization 167, 170, 171
'His Master's Voice' 253
Historia von D. Johann Fausten see Faust Books
The Historie of the damnable life, and deserued death of Doctor Iohn Faustus see Faust Books
hoax 60, 127
Hollywood, film scores 221
holocaust 213, 214
Homer 26
homosexuality 98, 220
homunculus 58
  see also Goethe, Johann Wolfgang von, *Faust. Eine Tragödie*

Hong Kong 158, 195
Hou, Chunhua (候春华) 190
hubris 26, 28
Humboldt, Wilhelm von 59
Hunt, Leigh 115
Hüttner, Johann Christian 131, 132
hydroelectric plant 77, 79
hypnotism 93

Iba, Takashi 156, 177
Ibsen, Henrik 177, 179
Ibsenism 179
Icarus 62, 209
idealism 94, 114, 195
idiom 37, 40, 41, 45, 112, 217
idyll 29, 75
Ife heads 254
illusion 23, 25, 27, 60, 66, 119, 130, 138, 164, 174, 254
immorality 136
immortality 25, 205, 207, 212, 214
improvisation 194, 250
indemnity 255
indeterminacy 120, 263
India 17, 149, 150, 153, 154, 158, 161, 162, 165, 166, 167, 168, 169, 174, 186, 248
individualism 271, 272, 273
industrialization 179
infidelity, marital 119
innatism, linguistic 59
inspector 89
intellectualization 267
internet 266, 270
intertextuality 90, 269, 273
intuition 95
in-yer-face theatre 259, 260, 261, 262, 269, 271, 273
irony 25, 92, 98, 108, 111, 112, 117, 118, 119, 121, 122, 196, 261
Islam 150, 152, 153, 154, 155, 158
  anti-Islamic propaganda 21
  Iblīs 150, 151, 152
  shaytān 150
Italy 29, 43, 45, 94, 108, 233, 249

Jackson, Michael 222
Jacobsen, Friedrich Johann, *Briefe an eine deutsche Edelfrau über die neuesten englischen Dichter* (*Letters to a German Noblewoman on the New English Poets*) 125, 133
Jagger, Mick, 'Sympathy for the Devil' 205, 216, 238
Japan 149, 155, 156, 157, 158, 159, 179, 180, 182, 186, 188, 195
Jeffrey, Francis 119
Jena 127
Jesus Christ Superstar 227
Jews 213, 252
Jones, Andy, *The Adventure of Faustus Bidgood* 214 (n.1)
Jones, Michael, *The Adventure of Faustus Bidgood* 205, 214 (n.1)
Jones, William 167
Johnson, Robert 216
Jove 19, 24
Jung, Carl Gustav 211
  Antwort auf Hiob (*Answer to Job*) 212
Junius 135
justice 18, 72, 75, 132, 173, 224, 247
  divine 96

Kabuki 188–9
Kaimal, Aymanam Krishna 161, 162, 165, 166, 167, 168, 170, 171, 172, 173, 174
Kalidasa, *Shakuntala* 153, 167
Kama 153
Kamadisundaran, Faust comparison 173
Kamiyama, Sojin 156, 177
Kane, Sarah 260
Kant, Immanuel 63, 114
Karaoke 192
Karāra, Muhammad Abdel Halīm 150
karma 154, 168, 174
Kathakali 161–76
  reception 163, 164, 165, 166, 167, 168, 170, 171
'kathodos' 211
Kentridge, William 252, 253, 254, 255, 256
Kerala 161, 162, 168, 172
Kikugoro, Onoe 188
Kimura, Kinji 156
Kimura, Naoji 156
KISS 228
Kley, Heinrich 248
Knebel, Karl Ludwig von 127, 134

'Knittelvers' 39, 253
knowledge 17, 18, 23, 38, 39, 41, 71, 107, 109, 111, 112, 113, 114, 116, 131, 132, 137, 138, 151, 153, 161, 168, 169, 179, 181, 185, 194, 197, 210, 219, 226, 250, 252, 262, 265, 266, 267, 269, 270
Kobe 156
Kohler, Adrian 253
Kolkata 161
Koran 153
Korea 155
Kortner, Fritz 66
Kottayam 163
Krishna 154, 162, 165, 174
Kubo, Sakae 156
Kyoto 156

labor, exploitation 73, 74, 246
Lacan, Jacques 262
Laing, Stewart, *Brainy* 262
Lambaréné, Albert Schweitzer Hospital 254
La Mettrie, Julien Offray de 78
Lamprecht, Pfaffe 18
language 50, 55, 58–63, 78–81, 115, 119, 126, 128, 129, 131, 132, 135, 136, 137, 138, 150, 152, 153, 154, 155, 158, 162, 171, 180, 188, 191, 212, 217, 226, 233, 234, 239, 265
Las Vegas 221, 227
Latin 40, 46, 90, 153
Latinium 76
Le Brun, Charles, *L'Entrée d'Alexandre le Grand dans Babylone* (*The Triumphal Entry of Alexander the Great in Babylon*) 28
LeCompte, Elizabeth, *House/Lights* 269
legend 231
    Alexander 18, 19, 20, 24, 26, 27, 28
    Faust 44, 110, 149, 150, 166, 167, 174, 218, 227, 231, 249, 259, 262, 266
    Rugmamgatha 165, 174
Leibniz, Gottfried Wilhelm 99
    Discours de métaphysique (*Discourse on Metaphysics*) 92
    Monadologie (*Monadology*) 98
Leipzig 44, 141, 168, 189
Lenau, Nikolaus, *Faust. Ein Gedicht* (*Faust. A Poem*) 37, 266

Lennon, John 216
Lenz, Jakob Michael Reinhold, *Der neue Menoza oder Geschichte des cumbanischen Prinzen Tandi* (*The New Menzoa or The Story of the Cumbanian Prince Tandi*) 45
Leo, Archpriest, *Historia de Preliis* (*The History of the Wars of Alexander*) 18
Leopardi, Giacomo 233
leper 254
Leroux, Gaston, *Le Fantôme de l'Opéra* (*The Phantom of the Opera*) 217
Lessing, Gotthold Ephraim 37
    Literaturbrief (*Letters on Literature*) 44
Leveson-Gower, Francis, Lord 124
Lewis, Matthew G. 109
    The Monk 107
Ley, Pablo, *F@usto Version 3.0* 270
Liberovici, Andrea 232
Libro de Alexandre (*Book of Alexander*) 18
Li, Fengbao (李凤苞) 178, 179
light 56, 57, 58, 71, 72, 75, 90, 92
lighting 164, 173, 189, 191, 195
Li, Jianming (李健鸣) 183, 189, 190
lily 169
linguistics 55, 58–63
Lin, Zhaohua (林赵华) 183, 185, 186, 187, 188, 189, 191, 193, 194, 195, 196
    Fushide (浮士德) (*Faust I and II*) 183, 184, 185, 186, 187, 188, 189–93, 197
    Hamlet 186, 188
    Richard III 188
    San jiemei. Dengdai geduo (三姊妹·等待戈多) (*Three Sisters. Waiting for Godot*) 187, 188
Locke, John 138
'logos' 56, 60, 136
Lombardi, Luca 231, 232, 234, 235, 236, 237, 238, 239, 240, 241
    Dmitri oder der Künstler und die Macht (*Dmitri, or the Artist and Power*) 241
    Faust. Un Travestimento (*Faust. A Disguise*) 232, 234, 235–41
    Lucrezio. Un oratorio materialistico (*Lucretius. A Materialistic Oratory*) 234
    Prospero 241
    Il re nudo (*The Naked King*) 241

London 118, 131, 254
  Actors Touring Company 262
  Covent Garden 126
  Royal Court 260
Los Angeles 264, 266
  1992 riots 264
lotus 172
  position 173
loudspeaker 66
Louis XIV 28
love 18, 23, 24, 26, 40, 94, 95, 98, 99, 100,
    107, 109, 111, 118, 120, 129, 135,
    137, 151, 152, 157, 159, 163, 168,
    169, 172, 173, 180, 192, 218, 221,
    222, 223, 227, 228, 239, 248
lower classes 42
Lucan 19, 22, 23, 24
Lucifer 20, 58, 89, 90, 91, 93, 98, 99, 111,
    112, 113, 114, 115, 120, 165, 166,
    167, 169, 170, 171, 174, 211, 222,
    223, 224
  see also Goethe, Johann Wolfgang von,
    Faust. Eine Tragödie and mythology
Lunarcharsky, Anatoly, Faust 253
Luther, Martin 88, 100
Lyly, John, Campaspe 23

Macao 158
MacDonald, Robert David 253
Macedonians 19, 25, 29
magic 17, 20, 23, 28, 41, 42, 46, 47, 49, 60,
    61, 63, 84, 93, 125, 138, 164, 169,
    172, 180, 225, 241, 253
magic lantern 66, 138, 250
magus tradition 206, 210, 211, 212
Mahabharata 167
Mahmud, Mohammad 151
Ma, Junwu (马君武) 157
Mamet, David 223
Manchu Dynasty 159
Manet, Edouard, Le Déjeuner sur l'herbe
    (Luncheon on the Grass) 239
'manga' 158
Mann, Klaus, Mephisto 269
Mann, Thomas 231
Manzoni, Giacomo 232
Marlowe, Christopher 22, 23, 210
  Edward II 23
  The Jew of Malta 23

Tamburlaine 23
The Tragical History of Doctor Faustus
    17–18, 22–6, 27, 36, 38, 129,
    158, 165, 166, 167, 174, 206, 253,
    262, 268
  Benvolio 24, 25
  Faustus 17–18, 23, 24, 25, 26,
    166, 167
  Helen 26
  Mephistopheles (Mephostophilis) 165,
    166
  Old Man 24–5
  Paris 26
marriage 94, 169, 172, 180
Mars, setting 196
martial arts 190
martyrdom 182
Marx, Karl 156, 177, 178
mask 163, 164, 188, 219, 234
masquerade 233, 234, 249
mass media 195
materialism 92, 138, 195
matter 63, 71, 73, 79, 90, 92, 212
Mawra, Joseph P., Olga's House of
    Shame 269
Max Müller Institute 153
Mayakovsky, Vladimir 186
McLuhan, Marshall 262
mediator 124, 138, 208
Mee, Erin B. 161, 162
megalomania 222
megaphone 64
Mehta, Vijaya 161
Meiji, Emperor 179
  reforms 179
Mei, Lanfang (梅兰芳) 187
Meirelles, Márcio, Fausto Zero 244–5,
    250–2, 256
melodrama 48, 233
Melo, Gustavo 251
Mencherini, Fernando 232
Menelaus 26
  see also 173
Meng, Jinghui (孟京辉) 191, 193, 194, 195,
    196
  Daoban fushide (盗版浮士德) (Bootleg
    Faust) 183, 189, 193–7
  Dengdai geduo (等待戈多) (Waiting for
    Godot) 194, 195

Meng, Jinghui (Cont'd)
    Fang xia ni de bianzi—woyicaike
        (放下你的鞭子·沃伊采克)
        (Put Down Your
        Whip—Woyzeck) 194
mermaid 209
metalepsis 79, 80
metamorphosis 59, 252
'metapherein' 79, 80
metaphor 72, 78, 80, 129, 217, 247
meter 39, 40, 126, 135, 136, 240
Methodism 115
Meyerhold, Vsevolod Emilevich 186, 190, 194
middle age 107
Middle Ages 97, 212, 226
Middle East 149, 150
Midrashim 211
Milan 66
Mill, John Stuart, *On Liberty* 155
Milton, John
    'On the Morning of Christ's Nativity' 56
    Paradise Lost 68 (n.26), 92, 108, 110, 117, 118, 208
mimesis 20, 72
mimicry 163
minorities, ethnic 181–2
Minotaur 266
Mishra, Abhay 153
misogyny 269
misology 137
missionary 253
Mnouchkine, Ariane, *Mephisto* 269
mode 21, 46, 75, 80, 107, 108, 109, 118, 121, 122, 233, 235, 273
modernism 233, 260
modernity 21, 70, 112, 231, 239, 245
modernization 78, 179, 233, 235
Mohammed 21, 22, 150, 153
Mommsen, Katharina 155
Monk, Egon 251
monologue 27, 39, 40, 49, 50, 188, 225, 247
Monroe Doctrine 248
montage 66, 218
Montaigne, Michel de 18
Moore, Thomas 135
morality 37, 42, 44, 118, 122, 127, 128, 155, 171, 247, 251, 252, 256, 259, 260, 261, 271, 272, 273

morality play 24
Mori, Ogai 155–6, 188
mortality 25, 29, 206, 209, 211, 212
Moses, Henry 124, 131, 135
mosquito 254
motivation 115, 136, 137, 218
motorcycle 66, 225
Motte-Fouqué, Friedrich Heinrich Karl, Baron de La, *Undine* (*Undine, or, The Spirit of the Waters*) 126
Mozart, Wolfgang Amadeus 252
    Don Giovanni (*Don Juan*) 118
'mudra', 163
Muhammad, Awad Muhammad 150
Müller, Maler 37
multimedia 195, 264
multiplicity 166, 231, 232, 236, 238, 239
Mumbai 161
Munich, Marionettes 206
    Residenztheater 66
Murray, John 124, 125, 126, 135
music 118
    African 255
    Afro-Brazilian 245, 250
    Austropop 217
    ballad 196, 218, 219, 220, 221, 225
    blues 187, 192, 216, 218, 219, 221, 225
    Cantopop-techno 196
    celestial 56
    chanson 217
    oratorio 56
    rock 65, 66, 216–30, 238, 263
        Chinese 187, 190, 191, 192, 193, 196
    see also Kathakali; opera
musicalization 65
Mussorgsky, Modest Petrovich 226
Mutran, George 150
mutuality 181
mysticism 168
mythology 38, 42, 56, 59, 60, 64, 76, 90, 92, 93, 98, 99, 149, 150, 167, 171, 172, 173, 195, 196, 208, 209, 210, 213, 226, 231, 239, 249, 250, 256, 265

Namibia 245
National Aeronautics and Space Administration (NASA) 196
National Socialism 213, 244, 248, 269, 270
nation-building 154, 178, 179, 244
Native American 251

naturalism 172
nature 19, 23, 28, 29, 39, 43, 44, 55, 62, 63, 71, 74, 75, 76, 77, 79, 80, 92, 113, 114, 118, 137, 158, 181, 211, 212, 213, 245, 247, 251
Near East 150
necromancy 21, 169
negativity 89, 91, 108, 110, 111, 117, 119, 121, 122, 260, 262, 266
Neo-Confucianism 177, 188
Neo-Platonism 99
Neptunism 58
The Netherlands 42
Neuber, Friederike Caroline 44
New Delhi 153, 161, 168
Newfoundland 205
New Labour 260
Newman, Randy
   Born Again 228
   Randy Newman's Faust 221–4, 227
new media 261
New Song movement 217
Newton, Isaac 138, 209, 214
   Opticks 57
New York, Broadway 221, 224
Das Nibelungenlied (*Song of the Nibelungs*) 37
Nielsen, Anthony 260
nightmare 112
Nine Worthies 18
nirvana 157
Nobel Prize for Literature 185, 206
noise 55, 58, 60, 61, 63, 64, 65, 66, 173
nostalgia 226, 228
nothingness 56, 92, 112, 114
novel, Gothic 107, 112
nuclear explosion 65
   weapons 179, 212
nursery rhyme 233

objectivity 111
O'Brien, Richard, *The Rocky Horror Show* 226
obscenity 96
occult 17, 20
ode 56, 130
Oedipus 268
Oenone 26
onomatopoeia 61
Ontario 205

opera 178, 206, 217, 219, 224–6, 228, 231–43
   Beijing 183, 188, 189
   Kunqu 189
   Shanghai 187
   Sichuan 187
Opium Wars 178
oral tradition 154
orient 19, 21, 91, 153, 167, 248
orientalism 167
Origen 89
   'apokatastasis panton' 99, 210, 247
orphan 172
Orpheus 62, 206
orthodoxy 116
Ortiz, Isidro 274 (n.11)
Osaka 156
ottava rima 119, 126
Ottawa 206
Ouyang, Yuqian (欧阳予倩) 183, 184

pact 17, 48, 49, 64, 90, 100, 111, 114, 130, 149, 151, 152, 166, 169, 174, 205, 206, 213, 218, 219, 220, 221, 224, 225, 241, 244, 250, 251, 253, 256, 262
Paganini, Niccolò 224
Palma, il Vecchio 239
Pamphylia 28
Panikkar, Kavalam Narayana 161
panopticon 254
pantheism 136
pantomime 25, 60, 66
Paracelsus 58, 206, 212
parliamentary system 179
parody 24, 50, 61, 115, 122, 131, 196, 222, 224, 227, 228, 233, 235, 238
passivity 186, 225
past crime 109
pastiche 271
patriarchy 207, 213
Pegasus 120
Pelagius 214
penance 165
perfection 75, 92, 99, 110
performance 37, 42, 43, 65, 122, 156, 161, 162, 163, 164, 165, 168, 170, 171, 184, 185, 186, 187, 188, 189, 190, 191, 193, 194, 195, 206, 216, 227, 232, 241, 249, 250, 251, 252, 253, 262, 269

perjury 94
Perkins, William 23
Perry, Matthew, Commodore 179
Persepolis 26, 29
Persia 19, 21, 22, 25, 28, 154, 248
personification 92, 127, 213, 269
Pfitzer, Johann Nikolaus 90
Philip, of Macedon 19
Philippou, Nick 262, 263, 264, 266, 269
   Brainy 262
philology 20
Philo of Alexandria 56
philosopher's stone 38, 212
philosophy 17, 24, 39, 109, 118, 135, 137, 210
   Aristotelian 19
   Chinese 155, 181
   Indian 153, 162
   natural 58, 155
   popular 99
   postmodern 259, 264–5, 267, 268, 270–2, 273
   see also language
phonosemantics 61
physics 56, 57
'physis' 79, 251
Picasso, Pablo 239
piety 64, 113, 114, 152
pilgrimage 152
Pinter, Harold 260
plasticity 63
Plato 23
   Kratylos (*Cratylus*) 61
   Politeia (*Republic*) 72
playbill 168–70
playing cards 255
Plutarch
   Bioi parallēloi (*Parallel Lives*) 17, 18, 22, 23, 24
   'Peri tēs Alexandrou tuhēs ē aretēs' ('On the fortune or the virtue of Alexander') 18, 23, 28–9
poet laureate 115
Pogwisch, Henriette von 132, 133
Pogwisch, Ottilie von 132
'poiesis' 76, 79–80
'polis' 72, 75
pop-art 194
possession 174

postmodernism 259, 264–5, 267, 268, 270–2, 273
Prati, Gioacchino de' 137
praxis 62, 74
prayer 173, 174
pre-Adamite beings 111
Presley, Elvis 216, 227
pride 49, 89, 99, 118, 120, 136, 212
projection 65, 190, 191, 253, 264, 270
   mental 113
Prokopets, Josef, *Fäustling: Spiel in G* (*Fäustling: Play in G*) 217, 226
Prometheus 110
props 163, 191, 192
prostitution 270
protest 115, 184, 205
pun 36, 37, 40, 46, 61
Punch and Judy 49
puppet theatre 72
   China 191, 192
   Faust 36–51, 90, 206, 249
      Faust 36, 37, 38, 39, 40, 41, 42, 44, 46, 47, 48, 49, 50, 51, 253, 254, 255
      Gretchen 254, 255
      Hanswurst 36, 40, 42, 43, 44, 45, 47, 50
      Helena 49, 254, 255
      Kasperle 36, 40, 41, 42, 45, 46, 47, 48, 49, 50
      Mephistopheles 38, 40, 47, 253, 254, 255
      Pickelhäring 36, 40, 43, 45, 49, 50
      reception 40, 41, 42, 43, 44, 45, 49, 50, 249, 253, 255
      South Africa 244–5, 252–6
      translation 37, 42, 46
      Wagner 40, 41, 42, 46, 47, 49, 254
   Japan 253, 255
Puranas 162
   Bhāgavata purana 162
   Padma purana 165
Pygmalion 209
Pythagoras 56

Qian, Chunqi (钱春绮) 157, 158

racism 216, 248, 252, 255
railway 248
Raimondi, Marcantonio 239

'raisonneur' 113
Raitt, Bonnie 223
Rampolokeng, Lesego 253
rationality 112
raven 93
Ravenhill, Mark, *Faust is Dead* 259–75
Razzi, Fausto 232
realism
  social 170, 260
  socialist 186
  Stanislavskian 185–6
reception *see* adaptation; Alexander the Great; Faust Books; film; Goethe, Johann Wolfgang von, *Faust, ein Fragment, Faust. Eine Tragödie* and *Urfaust*; Kathakali; Marlowe, Christopher, *Doctor Faustus*; music; puppet theatre; spectator; translation
recognition 38, 116, 205, 245, 255, 263, 265, 271
re-creation 159, 162
redemption 64, 91, 98, 99, 100, 116, 154, 155, 165, 166, 169, 223, 224, 245, 247, 255, 256, 272, 274
Reformation 166
rehearsal 163, 168, 190, 194
Reinhardt, Max, *Faust* 65, 268
rejuvenation 61, 151, 169, 249
remorse 22, 29, 100, 109, 115, 221, 223
Renaissance 177, 192, 211, 212, 249
Ren, Ming (任鸣) 187, 189
repentance 100, 169
repertoire 36, 42, 48, 161, 162
resistance 55, 79, 95, 111, 121, 156, 179, 255, 261
responsibility 95, 174, 181, 182, 186, 259, 267, 271
resurrection 24, 64, 171
Retzsch, Moritz 124, 131, 133, 135
revolving stage 65, 184, 190, 268
Rhine 77, 78
riddle 29, 41, 265
robot 196
The Rolling Stones 216, 220, 227, 238
Roma 212, 214
romance 18, 20
Roman culture 155, 177, 189, 249
  see also empire, Roman

Roman d'Alexandre 18, 21
Romanticism 58, 62, 63, 65, 231, 239, 266, 268
romanticization 270, 271
Ronconi, Luca 233
Ronstadt, Linda 223
Rufus, Quintus Curtius, *Historiae Alexandri Magni* (*History of Alexander*) 18
Rugmamgatha 165, 174
  Rugmamgatha Caritam 165
Russia 178, 179, 186, 205

Saaletal 132
Sabbath 63, 96, 208
sacrifice 165
safari 254
St Aegidius 210
St John's 205
St Tertullian 207
Salvador da Bahia 244, 250
  Teatro dos Novos 250
  Teatro Vila Velha 250
Salzburg, Kleines Festspielhaus 206
Sand, George, *Les Septs cordes de la lyre* (*The Seven Strings of the Lyre*) 253
San Diego 223
Sanguineti, Edoardo 231, 232, 233, 234, 235, 236, 238, 239, 240
  Faust. Un Travestimento (*Faust. A Disguise*) 231–4, 235, 236, 238, 239, 240
  Lucrezio. Un oratorio materialistico (*Lucretius. A Materialistic Oratory*) 234
  Orlando furioso 233–4
Sanskrit 167, 208
Santana, Rita 251
Santella, Marialuisa and Mario, Alfred Jarry 231
Sardanapalus 28
'satan' 90, 116
satire 42, 45, 98, 108, 115, 116, 117, 193, 194, 195, 196, 219, 228, 268, 271
scapegoat 112
Scaramouche 43
scenery 65, 163, 191, 196
Schelling, Friedrich Wilhelm 58
Schiller, Friedrich 128, 130, 180
  Die Räuber (*The Robbers*) 40
  Wallenstein 124, 127, 128, 130, 132, 138
Schmitt, Erich 247

Schönemann, Lili 109
Schopenhauer, Arthur, *Parerga und Paralipomena* (*Short Philosophical Writings*) 63
Schroth, Christoph 66
Schubert, Franz, 'Gretchen am Spinnrade' ('Gretchen at the Spinning Wheel') 239–40
Schwarz, Evgenij 241
science 17, 20, 23, 55, 109, 149, 158, 179, 181, 212, 214, 259, 264
science fiction 60, 205
Scodanibbio, Stefano 232
The Scorpions 225, 228
Scott, Walter, Sir 124, 125
sculpture 192
Secretum Secretorum (*Secret of Secrets*) 18, 29
seduction 70, 74, 94, 113, 150, 151, 165, 193, 195, 196, 254, 265
Seelentrost (*Soul's Consolation*) 18
self-censorship 96
self-mutilation 266
Senda, Koreya 156
sentimentality 260, 272
Septuagint 90
serialism 238
sexism 207
Shakespeare, William 37, 40, 91, 136, 137, 177, 187, 245, 250, 260
  Hamlet 268
  Henry V 23
  The Tempest 210, 241, 245
shamanism 206, 209, 210, 211, 213
Shanghai 157, 195
  see also opera
Sharma, Pandit Bholanath 154
Shelley, Percy Bysshe 114, 124
  Queen Mab 127
  'Scenes from the "Faust" of Goethe' 108, 115, 117, 121
Shen, Lin (沈林) 194
Shenzhen 195
Shiva 162, 171
shogunate 179
Simmons, Gene 228
Simon Magus 211
  Helena 211
Simrock, Karl 37, 38, 40, 47
simulation 234, 250, 262, 265, 272, 273
Singapore 195

Sinti 214
siren 65
Sirens 63
  see also Goethe, Johann Wolfgang von, *Faust. Eine Tragödie*
situationalism 260, 265, 270, 272
slapstick 36
slavery 129, 150, 151, 244, 250, 256
smith, underground 206, 207, 208, 209, 210, 211, 213, 214
snake 49, 93, 95, 96, 112, 113, 208, 209, 213, 214
Soane, George 124, 125, 126, 133
socialism 156, 158, 186, 272
social stratification 117, 167, 172
Socrates 23, 61, 72, 73, 75
solar system 56
soliloquy 38, 40, 41, 113, 169
Solomon, King 211
Somali 270
Song Dynasty 188
Sophia 211, 213
sorcery 24, 137, 167, 172
Sörgel, Herman, 'Atlantropa' 247–8
Šostakovič, Dmitri 241
Sotheby's 254
soul 42, 59, 63, 95, 97, 98, 110, 115, 116, 118, 128, 129, 130, 136, 138, 152, 154, 156, 166, 169, 170, 171, 173, 174, 196, 205, 211, 216, 217, 218, 219, 220, 221, 224, 228, 263
sound, imagery 55–69
  metaphysics 55–8
South Africa 244, 245, 252, 253, 254, 255, 256
Southeast Asians 172
Southey, Robert 118
  A Vision of Judgment 115, 116
space, interplanetary 57, 111
spaceship 196
  shuttle 226
Spain 19, 23, 24, 270
Spalding, Johann Joachim, *Die Bestimmung des Menschen* (*The Destiny of Man*) 99
spectacularity 249
spectator 74, 107, 111, 118, 196, 252, 259, 260, 261, 264, 270, 271, 272, 273, 274
speech, origins 58–60

Spengler, Oswald, *Der Untergang des Abendlandes* (*The Decline of the West*) 247
Spenserian stanza 126
spheres 56
Spies, Johann 249
  see also Faust Books
spirit 17, 22, 24, 25, 39, 41, 42, 46, 47, 50, 57, 58, 59, 60, 63, 89, 90, 91, 92, 96, 99, 109, 110, 111, 112, 114, 115, 116, 117, 119, 120, 121, 122, 126, 127, 137, 151, 152, 166, 171, 173, 206, 217, 247, 251, 252, 256
Spohr, Louis 224
spy 88
Staël, Madame de, *De l'Allemagne* (*Germany*) 107
Stalin, Joseph 205, 241
Stanislavsky, Konstantin, system 185, 186
Stanley, Paul 228
Steffens, Henrich 58
Stein, Gertrude, *Dr Faustus Lights the Lights* 253, 269
Stein, Peter, *Faust* 55, 66, 244, 267
Steiner, Rudolf and Marie 267
Steppenwolf, 'Born to be Wild' 225
stereotype 194, 195, 251, 271, 273
Storm and Stress 62
Straits of Gibraltar 24
Strasbourg 36
Strehler, Gorgio 66
Stuttgart 268
style 108, 135, 137, 156, 185, 186, 187, 188, 189, 193, 216, 219, 220, 221, 222, 226, 227, 228, 232, 233, 235, 238, 239, 240, 255, 260, 269
stylization 161, 162, 164, 172, 247
Styx 220
subconscious 62
sublime 27, 63, 110, 111, 114, 117, 118, 119, 120, 213, 233
submissiveness 182
suicide 64, 109, 111, 130, 137, 151, 169, 171, 218, 223, 267
Sun, Weishi (孙维世) 183, 184
superstition 22, 63, 113, 135, 222
surveillance 219
Süßmilch, Johann Peter, *Versuch eines Beweises, daß die erste Sprache ihren Ursprung nicht von Menschen, sondern allein vom Schöpfer erhalten habe* (*An Attempt at Proving that the First Language derived its Origin not from Man but from the Creator Alone*) 59
Swahili 254
Swedenborg, Emanuel 66 (n.3)
Switzerland 248
symbols, Judeo-Christian 64
syncretism 244, 245, 251, 255
synecdoche 73

Tagore, Rabindranath 159 (n.4)
Taipei 157
Takahashi, Goro 155, 156
talk show 264
Tanzania 245
Tasso, Torquato 126
taste 43, 44, 45, 62
Taylor, Bayard 154, 155
Taylor, James 223
technology 57, 65, 66, 70, 76–81, 149, 179, 181, 206, 219, 245, 247, 261, 262, 269
television 66, 178, 219, 264
  Chinese 191, 195, 196
Teweleit, Horst Lothar 151
Tezuka, Tomio 156
Thalheimer, Michael 66
Thanatos 212, 213, 214
Thatcher, Margaret 260
Théâtre du Soleil 259
'theatrum mundi' 247, 253
Thebes 26, 29
theism 136
theodicy 92
theosophy 56, 58
Tiananmen Square 179, 184, 185, 195
Tian, Han (田汉) 157, 180
  Fang xia ni de bianzi (放下你的鞭子) (*Put Down Your Whip*) 182
  Nü fushide (女浮士德) (*The Female Faust*) 180
Tieck, Ludwig 127
time 43, 48, 56, 73, 78, 107, 109, 111, 120, 191, 219, 231, 269
Timoleon 17
Tischbein, Johann Heinrich Wilhelm, *Goethe in der Campagna* (*Goethe in the Campagna*) 170, 174

Tokyo 183
    Imperial Theatre 156
    Imperial University 156
tone 50, 108, 120, 121, 129, 136, 163, 227, 237, 238
    sonic 60, 62, 63, 65, 129, 130, 222, 236, 237, 238, 240
Tor 56
Toto 220
tragedy 23, 36, 41, 48, 62, 70, 88, 93, 101 (n.16), 109, 110, 115, 118, 121, 124, 127, 131, 132, 161, 170, 174, 181, 235, 252, 254
tragicomedy 98, 194
transfiguration 98
translation 22, 76, 79, 90, 167, 170, 180, 184, 187, 188, 232, 233, 234, 249
    see also Goethe, Johann Wolfgang von, *Faust. Eine Tragödie* and *Urfaust*; puppet theatre
trauma 109
travelogue 20
trinity, Christian 90, 171
    Hindu 162
Troy 25, 26, 63, 118, 249
Truth Commission 255
Turkey 21, 22, 27, 150
tyrant 23, 26, 28, 29

Ulysses 63
uncanny 112
unconscious 211, 264
Union of Soviet Socialist Republics 186
United States of America 155, 161, 178, 179, 187, 194, 195, 217, 227, 256, 259, 262, 263, 264, 265, 267
unities, classical 43
university 93, 156, 194, 206, 207, 210, 211, 264, 265

Vancouver 205
Van Halen, Eddie 221
vanity 26, 64, 95, 112
ventriloquist 60
verisimilitude 48
Veronese, Paolo, *Alessandro e la famiglia di Dario (The Family of Darius before Alexander)* 29

Versailles 28
    Treaty 179
video 191, 219, 228, 264
    game 224
Vienna Festival 217
Vinkbooms, C. Van 126
Virgil, *Aeneid* 76
virtual reality 205
virtue 18, 25, 29, 58, 116, 224
Vishnu 153, 162, 164, 165, 171, 172
vision 49, 73, 81, 96, 110, 115, 117, 118, 120, 135, 173, 245
volcanic eruption 58, 66
Volz, Rudolf, *Faust: Die Rockoper (Faust: The Rock Opera)* 224–6, 228
Vulcan 208
Vulcanism 57, 58

wager 46, 70, 81, 90, 93, 97, 113, 122, 219, 221, 224
Wagner, Richard 60
    Tristan und Isolde (Tristan and Isolde) 240
Walter, of Châtillon, *Alexandreis (Alexandreid)* 18, 19, 28
Wang, Guowei (王国维) 181
Wang, Yin (王音) 189
waves, sound 56
Wayne, Philip 154, 157
weaponry 65, 149
webcam 264
wedding 45, 50, 172, 219
Weems, Marianne 178
Weimar 57, 107, 131, 153, 208, 244, 247
'Weltliteratur' 187, 197
westernization 179
Whitman, Walt 157
The Who, *Tommy* 223, 227
Wilde, Oscar, *The Picture of Dorian Gray* 217
Wilhelm, Richard 155
Wilkes, John 135
Williams, Paul
    The Muppet Movie 219
    The Phantom of the Paradise 217–19, 221, 224, 227
witchcraft 20
Wittenberg 26
The Wooster Group 259, 269

words, aesthetics 55–69
Wordsworth, William 131, 134, 135
    The Prelude 133
workshop 194, 263
world tree 211, 213
World War II, 238, 247

Xi you ji (西游纪)
    Journey to the West 181
        Sun Wukong, Faust comparison 181
Xue, Dianjie (薛殿杰) 185, 189

Yi, Liming (易立明) 190
Yin-Yang 193
youth 37, 62, 66, 93, 96, 107, 118, 130, 151, 156, 173, 180, 183, 184, 188, 189, 192, 193, 196, 210, 218, 219, 249, 260, 261
Yuan Dynasty 188

Zeng, Li (曾力) 189
Zen theatre 187
Zeus 56, 58
Zhang, Deming (张德明) 180–1
Zhang, Wentian (张闻天), 'Gede de fushide' ('Goethe's Faust') 180
Zhou, Enlai (周恩来) 183, 184
Zhou, Xuepu (周学普) 157, 158
Zong, Baihua (宗白华) 157, 180
Zoroasterism 151
Zulu 254